VISUALIZATION OF NATURAL PHENOMENA

Robert S. Wolff

Larry Yaeger

 CD-ROM included

 THE ELECTRONIC LIBRARY OF SCIENCE

Springer-Verlag

Robert S. Wolff
Apple Computer, Inc.
117 East Colorado Blvd.
Pasadena, CA 91105
USA

Larry Yaeger
Apple Computer, Inc.
20525 Mariane Avenue
Cupertino, CA 95014
USA

Publisher:	Allan M. Wylde
Publishing Associate:	Cindy Peterson
Production Manager:	Sue Purdy Pelosi
Promotions Managers:	Jacqueline Jeng / Paul Manning
CD-ROM Interface Designer:	Ming Cheng
Produced and Prepared by:	Black Hole Publishing Service, Oakland, CA
Production Artist:	Jim Predny
Cover Design:	Iva Frank
Copy Editor:	Andrew L. Alden
Permissions:	Laura Bonazolli

© 1993 Springer-Verlag New York, Inc.
Published by TELOS, The Electronic Library of Science, Santa Clara, California.
TELOS is an imprint of Springer-Verlag New York, Inc.

Cataloging-in-Publication data is available from the Library of Congress

Cover visualization of geophysical map courtesy of Research Systems Inc.

Printed in the United States of America.

9 8 7 6 5 4 3 2 1

ISBN 0-387-97809-7 Springer-Verlag New York Berlin Heidelberg
ISBN 3-540-97809-7 Springer-Verlag Berlin Heidelberg New York

THE
ELECTRONIC
LIBRARY
OF
SCIENCE

TELOS, The Electronic Library of Science, is an imprint of Springer-Verlag New York with publishing facilities in Santa Clara, California. Its publishing program encompasses the natural and physical sciences, computer science, mathematics, and engineering. All TELOS publications have a computational orientation to them, as TELOS' primary publishing strategy is to wed the traditional print medium with the emerging new electronic media in order to provide the reader with a truly interactive multimedia information environment. To achieve this, every TELOS publication delivered on paper has an associated electronic component. This can take the form of book/diskette combinations, book/CD-ROM packages, books delivered via networks, electronic journals, newsletters, plus a multitude of other exciting possibilities. Since TELOS is not committed to any one technology, any delivery medium can be considered.

The range of TELOS publications extends from research level reference works through textbook materials for the higher education audience, practical handbooks for working professionals, as well as more broadly accessible science, computer science, and high technology trade publications. Many TELOS publications are interdisciplinary in nature, and most are targeted for the individual buyer, which dictates that TELOS publications be priced accordingly.

Of the numerous definitions of the Greek word "telos," the one most representative of our publishing philosophy is "to turn," or "turning point." We perceive the establishment of the TELOS publishing program to be a significant step towards attaining a new plateau of high quality information packaging and dissemination in the interactive learning environment of the future. TELOS welcomes you to join us in the exploration and development of this frontier as a reader and user, an author, editor, consultant, strategic partner, or in whatever other capacity might be appropriate.

TELOS, The Electronic Library of Science
Springer-Verlag Publishers
3600 Pruneridge Avenue, Suite 200
Santa Clara, CA 95051

To our families

Book Table of Contents

CD-ROM Table of Contents

Interactive Visualization Browser

Video Greetings

Greetings from the authors

Greetings from David C. Nagel, Senior Vice-President and General Manager, Apple Computer Advanced Technologies Group and Macintosh Software Architecture Division

Greetings from Larry L. Smarr, Director, National Center for Supercomputing Applications (NCSA)

Interface

A state-of-the-art interface which allows the user to interactively explore a wide variety of scientific and medical data

QuickTime Scientific Visualizations

96 scientific visualizations, with accompanying text, coded by chapter, spanning a broad range of scientific and medical computing

12 visualizations for each chapter

12 visualizations for the Technical Notes section

QuickTime Interviews

A dozen researchers discussing current issues and research topics in computer graphics and scientific visualization on QuickTime MooVs.

Glossary

A glossary of terms for the book and the CD-ROM

Data and Software

QuickTime software

NASA Voyager and Viking images

Mathematica Notebooks from Theo Gray, Doug Stein, and Mark Yoder on computer graphics and image processing

Public domain visualization software from NCSA

Demo software from Spyglass, Wolfram Research, Vital Images, Cambridge Scientific

Foreword

by David C. Nagel

In the last five years visualization has gone from the lab to become a desktop technology for many scientists. Images and 3-D renderings of data sets and mathematical models have evolved from the high-priced hardware and customized software of graphics professionals to low-cost, off-the-shelf commercial software running on personal computers. As such, scientific visualization has taken its place beside mathematical modeling as an everyday means of interacting with one's data. This has significantly changed both the amount and the quality of information that scientists are able to extract from raw data, and has effectively established a new paradigm for scientific computing. In addition, new, low-cost hardware and software technologies such as CD-ROMs, digital video, and Apple's QuickTime time-based media and compression technologies have enabled large amounts of image and animation data to be easily accessible to the average researcher or teacher through the personal computer.

However, little has been done in the way of providing a context within which the researcher or teacher could learn which approaches might be best suited for a given problem. Furthermore, most scientists are unfamiliar with the terminology and concepts in modern computer graphics, which simply steepens the learning curve for them to apply the new technologies to their work. As a result, researchers and teachers are not yet taking full advantage of the new paradigm.

In *Visualization of Natural Phenomena* (VNP) the authors have bridged the gap between the computer graphics professional and the working scientist or educated layperson and, as such, have provided an important tool to those teachers and researchers who are strongly interested in scientific visualization, but have not yet incorporated it into their daily work. By using examples of real data sets from a variety of fields and researchers to illustrate basic concepts in image processing, computer graphics, and multimedia technology, VNP brings this complex world to the users' desktop in a form that they can readily understand.

If VNP were just a textbook alone it would be extremely useful. However, by incorporating a CD-ROM with animations, videos, and software, VNP has achieved a level of technology and information integration that no other product for this market ever has. This is exciting for both users and developers, and it sets a new standard for integrated text/software products in the future. I congratulate the authors and the publisher for their efforts in this landmark product, and I encourage scientists, educators, and students of all levels to enjoy the text, images, animations, and software in *Visualization of Natural Phenomena*.

David C. Nagel, Senior Vice-President and General Manager,
Apple Computer Advanced Technologies Group and
Macintosh Software Architecture Division
Apple Computer, Inc.
Cupertino, California

August, 1993

Foreword

by Larry L. Smarr

Human beings have evolved over millions of years interacting with a physical reality. We have developed a powerful eye-brain system, complemented by the other senses, with which to probe this physical world. As we walk through a forest or drive madly down a freeway, our visual "wetware" automatically sorts out the incoming photon field and connects it to a rich stored base of images, ideas, and interpretations. Just as transparently, this visual thinking is quickly coupled to our reasoning, decision-making, and motion capabilities.

Today these same humans are becoming exponentially immersed in a new information-based reality, pouring out of supercomputers, digital instruments, and stored databases. Instead of the hundreds of thousands of generations that our bodies had to adapt to the physical world, we have had to make this transition in less than one. In contrast to the physical reality in which nature automatically transforms the underlying numerical values of density, velocity, and material properties into light, color, and shape, all that comes out of the computer is an endless stream of numbers.

Scientific visualization was invented as the process whereby humans use software to do the work of converting number to image that nature does by physical processes. We have to invent ideas for how to represent the numbers as visual paradigms and then turn those ideas into software algorithms and computer programs. The fact that we have such a wide choice in how to transform numbers into various visual modalities is both the power and the pain of scientific visualization.

For computational scientists, this field has seemed like a set of black arts for many years. One marveled at the beautiful masterpieces that were produced by graphics professionals, but had little idea of how to do it oneself. This new book, *Visualization of Natural Phenomena*, gives us one of the first opportunities to explore systematically the subfields of scientific visualization. By demystifying the subject and giving us a sense of how to do it ourselves, the authors provide the community with a great service.

As supercomputers move toward being able to compute at over one trillion operations per second, visual output is the only sensible way for scientists to couple to this numerical reality. But the broader use of scientific visualization for communicating the results of scientific research to our colleagues in other fields and to the public at large is just as important as the discovery process itself. The power of visualization for this purpose lies in the fact that the image is a much more universal language than the underlying mathematics in which the science is couched.

Given that, the authors and publishers are to be congratulated for their pioneering use of an interactive CD-ROM created as an integral part of the writing process. This allows the reader to experience rapidly the power of visualization and then to "click" one's way to the text for deeper reading. This interactive visual interface is another step toward establishing as "natural" a mode for humans to live in an information reality as they now do in the physical universe.

Larry L. Smarr, Director
National Center for Supercomputing Applications
University of Illinois at Urbana-Champaign

August, 1993

About the Authors

Rob Wolff is the Project Leader of Advanced Applications in Apple's Advanced Technology Group where, since 1988, he has specialized in developing prototype environments for scientific computing. Before coming to Apple, he was a planetary astrophysicist for 11 years at NASA's Jet Propulsion Lab (JPL) where he worked on the interaction of the solar wind with nonmagnetic planetary objects. He was a Guest Investigator on Pioneer Venus and a member of the Voyager Plasma Science Team during the active lifetimes of those missions. He supported his research habit by designing distributed computing environments for planetary missions. In 1980 he began working with Jim Blinn on visualizing astrophysical systems. He has produced a number of visualizations and animations and has participated in several courses and panels on visualization at SIGGRAPH. He is currently Visualization Editor for Computers in Physics and is a Co-Investigator on the Volcanology Team on NASA's Earth Observing Systems (EOS) Mission. Dr. Wolff has a Ph.D. in astrophysics from Brandeis University.

Larry Yaeger's background includes computational fluid dynamics, computer graphics imaging, and neural network research. He carried out pioneering simulations of fluid flows over the Space Shuttle, in laser cavities, and over submarines. He was Director of Software Development at Digital Productions and one of the principal architects of its computer graphics rendering software. In this role he contributed to the design and development of the software tools and production techniques used in the film The Last Starfighter and Clio-award-winning television commercials. He also combined fluid dynamics and computer graphics to create the simulation of the planet Jupiter seen in the film 2010, and was technical director for the special effects creation of the flying owl in the opening title sequence of the film Labyrinth which received an NCGA animation award. As a Principal Engineer in Apple's Vivarium Program, he built neural network simulators on Apple's Cray and applied them to optical character recognition and text-to-speech translation, designed and implemented the software to give Koko the gorilla a computer-based "voice," and built and filmed a proof-of-concept system for integrating Macintosh graphics into routine film production for "Star Trek: The Next Generation." Now as part of the Adaptive Systems/Advanced Technology Group at Apple Computer, Inc. he is extending his character recognition work to pen-based micro-processors and he is currently combining computer graphics, neural networks, and genetic algorithms to study artificial life and artificial intelligence.

Preface

Since Apple Computer introduced the Mac II in the summer of 1987, the personal computer revolution has swept the scientific community from astrophysics to medical imaging. That year, for the first time, researchers could manipulate 8-bit color images in a low-cost, easy-to-use personal computer that had the speed of a VAX 11/750. Suddenly, the possibilities of imaging all sorts of pictorial, graphical, and volumetric data on a personal computer became real. However, two problems still remained:

 • There was no way to inexpensively network the new Macintosh to existing Unix and VMS data bases, and

 • There was no imaging or visualization software that ran on the new machine.

Apple and various third-party hardware companies solved the first problem by creating low-cost Ethernet cards that plugged into the Mac. However, solving the second problem was a little more difficult, since third-party software companies would not develop visualization packages for the Mac II until there were enough machines in researchers' hands to justify the development costs. For their part, researchers were somewhat reluctant to purchase a color Mac II until there were software packages that would improve their research productivity.

Apple broke this circle when it funded NCSA, the National Center for Supercomputing Applications, to develop public-domain visualization software for the Mac II. In the summer of 1988

Larry Smarr, director of NCSA, gave the keynote speech at the ACM SIGGRAPH meeting in Atlanta and, with a little help from a friend, demonstrated NCSA's visualization software on a Macintosh in front of a couple of thousand attendees. NCSA distributed its software over the Internet, and soon researchers and teachers throughout the country were creating images and animations on their desktops. At about the same time, a number of scientific software packages, like Mathematica™, were released. In addition, low-cost development systems such as Language Systems Fortran™ and Symantec's Think C™ became viable environments for the serious scientific developer. Scientists found that they could now compute, analyze, and visualize their data in classic Macintosh style. *Desktop visualization* had truly arrived and, with it, sufficient impetus for several other companies to upgrade or create software to take advantage of the new hardware.

Hardware in all areas of computing continued to improve, not only in speed, but in functionality as well. Today, personal computers run at several times the speed of the mid-1980s VAX minicomputers, 24-bit color is becoming standard, users can get up to 256 megabytes of RAM on their systems, and scientific users typically have over a gigabyte of disk space available to store data. With the introduction of Apple's QuickTime™ standard for manipulating digitized video, scientists worldwide can now create animations from data residing on Macintoshes or Unix hosts and play them back on Mac, Unix, or Windows™ machines through a wide range of software, from simple players to word processors. As a result of all of these developments, hundreds of thousands of well-endowed personal computers live on the desktops of researchers throughout the world, and there now exists a wide variety of imaging, analysis, and visualization software for the research or teaching scientist.

Visualization of Natural Phenomena (VNP) began as a project designed to teach researchers, university teachers, and students some of the basic concepts and techniques of scientific visualization. However, by its very nature of being a tightly coupled book and CD-ROM, we realized early on that an element of design needed to be incorporated that heretofore did not exist in print media. In particular, we felt that the CD should be more than just an interesting addition to the text, but should be able to stand alone as a unique product. As such we spent a fair amount of time, including prototyping several CD interfaces, trying to find the most effective way of incorporating this functionality in the design of the text. What we came up with was a system to use icons to link the text and the CD. On the CD, animations are played by clicking on an icon in a matrix, where the y-axis of the matrix lists the

chapters of the book, and the *x*-axis denotes the number of each animation in each chapter. Thus, for example, CD 5.3 indicates the third
animation in Chapter 5. In the text, the same icons from each of the
animations are placed appropriately in the margin of each chapter, along
with each animation's coordinates. This way users should be able to
navigate between the two media without much difficulty.

Of course, our goal of including a CD with over 100 animations
had technical problems of its own. Apple's QuickTime compression
technology enabled us to achieve that goal, and we describe Quick-
Time in several places throughout the text and the Tech Notes.
Unfortunately, QuickTime is not yet fully functional on Unix and
Windows platforms, thus it was impossible to build a CD-ROM that
ran on all environments. As a consequence, we had to ensure that the
book would be a valuable product by itself. So, although the CD-ROM
significantly enhances the text, it is by no means necessary in order to
understand the principles, techniques, and issues discussed in the text.
Correspondingly, for those Mac users who purchase the package
primarily for the CD-ROM, the 100-plus visualizations and animations
alone span a really interesting spectrum of science, and should be a
source of entertainment and learning for all educational levels.

Selected Mathematica notebooks described in the text, as well as
contributions from Doug Stein and Theo Gray of Wolfram Research
and Mark Yoder of Rose-Hulman Institute of Technology, are included
on the CD. Public domain and demo commercial visualization and
image processing software is also included on the CD as well as sample
data sets for image processing and visualization. We selected
Mathematica as the general medium of exchange in this regard, since
Mathematica runs on all platforms, although the Notebooks themselves
only work well on Macintosh and NeXT platforms. Those without
Macintoshes will be interested to know that some of the software
(certain NCSA software and the commands from the Mathematica
notebooks) is specifically designed to run on other platforms. However,
because of our intent to make the CD work properly on as many
Macintosh systems as possible, we pressed this current version of the
CD in Macintosh HFS format, rather than in an ISO 9660 format.
Pressing the CD in ISO format would enable text files to be read by
other systems, but it would cripple the interface to the QuickTime
animations, as well as severely limit their performance. We do intend to
provide the VNP CD to Unix and Windows environments in some
future release as soon as QuickTime technology is a bit more stable on
other platforms. Right now, however, the only really solid environment

CD 5.3

An icon like this one, placed
in the margin of the text,
indicates an animation on
the CD. In this case, the
animation is the third
animation in Chapter 5.

for playing compressed animations with sound (and, without sound, for that matter) is the Macintosh. However, we strongly encourage all readers to send in the registration card in the back of the package so that we can keep you updated on any new versions of the CD and other product announcements.

The text itself is organized into two major parts, a main text section consisting of seven chapters and a section of Tech Notes, comprising 15 short treatises on the most important technical issues referred to in the main text. The main text itself is designed to be read fairly easily, requiring minimal computer graphics or image processing background to understand it. At the end of each chapter are suggestions for further reading for those interested in pursuing topics in more depth. In contrast, most of the Tech Notes are fairly detailed, and several require a decent understanding of complex variables, differential and projective geometry, and differential equations. Some familiarity with advanced computer graphics concepts is probably helpful, but not necessary. Liberal pointers between the chapters and the Tech Notes ensure that the interested reader understands the overall context of a given technical issue. Three of the Tech Notes are written by colleagues of ours at Apple: Scott Stein wrote one on Apple's QuickTime technology and another on networking in scientific visualization, and Peter Hughes wrote the Tech Note on terrain rendering and *Mars Navigator*.

The text is constructed around the concept of an image, and we build on that basic notion as we discuss all of the various visualization and multimedia technologies. The chapter-by-chapter breakdown is as follows:

• Chapter 1 introduces the basic structure of an image, the nature of color, and some of the more common image processing functions.

• Chapter 2 extends the image display concept to more general data sets, including data from numerical simulations and various empirical data sets that would not necessarily be considered images.

• Chapter 3 looks at the complex issue of terrain rendering and the general problem of determining the altitude of an object from images of it.

• Chapter 4 takes us through multivariate visualization, the process of finding ways to correlate and visualize multiple scalar and vector data sets.

• Chapter 5 introduces the basic concept of volume visualization, and the most widely used methods are discussed from the perspective of the needs of the scientist.

• Chapter 6 delves into polygonally based three-dimensional rendering and animation—the kind of graphics used in motion picture special effects as well as some of the most striking scientific visualizations.

• Finally, Chapter 7 looks at the relationship between scientific visualization and the efforts made by the film industry to simulate reality. Chapter 7 can stand by itself, but it also closes the loop in a number of visualization areas since entertainment and scientific computer graphics have long had a mutually beneficial relationship. On a creative level, Chapter 7 reveals certain secrets of how various special effects are created, and this is interesting to anyone who has seen a science fiction film produced in the last 15 years.

• Chapters also have references appended at the end so that interested readers can simply copy the references that they need without having to keep flipping to the back of the book.

• The Tech Notes cover a range of topics from color to image processing to sound to algorithms in volume visualization and rendering and animation. Each Tech Note is designed to give an overview of the important concepts for that subject.

• Appendix A describes the making of *Visualization of Natural Phenomena*, the various hardware, software, and data management problems we had throughout the project's development, and how we managed to solve each of them. Appendix A also lists the different commercial software and hardware packages used in the production of VNP, along with the addresses and phone numbers of the developers.

• Appendix B is a Glossary of words and concepts as well as a complete list of references for the entire book.

This project required a fairly massive technological effort, both in producing the CD and producing the images for the CD. In addition, the production of the text and still images themselves was something that we, as the authors, were involved in throughout the entire process.

We hope that you find this book both informative and attractive. We've tried to mirror the combination of information and aesthetics that one finds in the best scientific visualizations, just as these two attributes are combined in our own perspectives.

Robert spent 11 years as a planetary astrophysicist at the Jet Propulsion Laboratory, the birthplace of digital image processing (as part of the 1964 Ranger 7 moon imaging mission) and home of some of the earliest 3-D rendering for scientific visualization (Jim Blinn's Voyager mission planning animations starting in 1977), and Larry spent 10 years as a scientist and programmer in the field of computational fluid dynamics and 5 years in the field of commercial computer graphics for the film and television industries. Both of us have been performing musicians as well, and both of us have produced a number of computer animations.

As it turns out, early in our careers, we both came to understand the great value of visualizing the results of numerical computations and empirical measurements. At first that often meant using a pencil and graph paper, yet the insights offered by processing the data through the world's best pattern recognizer—the human visual system—made the effort more than worthwhile. And, as a result of our need to understand complex data structures, both of us were quick to realize the potential of the digital computer. We feel strongly about the scientific (and ultimately the sociological) value of the techniques discussed in this book, and hope you find it both valuable and enjoyable.

While we've worked hard to ensure the correctness and usefulness of this book, everything can always be improved. In a project of this scope tradeoffs are always made, and we apologize if not all of the subjects we deal with here were treated in sufficient detail for all readers. If you find areas for improvement, including any technical errors, graphics errors, or omissions, please feel free to send an e-mail to *vnp@apple.com*. As we mentioned earlier, as cross-platform multimedia delivery systems start becoming a reality, we also hope to make the CD-ROM accessible to users of Unix and other operating systems; if you're interested in such a capability, let us know at the above e-mail address. So enjoy the short movies of fluids, planets, and other natural phenomena that populate the CD. We had fun making it, and it is our wish that you have fun viewing it.

Robert S. Wolff
Pasadena, California
August, 1993

Larry Yaeger
Los Gatos, California
August, 1993

Acknowledgments

Putting together this project required the help and support of lots of people. First off, we never would have completed the project if it were not for our publisher, Allan Wylde, who supported us and showed the patience of Job from start to finish of the project. Allan understood from the start that VNP was very difficult, and that we would be pushing technology throughout the entire project. Other Springer-Verlag folks who were critical to the project were Cindy Peterson, Publishing Associate, and Sue Purdy Pelosi, Production Manager, of the TELOS office in Santa Clara, California, who helped with project administration, and Paul Manning and Jacqueline Jeng in New York, who worked on advertising and promotion of VNP.

We thank Apple Computer for its strong support of the project, in particular, our management chain: David Nagel, Rick LeFaivre, Harvey Lehtman, Mark Miller, and Jim Spohrer for their support throughout this project, as well as all of our friends and colleagues in Apple's Advanced Technology Group for their friendship, advice, and encouragement. As far as the Macintosh itself goes, we realized several months ago that VNP would have been nearly impossible to do in any other computing environment today. Yes, we certainly have a long list of things that we feel need to be fixed or improved so that other people would have an easier time of it, but overall, there is not a better development environment today for this kind of project. The fact that we were able to put VNP together is a tribute to the engineers who have helped make the Macintosh environment what it is today.

Nearly all of the line art, as well as the development of the MacroMedia Director front-end to the animations on the CD, and much of the work in editing the visualizations for the cover was done by Ming Chen. His tireless efforts, often successively refining drawings, and doing countless iterations of the CD-ROM interface, working around MacroMedia Director QuickTime and screen-refresh bugs often times late at night and on weekends, enabled us to put together a first-class looking book with a CD-ROM interface to QuickTime MooVs that we feel is about as good as can be done with today's technology.

Our production manager, Jan Benes, is another saint, who put up with constant revisions and changes while attempting to maintain some sort of production schedule. Special thanks also go out to Andrew L. Alden for copyediting and proofreading. His ability to catch illogical statements, inconsistencies, and just plain dumb errors saved us many times. We thank Jim Predny for doing the skillful and tireless QuarkXPress page formatting. Bob Meyers and his staff at Robert Meyer's Studio in Pasadena, California handled the slide scanning and color separations with exceptional dedication and professionalism. Thanks to Iva Frank who designed the cover, and Laura Bonazolli who was responsible for the complex sets of permissions required.

We extend special thanks to the technical reviewers, who put in lots of time to help us get the bugs out of the first few revisions: Mark Yoder, of Rose-Hulman Institute of Technology (who also provided the Mathematica image processing notebooks on the CD-ROM); Bob Wolfe of the University of Rio Grande; Brand Fortner of Spyglass, Inc.; Mike Norman of NCSA; Jim Knighton of JPL; Peter Hughes of Apple Computer, Inc.; Doug Stein of Wolfram Research, Inc. (who also provided the Mathematica-to-HDF file converter and the Mathematica fractal generator for the CD-ROM); and Tom Wickham-Jones of Wolfram Research, Inc.

Many people contributed images, technical support, loaner equipment, and technical advice throughout the project. Some we had known for a long time; others who we knew only through a phone call or e-mail were willing to provide hardware, software, images, and animations; and there were a few people who we got to know fairly well as a result of their generosity in providing their data.

So, special thanks to Optical Data Corporation and their wonderful laser disks; Steve Goodman of FWB for loaning us a couple of large-capacity Hammer drives; John Chan of SuperMac for getting us a VideoSpigot card when they first came out; Don Johnson of Pinnacle

Micro, for loaning us a recordable CD-ROM drive so that we could master the test CD's; Jim Blinn of Caltech and Bob Holtzman of JPL for setting the initial sparks of the visualization fire; and Tim Taylor and Sandi Reda, of Radius, Inc., who went out of their way to loan us a Radius VideoVision card (and help with technical support) during the digitizing process.

Thanks to all of the people and companies who contributed images and animations to this project. Special thanks to:

Apple Computer, Inc., Advanced Technology Group, Eric Chen, Eric Hoffert, Peter Hughes, Todd Junkin, Michael Kass, Jean-Luc LeBrun, Pete Litwinowicz, Gavin Miller, Gary Starkweather, Scott Stein, Wendy Taylor, Doug Turner, and Lance Williams
Mike Backes, *American Film Institute*
CAROLCO
Ted Clark, *JPL's Galileo Project*
Gary Demos, *Digital Productions and Demographics*
Industrial Light and Magic
Bill Kroyer, *Kroyer Films, Inc.*
Lightstorm Entertainment, Inc., Geoff Burdick, Van Ling, and Caryn Mendez
Paramount Pictures, Inc.
Pixar, Inc., Loren Carpenter, Ralph Guggenheim, Pam Kerwin, and Deirdre Warin
Research Systems, Inc., Hal Elgie, Steve Richards, and Jim Wilson
Larry Smarr, *NCSA*
Lloyd Treinish, *IBM T.J. Watson Research Center*
Jack Van Eden, *Airborne Systems, Inc.*

We would also like to thank the following people and companies for contributing software and data:

Electric Image, Inc., Mark Granger, Chris Keller, and Jay Roth
Brand Fortner, *Spyglass, Inc.*
Susan Goode, *NCSA*
Theo Gray, *Wolfram Research, Inc.*
Michael Swartz, *Cambridge Scientific Company, Inc.*
Doug Stein, *Wolfram Research, Inc.*
Vital Images, Inc., Mark Rainbow and Kim Thomas
Mark Yoder, *Rose-Hulman Institute of Technology*

There are many people who offered very valuable support, advice, inspiration, and efforts:

David Block, *University of South Africa*

D. C. & H., Khasmere, Kiko, Kodi, and Michiko

Kevin Hussey and Patricia Lutges, *Jet Propulsion Laboratory's Image Processing Section*

Jim Knighton, *Jet Propulsion Laboratory's Earth and Space Sciences Division,*

The Los Angeles Kings

Skip McNevin and Jurrie van der Woude, *Jet Propulsion Laboratory's Public Information Office*

Trish Russo, *The Ohio University in Phoenix*

Lastly we thank our families: Donna, Tricia, and Sammy Wolff (Robert's clan); and Levi Thomas (Larry's wife) for their patience, understanding, love, and support throughout this project. Yes, we will be spending more time at home...real soon.

We wish to dedicate this book to two special men. The first is the late Clayne M. Yeates, for many years Science and Mission Design Manager for NASA's Galileo Project. Clayne funded much of the early visualization work at JPL, without which this project never would have been. As he was with much of his work and his life, Clayne understood the vision and gave us the freedom to dream. The second is Gino Moretti, who always insisted that the results of a simulation had to be plotted to be understood. He was right.

Images and Image Processing 1

Images of natural phenomena hold a particular fascination for us, especially if they show objects and events outside our normal range of perceptions or experience. Even commonplace phenomena like the rainbow swirls of oil on water attract us with their natural complexity, organic motion, and beauty. But we all share a special fascination for the mysterious and extraordinary phenomena that our senses are not normally capable of showing us. Telescopic images of galaxies or optical fiber-based videos of dividing cells draw and hold our attention the way each new experience fascinates a child.

However, the simple notion that an image of something will tell us all, or nearly all that we need to know about it is far from true, since the fundamental nature of an image is that it is dependent on the object being observed, the wavelength of the radiation being used to make the observation, and the technology being used to collect and display the observed data.

In this chapter we discuss the fundamentals of image creation and display, color theory, image processing, and image animation. Because image processing has its roots in space exploration and aerial photography, most of the examples we use will be from those domains. Space exploration also brings us to more general astronomical data and the concept of imaging in nonvisible wavelengths such as infrared, ultraviolet, X-rays, gamma rays, and radio waves. This chapter also forms the foundation for later chapters on imaging of numerical data, terrain rendering, and volume visualization. In this context the reader will find the material on color theory, image display, and image manipulation (image processing) to be generally useful in later chapters.

We need to establish a few basic terms for those readers who are only marginally familiar with imaging technology. These terms are also defined later in the chapter in the context of specific technologies and applications, but it's best to have a common working vocabulary at the outset.

Image processing refers to the manipulation of a digital image in order to extract more information than is apparent from an initial visual inspection. A *digital image* is composed of a matrix of numbers, each of which represents a particular color. Each of the numbers is called a "*pixel*," which is a contraction of "picture element." The *resolution* of an image is generally considered to be the number of pixels in each direction or, equivalently, the dimensions of the image matrix. Each pixel can represent one of a number of colors or gradations of gray. This is essentially the dynamic range of the pixel and is generally expressed in terms of the number of *bit-planes* (or simply bits of color). Thus, for example, a pixel with $2^8 = 256$ gray levels would have 8 bit-planes of gray-scale information. Alternatively, a color image might have 8 bit-planes for each of the three red, green, and blue (RGB) color *channels* represented by the electron guns in the computer's monitor. A detailed discussion of color is provided in **Tech Note 1**.

Imaging: Another Dividend from Space Exploration

The power of an image far exceeds that of the printed word or, for that matter, the matrix of numbers that compose the data set from which the image is generated. Nowhere has this been more apparent than in the public response to images taken by the robot spacecraft Viking and Voyager in the decade beginning in 1976. In fact, much of modern image processing technology comes directly from research in space exploration in the 1960s and 1970s. Thus it's fitting that our visual exploration of natural phenomena begins with the planets. One of the most awe-inspiring pictures ever produced was taken nearly 15 years ago by a robot spacecraft that was roughly half a billion miles from Earth. The image wasn't taken with film, but with a video camera. The spacecraft was Voyager 1 and, on February 13, 1979, when the spacecraft was about 20 million kilometers from Jupiter, the imaging system took the picture of Jupiter and two of its inner satellites, Io and Europa, shown in Figure 1.1a.

There are many remarkable things about this image: the accuracy of the spacecraft trajectory, the pointing accuracy of the camera, the stability of the spacecraft, the transmission of the data from Jupiter, the sensitivity of the receiving antenna on Earth, and so forth. However, for our purpose the imaging system itself is worth a close look. Since we use a number of Voyager and Viking images as examples throughout the book, it is valuable to understand something of the end-to-end process of the production of these images.

The video cameras on board the two Voyager spacecraft were fairly primitive by today's standards, but they did a job that no other camera has ever come close to. There are two cameras on each spacecraft, a wide-angle (200 millimeter focal length and field-of-view of about 3 degrees) and a narrow-angle (1500 mm focal length and field-of-view of 0.4 degrees) camera. Each Voyager camera's vidicon tube has a resolution of 800×800 pixels $\times$ 8 bits per pixel. The resolution of each optical system is roughly 10 microradians per pixel for the narrow-angle camera and 70 µrad per pixel on the wide-angle camera. This means that, at 100,000 km range, the camera can distinguish objects larger than about 1 km. The 10 µrad per pixel is the same resolution as the single camera on the much more recent Galileo spacecraft. To give you an idea of the actual structure of a pixel, we'll blow up a piece of Jupiter's volcanic moon

Figure 1.1a

Figure 1.1a
Voyager 1 image of Jupiter and two inner Galilean satellites, Io and Europa, taken on February 13, 1979. (Courtesy NASA/JPL)

Io (Figure 1.1b). Notice that a pixel here is simply a single gray square, and that there is absolutely no structure to it; usually there is no information about an image at resolutions below 1 pixel.

The cameras are attached to selenium-sulfur black-and-white vidicon television tubes—quite primitive compared to your home video-camera but nevertheless very impressive at a range of 500 million miles from Earth. Brightness levels are recorded at each element of the vidicon to an accuracy of 8 bits (1 part in 256), and that data was either stored on the spacecraft's tape recorder or transmitted directly to Earth, depending upon where the spacecraft was relative to Earth and Jupiter and what else the spacecraft was doing at the time. Color images were achieved by combining data from different images taken successively through different colored filters and then geometrically correcting the images on the ground for the motion of the spacecraft during the time that the images were taken.

Each Voyager image has a resolution of 800 by 800 pixels for a total of 640,000 pixels. Each pixel consists of 8 bits (1 byte) per image

CD 1.1

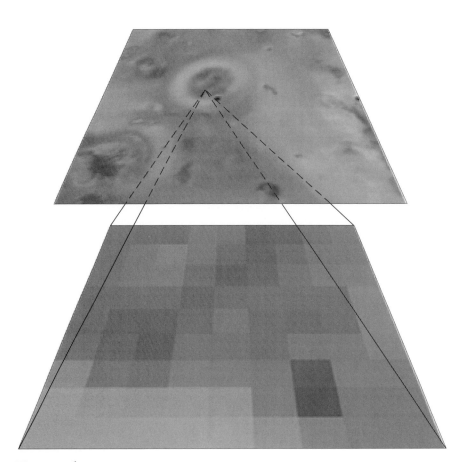

Figure 1.1b
Magnification of a gray-scale image of Io to the pixel level, showing how an image is composed from individual pixels. The circle in the center of the image is the volcano Pele.

Figure 1.1b

for a combined total of nearly 2 megabytes for each color image (three 8-bit channels) taken. Images taken by Voyager must either be transmitted directly to Earth or stored on the spacecraft's magnetic tape recorder and relayed later, as the spacecraft's active memory (RAM) is a mere 8000 bits. Obvious limitations in this process are the physical characteristics of the tape recorder and the data transmission rate from the spacecraft to Earth. In Voyager's case it took about a minute to transmit an image from Jupiter to Earth during the time that Voyager was traveling through the Jovian system.

IMAGE PROCESSING BASICS

In this section we discuss some of the concepts of image processing as a scientific computing tool:
- How a digital image is constructed from individual pixels
- Why image processing is important to scientists
- Some common image processing problems
- Basic image processing filters.

In the examples that follow, all of the image processing was performed in Adobe Photoshop™. A more mathematical treatment of image processing fundamentals is given in **Tech Note 2**. Readers so inclined will find image processing Mathematica™ Notebooks on the CD in the Image Processing folder.

Every image can be viewed as simply a two-dimensional (2-D) matrix of pixels, each with a different integer numerical value which represents a specific color or gray level. Since the eye has a nonlinear response to color, and small-scale features of a given brightness are easily lost in a sea of larger, brighter features, researchers turn to color and brightness manipulations to bring out specific features of an image. This task is made easier with the simple data structure of digital images. The process then resolves to developing mathematical methods for transforming images. The set of techniques that has evolved from these methods is called *image processing*. The individual techniques are generally termed *filters*.

Different filters are designed to perform different kinds of functions, but basically most image processing techniques fall into one of two classes:
- Filters that operate on the entire set of pixels at once in an image
- Filters that operate on a small subset of an image.

Examples of the first class include simple brightness or contrast variations of an image, or functional transformations of the brightness

5

distribution or histogram of the pixels in the image. In the second class fall such complex pixel manipulations as contouring, image sharpening or blurring, weighted averaging, and edge detection of features. These functions are discussed qualitatively later in this chapter, and the mathematical foundation of each kind of filter discussed here is detailed in **Tech Note 2**. However, first we need to get a better understanding of just why image processing is an important research tool to computational science, as well as some of the more common data analysis problems that image processing can address.

IMAGE PROCESSING AS A SCIENTIFIC TOOL

Scientific image analysis has very different requirements than, for example, artistic image manipulation. For the artist, creative control over individual pixels and collections of pixels is essential. Algorithmic manipulation of the image is of little use. In contrast, scientists need to be able to mathematically transform images from one state to another. Moreover, whereas artists usually work on a single image at a time, scientists often need to be able to apply the same set of functions repeatedly to hundreds or thousands of data sets. These distinct classes of functionality impose different requirements on an image processing system. As a result, a given commercial or public-domain image processing system cannot easily be optimized for both types of work.

In this book we're obviously concentrating on scientific computing. From that point of view we know that a scientist generally needs to perform one of two tasks with an image: (1) determine qualitatively and quantitatively the gross features of a dominant structure or phenomenon, and (2) find small-scale meaningful structures. These general requirements span the spectrum of scientific fields, from microbiology to astronomy. Given the needs of scientific image processing, the first question one needs to answer for a specific problem is whether to analyze the color or gray-scale representation of the data. Whereas it is true that intelligent use of colors can enhance specific morphological features of a given image, gray scale often provides better structural detail to the eye. This is especially true for fine details, so gray-scale mapping is often used in image analysis to pick out hard-to-discern features. Medical imaging is one area where gray-scale is used extensively, but it is used quite a bit in the studies of continuous systems, such as fluid dynamics, as well. For example, a researcher might be interested in ascertaining whether or not "artificial" numerical waves are propagating in the computational domain. A color palette designed to enhance small-scale structures, such as numerical waves, might also pick

CD 1.2

up other features, or simply produce artifacts associated with the choice of palette. Coupled with the nonlinear sensitivity of the eye, color is not necessarily the best choice for the problem. Gray-scale, which is simply related to the intensity discernible by the eye, should be much better for this task.

Many researchers in medical imaging are beginning to work with 12- and 16-bit gray-scale images, since the greater bit-depth gives a much larger dynamic range to the data represented by the image. With this dynamic range, image processing can bring out considerably finer detail than would be available with the 256 values in an 8-bit image. In the next section we'll look at a couple of examples from Earth and planetary sciences, and discuss some of the basic image processing filters that one might use to enhance small-scale and large-scale features of an image.

BASIC IMAGE PROCESSING FILTERS

Although hundreds of image processing filters have been developed over the past two decades, considerable information can be obtained from an image by the use of just a few. In particular, for the kinds of scientific problems we discussed earlier, a handful of basic filters should suffice for most applications. In this section we use some Voyager imaging data to illustrate the power of these basic tools.

As an example of the power of even simple image processing, consider Figure 1.2 where we process a Voyager image of Jupiter's Great Red Spot, first discovered by the English scientist Robert Hooke in

Figure 1.2a
Voyager 1 high-resolution image of Jupiter's Great Red Spot in natural color formed from three consecutive images. (Courtesy NASA/JPL)

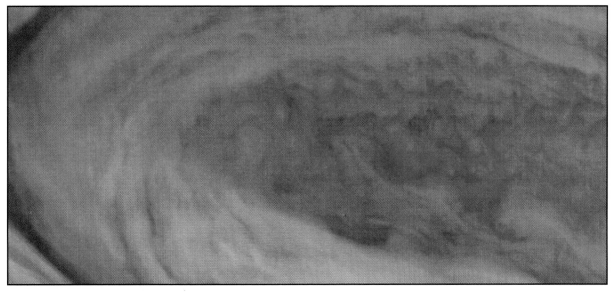

Figure 1.2a

1630 and subsequently drawn by the Italian astronomer Giovanni Cassini in 1631. Figure 1.2a shows a Voyager 1 high-resolution image (that is, an image from the high-resolution camera) of the Great Red Spot with surrounding vortices (in natural color) while Figure 1.2b shows a closeup in exaggerated color—false color—as a result of manipulating the color values of the image. In this simple case, color enhancement is achieved by taking all color values in a given range and adding a number to them, thus accentuating that range from others in the image. Notice how the enhanced color brings out some of the fine structure of the atmosphere surrounding the Great Red Spot.

A gray-scale image brings out subtle differences in brightness that are often masked in a color image. In Figure 1.2c we show a gray-scale image of Figure 1.2b

A more interesting filter is contrast enhancement, wherein one simply takes all pixels with brightness levels below a certain threshold value and decreases their brightness while at the same time taking all of the other pixels and increasing their brightness. Figure 1.2d shows a contrast enhancement of Figure 1.2c. Contrast enhancement is sometimes termed "stretching" the image, since poor contrast means that all of the pixels have numerical values that fall within a narrow range.

In the pixel world one of the most useful pieces of information we can obtain is a *histogram* of the image. A histogram plots the color values of pixels in a given channel against the total number of pixels with those values in the channel. In the case where a single (gray-scale) channel is selected, the histogram gives us a distribution of

Figure 1.2b
Voyager 1 closeup image of the Great Red Spot in false color. Note how small-scale features are exaggerated compared to the natural color image in Figure 1.2a.

Figure 1.2c
A gray-scale representation is often a useful transformation to do before performing basic image processing.

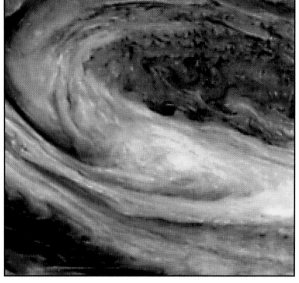

Figure 1.2b   **Figure 1.2c**

gray-levels of the image. In terms of the histogram, increasing contrast stretches the image data out across the histogram. In the Photoshop context, 100 percent contrast yields the widest separation of grays yielding just black and white, whereas 0 percent contrast reduces all grays to a single, median gray. Functionally, most contrast enhancement functions compress all gray-level values below the threshold into a narrow range toward 0 (black) while compressing all gray-level values at or above the threshold into a narrow range toward 255 (white). The simple brightness enhancement increases or decreases the gray-level of every pixel in the image, thus shifting the entire range of grays in the histogram. Brightness filters can therefore be considered to be a subset of contrast enhancement. The histogram model shows us that contrast enhancement is basically a scalar transformation of gray-levels in an image.

We can enhance small-scale features even further by applying a simple filter, called a *histogram equalization*, to the false-color image. Histogram equalization is discussed in depth in **Tech Note 2** but, for the purpose herein, we can consider it as just a redistribution of color and intensity values of the image such that each combination of color and intensity is assigned the same number of pixels. Figure 1.2e shows a histogram equalization of Figure 1.2b.

Another powerful filter is *edge detection*. Edge detection filters look for sharp changes in color or gray-scale level in an image and blacken out the surrounding region. This tends to enhance small-scale structure of the image. In **Tech Note 2** we discuss the functional basis

Figure 1.2d
Contrast enhancement of Figure 1.2c. Notice the increased sharpness of small-scale features.

Figure 1.2e
Histogram equalization of Figure 1.2b.

Figure 1.2d   **Figure 1.2e**

for edge detection. In Figure 1.2f we've applied an edge detection filter to the image to observe small-scale turbulent flow structure within the Great Red Spot.

The image processing filters discussed above can be used to "make visible the invisible," so to speak, and Voyager 1's journey to Jupiter provides excellent examples to illustrate this point. In particular, we consider the discovery of Jupiter's ring (Figure 1.3), a planned-for observation of an object that had never been seen, and the discovery of volcanic activity on Io, when the imaging system was being used not for scientific observations, but for optical navigation of the spacecraft (Figure 1.4). In the case of Jupiter's ring, the observation to search for the ring was planned for based on theoretical models of existing ring systems around Saturn and Uranus. However, in the case of Io, the discovery of active volcanism was unexpected and unplanned for. In both cases, a lot of image processing was required to determine the validity as well as the precise nature of the observations. To give you a feel for both the sensitivity of Voyager's cameras and the difficulty of observing Jupiter's ring, consider that Jupiter's ring is roughly ten thousand times more transparent than the best glass made.

MORE EXAMPLES

In this section we apply a variety of filters of the types discussed above to a couple of images. Since there is no better teacher than example, this exercise is intended to give the reader a feel for several

Figure 1.2f
Edge detection filter applied to Figure 1.2d to bring out some of the small-scale structure of the image. Part of what we're seeing, however, is likely due to artifacts of the edge detection algorithm applied to a highly contrasted image.

Figure 1.3
This image from Voyager 1 shows, for the first time, a faint ring encircling Jupiter (thick gray line in center of image). The faint lines parallel to the ring are star tracks, and the regular array of dark dots are calibration marks on the image known as reseau marks.

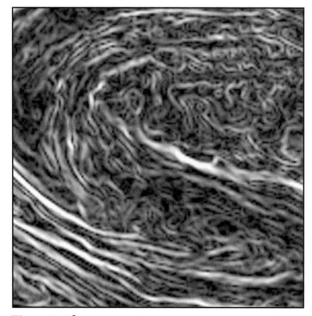

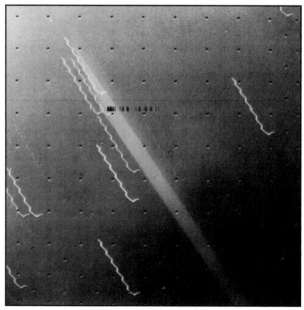

Figure 1.2f   Figure 1.3

kinds of filters. One of the most dramatic examples of the success of image processing as a research tool is a Voyager 2 image of Saturn's rings taken from a range of about 3 million kilometers (Figure 1.5). The theory was that, although Saturn's rings are composed mostly of water ice, differences in color across the rings might be able to be used to determine the presence of possible trace constituents of other materials. These color differences are too small to show up in an ordinary image, but they can be brought out by special processing of the image. In Figure 1.5 the image of Saturn's B and C rings was made from three pictures taken through separate green, blue, and ultraviolet filters by Voyager and then combined to form a single false-color image later during processing at the Jet Propulsion Laboratory (JPL).

In Figure 1.6a we show the full disk of Io in natural color as imaged by Voyager on March 5, 1979. Io is the most volcanically active object in the solar system, and its color (largely due to sulfurous deposits on the surface) and pockmarked surface are principally due to ongoing volcanic activity. In Figures 1.6b, c, and d the composite image is broken down into component red, green, and blue bands, respectively. Each band has a resolution of 8 bits. In addition to getting a better feel for the color composition of the image, it's much easier to work with an individual band when performing most image processing operations. In Figure 1.6e we apply a weighted average filter to the red band. The filter sharpens the image considerably and, if we look at the region encircled in red, allows us to see a lot more structure than was apparent in the

Figure 1.4
This image taken by Voyager 1 as it flew by Jupiter, showed the first evidence of extraterrestrial active volcanism. The umbrella-shaped plume is volcanic gas and dust spewed outward by the volcano, named Pele, after the Hawaiian god of volcanism.
(Courtesy NASA/JPL)

Figure 1.5
Voyager 2 image of Saturn's B and C rings taken from about 3 million kilometers. Images from the green, blue, and UV filters were combined to produce this false color image. Notice how the fine structure of the rings stands out.
(Courtesy NASA/JPL)

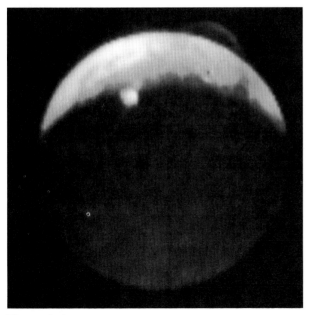

Figure 1.4

Figure 1.5

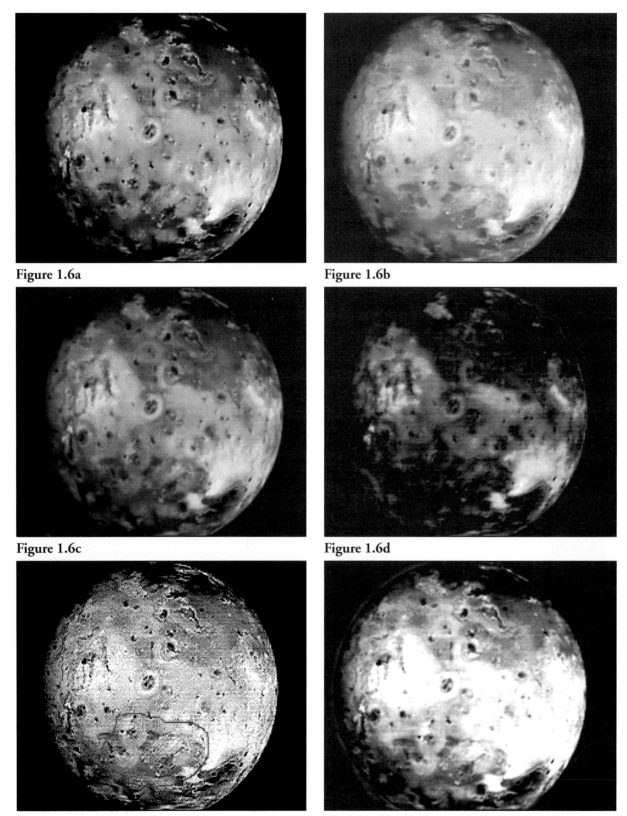

Figure 1.6a

Figure 1.6b

Figure 1.6c

Figure 1.6d

Figure 1.6e

Figure 1.6f

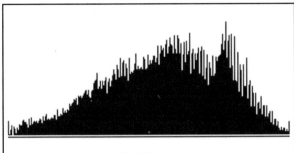

Mean: 142.33

Std Dev: 54.08

Median: 146

Pixels: 43392

Figure 1.6g

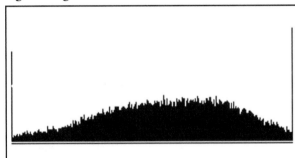

Mean: 142.27

Std Dev: 62.47

Median: 146

Pixels: 43392

Figure 1.6h

Mean: 139.72

Std Dev: 91.32

Median: 148

Pixels: 31428

Figure 1.6i

Figure 1.6a
This image of Io taken by Voyager 1 on March 5, 1979 shows clear evidence of volcanic activity through extensive mottling and erosion of the satellite's surface, confirming a prediction made by planetary geologist Stanton Peale. (Courtesy NASA/JPL)

Figure 1.6b
"Red" channel from Figure 1.6a.

Figure 1.6c
"Green" channel from Figure 1.6a.

Figure 1.6d
"Blue" channel from Figure 1.6a.

Figure 1.6e
A weighted average filter applied to Figure 1.6b. Note the sharpness of the structures visible in the red-circled region compared to the same region in Figures 1.6a and b.

Figure 1.6f
Contrast enhancement to Figure 1.6b. Although it makes the bright regions brighter, we see no additional structure beyond the previous enhancements.

Figure 1.6g
Histogram of Figure 1.6b. Note the median of the distribution at 146, with a fairly wide standard deviation.

Figure 1.6h
By applying a weighted average we can spread out the pixel distribution, as in this histogram of our test image.

Figure 1.6i
This histogram of the contrast-enhanced image (Figure 1.6f) shows how the number of pixels per gray level is spread out fairly evenly over the range of gray-scale values.

CD 1.3

original image. Finally, in Figure 1.6f we apply a contrast enhancement to the red-filtered image. Although the contrast enhancement makes the bright areas brighter by stretching out the distribution of pixels among the available 256 gray-scale values, in this case it does not provide us with any better detail of the image. That's because the weighted average filter has already brought out the interesting features in the image.

Figures 1.6g, h, and i show the histograms of pixels among the gray-scale values for Figures 1.6d, e, and f, respectively. The horizontal axis of the histogram is the gray level and the vertical axis is the number of pixels. The "mean" is the average brightness value, while the "standard deviation" and "median" are the usual definitions, and "pixels" signifies the total number of pixels in the image.

We should note, for those who want to try these exercises at home, that all processing in these examples was done in Adobe Photoshop 2.0 with a 16 MB RAM partition running on a Mac IIfx with 32 MB RAM, under System 7.0.1. The memory partition only affects the speed of the computation since, if the partition is large enough, all of the image can be loaded into memory at once. Otherwise the data must be continuously read in from disk. The other problem with Photoshop is that it creates a "virtual memory" space on the hard disk, and for large size images this could take quite a while. The virtual memory is equal to the size of the image you are opening.

Figure 1.7a
A Voyager 1 single-filter image of Saturn's ring system. Note the gross structure of a few large rings, although there appears to be a hint of some smaller scale structure. (Courtesy NASA/JPL)

Figure 1.7b
Contrast enhancement of Figure 1.7a. Radial structures (the "spokes" of Saturn's rings) appear in the center of the ring system. These structures were not visible to the unaided eye in Figure 1.7a.

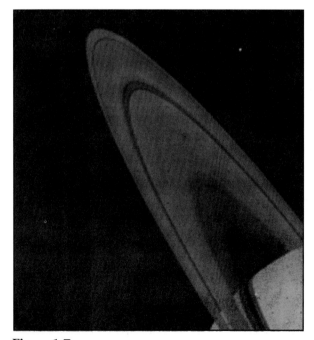

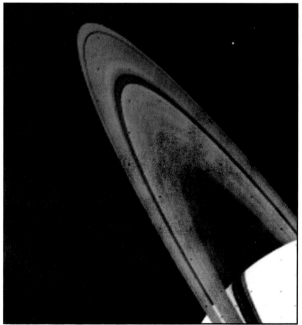

Figure 1.7a   Figure 1.7b

If there is not enough contiguous space, the image opens extremely slow. The raw image data for each of these examples is provided in the CD in the "Image Processing" folder. Each particular computation that we performed here took about 5 to 10 seconds to process in this environment. However, the processing time depends strongly on a variety of factors such as the size of the image in pixels and the complexity of the algorithm.

  Simple contrast enhancement and sharpening filters can be powerful techniques, as we illustrate in Figure 1.7 using a Voyager 1 single-channel image of Saturn's ring system. Figure 1.7a shows the original image, while 1.7b shows the image with a fair amount of contrast enhancement. In the original image Saturn's rings appear to be five or six fairly homogeneous structures. However, upon applying the contrast enhancement filter we can see considerably finer structure in the rings. Notice also that just inside of the dark band (the Cassini division) there appears to be a hint of radial structure in the form of dark streaks. These were identified by planetary scientists as "spokes" and appear to be dark dust electrostatically elevated above the ring plane and partially coupled to Saturn's magnetic field. In Figure 1.7c we apply a *sharpening* filter to the contrast-enhanced image in Figure 1.7b. This is another type of filter that enhances small-scale features in an image. The first thing we notice is that the ring system is made up of literally hundreds of smaller rings (as Figure 1.5 showed in detail). In addition, the spokes become a

Figure 1.7c
A sharpening filter applied to Figure 1.7b really brings out the small scale structure of the rings as well as the spokes.

Figure 1.7d
Another contrast enhancement clearly shows the two inner ringlets, which otherwise would only be faintly visible.
(Courtesy NASA/JPL)

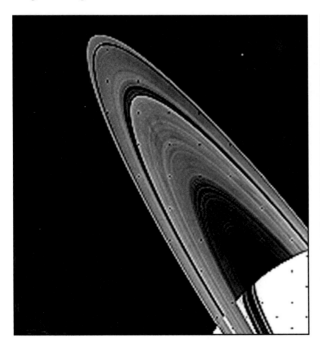

Figure 1.7c

Figure 1.7d

bit more visible under this filter and are clearly identified as radial features. We also see some faint ring structure at the very inner edge of the ring system. Another contrast enhancement (Figure 1.7d) enables us to clearly see two thin rings at the inner edge of the ring system.

IMAGE ANIMATION

For a long time films or videos of sequences of images were considered an extravagant luxury for researchers or, at best, a tool that management and public information folks could use for public lectures and program reviews. Exceptions to this were projects like E.E. "Doc" Edgerton's work at MIT on high-speed photography; satellite-based meteorological data; and fluoroscopy for seeing a patient's gastrointestinal tract at work. But these were specialized technological approaches toward specific scientific or medical problems, and the techniques were not easily generalizable to other content areas.

However, partially as a result of Voyager's observations over the past 15 years, the attitude toward animation has changed considerably. Part of this prejudice had to do with cost: until 1990 or so it was just too expensive to create films or videotapes of large numbers of images as a regular course of research. However, today it is fairly easy for researchers and teachers to create videos of sequences of images, and since videos are a basic medium of exchange of time-dependent, visual

Figure 1.8
This sequence of four images taken by Voyager 1 illustrates the importance of studying the time-dependence of systems. Note the movement of the small vortex in the lower right-hand edge of the red spot. By measuring the distance that this vortex has moved over the course of the four rotations, researchers can obtain local wind-velocity information about Jupiter which would otherwise be difficult to impossible to determine. (Courtesy NASA/JPL)

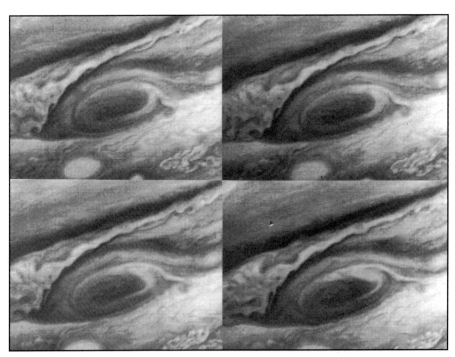

Figure 1.8

information, more and more scientists are using animations as a regular part of their work. As a result, it is now widely accepted that sequences of images of phenomena in any field can clearly be of value when one is interested in time-dependent as well as spatially varying problems.

In Figure 1.8 we show a sequence of images of Jupiter's Great Red Spot that clearly shows the dynamics of the atmosphere in that region. These images were taken by Voyager 1 on its approach to Jupiter approximately 10 hours (one Jovian rotation period) apart. They were the first direct observations of dynamics in Jupiter's atmosphere, and gave researchers an opportunity to study the large-scale structure and dynamics of a planetary atmosphere other than our own. This knowledge has enabled meteorologists to gain a much broader perspective on our own weather systems here on Earth. Figure 1.9 shows the same observational technique applied to Saturn's rings; as a direct result of these images, planetary scientists found that the mysterious radial spokes were partially coupled to the rate of rotation of

CD 1.4

CD 1.5

Figure 1.9

Figure 1.9
A sequence of images of Saturn's rings taken by Voyager 1 enabled researchers to determine that the spokes in the rings were tied to the rotation period of Saturn's magnetic field, rather than to the much more slowly rotating rings themselves. (Courtesy NASA/JPL)

Saturn's magnetic field. This was an unexpected result, leading researchers to consider the broader aspects of electromagnetic forces in the evolution of planetary systems.

In both of these cases, the knowledge gleaned by simply taking a time-dependent data set rather than a single image has changed our knowledge of those systems forever. In Chapter 2 we discuss the process of image animation in some detail from the perspectives of producing videotapes as well as creating sequences of digital images to be viewed on a personal computer.

Beyond Visible Images

Another variable in the imaging world is wavelength. So far we have been discussing images taken primarily in visible light. But what if we branched out from the visible spectrum and looked at wavelengths in the infrared, ultraviolet, X-ray, and radio regions of the electromagnetic spectrum? Just as different colored filters give different views of a scene, each spectral region provides a completely new window on the world. In addition, within each spectral regime different observational techniques and technologies are needed to obtain the data, and different analysis and visualization techniques are required to understand the data. Recent advances in detectors have enabled researchers in many fields to gain insight into processes and phenomena that were once hidden. Moreover, different spectral images of an object often produce such radically different results as to put into question how we classify and analyze many astronomical objects.

As an example, consider the galaxy M31, the famous Andromeda galaxy. In Figure 1.10a we show an image, taken in visible light, from the 200-inch telescope at Palomar Observatory, while in Figure 1.10b we show M31 as imaged in the infrared by IRAS (Infrared Astronomy Satellite) in 1979. Note the distinct difference in structure of the galaxy in the two wavelength bands. A more dramatic example is an image taken recently of the galaxy NGC 309 (Figure 1.10c), which in visible light appears similar to the Milky Way, having three bright arms that spiral out from a central disk. NGC 309 is classified as a classic spiral galaxy. Standard theories of stellar evolution maintain that the luminous arms are the regions of the galaxy where starbirth takes place. However, viewed in the near-infrared at a wavelength of 2.1 μm one of the galaxy's three arms disappears and the central disk appears more like an ellipsoid (Figure 1.10d). This image indicates that the galaxy could belong to an entirely different class of objects, the barred spirals, which differ significantly from classic spiral galaxies in a number of aspects. Whereas the visible image of NGC 309 suggests that the luminous arms are the likely regions of star formation, the infrared image indicates that the central ellipsoid is the principal region of starbirth.

Figure 1.10a

Figure 1.10a
The Andromeda galaxy as photographed in visible light by the 200 inch Mount Palomar telescope. (Courtesy California Institute of Technology)

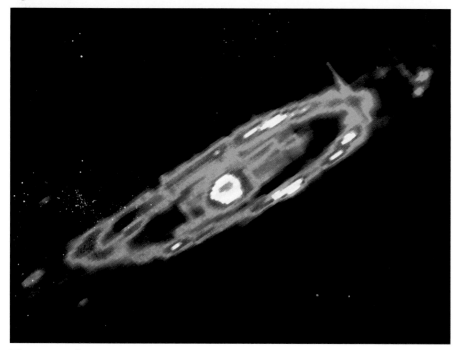

Figure 1.10b

Figure 1.10b
The Andromeda galaxy as viewed in the infrared by the IRAS satellite in 1979. (Courtesy NASA/JPL)

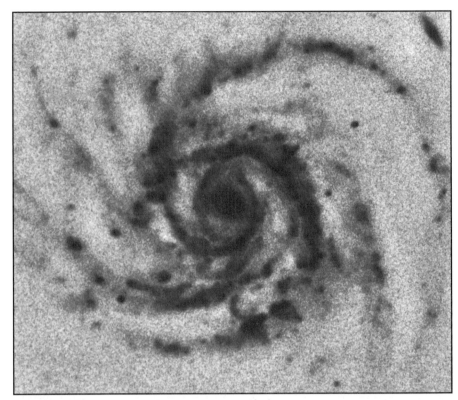

Figure 1.10c
In visible light, NGC 309
appears to be a classic spiral
galaxy with several arms.
(Courtesy David L. Block,
Richard J. Wainscoat, and
T. Kinman)

Figure 1.10c

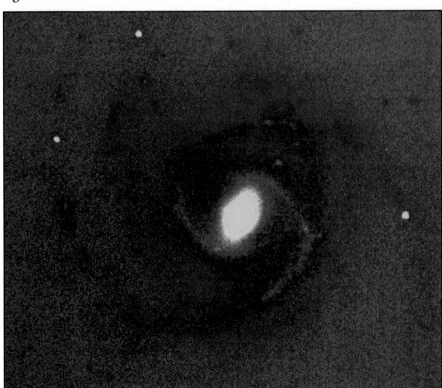

Figure 1.10d
This image of NGC 309,
taken in the infrared and
shown here in color, indicates an entirely different
type of galaxy than is seen
in visible light, and calls
into question the very
process that is used to
classify the structure and
evolution of galaxies.
(Courtesy David L. Block,
Richard J. Wainscoat)

Figure 1.10d

The infrared observing technology used for this image is extremely new, being essentially a prototype of a new infrared detector called NICMOS (Near-Infrared Camera and Multi-Object Spectrograph), which is planned to be installed on the Hubble Space Telescope in 1997 (Block and Wainscoat, 1991). High-resolution infrared astronomy clearly has potential to alter traditional astronomy. In fact, it is now reasonable to conjecture that astronomers must look in both the visible and the infrared windows to truly comprehend many astrophysical phenomena that were typically considered understood. As we've seen, this implies that new forms of data analysis and visualization must be developed to take full advantage of the new observing technologies. Obviously, many galaxies are likely to be reclassified. As our last foray into galactic astronomy, we show the galaxy M83, a prominent radio source, in Figure 1.10e. Note that this image does not resemble anything that we would normally consider to be a galaxy in visible light.

By far the most studied object in the solar system, aside from the Earth, is the Sun. The Sun has been photographed for nearly 150 years, and observed extensively in a variety of wavelengths since 1892 when George Ellery Hale invented the spectroheliograph. The spectroheliograph is an instrument that allows the entire disk of the Sun to be observed

Figure 1.10e
The galaxy M83, a prominent radio galaxy that has a spiral structure when viewed in the visible, looks nothing like any of the spiral galaxies that we've seen in the visible or the infrared. This particular color-contour image shows the distribution of polarized radio continuum emission around M83, as observed with the Very Large Array radio telescope in New Mexico at a wavelength of 20 cm, and processed at NCSA. The image of the galaxy visible at optical wavelengths lies almost entirely within the darker central regions of this figure, indicating that the magnetic field (which must also be present in the bright parts of the galaxy disk) is tangled on length scales of several kiloparsecs. Turbulence in the interstellar gas, driven by the star formation process in the disk of the galaxy, is thought to be the explanation for the magnetic field morphology which results in this remarkable image. (Courtesy S. Sukumar and R. J. Allen, NCSA)

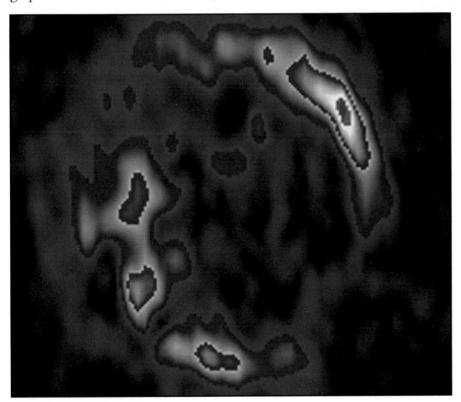

Figure 1.10e

Figure 1.11a
The solar corona in white light taken during a 1973 eclipse. (Courtesy NASA & Optical Data Corp)

Figure 1.11b
Coronal hole stucture as observed by Skylab in an X-ray photo. (Courtesy NASA & Optical Data Corp)

Figure 1.11c
Hydrogen-alpha image of the solar disk with "great sea-horse flare" circled in red. (Courtesy NASA & Optical Data Corp)

Figure 1.11d
Closeup image of the great sea-horse flare (Courtesy NASA & Optical Data Corp)

at any wavelength. Because of the variety of phenomena the Sun exhibits, and the widely varying length-scales over which solar physics is studied, the Sun provides perhaps the best example of an object that presents many faces depending upon the wavelength that you observe it in.

The Sun, a typical star, is a tremendously active object. Most people are familiar with the terms sunspots and solar flare, and many people have even observed them through pinhole cameras or telescopes. However, the Sun exhibits many other kinds of active phenomena, and often a particular event or physical process can only be observed in a specific wavelength region. Only by observing the Sun across a wide spectrum can researchers obtain an accurate understanding of the physics of the solar atmosphere. The different parts of the Sun, which we briefly review below, are active at different wavelengths.

The Sun has a radius of about 700,000 km, however the visible surface of the Sun—the disk that we can see in the visible wavelengths,

Figure 1.11a

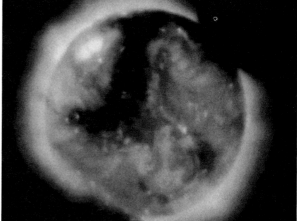

Figure 1.11b

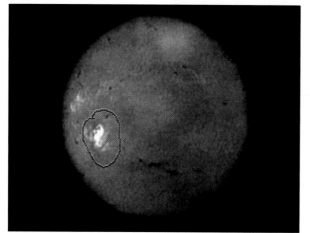

Figure 1.11c

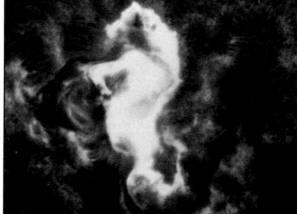

Figure 1.11d

22

called the photosphere—is a shell of gas only about 400 km thick with a temperature (at the top) of about 6000 degrees Kelvin. Nevertheless, this is the region from which nearly all of the Sun's light is emitted. Above the photosphere is a thin, gaseous region about 1000 km thick called the chromosphere. The temperature at the top of the chromosphere is about 50,000 K. Above the chromosphere, extending for several solar radii, is the corona, a hot ionized gas (plasma) with a temperature ranging from several hundred thousand to several million degrees. Beyond the corona is the solar wind, which blows hot plasma at several hundred kilometers per second into interplanetary space.

Figure 1.11 shows images of the photosphere, chromosphere, and corona over several wavelengths taken by a variety of sources from the visible through the extreme ultraviolet and X-ray regions of the spectrum. Figure 1.11a shows the solar corona in white light taken during a 1973 eclipse, while Figure 1.11b shows the coronal hole structure as an

CD 1.6

CD 1.7

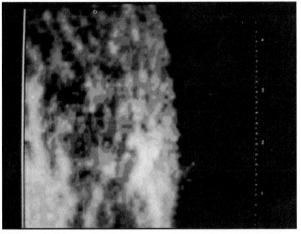

Figure 1.11e

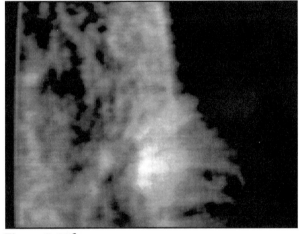

Figure 1.11f

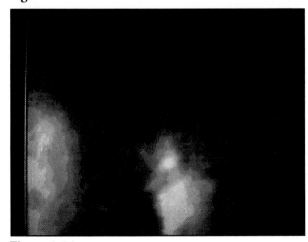

Figure 1.11g

Figure 1.11e
Lyman-alpha UV (122 nm) filter image of the chromosphere taken by Skylab on September 11, 1973.
(Courtesy NASA & Optical Data Corp.)

Figure 1.11f
An O(IV) UV (104 nm) image of the solar chromosphere.
(Courtesy NASA & Optical Data Corp.)

Figure 1.11g
An Mg(X) filter (62 nm) of the chromosphere taken on the same day as Figure 1.11f. Note the strong differences in structure in the two different wavelengths.
(Courtesy NASA & Optical Data Corp.)

CD 1.8

Figure 1.12a-d
An eruptive prominence observed at the Sacramento Peak Solar Observatory on September 1, 1956. (Courtesy Sacramento Peak Observatory & Optical Data Corp.)

X-ray photo taken by Skylab in 1973. Figure 1.11c shows the solar disk in red H-α light on August 7, 1972, including a giant flare known as the "great sea horse flare." Figure 1.11d shows a closeup of this flare. Figures 1.11e, f, and g show the chromosphere photographed in three ultraviolet wavelengths by Skylab on September 11, 1973. These images show that the chromosphere has a widely varying structure depending upon the wavelengths it is viewed in.

The last bit of solar physics we'll do is to study some dynamics as observed by a couple of optical solar observatories over the years. These images were digitized from a laserdisk (*The Universe*) produced by Optical Data Corp. using SuperMac's Video Spigot card. Figures 1.12 show the major eruptive prominence observed at the Sacramento Peak Solar Observatory on September 1, 1956. These four images show a very dynamic system in the upper layers of the solar atmosphere. Conversely, in Figures 1.13 we see closed magnetic loops that appear to

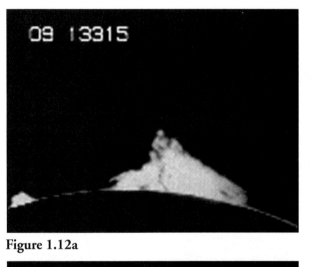

Figure 1.12a

Figure 1.12b

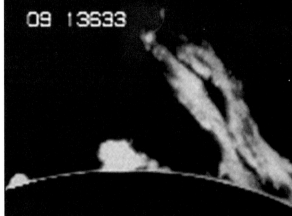

Figure 1.12c

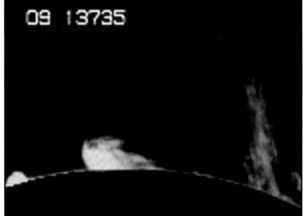

Figure 1.12d

be fairly stable, structurally, although they most likely are channeling plasma through them. These images were also taken at Sacramento Peak on June 28, 1957. Finally, Figure 1.14 shows a giant ascending arc observed on June 28, 1945. The arc appears to be quasi-stable, eventually expanding and dissolving, but nowhere nearly as rapidly as the September 1 prominence.

By combining knowledge gained from studying the Sun throughout the entire spectrum, astronomers can gain a fairly complete picture of the physics of our local star, one which would be impossible to construct with strictly visible-wavelength observations.

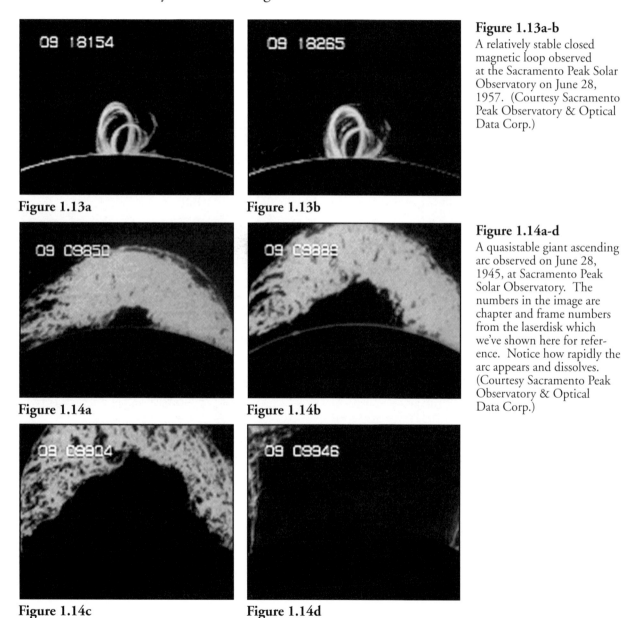

Figure 1.13a   **Figure 1.13b**

Figure 1.14a   **Figure 1.14b**

Figure 1.14c   **Figure 1.14d**

Figure 1.13a-b
A relatively stable closed magnetic loop observed at the Sacramento Peak Solar Observatory on June 28, 1957. (Courtesy Sacramento Peak Observatory & Optical Data Corp.)

Figure 1.14a-d
A quasistable giant ascending arc observed on June 28, 1945, at Sacramento Peak Solar Observatory. The numbers in the image are chapter and frame numbers from the laserdisk which we've shown here for reference. Notice how rapidly the arc appears and dissolves. (Courtesy Sacramento Peak Observatory & Optical Data Corp.)

Summary

CD 1.9   **CD 1.10**

CD 1.11   **CD 1.12**

Images of natural phenomena throughout the electromagnetic spectrum play a large part in our understanding of physical and biological processes. Whereas traditional images in fields such as medicine and astronomy had been typically taken with film, and strictly relied on human eyesight and experience for their analysis, many modern imaging techniques are virtually entirely digital, enabling a vast array of image processing and computing techniques to be applied in both the discovery and analysis ends of the imaging process. In addition, the ability for users to access desktop image animation software is enabling researchers to study time-dependent phenomena in ways that were impossible only a few years ago. Animations CD 1.9 through 1.12 illustrate several other applications of image animation.

Suggested Reading

1. *Digital Image Processing,* by Raphael C. Gonzalez and
   Richard E. Woods, Addison-Wesley, 1992.

2. *Illumination and Color in Computer Generated Imagery,*
   by Roy Hall, Springer-Verlag, 1988.

3. *Computer Graphics: Principles and Practice,*
   by James D. Foley, Andries Van Dam, Steven K. Feiner, and
   John F. Hughes, Addison-Wesley, 1990.

4. *Video Technology for Computer Graphics,* ACM SIGGRAPH
   '92 Course Notes #4, by Dean Winkler, 1992.

5. *Color Theory and Models for Computer Graphics and
   Visualization,* ACM SIGGRAPH '92 Course Notes #10,
   by Haimi Levkowitz, 1992.

Imaging Numbers 2

In Chapter 1 we explored the range of capabilities of image processing and the methodology for analyzing images, enhancing features, and extracting information that is otherwise not readily visible. However, the images we dealt with were usually pictures of objects, even if those objects were amorphous in nature or were imaged in the nonvisible range of the spectrum. The point is that the image of the object was obtained with some sort of imaging device, be it a camera on a spacecraft, a telescope, or an X-ray machine in a doctor's office. Hence, our mindset when we study these objects is one of looking at a well-defined structure in an attempt to discover new information. From another perspective, imaging data as we had implicitly defined it in Chapter 1 is usually confined to an 8-bit dynamic range (zero to 255) in the case of gray-scale imaging or 8 bits per channel in a "full-color" RGB image.

If we abstract the concept of an image away from the picture metaphor to simply a pixel representation of an arbitary function or dataset $f(x,y)$, then we potentially have a powerful tool for visual analysis of arbitrary numerical data. Unfortunately, we immediately run into problems. First, whereas a gray-scale image necessarily has an integer dynamic range from 0 to 255, an actual data set of floating-point numbers can have any value within an almost unlimited dynamic range. Thus, if we apply imaging techniques to nonimage data we need to carefully consider the conversion between the floating-point representation of the data and the integer representation of gray-scale or color channel image data (see **Tech Note 3**). Second, in contrast to pictures of planets, for example, images of arbitrary data have no natural color representations, and we therefore are forced to construct arbitrary color mappings of the data. This is more of an art than a science and, at best, is a tricky operation, since the researcher may not know the values or dynamic range of the features of interest.

In this chapter we consider the general problem of imaging arbitrary floating-point data sets and the intrinsic value of these kinds of visualization techniques to the working scientist.

• First, we introduce the subject through historical examples from space physics and astrophysics.

• Next we develop the general image model by first examining the next closest visualization technique—contour plots—using several examples from a variety of researchers to illustrate the points made.

• We then discuss animation techniques as a way to visualize time-dependent systems.

• Finally, we cover the pitfalls as well as the productivity advantages in using desktop imaging and animation capabilities as a daily tool.

Historical Background

In this section we look at some of the historical roots of data imaging, identify the kinds of data-imaging problems that today's researchers confront, and see how the capabilities of today's desktop systems address these problems. Much of the work in this area stemmed from the needs of astrophysicists and space physicists, who had large amounts of data to sort through in short periods of time. These needs led researchers to try to convert floating-point data of the form $f(x,y)$ to images.

In Chapter 1 the examples that we gave were based on data with integer values; we dealt with the issue of noninteger data by using a linear map from the data space to the image space. That works fine for systems with small dynamic range. But what if, for example, you have an array of floating-point numbers that represent, say, the density (number of particles per cubic meter) or flux (number of particles per second) of a plasma in a region of space? Such a data set could easily span several orders of magnitude, as in crossing the boundary between the ionosphere of Venus and the solar wind, or a simple expansion of a high-density jet into interstellar space. In these cases a linear mapping into the 8-bit dynamic range of our gray-scale or pseudocolor image isn't sufficient to provide any detail within the range of values in the physical phenomena under consideration. Twenty-four-bit color would be fine, if it were a continuous scale, but the reality is that 24-bit color is usually divided up into three bands for any display or output device, and arbitrarily separating a function into red, green and blue ranges leads to artificial discontinuities. The issue then resolves to representing an arbitrary dynamic range of a parameter with a given color map. This is not easy since one cannot really build a comprehensive theory of this process, but if one takes an empirical approach, quite good results can be achieved. For those readers interested in a more quantitative discussion of this subject, **Tech Note 3** goes into more detail about color transformations, and how improper considerations in mapping data into a color range can lead to false results.

Space exploration has always produced spinoff technologies according to the adage "necessity is the mother of invention". So it was with images of plasma data, which were, as far as we can determine, the first color images of any digitally recorded fluid phenomena, being produced in 1969 as part of the Injun-5 program to study the auroral arcs at high latitudes in the northern hemisphere. The work was done by Louis A. Frank and his team at the University of Iowa, in Iowa City. These crude, but very valuable images of the energy spectra of spacecraft plasma showed the energy on the y-axis versus time on the x-axis. Color indicated the number of particles per second observed at any point in time in a given energy range for the plasma (Figure 2.1a). Other experimenters followed Frank's lead, and now spectrograms are commonplace forms of data visualization in space plasma physics. In 1985, one of us (Wolff) and Stephen Philipson took Frank's basic spectrogram technique and built a system for the Voyager Plasma Science Experiment designed to rapidly analyze and visualize plasma data for the Uranus encounter. John Belcher, the current Principal Investigator of the experiment, and colleagues at MIT have since gone back and reanalyzed much of the previous Voyager data using this visualization method (Figure 2.1b and c). However, in 1985 we still needed custom software and relatively expensive hardware that was not very easy to use.

Another important development occurred in 1985 with the birth of the National Center for Supercomputing Applications (NCSA). As it turns out, the developments at NCSA led directly to the desktop visualization capabilities that researchers have available today. In October of that year one of us (Wolff) was invited by Larry Smarr, the fledgling center's director, along with Mike Norman (then at Los Alamos) and

CD 2.1

Chuck Evans and John Hawley (then of Caltech) to "test-drive" the first Cray supercomputer being installed at the new national center.

Hawley and Norman had brought some code with them that enabled a Sun 2-170 workstation to create an image using the data from their interstellar shock simulation. Figure 2.2a is an image of the diver-

Figure 2.1a

This energy-time spectrogram from plasma data produced by the Injun-5 spacecraft in 1969 is one of the first published images of floating-point data. In the image, energy is along the *y*-axis, time is along the *x*-axis, and color represents the number of particles per second observed at any point in time in a given energy range. At the time, to produce an image like this required very specialized hardware and software running on a mainframe computer. (Courtesy Louis Frank, University of Iowa)

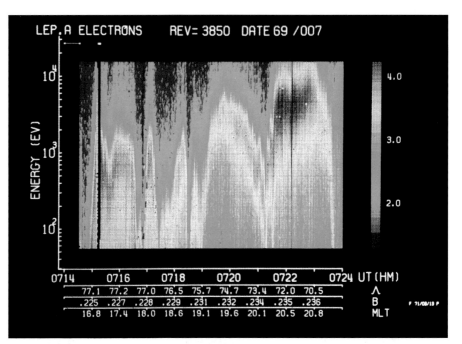

Figure 2.1a

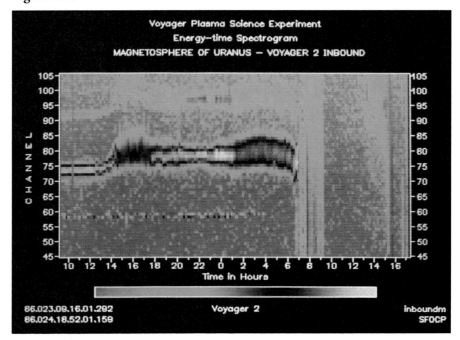

Figure 2.1b

This color spectrogram from the Voyager Plasma Science Experiment was produced in January 1986 in near real-time on a Sun 2-170 during Voyager 2's encounter with Uranus as part of a prototype experiment in real-time data analysis at JPL. The *y*-axis is energy. The *x*-axis is time, and color represents the plasma flux per square centimeter. The total time from receipt of the spacecraft data at JPL to the production of the slide was under two hours. (Courtesy John Belcher, MIT)

Figure 2.1b

gence of the velocity field of a Mach 6 shock wave arising from a jet with a density of 0.1 of the ambient density. This particular simulation is computed on a 300-by-600 grid in the upper half-plane and symmetrically reflected about the x-axis. The original calculation by Norman et al. (1981) was computed on a 60-by-240 grid. Figure 2.2b is an image of the density field from the same shock wave as in Figure 2.2a, but with a color palette selected to accentuate the structure along the bow shock and the central axis. The imaging technique had been pioneered in 1982 in Germany by Karl-Heinz Winkler and Mike Norman. However, the Winkler-Norman work on this imaging technique, called MUNA-COLOR (Norman and Winkler, 1986), was viewed as being beyond the average scientist's capability. The mapping from data space to 8-bit color space was a simple logarithmic function (see **Tech Note 3** for more discussion on this general technique), and the colors showed up brilliantly on the screen—especially late at night when everything else in the building was pitch black. Hawley's image on the monitor showed fine structure in the calculation which had rarely, if ever, been observed before in any fluid simulation. That vision changed the way that the four of us viewed numbers and, more important, fired one of the first volleys in the scientific visualization revolution that was to come. Hawley also took his simulation results to the commercial computer graphics company Digital

CD 2.2

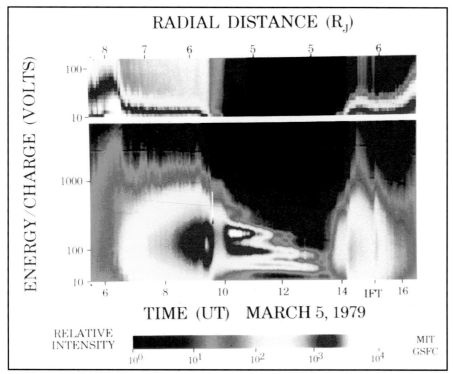

Figure 2.1c

Figure 2.1c
As a result of the Uranus encounter work, the Voyager Plasma Science Team went back and re-analyzed the old Jupiter and Saturn data using the spectrogram tools developed for the 1986 Uranus encounter. This slide shows one such analysis of the crossing of the Io torus. (Courtesy John Belcher, MIT)

Productions (along with Joan Centrella and a number of other researchers), as part of the National Science Foundation's National Supercomputer Initiative (from which came part of the funds to help found the NCSA), and participated in the production of one of the first in a new wave of high-quality scientific animations. (Chapter 7 discusses this cross-fertilization between science and Hollywood, and contains images and movies from a number of researchers at Digital Productions.)

A few months later Norman, who by then had joined NCSA, and Carol Song, a graduate student in computer science, began working

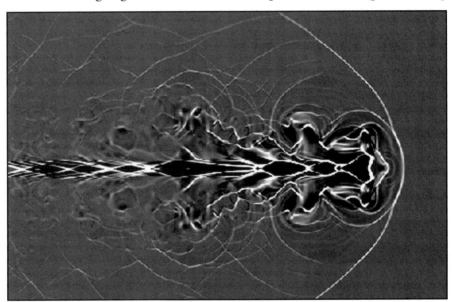

Figure 2.2a
An image of the divergence of a Mach 6 shock wave arising from a jet with a density of 0.1 of the ambient density. (Courtesy Michael Norman, NCSA)

Figure 2.2a

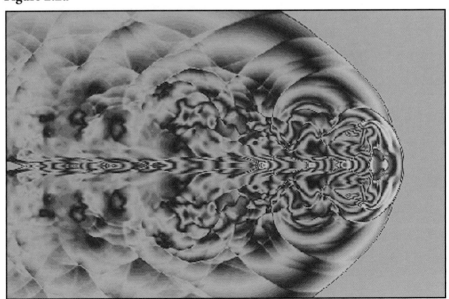

Figure 2.2b
An image of the density field from the same simulation, but with a color palette selected to highlight the bow shock and central axis structure. (Courtesy Michael Norman, NCSA)

Figure 2.2b

on a program called *ImageTool* that was an interactive version of the software that Hawley had demonstrated. ImageTool ran on a Sun 3-160 and, in addition to simply displaying images, it allowed the user to interactively manipulate the color palette—the mapping of the image data to color space—so that one could examine various structural details of a given image by cueing a particular color to a specific feature. If used properly, color palettes can be used to illustrate specific features of a function or a data set.

Contour Plots and Related Techniques: Pre-Images

In Chapter 1 we represented an image as an array of integers, where each integer corresponded to a particular color or gray-scale value. This chapter has so far focused on extending the image metaphor to include floating-point data of the form $f(x,y)$ and the transformations of those data into images. However, before researchers imaged data they computed contour maps, and contours still play a major role in data analysis and visualization. In this section we use *contour plots* (or *contour maps*) as a tool to study the structure of 2-D scalar functions, and we examine the differences between contour plots and images of a given data set.

One traditional way of approaching the general visualization problem is to simply begin with contour plots and expand the various visualization schemes from there. As we shall see, contour plots can be considered in many ways to be "pre-images" of floating-point data, and it is interesting to study them as a separate entity. Contour plots are revisited in Chapter 4 as a component in the visualization of multi-dimensional, multivariate data sets.

On a basic level, contour plots are simply visual representations of $f(x,y)$ such that the only points drawn are those satisfying $f_i(x,y) = C_i$, where the C_i are contours, curves representing specific levels in the data space. These contours are usually drawn as 2-D curves in a plane, and there are a wide variety of algorithms that are used in commercial as well as public-domain programs to compute contours of a data set or continuous function. In Figure 2.3 we use Mathematica to compute a contour plot for a simple electric dipole field

$$f(x, y) = \frac{x^2}{\left(x^2 + y^2\right)^2}$$

Notice that the function as plotted is not "smooth"—that is, you can see the line segments in a given contour, especially in the low-resolution image. This is a result of aliasing at low-resolution sampling, a concept introduced in **Tech Note 2** when we discussed sampling theory and the structure of a function in Fourier space. Also notice that, as the plot resolution is increased, more structure appears, and the asymptote toward the singularity at the origin becomes more properly defined.

For reference, the images in Figure 2.3 were generated on a Mac IIfx in Mathematica in less than a minute with a one-line command:

ContourPlot[x^2/(x^2+y^2),{x,-Pi,Pi},{y,-Pi,Pi},
PlotPoints->n,Contours->c, ContourShading->False]

This command simply says, "Take the Mathematica function "**ContourPlot**" and apply it to the function $f(x,y)$ in the range $-\pi \le x \le \pi$ and $-\pi \le y \le \pi$ with n points along each axis and the number of contour levels set equal to c. Do not apply any shading to the contours." (Not all that long ago this simple command would have required days to weeks of work, not to mention the hundreds to thousands of dollars in "computing time.")

An aspect of the contour plot from the visualization perspective is that it is usually difficult to remember specific features of a contour plot when you're not staring at it. This is likely due to the fact that, in any contour plot, the amount of "information" is small compared to the amount of "white space." As a result, particular features stand out less than, say, a full image of the same data would. Moreover, gaining an understanding of the contour of a function often requires reading the labels on the plot and following the contours around. In addition, whereas the user can clearly obtain some information from a contour plot about the global structure of the data set, virtually all the local structure (the function's value at a given point, gradients, singularities, and so forth) is lost. Nevertheless, the contour plot is a well-established analytical tool in the physical sciences. Indeed, researchers have been publishing contour plots of their data for several decades and, for the most part, contour plots have been the principal means by which researchers have visualized scalar functions of two variables. Pavlides (1982) has a good technical discussion on the geometric issues of defining contours on a grid.

Some of the problems discussed above can be mitigated by going to finer grids and contour levels. In other words, as we reduce the parameter value distance we pick up structure that was not visible in the coarse-grained contour representation. However, as the number of contours becomes large the graph becomes more of a continuous black image rather than a set of contours. Moreover, the contour labels rapidly become impossible to discern. Thus, simply increasing the

CD 2.3

number of contour levels has limits for utility. However, if, in addition to increasing the number of contour levels, we also assigned a particular color or gray-level to each contour level, the user would be able to begin to visually discern *x*- and *y*-gradients along the contour surface. In this

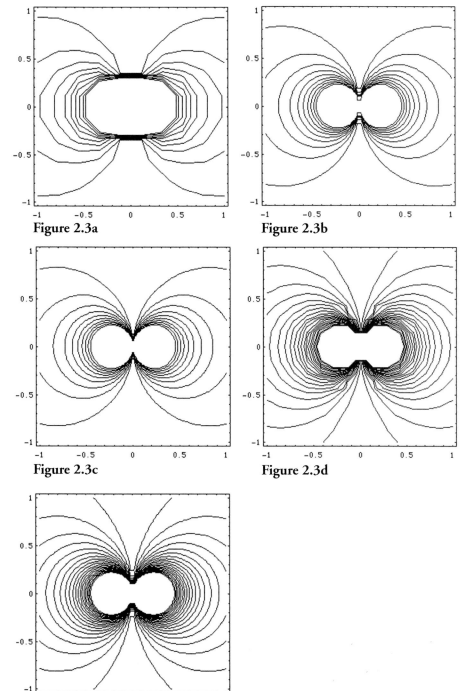

Figure 2.3a

Figure 2.3b

Figure 2.3c

Figure 2.3d

Figure 2.3e

Figure 2.3a
Contour plot of a dipole field with number of samples along each axis $n = 10$ and number of contour levels $c = 10$ (see text for details).

Figure 2.3b
Same as Figure 2.3a, but with $n = 50$, $c = 10$.

Figure 2.3c
Same as 2.3a, but with $n = 100$, $c = 10$.

Figure 2.3d
Same as 2.3a, but with $n = 15$ and $c = 20$.

Figure 2.3e
Same as 2.3a, but with $n = 50$, $c = 20$.

context, as the number of contour levels grows, the contour plot approaches an image of the function. Thus, contour plots can be considered to be "pre-images," in the sense that one can build an image of a data set by properly transforming its contour plot. Figure 2.3 illustrates this progressive approach. Taking our test function as an example, we can create a "false image" in gray-scale that gives us a much better visual feel for the structure of the function than the simple contour plot itself (Figure 2.3f). This is because the gray scale can give us visual cues on local structure, gradients, and other attributes that simple contour lines cannot. There's simply more information available in an image. On the practical side of things, to produce this image in Mathematica all we had to change in our generating equation is to set

ContourShading->True

That's a far cry from a few years ago, when it generally required generating and compiling new FORTRAN code to produce an image from the contour plot. However, the gray-scale image produced with the contour plot was not a true pixel representation of the data. It was more of a gray-scale representation of the contour plot. We can plot just the true gray-scale image of the data with a command similar to "ContourPlot". The difference between a true image and an image generated with "ContourShading" is that the true image is actually a pixel representation of the data. This gives all of the small-scale structure that we need in order to understand and thoroughly analyze the

Figure 2.3f
Same as 2.3c,
but with Contour
Shading -> True.

Figure 2.3g
Same resolution as 2.3c, but
with the imaging function
"DensityPlot" turned on.

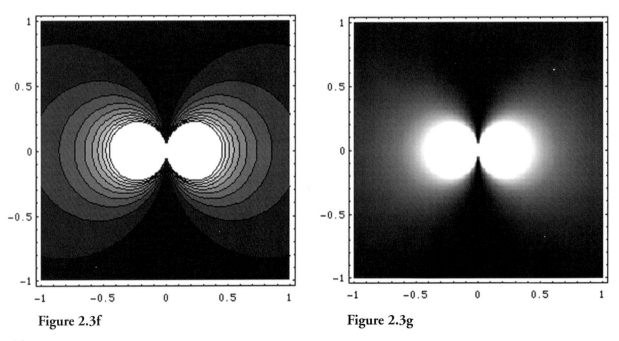

Figure 2.3f   **Figure 2.3g**

data. The new command is

$$\text{DensityPlot}[x\text{\textasciicircum}2/(x\text{\textasciicircum}2+y\text{\textasciicircum}2),\{x,\text{-Pi,Pi}\},\{y,\text{-Pi,Pi}\},$$
$$\text{PlotPoints-}{>}200,\text{Mesh-}{>}\text{False}]$$

and the results are shown in Figure 2.3g, which is essentially an image of the test function produced by the Mathematica routine **DensityPlot** with the parameter **Mesh**—which produces a grid on the image— turned off. Next we will extend this metaphor and apply imaging techniques to a variety of floating-point data.

More Imaging Examples

In Figure 2.4 we show polar images of the wave-function for a hydrogen orbital. The data represents a two-dimensional slice through a particular wave-function of the electron in a hydrogen atom. The selected wave-function is one of the $3d$ orbitals (where n=3, l=2, m=0). The general equation used is

CD 2.4

$$r^2 \sin(\theta)\cos(\theta)e^{-(r/c)}$$

where r is radius, θ is the angle in radians, and c is a constant. The images were generated using "Polar Image" in Spyglass Transform.

In Figure 2.5 we show several images of a supercomputer simulation of the nonlinear growth of a Kelvin-Helmholtz kink instability in a Mach 3 supersonic jet. The simulation was performed in two space dimensions on a numerical grid of 600×320 zones, and required 20 hours of CPU time on the NCSA Cray X-MP. Note how the different palettes accentuate different features of the flow in these images.

Figure 2.6 shows a different use of imaging, in this case to visualize the height of different regions of the Earth relative to sea level. Figure 2.6a shows a relief map of the world while Figure 2.6b shows the sea depth. Note how a good choice of palette and some relief to the data (apparent height as a function of latitude and longitude) dramatically visualize the data sets. Figure 2.7 shows the surface elevation and bedrock structure of Antarctica using two different palettes.

Figures 2.8 to 2.17 show a variety of images of data sets from a number of research areas. The variety is endless, and essentially all fields can benefit from application of this simple technology. Computationally, a program like Spyglass Transform takes only a few seconds to generate a 300×300 image on a Mac IIfx.

Figure 2.4a

This is a polar image of a 2-D slice of the wave function for a 3-D hydrogen orbital. In this series of images we can see how different palettes bring out different structural features of a data set and can lead to very different scientific interpretations. In addition, different palettes can introduce artifacts such as banding into the image which can mask the real science. This image is displayed with NCSA palette "Rain.Band."

Figure 2.4b

Same as 2.4a, but with NCSA palette "Rainbow."

Figure 2.4c

Same as 2.4a, but with NCSA palette "Apricot."

Figure 2.4d

Same as 2.4a, but with NCSA palette "Morning Glory."

Figure 2.4e

Same as 2.4a, but with NCSA palette "Metal."

Figure 2.4f

Same as 2.4a, but with NCSA palette "Gray-Banded."

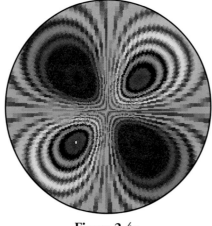

Figure 2.4a

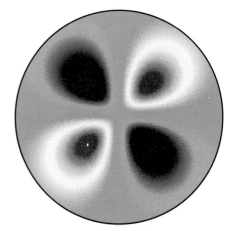

Figure 2.4b

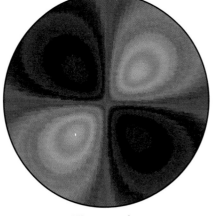

Figure 2.4c

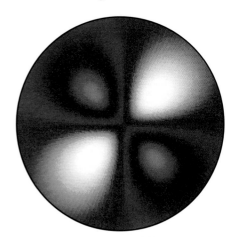

Figure 2.4d

Figure 2.4e

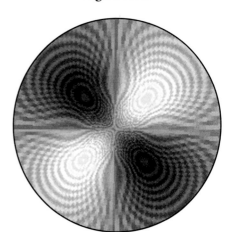

Figure 2.4f

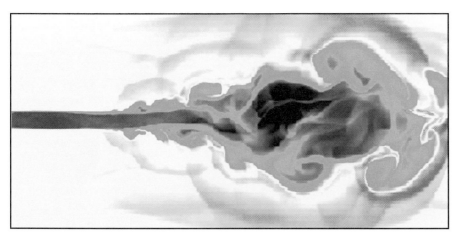

Figure 2.5a

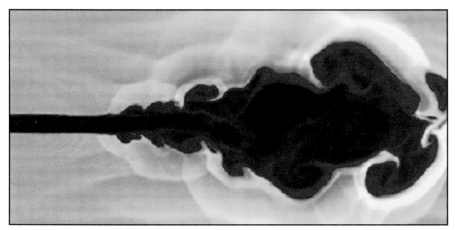

Figure 2.5b

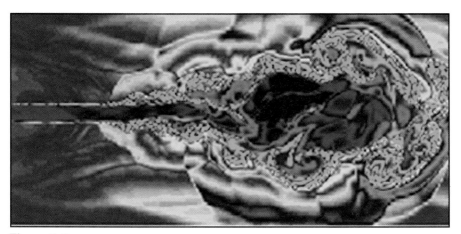

Figure 2.5c

Figure 2.5a-c
Images of the density of a gas dynamic simulation of nonlinear growth of a Kelvin-Helmholtz kink instability in a Mach 3 supersonic jet. This sequence of images illustrates the same concept of color mapping that we showed in Figures 2.4, however, in this case the data is discrete as opposed to a continuous function (see text for details). (Courtesy Michael Norman, NCSA)

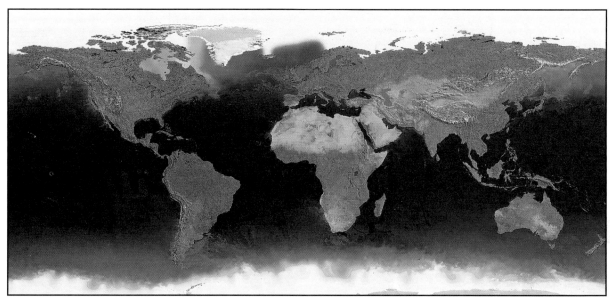

Figure 2.6a

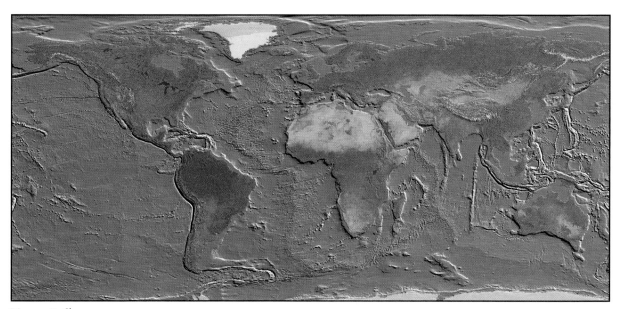

Figure 2.6b

Figure 2.6a

A relief map of the world showing terrain and vegetation features constructed from three component data sets.
The first data set is ETOPO5 (Earth topography at 5-minute resolution from NOAA with a vertical resolution of 100 m).
The second component is the 18 km sea-surface temperature created from AVHRR (Advanced Very High Resolution Infrared Radiometer), an instrument on Nimbus-9 from the University of Miami. The third component is a re-coloration of AVHRR Global Area coverage (GAC) infrared and visible which just shows land-surface features. (Courtesy Jim Knighton, Van Warren, Tom Van Sant, Erik Bruhwiler, NASA/JPL)

Figure 2.6b

The same as Figure 2.6a, but with the sea-surface temperature component removed via Photoshop. Note how that, when viewed in this manner, the ETOPO5 data set provides a very visual map of the world's ocean floor, showing undersea mountain ranges. (Courtesy Jim Knighton, Van Warren, Tom Van Sant, Erik Bruhwiler, NASA/JPL)

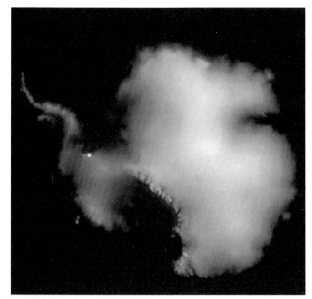

Figure 2.7a

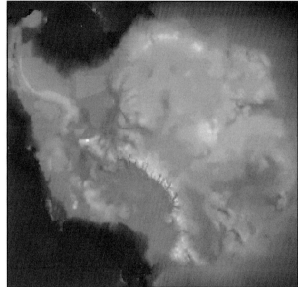

Figure 2.7b

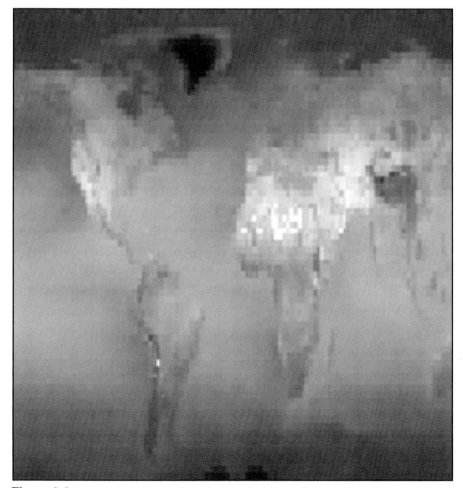

Figure 2.8

Figure 2.7a
Antarctica surface elevation.
Data is public domain taken
from the British Antarctica
survey, Drewry, 1983. (Image
courtesy Doug MacAyeal,
University of Chicago)

Figure 2.7b
Antarctica bedrock structure.
Data is public domain taken
from the British Antarctica
survey. (Image courtesy
Doug MacAyeal, University
of Chicago)

Figure 2.8
This image is the average
global surface temperature
for July 1979 from the
TIROS-N NOAA satellite.
Two instruments on board,
HIRS2 (infrared) and MSU
(microwave), are used in the
processing. Note the bright
(hot) spots in the U.S.
Southwest and the dark (cold)
area in Greenland and South
America. Combined with
actual surface temperature
information, ice and snow
cover can be deduced.
(Courtesy Bob
Haskins/NASA/JPL)

Figure 2.9
An image of the Lyapunov
function in chaos theory,
produced in IDL. (Courtesy
Research Systems, Inc.)

CD 2.5

Figure 2.10
Nimbus-9 Total Ozone
Mapping Spectrometer
(TOMS) data of the monthly
average total ozone over the
Earth during a northern
winter month (note the
absence of data in the north
polar region). The ozone level
is measured in Dobson units,
which is the total column
density of ozone between
the point of observation and
the ground. In this image the
"qualitative" color table ranges
from dark brown (low ozone)
to light yellow (high ozone).
(Courtesy Jim Knighton,
Simon Simpson, NASA/JPL)

Figure 2.9

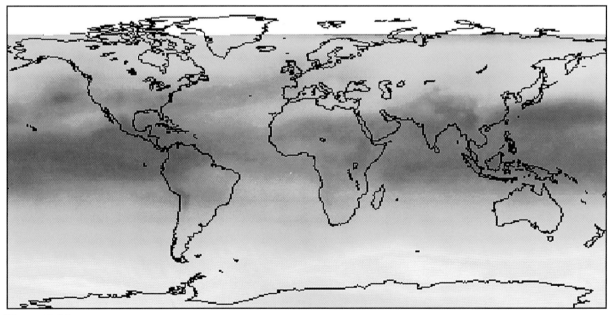

Figure 2.10

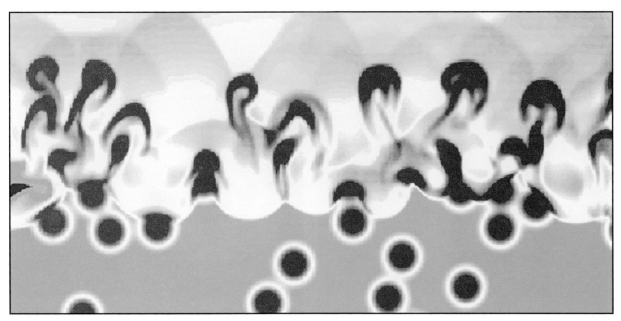

Figure 2.11

Figure 2.11
Simulation of supernova shock
wave interacting with clumps
of matter. Colors represent
the local density of matter.
(Courtesy Michael Norman,
NCSA)

Figure 2.12
Mandelbrot Set fractal image.
Colors are a qualitative
indication of how long it
takes for a point to escape to
infinity. Image produced in
NCSA Image (For more
information on fractals see
Peitgen and Richter, 1986,
or Peitgen et al., 1992.)
(Courtesy NCSA)

Figure 2.12

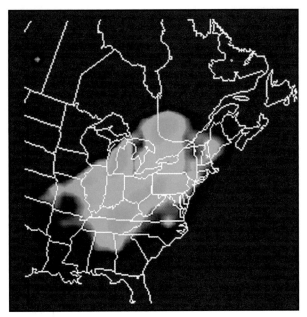

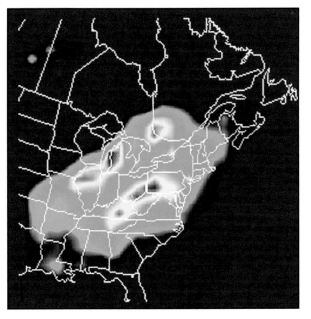

Figure 2.13

Figure 2.13
Sulfate concentrations as an indicator of acid rain. The image was created from data generated from a 3-D Eulerian model, referred to as the Acid Deposition and Oxidant Model. The model simulations were generated on a Cray X-MP at the Canadian Meteorological Center in Montreal. Scientists at ENSR used Spyglass Transform and Format to create and annotate the images, and AtlasPro to create the map. The image is from an animation showing the pattern of sulfate wet deposition, which is the main contributor to acidic deposition in the Eastern United States. (Courtesy A. Venkatram, P.K. Karamchandani, G. Kuntasal, Gürkan Kuntasal, ENSR Consulting and Engineering)

CD 2.6

CD 2.8

Figure 2.14
Frame from a time-dependent simulation of the forces on the San Andreas fault. Color indicates shear stress, with blue being lowest and red being the highest. (Courtesy Gregory Lyzenga, NASA/JPL)

Figure 2.14

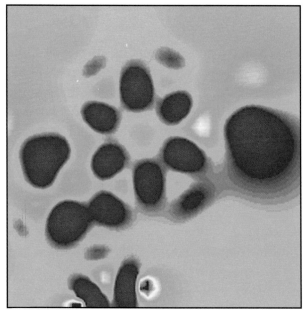

Figure 2.15

Figure 2.17

Figure 2.15
Electrostatic potential of serotonin calculated in a plane for $x = -4$ Å to 4 Å and $y = -1$ Å to 7 Å. The electrostatic potential at each of these points is computed using the electrostatic multipoles (monopoles, dipoles, and quadrupoles) calculated from a finite-expansion technique. (Courtesy Harel Weinstein, EPA and NCSA)

CD 2.7

Figure 2.16
Electropheresis gel of DNA.   (Courtesy Thomas Jacobs, University of Illinois)

Figure 2.17
Radius vs. time image of a simulation of mass accretion onto a neutron star where color represents density. The periodicity observed here was discovered by imaging the data set. (Courtesy Brand Fortner, Spyglass, Inc.)

Desktop Animation

From a researcher's perspective, often one of the most frustrating issues in scientific computing is the question of how to show an animated sequence of images. Since most phenomena exhibit some time dependency, the question is, "Can personal computer and workstation software be developed to make near real-time display of a sequence of images?" The answer is a qualified yes, as we'll explain below. In addition, since it is important to be able to present these animations at scientific meetings, or to show to students in a class, the researcher also needs to know how to make videotapes of the animations. Desktop animation and video production are quite normal activities in what can be considered "personal multimedia computing" today. Unfortunately, most scientists are unaware of the advances that have been made in this area over the past couple of years. Moreover, virtually all of the multimedia technology has ignored the specific needs of scientists and engineers. Thus, even though researchers spend several billion dollars a year on personal computers, it was only in 1992 that a few multimedia companies began to ship products that can deal with scientific data formats such as HDF. No wonder the average scientist feels left out of the technology revolution!

As far as animation is concerned, there are two aspects we can consider. First, there is what we shall term "desktop animation," that is, rapid display of a sequence of images on the computer. This function is invaluable for analyzing large amounts of data. Take, for example, the kinds of hydrodynamic simulations discussed in the previous section. One of the things that researchers from NCSA to Los Alamos discovered in the mid-1980s is that, unless one could display images at a rate of at least 10–15 frames per second, many of the time-dependent phenomena of interest would not be discernible. That's because the maximum time interval that the eye-brain system can perceive two sequential images as continuous is around 0.1 second. Thus, for example, a sequence of images played at, say, five frames per second looks too jerky and disconnected to easily be perceived as a continuous animation. On the other hand, standard video frame rates are roughly 30 frames per second (film is 24 fps), so it's clear that somewhere between 10 and 30 frames per second is a reasonable number to shoot for in a screen animation. More than 30 frames per second really doesn't have much effect on the viewer.

The second kind of animation we'll talk about is video animation, or how to go from computer to videotape. The basic concepts are discussed in detail in the following section, and some of the hardware considerations are detailed in **Tech Notes** 4 and 5.

In order to even begin an animation sequence on your computer you need to have each of the frames (or timesteps) in your data in a form that can be displayed as an image. In NCSA and Spyglass tools this is done automatically, especially for data in HDF (Hierarchical Data File) format. Given that, the simple way to think of the general animation problem is that a given computer has a certain bandwidth, and within that bandwidth must fit a body of data with three parameters: (1) a certain number of frames per second at (2) a certain resolution or image size (3) at a certain color, or bit depth.

The bandwidth is limited by the slowest member in the data path. This could be the internal bus architecture of the computing environment (on the Macintosh, for example, the NuBus has a bandwidth of about 4.4 MB/s) if, for example, all of the data is stored in memory. On the other hand, if the data is stored on disk you're most likely limited by the speed that the hard disk transfers data to the CPU, or central processing unit. Typical personal computer SCSI (Small Computer System Interface) data rates today are in the 1–2 MB/s range for continuous file transfer, less in the case of sequences of files transferred. As this book is being written, however, SCSI-2 standards are being implemented, which will increase disk transfer rates by factors of two to several, although most users won't see any improvement until SCSI-2 CPUs and peripherals become widely available. Alternatively, in a distributed environment like an X-window system, the limit is imposed by the network; for example, Ethernet clocks in at at roughly 1 MB/s, although actual rates are often much slower. Again, these limitations will change as higher speed networks become commonplace over the next few years that support both large single file transfers and the kinds of data "streaming" that are needed for desktop animation. (Networked desktop animation issues are discussed further in **Tech Note** 6.)

From the above analysis we can then develop an equation to predict the frame rate (R) for a given animation as a function of bandwidth (B), in megabits per second, the size of each image in pixels per frame (A), and the color-depth (N) in bits per pixel of the image:

$$R = B/AN$$

Thus, given a limiting bandwidth from network, disk transfer, or bus speeds, we quite reasonably find that the larger the area or bit depth, the lower the frame rate will be for the animation. This was a

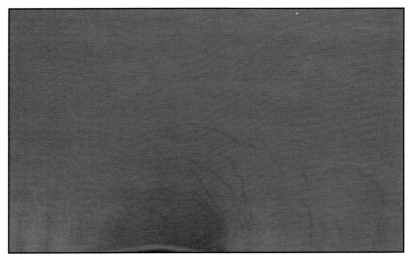

Figure 2.18a

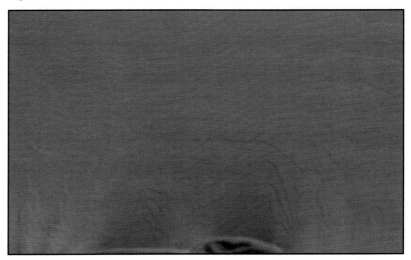

Figure 2.18b

Figure 2.18a-e
Frames from a simulation of
the solar wind interaction
with the ionosphere of Venus
(by R. S. Wolff and M. L.
Norman). Notice how
quickly the plasma "blob"
moves across the frame.
Without animated visualization this effect would have
been very difficult to capture
and study.

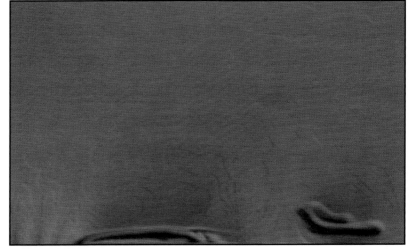

Figure 2.18c

problem that Mike Norman and Carol Song surmounted when their Imagetool program was modifed to include the capabilities to animate data. Using it, one of us (Wolff) was able to identify a rapidly forming and moving plasma cloud in a simulation of the solar wind interaction with the Venus ionosphere (Figure 2.18). The cloud formed and traversed the frame width in about 10 frames or so, and would likely have been missed in a systematic examination of the simulation data every, say, 20 frames. We can see this dramatically in the accompanying images of Figure 2.18, at frames 25, 50, 60, 75, and 80, respectively. The plasma cloud forms at around frame 60. By frame 75 only a slight image of the cloud's trailing edge remains in the image, and by frame 80 the cloud is entirely out of the picture. Although the transport physics

Figure 2.18d

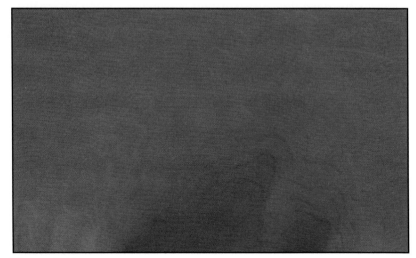

Figure 2.18e

of the cloud was consistent with solar wind plasma accretion theory, and hence we expected the cloud to be transported out of the image within 10 to 15 frames, we had no idea just when the cloud would form. Consequently, without the ability to use animation, it would have been very difficult to "trap" the cloud. (We visit this simulation again in Chapter 4.)

As an example, let's say that you determine that you need a 200×200 pixel, 8-bit-deep image at 15 frames per second to have a reasonable animation of your data. (Though many manufacturers are touting high-resolution, million-plus pixel displays, for most scientific needs, 200×200 is usually sufficient. As we'll see below, image size is a significant determinant in system requirements.) Thus, you need a bandwidth of at least 6 MB/s in order to view the data. This automatically imposes several real-world constraints. First, if you have, say, 3000 time steps, a nominal amount for most numerical simulations, then each parameter you wish to animate needs 120 MB of storage on your system.

Typical hydrodynamic simulations usually have at least 10 (scalar plus component vector) parameters, which means that, somewhere, you need 1.2 GB of disk space just to keep the data from the animation while you view it! But this 1.2 GB is most likely generated not on your desktop system, but rather, on some high-speed departmental, university, or labwide supercomputer. So, you then have to get the data over to your machine which takes, in a typical Ethernet configuration, about 1000 seconds or so, assuming that you have the disk space available and the Ethernet is running efficiently. However, if you listen to some hardware manufacturers, you'd be sending 1000×1000 pixel images, or 30 GB of data to your machine, which would take about 7 hours, assuming that you had a small disk farm.

Alternatively, you could animate from your computer or file server, which even at typical Ethernet speeds (10 Mbits/s) would mean about 25 frames per second (at $200 \times 200 \times 8$ bits or 40 kB per frame), which is perfectly sufficient for analysis—assuming, of course, that the network was running efficiently. Notice that our assumption all along is that we are working with 8-bit images. If, however, you need 24-bit images, or you need to see more than one parameter animating at a time, then all bets are off as far as most local area networks are concerned, and you need to consider higher-speed networks. This should not be as much of a problem in the latter part of the 1990s as it is today, as gigabit-per-second networks will be fairly commonplace by then.

Data Compression

Since it will most likely always be the case that users will bump up against the bandwidth limiters for desktop animation, many people are considering various ways to compress data. While a detailed discussion of data compression algorithms is beyond the scope of this book, we can explore the basic concepts, referring the interested reader to some of the references provided at the end of the chapter.

Basically, the objective of any data compression scheme is to represent a given set of data with fewer bytes than the original data set. Data compression takes two forms: lossless and lossy. In the first case, no data is lost; rather, it is reformulated so that, for example, all locations of 0 are described, rather than indicated on a point-by-point basis. Lossless compressions are almost always applied to text, but not as frequently applied to images. Lossless compression schemes can usually save a factor of 2 to 5 in data storage (possibly more if large regions of the image are the same color, possibly less for scenes with fine-scale naturalistic content). Lossy compressions, usually in the form of approximations or averages to an image (whether through manipulations in frequency space or as the result of "codebook" substitutions derived from vector quantization), or sequences of images, can save a lot more file space, but at the price of missing a small, but possibly significant feature in the image. Structures that are averaged out might be precisely the things that the researchers are looking for.

Apple's QuickTime environment approaches data compression from several perspectives and supports both lossless and lossy schemes for single images as well as sequences of images. Animations, for instance, are generally dealt with in QuickTime through the use of "frame-differencing" techniques, which examine a sequence of images to see which pixels have changed, then keep track of only the changed pixels. Each type of compression scheme is designed for a specific application—videotape digitization, for example, or animation of continuous images—and each has a corresponding decompression scheme. There are many compression-decompression algorithms, or *codecs*, available from Apple and third-party developers. From an application perspective, QuickTime is disk-based, rather than RAM based, which means that it is designed to continually feed data into video-RAM from disk, thus enabling animations tens of megabytes in size to be played back at frame rates approaching 30 frames per second on machines with only 8 MB of RAM. All of the animations on the accompanying CD were done in QuickTime. In addition, QuickTime is designed to work with any "time-based" medium, thus we include sound in our animations. QuickTime is also designed to be used with various video digitizing boards to digitize existing video footage into QuickTime movies. Finally, although QuickTime is designed for Apple hardware platforms working under the Macintosh operating system, it is licensed in various forms to developers working in other operating environments, including Microsoft Windows and various Unix systems.

Putting It on Tape

Now that we understand the basic elements of desktop animation in the modern personal computing environment, we can address the next major problem on the list: how to get these images to videotape. Videotape grew up in the broadcast television industry, and many of the terms and technologies are directly derived from this culture. Towards that end there are two important concepts to keep in mind as you go through this section. *Component video*, which separates the video signal into separate color and intensity (that is chrominence and luminence) signals, and *composite video*, which merges both signals together. Component video is much higher quality and is generally found in industrial or professional environments and comes in a number of flavors: Beta Cam, U-Matic SP, Hi-8mm, SVHS, and one-inch. Correspondingly, composite video is considered "consumer quality" and is usually VHS or 8mm video. (For an excellent reference on video technology as applied to the computer graphic world see [Winkler, 1990, 1992].) Moreover, many of the quality considerations that plague broadcast professionals are irrelevant to scientists and engineers. Rather than deliberate production values and aesthetics, the researcher or teacher simply wants to get the data onto videotape to show to colleagues and students. Broadcast people cringe when we say this, but it really doesn't matter much how the animations look as long as they get the basic point across. This philosophy solves many problems, but it also creates others.

Unfortunately, despite the fact that there are considerably more scientists and engineers than broadcast video professionals, obtaining a videotape of your research has, until very recently, been an expensive nightmare. Either you had to invest in tens of thousands of dollars of video equipment and an expert from a local university or lab graphics arts department to learn how to run it, or you had to ship your data off to a service that would give you back a video that marginally met your needs.

Basically, there are three ways of obtaining a video of an animation, although only the third is useful for anything other than informal purposes. First, you can video the screen in real time by pointing a camera at it. This works if your monitor can adjust to 60 Hz, roughly the camera rate, your animation moves fast enough on the screen that recording it makes sense, and you have good lighting and know how to use a video camera to record off of a monitor. This method has distinct advantages: it is simple, cheap, and fast, you can narrate your video as you shoot, and there's no need to convert data sets to some standard format.

However, the drawbacks of this method are obvious, starting with "video roll," that is, the difference in frame rates between what the screen is displaying and the frame rate of the camera. (A public-domain utility called VideoSync, available from Apple, permits you to set certain Macintosh displays to NTSC frame rates for just this purpose.) There may be problems with room light and reflections from the screen, though these can be somewhat mitigated by having good, indirect lights (or none at all, depending upon the quality of the camera and the nature of the animation being recorded). You will also have an aesthetic and composition problem if the animation appears in a window on your monitor. If, for example, the animation is in a 200×200 window in a 640×480 screen it will either appear very small in your video or, if you choose to zoom in on the window, you it will be of marginal video quality since you'll be enlarging a 200×200 image. If instead you expand the image on the monitor, it may take quite a while for the computer to paint each image on the screen, and the video would clearly not be a "real-time" animation.

QuickTime movie images can be expanded to whatever resolution you desire, but the results still are generally poor, with "boxy" images of individual pixels and slow frame rates. Finally, there's the overall quality of the video itself, from the effective sampling that your camera takes of your computer screen resolution, to the type of camera and recording system (Betacam SP, SVHS, Hi-8mm, etc.) and quality of tape used.

The second way of obtaining video of an animation is to record directly from a board in the computer to a video deck. This method has several advantages over videotaping the monitor: there are no problems with lighting, distortion from the monitor glass, or video roll. The disadvantages of this method are that (1) again, you are getting only the screen resolution, so it will often look "blocky," (2) most boards send the entire screen, not just the window of interest, (3) sound has to be put on afterward, (4) you must pay the cost of a board (but this is generally under $1000 for most boards that are sufficient for scientific computing purposes), (5) you may get artifacts and color conversion problems between your monitor, board, and tape deck, and (6) there is still a problem when images take a long time to draw. If it takes several seconds to dump a frame to the screen, then that "drawing process" is what the VCR picks up.

The best method for creating videos is to create single-frame animations from the individual images making up the set of data. This is how commercial computer graphics companies produce their work. They create a scene, using commercial or homegrown computer graphics software, and then render each frame to video. In single-frame animation each individual frame gets recorded separately, as opposed to the real-time video approach we described above. This method yields the best quality possible outside of a broadcast environment. There is no problem with the playback rate of the images—each one is brought up on the screen as an individual image before being recorded as a frame. You can also edit the images, since they are recorded individually with time code burned in; furthermore there are full-screen images, not windows. However, single-frame animation is expensive: the hardware costs a minimum of $10,000 in addition to the computer (see **Tech Note 4** for a more in-depth discussion of single-frame animation). Single-frame animation also takes time. Besides the time needed to render the frame on the computer, there is usually an additional overhead of 5–30 seconds per frame to let the tape deck do a "pre-roll" (unless you are fortunate enough to have a recordable laserdisk system). Thus, if you have thousands of frames of data times several parameters, the entire video can take a week or longer. Nevertheless, single-frame desktop animation has arrived at the consumer level, at least for scientists.

Summary

In this chapter we've covered the elementary concepts of imaging numbers and dynamic phenomena and we've also gotten into some specific issues regarding color mapping, video, and data compression. The next chapter deals with a different application altogether—terrain rendering—which forms a central core around which we can develop other themes in visualization, modeling, and animation. Animations CD 2.9 through CD 2.12 show visualizations of different empirical and computational data sets.

CD 2.9

CD 2.10

CD 2.11

CD 2.12

Suggested Reading

1. *The Data Analysis Handbook*, by Brand Fortner, Spyglass, 1992.

2. *The Elements of Graphing Data*, by William S. Cleveland, Wadsworth, 1985.

3. *Envisioning Data*, by Edward R. Tufte, Graphics Press, 1990.

4. *Algorithms for Graphics and Image Processing*, by Theo Pavlides, Computer Science Press, 1982.

5. *Digital Image Processing*, by Rafael C. Gonzalez and Richard E. Woods, Addison-Wesley, 1992; Chapter 6, "Image Compression".

Through Canyons and Planets 3

In Chapter 1 we looked at a number of planetary images taken by various spacecraft. One common element of these images is that they were flat; that is, the image was two-dimensional. Furthermore, our viewpoint was always at some distance from the planet. However, we know that planets have structure—craters, mountains, canyons, and so forth. Given that, it would be really interesting if we could somehow "fly over" the surface of the planet. The question is, then, how can we apply computer graphics technology, along with available data, to effect a planetary flyover?

We've encountered height fields before, in Chapter 2, where we visualized a dipole field as $z(x,y)$. We also examined terrain data with the global relief maps and the Antarctic altitude data sets in Figures 2.8 and 2.9. In the case of the dipole field, which is a continuous function everywhere except at the origin, the resolution is arbitrary, since for every possible value of $(x,y) > (0,0)$ a finite value of $z(x,y)$ exists and can be easily computed from the governing equation. On the other hand, with an empirically measured data set, such as the Antarctic data, actual altitude values only exist at those points that were measured; everything else is interpolated. Thus, our altitude data is *discrete* rather than continuous, and we need different methods to properly analyze and visualize it. If we can imagine "flying over" such a discrete data set we would actually see a field of different height spikes in front of us and all around, unless we employed some reasonably clever interpolation

CD 3.1

scheme. However, even if we were able to properly interpolate the height field so that we had a continuous function, instead of a discrete one, we would still only have the kind of structure that we observed with the Antarctic altitude visualization. There would be no "image" of the region—no trees, no colors, no lakes—just a smooth altitude function. And, without an image, you aren't really flying over anything very interesting. So, what's the solution?

The answer lies in understanding the nature of a given image of a region and how that image was acquired. As we observed in Chapter 1, an image is a matrix of pixels, $f(x,y)$, each pixel being a particular color that represents, say, the average of the colors of the area in the image covered by that pixel. With terrain data, in addition to a color value, each pixel can also be considered to be at a given altitude, averaging the altitude of all data points within it. However, whereas an image of a region can be easily obtained with a camera and film, the altitude at each point must somehow be derived.

In Chapter 2 we said that contours can be treated as "pre-images," which can evolve into images by increasing the number of

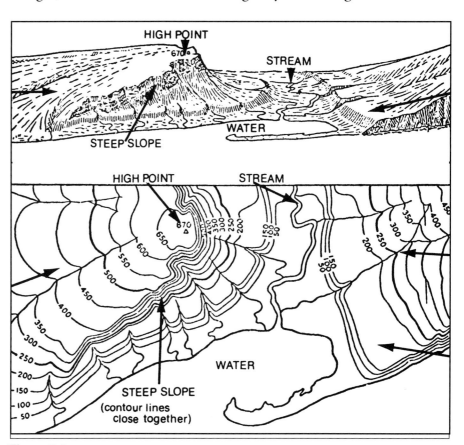

Figure 3.1a

This image shows the relationship between a contour map and its corresponding 3-D terrain image. Note how contours are closer together in steeper (large gradient) regions.

Figure 3.1a

58

contour levels and assigning color to each level. We saw that although contour plots provide important quantitative information about the data set, they don't display all the information available. But in reality, contour maps are simply 2-D projections of height fields. An example of this is a contour map of a hiking trail. In the United States, for example, virtually every piece of land has been surveyed, measured, and cataloged by the United States Geological Survey (USGS). Topographic (contour) maps of any region of the country are available at local sporting goods and book stores for a few dollars. In a typical contour map each closed contour line refers to a particular altitude, usually demarcated in units of 10, 20, or 40 feet, depending upon the spatial resolution of the map (the size of the area that it covers). In Figure 3.1a we show the basic idea behind a contour map and its relationship to the corresponding three-dimensional terrain, while Figures 3.1b and c show pieces of USGS contour maps from a popular area in Sequoia National Park.

Contour maps are fine as far as they go, but without practice one cannot get a feel for the terrain structure from them, let alone the trees, lighting conditions on the trail, or the rockiness of the ground. Those

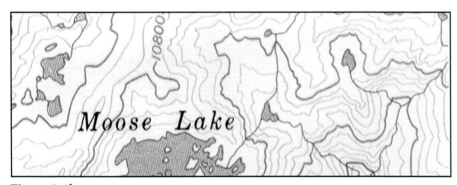

Figure 3.1b

Figure 3.1b
USGS contour map of a popular area in Sequoia National Park. Notice that it's difficult to get an intuition of the altitude variation in the vicinity of Moose Lake.

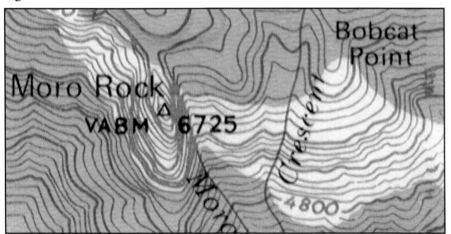

Figure 3.1c

Figure 3.1c
This USGS contour map of the Moro Rock area of Sequoia National Park shows a number of distinct features such as sharp gradients (steep slopes) at Moro Rock itself, a stream, and gently sloping hills. However, without the 3-D image it is very difficult to get a true perspective of the area.

would require an image of the trail with submeter resolution. But then the image alone wouldn't give the overall change of altitude information needed to plan a hike—precisely what the contour map does well.

A solution to this problem is to overlay the contour map onto the image. This technique has a couple of advantages. First, the contour map enhances the overall structure of the image, so that the user is drawn to the major changes in the data as indicated by the contour levels. Second, by viewing the contours on top of the image we can determine if the color map of the image accurately represents the phenomenon we're trying to visualize. We've already seen an example of this in **Tech Note 3**, where the concept of color transforms is discussed in detail. However, even if we had a contour map overlaid on an image, we're still missing true 3-D structure.

Another solution entirely, which addresses the 3-D problem, is to compute a 3-D wireframe or a shaded surface of the function. This is done for the electric dipole function in Figure 3.2. The term wireframe comes from what it appears to be: a set of wires hooked together to make a 3-D plot of a function. Notice that you can't "see through" the wires to the back of the function, thanks to the "hidden line" algorithm used to hide those lines from the viewer. If those lines were visible, the function would be much more confusing to view. Three-dimensional data plots have been employed in scientific computing since the early

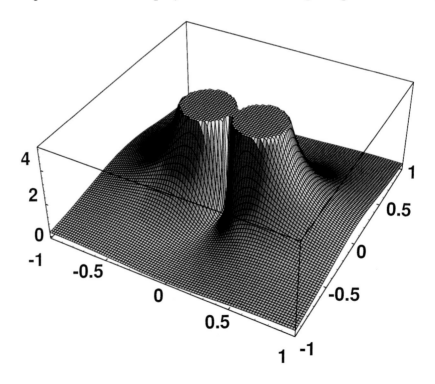

Figure 3.2
This 3-D wireframe map of the electric dipole function that we computed in Chapter 2 shows how dramatic a 3-D view of a dataset can be.

60

1960s, and the 3-D wireframe was definitely a sign of prestige for researchers for a couple of decades. This is because, except in well-equipped places like the National Center for Atmospheric Research (NCAR) in Boulder, Colorado, or the Lawrence Laboratories in California, 3-D plots were hard to come by, since they were compute intensive at the time and generally needed expensive plotters to be printed. That was before the age of personal computers.

Wireframe plots provide a different set of information about the data than a simple contour plot does. This is due to the fact that each point generally has the height resolution of the gray-scale image (a value between 0 and 255), but without the artifacts of color getting in the way. Despite their value and popularity, 3-D surface plots don't solve all of our problems. For one thing, it is generally impossible to see the entire data set at once when points with greater height obscure parts of the graph that are lower. Thus, the user often needs to rotate the data set to find the information of interest, which brings in the requirement that hardware be fast enough to rotate the 3-D object in real time. Also, in contrast to contour plots and images, where labels are relatively unambiguous, it's difficult to get a good quantitative understanding of a 3-D wireframe structure on a 2-D screen. Despite these shortcomings, 3-D plots are a useful addition to the researcher's visualization toolkit.

If we now shift back to the terrain problem we can see a general applicability of basic wireframe computer graphics to terrain data and, in this chapter, we will explore a number of aspects of this rapidly growing visualization technique. Our "back to basics" approach will take us through a bit of computer graphic and scientific computing history, with the objective of understanding how to determine altitude from image data and the general concepts behind 3-D animation techniques.

Methods of Altimetry

Most contour maps were created by careful manual surveying: people trudging up and down mountains with surveying and photographic equipment, often spending several days obtaining data for a small region. Most of this data was then stored on paper, as opposed to creating a digital record. Access to the original data is difficult and limited, and one has to be an expert (or have expert help) in order to interpret the data. Applications such as creating a computer animation of a flyover of the Grand Canyon end up requiring a significant amount of labor just to acquire the data. To do these sorts of things we need to find other means of acquiring altitude data. This usually entails acquiring detailed photographs of the area under consideration and applying various analytical techniques which we discuss below. Photographic data is obtained either from satellite images such as Landsat (or, in the case of planetary data, from spacecraft like Voyager or Viking) or from aerial photography companies which specialize in taking geometrically accurate photographs of different geographical regions.

Over the years, several techniques have been developed to compute altitude data from photographic images acquired from airplanes or spacecraft. We will discuss three of them here: *relief displacement*, *stereo pairs*, and *low-Sun-angle photography*. Each of these has its uses, advantages, and disadvantages, but within specific contexts each can provide valuable altitude data which is otherwise unavailable.

The simple derivations and explanations provided herein are conceptual tools to enable the reader to understand the principles involved in creating altitude data from image data. They are not nearly 100-percent accurate since there are many sources of error in all of these methods, including the curvature of the planetary surface, local geological anomalies, motion of the airplane or spacecraft during image acquisition, atmospheric distortion, and refraction. Any calculations we do are only as good as the accuracy of the input data and the applicability of the stated assumptions to the problem at hand.

RELIEF DISPLACEMENT

In the case where we need to find the height of various features or structures on the ground and all we have is an imaging camera on a low-flying aircraft, we can take advantage of the geometric relationships between the focal length of the camera's lens, the horizontal spatial resolution of the film or imaging device, the altitude of the camera (as measured by the plane of the lens), and the height of a given object on the ground. The geometry is shown in Figure 3.3a: given a camera with focal length f, with a resolution in the image plane of δ (the width of a pixel in the imaging system) and an altitude H, by applying elementary geometric relationships of similar triangles the minimum spatial resolution on the ground is given by $\Delta_{min} = \delta H/f$. Thus, for example, given a lens with a focal length of 1000 mm, a film resolution of 0.1 mm/pixel, and a camera altitude of 10 km, the minimum ground resolution would be 1 meter. Figures 3.3b and c shows typical aerial photos at different spatial resolutions.

Spatial resolution puts an upper bound on the accuracy of any altitude data obtained from the image. To go further, we can exploit the fact that all objects appear to lean outward from the center of the

CD 3.2

image. This is shown in Figure 3.4, a photo of Century City in Los Angeles taken from an airplane. Note, in particular, quantities h and d, which we drew on the photograph, and how all structures in the image appear to lean outward from the center of the photograph. To understand how this effect can be used to determine altitude we look at Figure 3.5, where it can be shown (see Sabins, 1978, and references therein) that the actual height of an arbitrary object in a photographic image can be obtained through the relationship

$$h = Hd/r$$

where H is the camera height and r is the distance from the center of the photograph to the top of an object of height h. The quantity d, called the *relief displacement*, is the effective "photographic distance" between

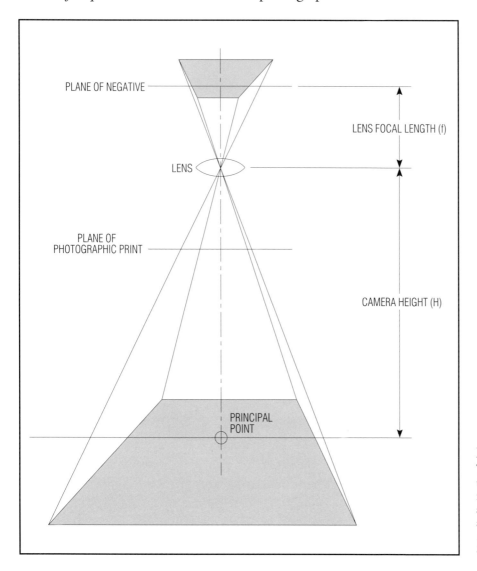

Figure 3.3a
This figure illustrates how to find the height of a given feature in an image taken by a camera of focal length f at a resolution d and a height H from the ground (After Sabins, 1978, Figure 2.6).

Figure 3.3b
This image, taken from an airplane with a highly accurate camera shows a portion of the southern California coast at a fairly low resolution. As altitude (spatial resolution) increases (decreases) it becomes more difficult to determine the height of an object. (Courtesy Airborne Systems, Inc.)

Figure 3.3b

Figure 3.3c
This image of downtown LA shows considerable structure and detail. At this resolution we can reliably obtain height data either from studying shadows or from measuring displacement. (Courtesy Airborne Systems, Inc.)

Figure 3.3c

Figure 3.4

Figure 3.4
High-resolution photograph of Century City in Los Angeles designed to show building shadows. Notice how the farther away an object is from the center of the image, the more the object appears tilted toward the edge of the photo. This artifact, called relief displacement, can be used to compute the height of the object. (Courtesy Airborne Systems, Inc.)

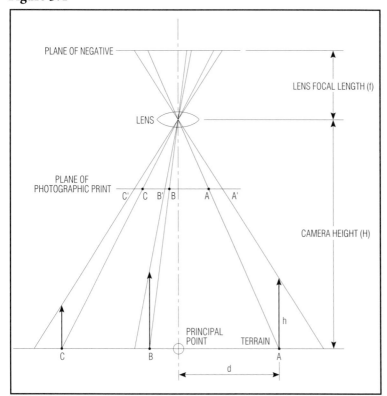

Figure 3.5

Figure 3.5
The effect of relief displacement in determining the height of an object in an image (after Sabins, 1978, Fig. 2.9).

the point in the photograph that it should be and the point that it appears to be at due to the effect of the lens.

We can intuitively understand the relationship between h and d by solving this equation for d to get

$$d = hr/H$$

If we examine this equation we see that, as one would expect, the taller the object (the greater h), the greater the effect. We also find that, as we would also expect, the higher the camera (the larger H is) the smaller the effect, since the angle that a ray from the top of the object to the center of the camera lens makes with the normal to the lens decreases with alititude. Finally, we would clearly expect d to increase with r. An important consequence of this equation is that if d is smaller than the ground spatial resolution, we cannot use this method to resolve the altitude of objects. Thus, for planetary missions like Voyager, where the imaging system is tens of thousands of kilometers from the target planet, the method of relief displacement cannot be used to resolve altitude. However, on a mission like Viking, where the spacecraft orbited Mars for several years at a relatively low altitude above high-relief landforms, one could employ this technique under limited circumstances.

STEREO PAIRS

Another method of obtaining altitude data from two-dimensional images is by taking *stereo pairs*, images of the same area from two different angles. This method is particularly well suited to spacecraft observations, since the distance of the camera from the target object does not enter into the calculation of the altitude. When images taken from different perspectives have an overlapping region, the common region can be made viewable in stereo with appropriate glasses (Foley et al., 1991, p. 616; Sabins, 1978, p. 29).

More important than simply viewing stereo images of a particular region, however, is using the overlapping image data to build a terrain data base from the original image data base. The details of the method are presented in **Tech Note 7**.

In contrast to the process of relief displacement, deriving altitude data from overlapping images does not require any information about the camera such as the focal length of the lens. Nor does it require any range data, such as the height of the aircraft or spacecraft from a particular point on the ground. All that is needed are the position of the camera (that is, the spacecraft) and the direction that the camera is pointing for each image. The spacecraft position and orientation are continually updated via the radio link between the spacecraft and the Earth with extremely small error. Figure 3.6 diagrams the problem using the spacecraft position data from two images of Arsia Mons on Mars (see **Tech Note** 7 for a detailed analysis). If we examine this drawing we find that we have enough information to determine the altitude of the object of interest. This is how terrain data is generally obtained from planetary image data.

Once we have computed a height for every pixel in the image we need to map the image data onto the terrain (height) data. Since, in many cases (including the Arsia Mons image), the number of pixels in the image and their orientation is the same as the number of known altitude points, all we need to do is to assign a particular z-value to each pixel and project that on the screen. This is shown in Figure 3.7 where we show the process used to map the Arsia Mons image data set onto the corresponding terrain data. Figure 3.7a shows the image, Figure 3.7b shows a gray-scale image of the terrain data, and Figure 3.7c shows the composite image mapped onto the terrain data. The rendering was done with Electric Image rendering software, which enables us to choose a viewpoint anywhere in space.

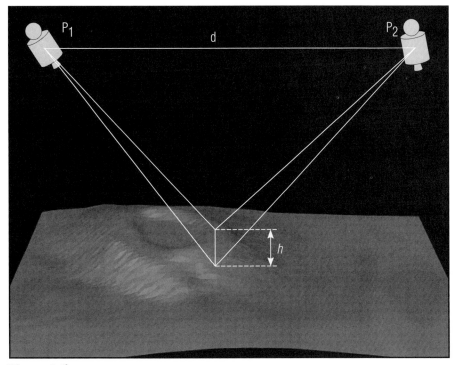

Figure 3.6

Figure 3.6
This image illustrates how overlapping images are used to determine the height of a feature. The image used in this example is a Viking image of Arsia Mons, one of the Martian shield volcanoes. This method works because the spacecraft position is well known at all times (see **Tech Note 5**).

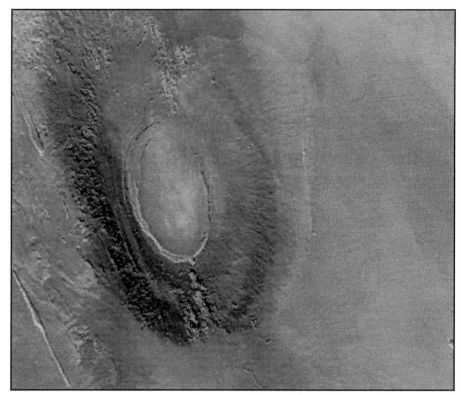

Figure 3.7a

Figure 3.7a
Viking Orbiter image of
Arsia Mons, one of the
shield volcanoes on Mars.
(Courtesy NASA/JPL)

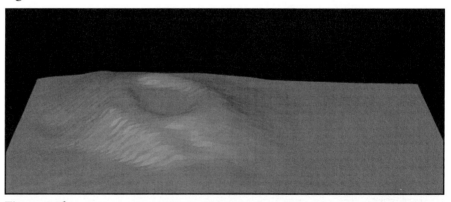

Figure 3.7b

Figure 3.7b
Digital terrain data of Arsia
Mons, rendered in Electric
Image, shows the altitude
structure of the volcano.
The terrain data, computed
by USGS researchers from
the image data, is at the
same resolution as the image
data. (Data supplied by
USGS and NASA/JPL. Data
conversion help by Mark
Granger of Electric Image)

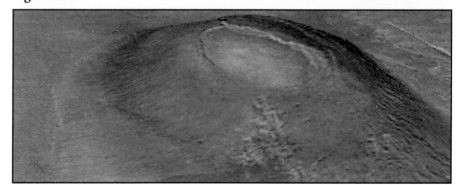

Figure 3.7c

Figure 3.7c
This image was computed in
Electric Image by mapping
the Arsia Mons image from
Figure 3.7a onto the terrain
data shown in Figure 3.7b.
The mapping was done
with Electric Image's texture
mapping function.

LOW SUN-ANGLE PHOTOGRAPHY

In those cases where there are no overlapping regions and the camera is too high off the ground to use relief displacement, shadows can be used to estimate the height of various structures. This is shown in Figure 3.8a, a simple derivation of the technique, and in Figure 3.8b, another photo of the Century City building with the shadows marked off. In this method, the spacecraft or airplane position is accurately known, as is the position of the Sun. However, since the shadow length is proportional to the cosine of the angle formed by the observer, the top of the object, and the bottom of the object, it is clear that the most accurate observing conditions are when the shadow is the longest. Thus, low Sun angles provide the best lighting conditions for determining altitude by this technique.

CD 3.3

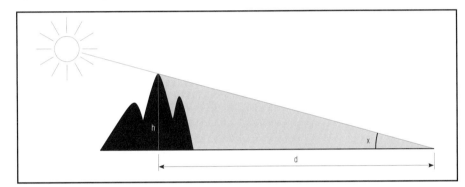

Figure 3.8a

Figure 3.8a
Geometry of determining altitude by shadows. The lower the Sun, the greater unobstructed distance is needed to determine the height of the object.

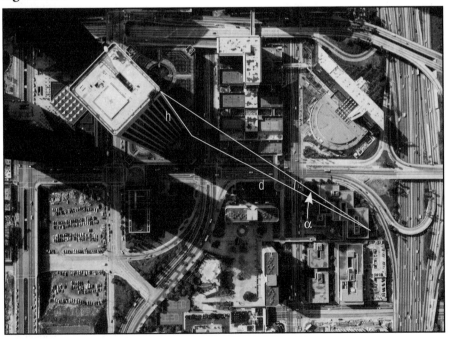

Figure 3.8b

Figure 3.8b
The principles described in Figure 3.8a are applied in this image of Century City. Notice the structure of the shadows, in addition to the relief displacement of the buildings. (Century City Image courtesy Airborne Systems, Inc.)

CD 3.4

Figure 3.9a
Typical camera path over sample elevation data set. This particular data set is of Mount St. Helens, and the flyover is designed to look into the crater. This is a screen shot of Electric Image software, which was used to do the rendering. (Courtesy Jim Knighton, NASA/JPL.)

3-D Animation: Flying Over Terrain

Once the digital elevation (terrain) data have been computed, the researcher may want to "fly through" the 3-D region now represented by the data. This requires understanding several things, including the notion of a "camera" moving over the data set snapping pictures of the 3-D structure. Figure 3.9 illustrates a typical path that a camera might take over a sample elevation data set: by traversing a particular path and snapping pictures as you go along, you end up with a sequence of images that appears as if you are "flying" along the path. The camera in this instance is simply a computer graphic object that enables the researcher to frame the image, much like a real camera. The collection of images along the path can be combined to form an animation that appears to the viewer like a plane ride over the terrain. Obviously the observer can determine the altitude of the camera at any

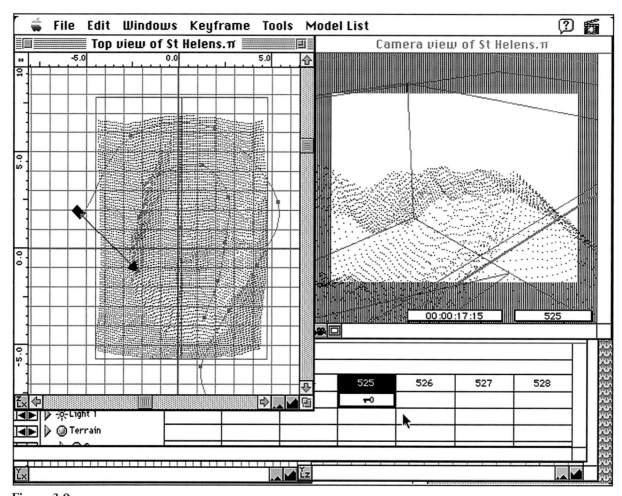

Figure 3.9a

point along the path and, in fact, can invoke a "terrain-following radar," as described in **Tech Note 8**.

In addition to the path of the camera, the orientation of the plane of the camera lens—where the camera is pointed—is critical to the outcome of the animation. Imagine, for example, that you're on a roller coaster with a video camera and you're trying to hold the camera steady in front of you throughout the ride. Clearly if the camera is bouncing all over the place you won't get a very good video because the orientation of the plane of the camera lens is changing too rapidly. However, if you keep the camera completely steady or bolt it to the car pointed straight ahead, with the normal vector to the plane of the camera always following the tangent to the curve of the roller coaster, you will never get an interesting shot (unless you're interested in the back of the head of the person in front of you). So, to obtain an interesting video you must move the camera in an artful fashion, keeping in mind that the roller coaster is continually moving along a complex, rapidly varying path. In the 3-D animations that accompany this text, observe the smooth camera motions throughout each visualization. This is an acquired skill, and one must adapt the changing camera position to the problem at hand. Thus, for example, in the animated flyaround of Arsia Mons, we were mostly interested in obtaining different perspectives on the volcano's caldera, or central crater, whereas in *Mars Navigator*, described below and briefly in **Tech Note 8**, we were more interested in general panoramic views of the surrounding terrain.

Figure 3.9b
This image shows the actual Mount St. Helens terrain data in gray-scale, as we had done with the Arsia Mons data previously. (Courtesy Jim Knighton, NASA/JPL)

Figure 3.9c
This rendered image of the Mount St. Helens crater shows the path that the camera took in computing frames for an animation. Key-frames are indicated by circles. The rendering software is Electric Image. (Courtesy Jim Knighton, NASA/JPL)

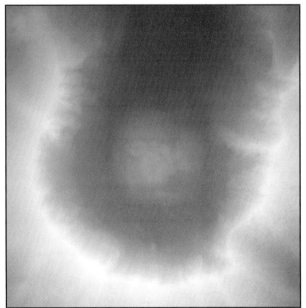

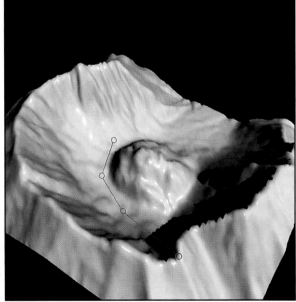

Figure 3.9b

Figure 3.9c

Consequently, the camera movement employed in each of those two animations was different.

We discuss the general problem of cameras, lighting, and 3-D animation in a bit more depth in Chapter 6 and **Tech Notes 14** and **15**, where the entire notion of *key-frames*, or control points for the path that the camera will follow, is developed. For current purposes, however, one can assume that, after the key-frames are set up, it is straightforward to fill in the frames between them. This process is called *in-betweening*, and is generally done these days automatically with software that constructs *splines* between the key-frames. The splines interpolate parameters of the camera, or of objects if they're moving as well, between successive key-frames to approximate a smooth, natural motion (see **Tech Note 9**). The key-frame concept was developed for traditional animations like Disney's *Snow White*, and continues today for traditionally produced animations for television and film. Film and TV studios typically hire dozens of "in-betweeners" to fill in the frames for an animation manually. This extremely labor-intensive task is many orders of magnitude less efficient than a spline-based computer animation system and is pretty much impossible to use in a 3-D animation. In fact, today when Disney wants to have realistic 3-D movement in otherwise traditional animations, it employs 3-D computer graphics to guide the hand animations. (It has even been known to blend backgrounds rendered entirely by computer graphics techniques with hand-animated foreground characters; such was the case in *Beauty and the Beast*.)

Examples

The following images and animations provide a few examples of the dramatic effect of employing terrain data with image data to visualize geographic regions. Corresponding animations can be found on the CD accompanying this text. For historical purposes, the first perspective animation of real topographic data using ray-tracing was done by Michael Kobrick in his 1985 animation "Topo Follies" which was a 3-D journey around Mt. Shasta in Northern California.

LA: The Movie

Figure 3.10 shows a frame from *LA: The Movie*, created in 1987 by Kevin Hussey, Bob Mortenson, Helen Mortenson, and Jeff Hall of JPL. It was created with data from a single Landsat satellite image taken from an altitude of 918 km on July 3, 1985. The image was combined with digital elevation data provided by the Defense Mapping Agency and then processed to simulate 3-D.

The raw image data came from the Thematic Mapper instrument on the Landsat spacecraft. The Thematic Mapper can generate data from seven spectral bands covering the visible and infrared regions of the electromagnetic spectrum. In *LA: The Movie* the three visible spectral bands were used. The resolution of each of these spectral bands was 7000 × 5000 pixels, with each pixel being 8 bits deep. Thus, the image data alone was 35 MB. The horizontal resolution of the data is 30 meters (both *x* and *y* resolution). The three spectral bands were separately enhanced so that their histograms approximated a Gaussian (bell curve) distribution. The Landsat image was then transformed to fit the existing terrain data (Hussey et al., 1988).

One problem that occurred in the production of the movie was that the digital elevation data was at a spatial resolution of 90 meters, one-third that of the Landsat image data. Hussey's team solved this problem by resampling the digital elevation data, effectively increasing the number of pixels in the image. This is often the case with Earth-based data where the spatial resolution of the terrain data differs from the spatial resolution of the image data. In the general case where the image data resolution is less than the terrain data resolution, the terrain data needs to be averaged such that each point of the terrain data set maps uniquely into a pixel from the image data set. Conversely, if the image

CD 3.5

Figure 3.10

Figure 3.10
This image of Los Angeles was computed as part of the JPL animation *LA: The Movie.* The original data was from a single LANDSAT Thematic Mapper satellite image taken from an altitude of 570 miles on July 3, 1985. The image was combined with digital elevation data provided by the Defense Mapping Agency and processed at JPL to simulate 3-D. (Courtesy Kevin Hussey, NASA/JPL.)

data resolution is greater than the terrain data resolution, the image data needs to be averaged so as to achieve the appropriate 1-to-1 mapping. This mapping process is termed *registration*, and the general problem of registering image data has grown into a branch of research itself.

All of JPL's software was homegrown, since no commercial software for this sort of thing existed at the time. Although there were often problems with the software, the fact that the people who wrote it were also the users meant that it could be fixed more easily than it would if a third-party company had to respond to each particular complaint. It also had the advantage that the users/developers could build on their previous experience and design features into the software that were specific to their computing environment, such as data formats, color calibrations, geometric corrections, and map projections. This level of control had its disadvantages as well, since the users often had to interrupt the production process in order to fix a bug or add a needed feature. In the production of *LA: The Movie*, for example, each of the more than 3300 frames computed consisted of 512×512 pixels $\times$ 24 bits per image (roughly 2.6 GB of data). Once all the frames were computed, the JPL team single-framed them onto videotape in the manner described in Chapter 2. When the production team ran into a problem there was no expert to call in to help. This is a serious issue when you consider whether to build your own terrain-rendering software. On the other hand, there really isn't any robust, feature-laden terrain-rendering software on the market today, so you might have to do your own development anyway. JPL has lots of experts of various kinds in the immediate neighborhood, so the team could afford to take that risk.

The JPL work also provides good examples of the kind of customization that one needs in homegrown software. In *LA: The Movie*, for example, the precise camera view of each frame was determined by eight parameters which defined the location and orientation of the plane of the camera lens, the angle of the field of view, and the resolutions of the input image and elevation data. Key frames incorporating all of the eight parameters were selected along the "flight path" and a separate cubic spline (see **Tech Note 9**) for each of the parameters was computed to determine the in-between frames.

One problem that occurs in nearly all computer-animated flyovers is perceived versus actual altitudes of the features. This is a consequence of a number of fairly complex effects coming together and is addressed in some detail in **Tech Note 8**. The usual solution, which represents an accuracy problem in itself, is to vertically exaggerate (scale up by some factor) all of the terrain altitude data. In *LA: The Movie* the vertical exaggeration is a factor of 4, so, for example, a mountain that is actually 5000 feet is rendered as if it were 20,000 feet tall. On the other hand, without the vertical exaggeration many of the features that are currently visible in the animation would be less then one pixel high. So, clearly there is a trade-off between accuracy and visibility.

Miranda: The Movie

LA: The Movie was created from satellite data in which the resolution of features on the ground is very high, and the heights of features are determined elsewhere and are well known. A more difficult problem is to take low-resolution spacecraft imagery of an unfamiliar object, compute a corresponding digital elevation data set, and compute a 3-D flyover. Such was the case with Uranus's moon Miranda which, in addition to not having a high-resolution data set, has a small radius—240 km—and thus a large curvature relative to the resolution of the images (in contrast, LANDSAT images, with resolutions on the order of 30 m, are on the Earth, whose radius is roughly 6400 km). With the Miranda data in hand, the same team that did *LA: The Movie* turned its efforts to this interesting problem. This was a good test of their homegrown software as the JPL team could take advantage of the development that they had done in their previous work.

The input data for *Miranda: The Movie* consisted of nine Voyager 2 images of the southern hemisphere of Miranda (Figure 3.11). The images were obtained at distances of 30,000 to 40,000 km with a

CD 3.6

Figure 3.11a-e
These images are from the JPL animation *Miranda: The Movie.* The original data consisted of a mosaic of nine Voyager 2 images of the southern hemisphere of Miranda with a resolution of 560 to 740 m/pixel. (Courtesy Kevin Hussey, NASA/JPL)

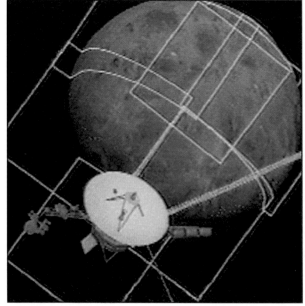

Figure 3.11a

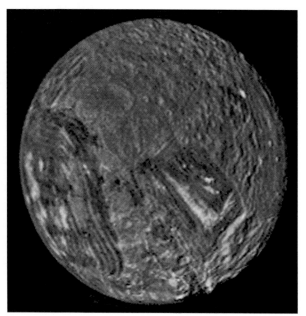

Figure 3.11b

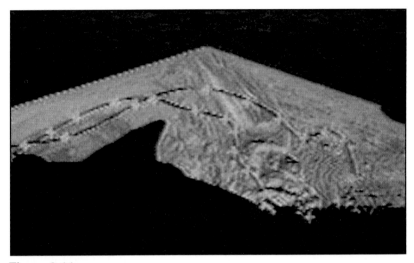

Figure 3.11c

Figure 3.11d

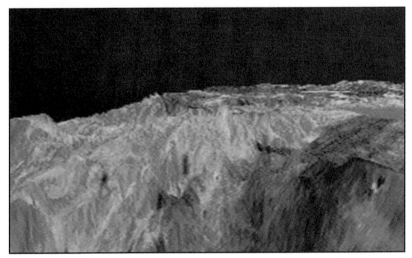

Figure 3.11e

resolution of between 560 and 740 meters per pixel. The elevation data was obtained from stereo pairs of each image.

When it came to creating the animation, there were two main problems with the image data. First, since each image was taken under different lighting conditions, each raw image needed to be radiometrically corrected (that is, corrected for lighting and color) to allow the assemblage of a final mosaic with effectively equal lighting conditions across the satellite's surface. Second, each of the images needed to be geometrically corrected to remove distortion created by the moon's curvature and any attributes of the camera that might contribute to it. Once the images were put together in a preliminary mosaic, the edges between pairs of images had to be eliminated, so more image processing was performed to remove blemishes and to adjust for any camera-induced distortions. From this point on the JPL group gained considerable advantage by using their homegrown software since the process for producing *Miranda: The Movie* was nearly the same as it was with *LA: The Movie*.

ARSIA MONS ON A MAC

We now move from the custom software environment of the minicomputer of the mid-1980s to the commercial software world of the 1990s personal computer. In Figure 3.7 we showed an image and a terrain rendering of Arsia Mons, one of the shield volcanoes in the equatorial region of Mars. This work was done in early 1990, and even though the time between *LA: The Movie* and this work was less than three years, the evolution of technology was substantial. One of us (Wolff), working with Mike Backes, a screenwriter and special effects consultant who was one of the first Mac 3-D animators, took this data and created a 90-frame animated flyaround of the volcano in a single afternoon on a stock Mac IIci with 8 MB RAM using Electric Image rendering and animation software. Whereas the JPL work in 1985–88 required months of work with custom software running on a Vax 8600 minicomputer, we were able to do the Arsia Mons animation on a personal computer with commercial software.

The actual rendering process took about 2 minutes per frame. The principal difficulty we had was not the rendering, but getting the USGS derived digital terrain data into a form that Electric Image could read and interpret correctly. To do this, Mark Granger, one of the architects and principal programmers of Electric Image, developed a filter that would read the USGS digital terrain data in and output it correctly.

The other problem we encountered was creating a reasonable key-frame sequence that would take the viewer around the volcano, keeping a focus roughly on its center. This took a bit of artistry, first, to ensure that the first and last key-frames matched up in a smooth fashion and, second, to move the camera in such a way that the viewer did not get motion sickness. This is an important point, because without the help of an experienced animator, viewers could get seasick. Figure 3.12 shows a few frames from the animation.

MARS NAVIGATOR

To do something entirely new in visualization or multimedia computing generally means pushing the envelope of several technologies. These high-risk projects often aim a little too high for the available technologies, and producers, animators, engineers often find themselves in a footrace between the rapidly approaching delivery date and the development of the technology that they critically need to complete the project. This was certainly the case with *Mars Navigator*, a project that Apple's Advanced Technology Group developed in collaboration with Volotta Interactive Video, Inc. for the Tech Museum of Innovation in San Jose, an interactive museum about Silicon Valley technologies designed to showcase high technologies and visions of the future. One of us (Wolff) was the project leader for *Mars Navigator*, and it is a textbook case of a technological race against time. Tom Volotta, a very experienced multimedia developer, was the producer of the project, and was responsible for both the look and feel of the final exhibit, as well as delivering two working systems to the museum.

Mars Navigator is an interactive multimedia exhibit that allows the user to fly through the equatorial region of Mars, visiting canyons, craters, and volcanoes, while occasionally stopping to explore the surrounding area. The data consists of 30 GB of rendered Viking image and terrain data recorded onto dual laserdisks, with an accompanying Supercard front-end and a surround-sound soundtrack developed by Gary Rydstrom of LucasFilm, Inc.

The actual terrain flybys incorporate a variety of perspectives and points of view for the user controlling the system, such as high-speed travel, terrain following, and, just for the fun of it, crashing into obstacles on Mars. Unlike previous 3-D animations of Mars and other planets, *Mars Navigator* has an "atmosphere," derived from realistic models of the Martian atmosphere and incorporated by Peter Hughes of Apple Computer into his terrain renderer (see **Tech Note 8**). Thus, each frame computed also has a calculated Martian atmosphere. The atmosphere is important both from a scientific perspective and from the vantage point of the user, since it adds an element of realism which helps

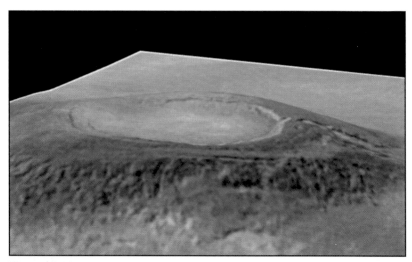

Figure 3.12a

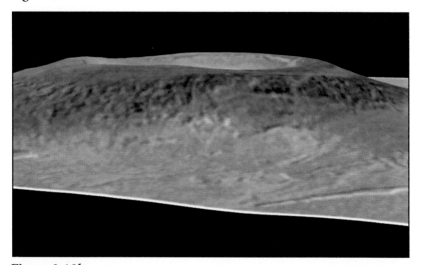

Figure 3.12b

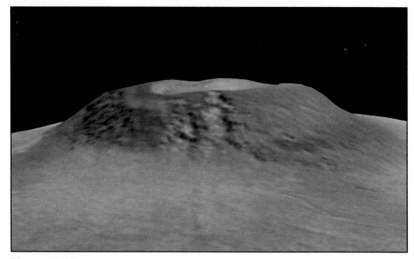

Figure 3.12a-c
These images are from an animated flyaround of Arsia Mons. This animation was done on a Mac IIci in a couple of hours using Electric Image. (Mars data courtesy NASA/JPL)

Figure 3.12c

draw them into the overall experience. Users make choices about which paths to fly by touching one of the three video "buttons" below the main viewing screen, showing scenes of the locations on Mars that they can fly to (Figure 3.13).

   In addition to the interactive flyby, users can browse through a multimedia database containing more than sixty 10- to 15-second information clips about the exploration, geology, and future of Mars. A map of the flyby region can also be accessed and users can see the various paths available and preview their flight over the Valles Marineris labyrinth, the shield volcanoes, the Viking 1 Lander site, and other locations.

   The actual working *Mars Navigator* system consists of an Apple Macintosh IIfx computer with 8 MB RAM and an 80 MB internal hard drive. Two Pioneer LD-V8000 videodisk players, each with an identical disk, are used and enable the seamless path switching during the flybys. Video from the disk players is routed into a Mass Microsystems ColorSpace FX board, then to a ColorSpace IIi to enable scan-rate conversion so a noninterlaced signal can be combined with real-time color graphic overlays from the Macintosh. Switching between the two videodisk sources is controlled by the Macintosh, through the ColorSpace FX board. Special sound effects and voiceovers during the flyby are stored as sound files and played back through a

CD 3.7

Figure 3.13
This image of *Mars Navigator* shows the interface and screen that users see as they navigate through the canyons of the Red Planet. *Mars Navigator* allows users to navigate their own path through the planetary terrain, in contrast to a movie fly-through, where the user is presented only one viewpoint. *Mars Navigator* was produced by Volotta Interactive Video in cooperation with Apple Computer, Inc.

Figure 3.13

Digidesign AudioMedia board. Versions in French, German, and Japanese are planned. Eight languages can be handled easily by the system. A wide variety of displays, from an ordinary color monitor to big-screen multisync projectors, can be used in the system. The system in the museum is designed to operate with a touch screen fitted to a multisync monitor as the user interface device, but a mouse, trackball, or joystick can also be used.

Perhaps the most difficult part of building *Mars Navigator* was developing the terrain renderer. As was the case at JPL, we found that no commercial software existed for what we needed to do. Furthermore, obtaining decent image and terrain data on Mars was considerably more difficult than any of us had anticipated. Although the data is considered public domain, there is no organization or individual whose job it is to actually provide that data. It took us nearly two years to get a usable data set. What you see in the exhibit is essentially created from the same data set that Kevin Hussey and collaborators used in *Mars: The Movie*, another in the series of JPL simulated planetary flyovers. Hussey's group generously allowed us to use the data that they had spent considerable time processing for their animation.

Mars Navigator may be a model for future interactive multi-media designs. By taking the flying camera metaphor a step further, users could be able to fly through different databases, whether they be scientific or even financial, in a rapid-paced, almost impressionistic style of simulation. Imagine, instead of different visual paths to fly on Mars, flying through the complex structure of the Sun's magnetic field. Or imagine traveling though a variety of "what if" simulations where users must make life-style choices, and by doing so affect biological and social elements of their and other people's lives. *Mars Navigator* demonstrates that these new ways of using interactive multimedia are within the grasp of current technology.

MAGELLAN: SYNTHETIC APERTURE RADAR IMAGING OF VENUS

A completely different approach to imaging uses radar (usually defined to be in the 1 mm to 1 m wavelength regime) to determine the surface characteristics of Venus, a planet perpetually shrouded by a thick cloud cover that is impenetrable to optical imaging devices. Radar imaging has been used by military aircraft since the 1950s as a reconnaissance technique to obtain images of a target without having to fly over hostile air space. Initially called Side-Looking Airborne Radar

CD 3.8

(SLAR), the technique today is known as SAR, for *synthetic aperture radar* (see Sabins, 1978, p. 177, and Curlandur, 1991, and references cited therein for a more complete discussion of the technology.)

    In SAR imaging, radar (radio wave) pulses are sent out from the airplane or spacecraft antenna and illuminate a narrow strip of terrain oriented normal to the airplane or spacecraft's flight direction (Figure 3.14). Echoes are recorded and plotted as a function of two-way travel time, with the near side (the part closest to the aircraft) of the image strip being the shortest and the far side being the longest. Brightness, or intensity of the reflected radar pulse, is a function of material composition and surface roughness. Smooth surfaces such as lakes, highways, or lava fields, give mirrorlike (specular) reflections of radar energy, whereas rocky or gravelly areas do not. The radar image itself has no color. Radar altimetry (using radar pulses sent straight down) is often used in conjunction with radar imaging to obtain altitude data that can be geometrically registered with the radar image data.

Figure 3.14
This illustration shows how synthetic aperture radar (SAR) works. Radar pulses are sent out from the airplane or spacecraft antenna which illuminate a narrow strip of terrain. Radar pulses for each image are ordered as a function of two-way travel time. Brightness is a function of material composition and surface roughness (after Sabins, 1978, Fig. 6.3).

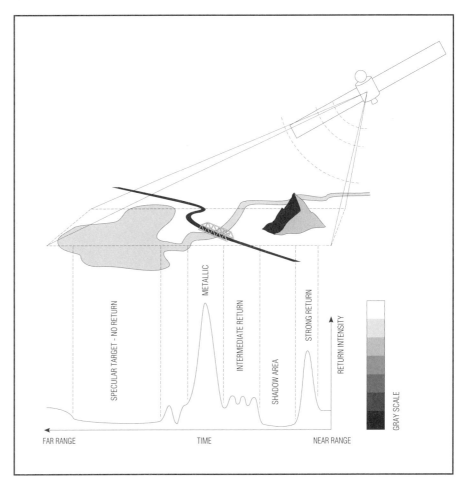

Figure 3.14

Magellan, NASA's Venus radar imaging mission, designed and managed by JPL, obtained nearly complete imaging and altimetry coverage of Venus at fairly high resolution before its mission life ended in 1992. In Figure 3.15 we show several images based on Magellan data in the neighborhood of Gula Mons, a 3-km-high volcano located

CD 3.9

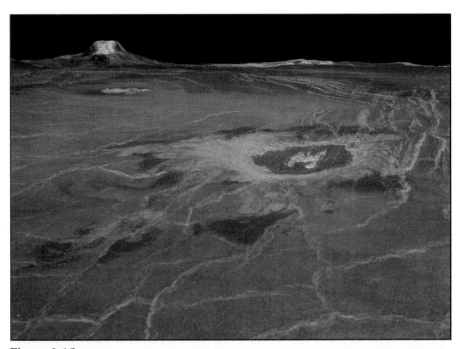

Figure 3.15a

CD 3.10

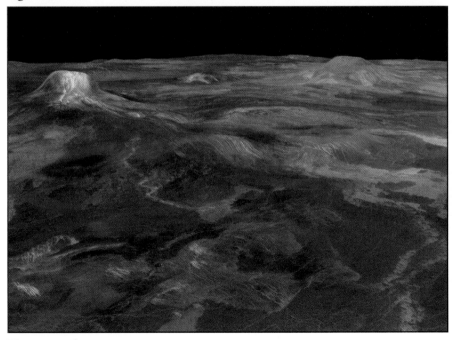

Figure 3.15b

Figure 3.15a-d
Frames from a fly-around of the Gula Mons region of Venus. The original data set is from the Magellan mission's SAR system. (Courtesy NASA/JPL)

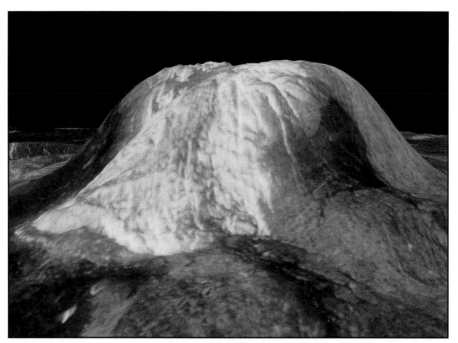

Figure 3.15c

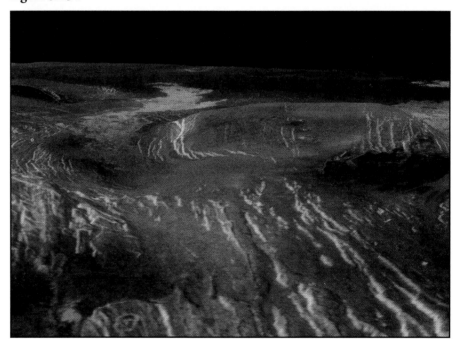

Figure 3.15d

roughly at 22 degrees north latitude, 359 degrees east longitude on Venus. The images are registered with their corresponding altitude data and are from an animated visualization of a Venus flyover done by the same JPL group that did *LA: The Movie* and *Miranda: The Movie.* The complete animation is on the CD-ROM as a QuickTime movie.

Summary

This chapter has explored techniques and applications of terrain measuring and rendering, which is an increasingly valuable tool for researchers and teachers alike. Most altitude data is obtained indirectly, using secondary measurements from which the altitude at a given point can be inferred.

We also examined several applications of terrain rendering in Earth and planetary sciences that show that these problems are, in general, very difficult to solve. These examples point to a need for more general tools to help the researcher or teacher develop applications without having to resort to major efforts by national labs or large companies. Given the increasing demand for this capability, the power of today's desktop systems, and the millions of gigabytes of image and terrain data that currently exists, commercial software developers ought to look at developing products for this market. Animations in CD 3.11 and 3.12 show different applications of this technology.

CD 3.11

CD 3.12

Suggested Reading

1. *Mathematical Elements for Computer Graphics, Second Edition*, by David F. Rogers and J. Alan Adams, McGraw-Hill, 1990.

2. *Remote Sensing: Principles and Interpretation*, by Floyd F. Sabins, Jr., W. H. Freeman and Company, 1973.

3. *Mars Navigator*, Masters Thesis in Computer and Information Sciences by Peter Hughes, University of California at Santa Cruz, 1991.

4. *An Introduction to Splines for Use in Computer Graphics and Geometric Modeling*, Richard H. Bartels, John C. Beatty, and Brian Barsky, Morgan Kaufmann Publishers, 1987.

5. *Synthetic Aperture Radar: Systems and Signal Processing*, by John Curlander, John Wiley and Sons, 1991.

Visualization of Multivariate Systems

4

      The principal objective of visualization in scientific computing is to develop techniques that make perceptible the most important informational aspects of a data set. In this chapter we look at the variety of ways that researchers commonly visualize data, and examine some of the problems that are routinely encountered. There are virtually limitless techniques for graphically representing a set of numbers. The trick is to pick the right one for a given problem. Many times this is not very obvious, and the researcher often ends up simply using the tools at hand.

      Up to this point we have talked mostly about visualizing single scalar functions in 2-D or 3-D space under stationary or time-dependent conditions. But the real world usually isn't that simple, and neither are the simulations that attempt to model it. In this chapter we describe practical and easy-to-use techniques that allow researchers to analyze complex multiparameter vector and scalar systems in virtually any scientific field. Each technique has its strengths and weaknesses, which we will explore using different examples. The visualization techniques we illustrate here are commercially available for most 32-bit operating systems used in scientific computing, as well as in the 16-bit MS-DOS and Windows environments. However, memory configuration problems can seriously impede the performance and functionality of many visualization techniques in a 16-bit environment, especially when dealing with large data sets.

Most scientists today employ a basic set of visualization and analysis techniques to help them understand a particular empirical data set, simulation, or theoretical model. These include scatter, line, contour, and vector plots, as well as 3-D wireframes, 2-D imaging, and various combinations of the above. These basic techniques have been around for decades. However, until a few years ago researchers have either had to write their own software (or have students write it) that would perform even the most elementary of functions, such as plotting a line; or purchase expensive commercial packages of library routines. In both of these cases the software was specific to a particular kind of computer as well as to specific output devices, such as a Tektronix graphics terminal or a CalComp or HP (Hewlett-Packard) plotter. Today's off-the-shelf commercial software that runs on integrated 32-bit personal computers and Unix workstations allows scientists to bypass these problems. Moreover, since there is no complex programming involved, researchers can actually do the interactive analyses themselves, without hiring legions of students and programmers. The result is both a tremendous increase in productivity and a deeper understanding of the data being analyzed.

The objectives of this chapter are fairly straightforward. First, we want to give the reader the awareness of the kinds of off-the-shelf capabilities that are available to the researcher or student today. Second, we want to try to instill a rigorous aesthetic about effectively communicating information in a visual context. We conduct the discussion in two sections: *basic visualization techniques* and *advanced visualization techniques.*

By "basic" we mean the kind of "scientific computer graphics" that has been mainstream for the past couple of decades and can be done easily with low-cost personal computer software. These include the visualization of scalar and vector data using point plots, bar graphs, contour maps, vector plots, wireframes, and multiparameter plots.

As we move into advanced visualization techniques, we will discuss methods like parametric plots and particle systems. We will also study the general problem of visualization of continuous functions, a subject of deep interest to mathematicians and theoretical physicists, as well as to students studying mathematics, physics, and engineering. Finally, we look at some specific examples in molecular visualization as well as in planetary astrophysics and geophysics.

Basic Visualization Techniques

POINT PLOTS AND BAR GRAPHS

The most basic visualization technique is simply plotting points of data on a piece of graph paper. We all learned this in grade school, but it applies to even the most sophisticated researcher. A simple graph gives a picture of the most fundamental entity that scientists look for in any problem—a relationship between two variables. If parameter B changes when we alter parameter A, then we've learned something. Correspondingly, if parameter B does not change when we vary parameter A, then we've also learned something. In fact, all of the material in this book is built on this basic principle. The problem is knowing how best to present the information, and that usually takes experience. The other end of this is what Edward Tufte calls "chartjunk" (Tufte, 1990). To get an idea of this concept, simply page through any scientific journal or attend any corporate presentation. You'll rapidly discover how poorly even the simplest data is usually represented (or, rather, misrepresented), often to the point of total confusion to the audience.

As a simple example, consider the data in Table 4.1, which is a brief listing of sunspot activity between January and June from the years

Table 4.1 Monthly Sunspot Numbers

Year	Jan	Feb	March	April	May	June
1950	101.6	94.8	109.7	113.4	106.2	83.6
1951	59.9	59.9	59.9	92.9	108.5	100.6
1952	40.7	22.7	22.0	29.1	23.4	36.4
1953	26.5	3.9	10.0	27.8	12.5	21.8
1954	0.2	0.5	10.9	1.8	0.8	0.2
1955	23.1	20.8	4.9	11.3	28.9	31.7
1956	73.6	124.0	118.4	110.7	136.6	116.6
1957	165.0	130.2	157.4	175.2	164.6	200.7
1958	202.5	164.9	190.7	196.0	175.3	171.5
1959	217.4	143.1	185.7	163.3	172.0	168.7
1960	146.3	106.	102.2	122.0	119.6	110.2
1961	57.9	46.1	53.0	61.4	51.0	77.4
1962	38.7	50.3	45.6	46.4	43.7	42.0
1963	19.8	24.4	17.1	29.3	43.0	35.9
1964	15.3	17.7	16.5	8.6	9.5	9.1
1965	17.5	14.2	11.7	6.8	24.1	15.9
1966	28.2	24.4	25.3	48.7	45.3	47.7
1967	110.9	93.6	111.8	69.5	86.5	67.3
1968	121.8	111.9	92.2	81.2	127.2	110.3
1969	104.4	120.5	135.8	106.8	120.0	106.0

1950–1969. The scientist asks the obvious question, "Is there any pattern here?" By just looking at the numbers it's hard to tell, although it seems that there may be some kind of periodic, or near-periodic variation over the years. But exactly what that variation looks like is a mystery without visualizing the data.

In Figure 4.1a we've plotted the data for January and June using Synergy Software's Kaleidagraph data analysis software. The graph indicates a definite periodic variation of sunspot numbers over the years, although there is nothing that leads one to believe that January is significantly different from June in any given year. This is what one would expect, given that the physics of the Sun has nothing whatsoever to do with Earth's calendar.

In Figure 4.1b we've taken the January data and plotted it in a traditional bar-graph form. Even though bar graphs are the traditional means of graphing business or commercial data, and grade-school kids learn to plot bar graphs as soon as they can draw a straight line, bar graphs can often obscure more information than they represent. This simply illustrates the concept that one must be judicious in choosing a particular visualization technique. A given technique can either enhance or hide the information that one is trying to show. This general principle is articulated at length by Edward Tufte in *The Visual Display of Quantitative Information* (Tufte, 1990), a book that we would recommend to anyone interested in understanding and presenting data.

This sunspot data set is a case in point. Although the temporal variation is still clearly visible in the bar graph, the visual structure of the bar graph itself seems to show off the periodicity a lot less than the simple point plot in Figure 4.1a.

If Figure 4.1b isn't as clear as Figure 4.1a, then Figure 4.1c muddles the picture even further, where we show both the January and June sunspot numbers on the same bar graph. This graph, called a stacked bar graph, is popular in business computing, although it is difficult to make much sense of time-varying trend data when the eye is confused by the graphical addition of two separate data sets. It's very hard to look at Figure 4.1c and separate the January trend from the June trend or the sum of the two.

Figure 4.1d goes the other way entirely. Here we use a cubic spline to connect the different points in the January and June graphs. These are the same data, but the graph's more open appearance allows one to view the data in a more critical fashion. We not only obtain an instant visual sense of the periodic variation of each data set, but we also get an immediate feel for the relationship between the two data sets, something impossible to obtain from the stacked bar graph in Figure 4.1c.

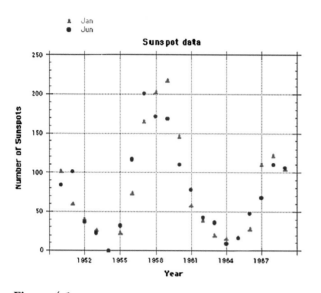

Figure 4.1a

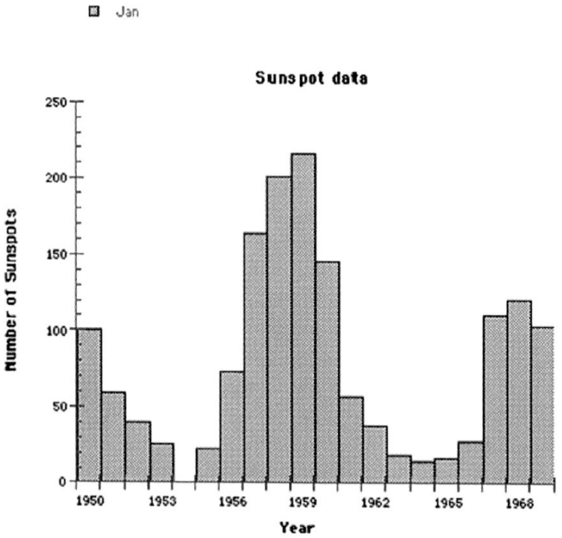

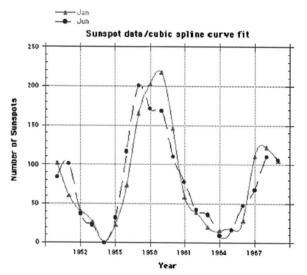

Figure 4.1b

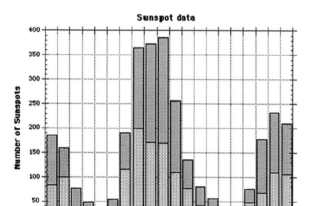

Figure 4.1c

Figure 4.1d

Figure 4.1a
This figure of sunspot data, produced in Kaleidagraph, shows definite periodicity in sunspot activity over the interval from 1950 to 1989. However, the differences between the January and June data sets are much more difficult to discern.

Figure 4.1c
The stacked bar graph, another business favorite, is less than useless for displaying comparative data, as shown in this image of the January and June sunspot data.

Figure 4.1b
Bar graphs may be good for displaying sales data, but they often miss the mark, visually, for many kinds of scientific data sets. This is the same January sunspot data as in Figure 4.1a.

Figure 4.1d
By far the most interesting and meaningful display of these data is these connected curves. Both amplitude and phase information can be obtained from this with a simple visual inspection.

CONTOURS AND IMAGES

Moving up the hierarchy in visualization sophistication, we come to contours and images, data sets where one is looking at $f(x,y)$ rather than $f(x)$. We examined these visualization techniques in previous chapters, but we take a slightly different approach here, using off-the-shelf software tools to analyze a data set. The data set we will use is the weather of the United States observed on January 2, 1991, and is from the National Weather Service, courtesy of the Department of Atmospheric Sciences of the University of Illinois at Urbana-Champaign. Data is recorded at 694 stations: temperature in degrees Fahrenheit, pressure in millibars, and wind velocity (north-south and east-west) in meters per second. All of the work that follows is done in the Spyglass Transform environment.

In Chapters 1 and 2 we discussed images and how they are generated. Here we'll use those concepts together with more complex analysis techniques. If we begin with the concept of an image as a matrix of data points, we can obtain some interesting structures. However, a critical point, emphasized in Chapter 2 and in **Tech Note 3**, is that all manipulations on a given data set should be performed directly on the floating-point data. This is so that any features discovered in the resulting image are representative of something in the original data, and not artifacts of the image processing. Still it is important to remember, as we go through the examples, that it is easy to be

Figure 4.2a
This image, produced in Spyglass Transform, is an interpolation of the average temperature in the United States on January 2, 1991, from 694 weather stations. (Courtesy Brand Fortner, Spyglass, Inc.)

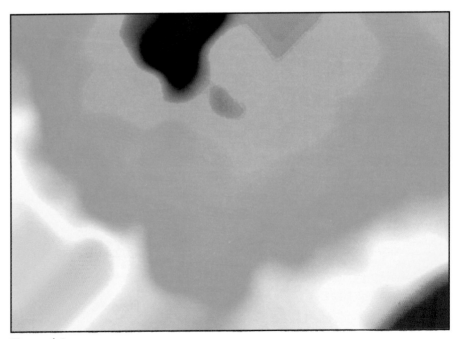

Figure 4.2a

misled by images that reflect arbitrary mappings in color space.

To begin with, consider Figure 4.2a, an image of the temperature on January 2, 1991 over a rectangular area encompassing the continental United States. The image is an interpolation of the data from 694 weather stations. Figure 4.2b shows the same temperature field with a map overlaid on top of the temperature field and appropriate contour labels added. The map and the temperature labels were created as PICT files and pasted into Transform as an overlay onto the image.

CD 4.1

VECTORS

So far we've dealt primarily with scalar data, showing a variety of ways of visually examining a particular data set. Now consider what happens when the data set happens to have a magnitude and a direction. In that case we need a vector representation. Although we typically think of vectors as a tool for visualizing multiple components of quantities like wind-velocity and magnetic fields, vectors are also useful to understand multidimensional gradients of scalar functions, as well as simply the relationship of any normalized or dimensionless parameters of a data set. Examples of the latter include comparisons of the number density (that is, particle density or concentration) of trace chemicals in a solution, or the kinetic versus gravitational potential or electromagnetic energies of a gas or plasma.

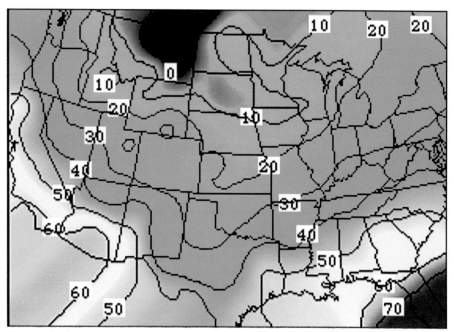

Figure 4.2b

Figure 4.2b
This image shows the temperature data of Figure 4.2a with a map overlaid on top of the temperature image. Temperature contours are also shown in degrees Fahrenheit. (Courtesy Brand Fortner, Spyglass, Inc.)

Vector fields (in 2-D) come in three flavors, so to speak: the traditional x-component versus y-component plot, such as velocity or magnetic field; the gradient vector field of a real-valued scalar function, f, which plots $\partial f/\partial x$ against $\partial f/\partial y$; and the Hamiltonian gradient field, which plots $\partial f/\partial x$ against $-\partial f/\partial y$. Figure 4.3a is a vector representation of the wind velocity field for the January 2, 1991, data set. The

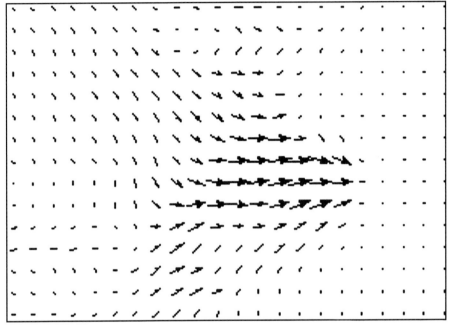

Figure 4.3a

Figure 4.3a
This image of the velocity field over the United States illustrates the power of a simple vector field visualization.
(Courtesy Brand Fortner, Spyglass, Inc.)

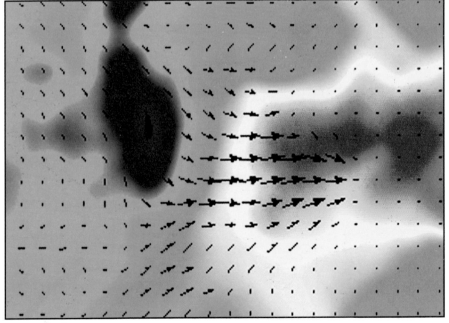

Figure 4.3b

Figure 4.3b
In this image we overlay the velocity vector field on top of the pressure image. Correlating two parameters in this manner often reveals causal relationships that are not evident in examination of the individual data.
(Courtesy Brand Fortner, Spyglass, Inc.)

horizontal axis is east-west and the vertical axis is north-south. This doesn't really tell us much as it stands. However, since wind velocity generally results from the acceleration of air generated by a pressure gradient, perhaps it would be instructive to correlate velocity with atmospheric pressure. In that context, another interesting use of vectors is to plot a vector field over a scalar field, so as to obtain a correlation between the two data sets. The results of that exercise appear in Figure 4.3b.

As another example of the use of vectors, consider the visualization of a potential $g(x,y)$. One obvious thing we could do is to compute the gradient vectors at every point on the grid and plot them. That's always important since, in the case of a potential field, for example, the gradient, in addition to being in the direction of the force, also defines an important geometrical quantity that is normal to the tangent vector field of the potential. From there, one can begin to do differential geometry on the system. However, as we mentioned, in addition to the simple gradient one can define the "Hamiltonian gradient," which gives a measure of the asymmetry of the function being analyzed. It gets its name from the Hamiltonian equations of motion of a test particle in a potential field $V(\mathbf{r})$. For a 2-D potential in Cartesian coordinates, the equations of motion in phase space are

$$\frac{\partial H}{\partial x} = \frac{\partial V}{\partial x}$$

$$\frac{\partial H}{\partial y} = -\frac{\partial V}{\partial y}$$

In Figure 4.4 we compute both vector fields for a simple function $f(x,y) = \sin x \cos y$. This function is a good one to illustrate the differences between these two techniques. Figure 4.4a shows the shaded contour plot of $f(x,y)$, while 4.4b and c show the gradient and Hamiltonian vector fields, respectively.

THE MULTIPARAMETER PROBLEM

As we continue to add parameters, the visual representation of the information that we are interested in becomes a bit cluttered, and one is faced with several options to try to get around this problem. By far the most common approach is to simply pile more visual information on until the reader is hopelessly confused (although the paper will generally get published!). Thus, for example, to represent clouds or smog concentration on the weather map we could add patterns or

CD 4.2

textures to the temperature, pressure, and velocity map. However, these would clearly interfere with the visual analysis of the pressure contours and the velocity vectors.

The next most common approach is to split the data into two or more images, each with a different set of parameters. This approach solves certain kinds of problems, but generates others. For example, we could correlate temperature and velocity with smog level, and pressure with temperature and velocity, but it would take a fair amount of effort

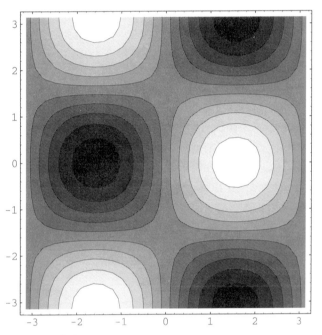

Figure 4.4a

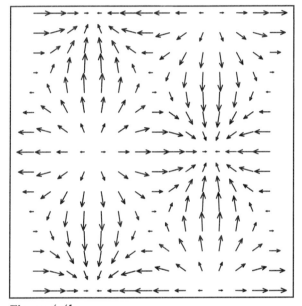

Figure 4.4b

Figure 4.4a
These images of sin x cos y in a shaded contour plot, bring out the symmetry of the function. The Mathematica function that generated this image is:
ContourPlot[Sin[x] Cos[y],{x,-Pi,Pi}, {y,-Pi,Pi},PlotPoints->30]

Figure 4.4b
This image shows the gradient vector field of sin x cos y.
Note the different structural features from the shaded contours that this visualization brings out. The Mathematica command to produce this image is:
PlotGradientField[Sin[x] Cos[y],{x,-Pi,Pi}, {y,-Pi,Pi}]

Figure 4.4c
This image of the Hamiltonian vector field of sin x cos y gives more insight into the geometrical structure of the function. In particular, one can discern antisymmetries that are not obvious from either of the other techniques. The Mathematica function is given by:
PlotHamiltonianField[Sin[x] Cos[y],{x,-Pi,Pi}, {y,-Pi,Pi}]

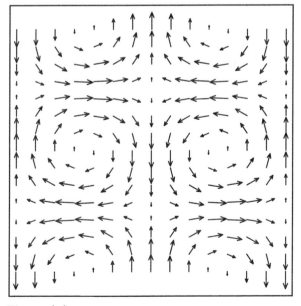

Figure 4.4c

to determine where all of the parameters came together to identify a particular event.

A third way is to assign one of the scalar parameters to time and to simply animate the entire data set. Within the past few years many researchers have concluded that animation is the first resort for most types of multiparameter visualization problems. Unfortunately, although this approach works well for certain kinds of data sets, it is confusing for nearly all data that is entirely spatially dependent. In addition, time is a scalar and, as such, animation can only account for one scalar variable, so that having more than one excess parameter leaves one in the same predicament again, although this time with animated data.

Yet another way is to produce 3-dimensional graphs, with one parameter suspended in space above a couple of others. While this technique has gained popularity recently because of the kinds of exciting displays one gets, there are still many of the visual problems associated with looking at multiple data sets on the same image. A correlary of this approach is to have one parameter represented as a height field, with the other parameters overlaid on top of it. This technique can be effective, but only for small numbers of parameters. As an example, in Figure 4.5 the color temperature image from the January 5, 1991, data set is overlaid onto a 3-D wireframe surface of the barometric pressure. And, of course, the cover of this book has one parameter rendered as a height field, with two others "stacked" above it.

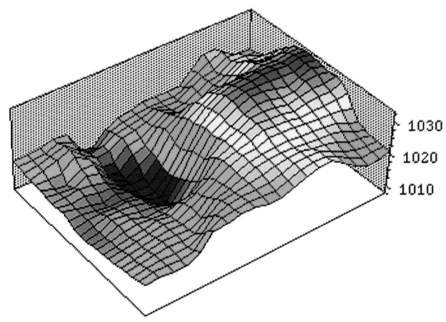

1030
1020
1010

Figure 4.5
This image shows the January 5, 1991, temperature data set overlaid onto a 3-D wireframe surface of the pressure. Observe that this correlation, while interesting in its own right, is somewhat more difficult to discern than the correlation of velocity and pressure shown in Figure 4.4c. The scale on the right-hand side indicates pressure in millibars. (Courtesy Brand Fortner, Spyglass, Inc.)

Figure 4.5

Advanced Visualization Techniques

High-performance workstations and 32-bit color personal computers have brought unique capabilities to the desktop, and researchers have begun to exploit the new generation of hardware and software. In this section we illustrate several novel approaches toward visualizing multiparameter scalar and vector data sets. All of the images shown here were done with commercial software packages. We begin with a simple mapping of scalar ozone optical depth data onto a sphere, done in IDL (Figure 4.6). The spherical mapping enables the viewer to gain a much better perspective of the data set than normal rectilinear mapping schemes. The IDL ozone visualization is a simple variation of the imaging technique used in Figure 2.10, although here the mapping is done on a sphere.

In Figure 4.7 we use the ozone data from Nimbus 7 to illustrate the range of techniques beyond simple imaging that one can apply to a particular problem. Each technique provides unique insight into the nature of the physical problem. First, Figures 4.7a and b use the simple imaging technique of Figure 2.10 to show the average ozone optical depth for the month of October for 1979 and 1990. Notice the difference between the two images in the south polar region, where both the extent and the intensity of the ozone depletion are considerably greater in 1991 than in 1979. Figures 4.7c and d used IBM's Visual Explorer software to show the ozone data from October 1, 1979 and October 1,

CD 4.3

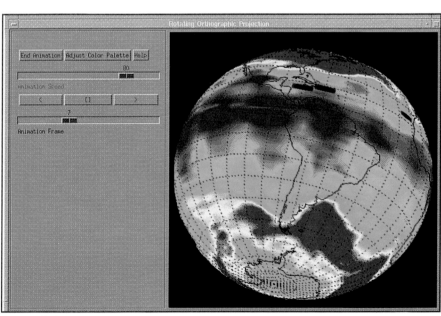

Figure 4.6

Figure 4.6
This image of total columnar ozone (the total amount of ozone contained in a cylindrical column between the observing spacecraft and the Earth's surface), computed in IDL, shows a banded structure of the stratospheric ozone layer, with a local minimum encompassing the South Pole region. (Courtesy Hal Elgie, Research Systems, Inc.)

1991. Using a 3-D mapping of the data, along with color, provides a much more dramatic view of the phenomenon than does the simple imaging technique. However, the imaging technique in Figures 4.7a and b allows us to draw quick quantitative relationships between different latitude and longitude regions. Figure 4.7e shows a polar projection of an image of the ozone data for October 1991. This visualization technique gives us a complementary view to the rectangular projection in Figures 4.7a and b. Finally, in Figure 4.7f IBM Visual Explorer was used to produce a transparent view of the October 1, 1991 data. While interesting from a computer graphics perspective, this particular method is not as effective in communicating the basic nature of the problem—that there is a significant decrease in the amount of stratospheric ozone over the south polar region—as the other techniques that we have shown.

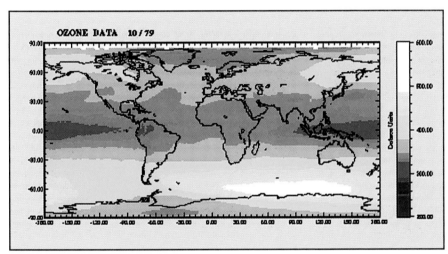

Figure 4.7a

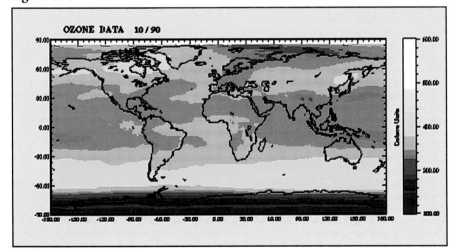

Figure 4.7b

Figure 4.7
These visualizations of the total columnar ozone from the TOMS experiment on Nimbus-7 illustrate the variety of ways that simple $f(x,y)$ data can be displayed to provide the viewer with different perspectives on the same data set.

Figures 4.7a and **b** use the same technique as Figure 2.12 to show the average daily ozone optical depth for October 1979 and October 1990. This view gives us an intuition of the relationship between different geographical regions.

Figures 4.7c and **d** use a combined depth-color technique to show daily averages for October 1, 1979, and October 1, 1991. In this view the quantitative relationships between different geographic regions are not as obvious, although the intensity and magnitude of the physical phenomenon are more obvious.

Figure 4.7e shows a polar projection of the October 1, 1991, data that combines elements from both previous techniques.

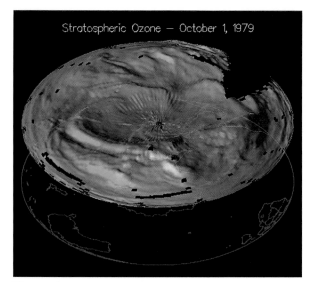

Figure 4.7c

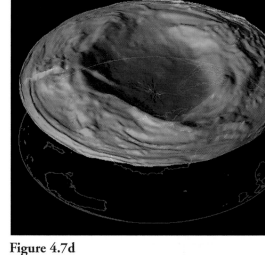

Figure 4.7d

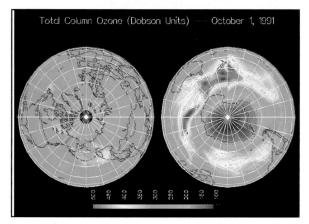

Figure 4.7e

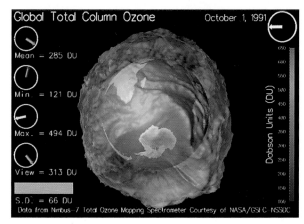

Figure 4.7f

Figure 4.7f shows a "transparent" view of the global column ozone data for October 1, 1991. This image provides additional insight into the 3-D structure of the total column ozone, but does not provide the intuitive insight into the nature of the problem that the other figures do (4.7a and b courtesy Jim Knighton NASA/JPL; 4.7c-f courtesy Lloyd Treinish, IBM; NASA/GSFC)

Figure 4.8 shows a variety of visualizations of air flow past different aerodynamic objects. Designing aerodynamical systems requires an understanding of the relationship between the multiple variates air pressure, velocity, vorticity, and friction on the body being flown. Figures 4.8a-c show flow parameters for gasdynamics flow past airplanes and the Space Shuttle while Figure 4.8d, from NASA Ames, shows a particle system approach (described in Chapter 6) towards modeling streamlines of blood flowing through the heart. All images were done on Silicon Graphics IRIS machines.

A completely different approach to the multiparameter problem is being pursued by researchers at the University of Lowell, in Massachusetts (Grinstein et al., 1989, Grinstein and Smith, 1990) in

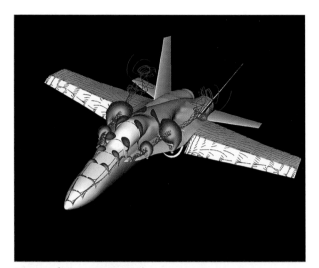

Figure 4.8a

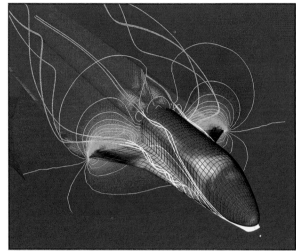

Figure 4.8b

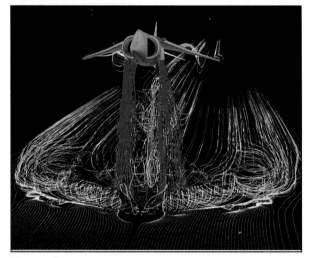

Figure 4.8c

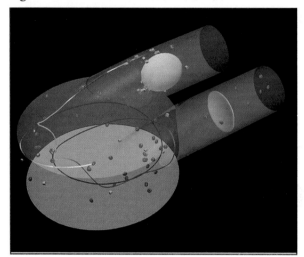

Figure 4.8d

Figure 4.8a

This visualization of the flow field around an F-18 shows the flow field represented by particle traces with helicity density (the product of vorticity and velocity) in cross sections of the flow field with simulated flow lines on the wing's surface.(Courtesy Val Watson, NASA/Ames Research Center)

Figure 4.8b

Too much visual information can produce visual clutter that makes it difficult to ascertain the key features of a simulation or observation. (Courtesy Val Watson, NASA/Ames Research Center)

Figure 4.8c

This visualization of a Harrier jet hovering at take-off shows an effective use of particle traces to understand flow lines. (Courtesy Val Watson, NASA/Ames Research Center)

Figure 4.8d

Techniques developed for visualizing airflow over fighter jets is applied to this simulation of blood flowing through the heart. (Courtesy Val Watson, NASA/Ames Research Center) their Exvis experimental visualization environment. Their work is specifically designed to address the problem of visualizing multiple vector and scalar parameters and uses geometric coding, in the form of *iconographic* representations of data. These researchers have applied the technique to several fields, including tomographic medical images and multispectral satellite images, and have had some interesting results. The basic concept is to introduce a small icon called a *generalized icon (gicon)*, which is essentially a "generalized pixel" with several attributes including shape, orientation, length, density (number per unit area), and color. An example of this technique is shown in Figure 4.9.

Finally, there is sound, which can be effectively used in conjunction with visual displays to extract multiparameter data from a complex data set. In **Tech Note 10** we describe approaches toward sonification by different researchers, and the CD includes a Mathematica Notebook with several computations and sonifications to give you a feel for the use of sound as a data analysis tool.

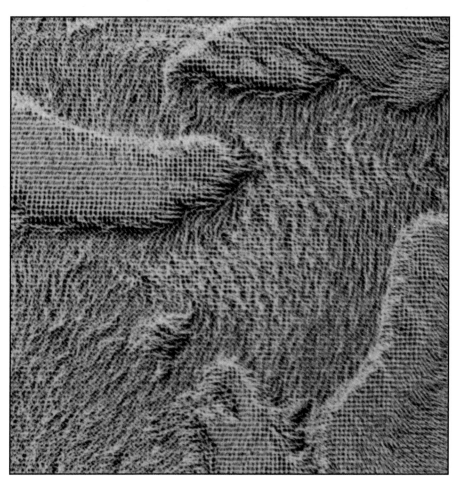

Figure 4.9
This Exvis image is from data from the NOAA-7 AVHRR weather satellite. The iconographic picture is a composite of five photographs, three at different infrared wavelengths and two in the visible range. The picture covers a region including the eastern end of Lake Erie, the western end of Lake Ontario, most of Lake Huron, and Georgia Bay.

Figure 4.9

Special Problems

In this section we focus on areas where the common data visualization techniques are not enough. In particular, we'll study the problems of visualizing complex mathematical functions, as well as certain specialized applications such as geophysics, planetary science, and molecular visualization. This latter field is becoming increasingly important as pharmaceutical and molecular biology researchers move toward the "simulated laboratory" as a way of quickly and cheaply studying different variations of well-known molecules. Researchers in this field also demand interactivity, which brings in the entire question of the user interface in a personal computer environment.

VISUALIZATION OF CONTINUOUS FUNCTIONS

The notion of being able to rapidly visualize any arbitrary function or data set is extremely attractive to mathematicians, physical scientists, and probably any student or teacher who's ever had to struggle with understanding a mathematical object or a theoretical representation of a physical process. Several commercial software developers have begun to provide this sort of capability which, for the average university, corporate, or government lab researcher would significantly reduce costs associated with hiring programmers to develop custom graphing packages. The marriage between these two groups has since fueled the commercial software industry, which now sells hundreds of thousands of packages of software per year to scientific R&D users for the express purpose of visualizing continuous functions. Continuous functions provide certain advantages over discrete data sets, and they pose certain problems as well. In this section we examine some of the capabilities of these packages and show how useful different visualization techniques can be for mathematical structures.

Dozens, if not hundreds, of new ideas are continually being developed throughout the scientific R&D and commercial software development communities, but for many 3-D scientific visualization problems there is a fairly well defined canonical set of representations that encompass most problems. This set of representations becomes even smaller when the object being visualized can be represented by a closed-form function. With that in mind, we will display a number of examples of these techniques. With the exception of Figure 4.10, which was computed in IDL, each of the examples shown in this section can be found in a Mathematica Notebook on the CD. Finally, to underline just how these visualization techniques empower users to analyze their data more deeply, we've selected a few astrophysical problems to demonstrate how useful and powerful these methods are.

Below we reproduce a variety of 3-D graphics images created by visualizations of continuous functions. All of the Mathematica images were computed on a Mac IIfx with 32 MB RAM (Mathematica was running under a 25 MB partition). Most of the images took 1 to 5 minutes to compute, although a few took considerably longer.

In Figure 4.10 a solution to the Schrödinger equation is shown with the results displayed as a 3-D plot with "shadow" contour and image plots displayed on the inside of the bounding box. In Figures 4.11 we've computed a series of continuous parametric plots and 3-D point plots of a helix

$$f[x(t), y(t), z(t)] = \{t\cos(t^2),\ t\sin(t^2),\ t\}$$

over the range $0 \le t \le \pi$ under different resolutions. The objectives of this exercise are twofold: (1) to illustrate how important sampling rate (resolution) is and (2) to show that sometimes unobvious ways of visualizing something are equally as good as, if not better than, the traditionally accepted modes. Normally one would think the best way to visualize a continuous function is to plot a continuous curve. However, notice how the 3-D point plot seems to stand out more than the curve.

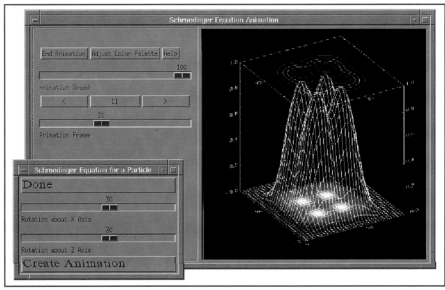

Figure 4.10
This IDL visualization of a solution of the Schrödinger equation incorporates a 3-D plot coupled with a shadow contour and image plots displayed in the bounding box. (Courtesy Hal Elgie/RSI, Inc.)

Figure 4.10

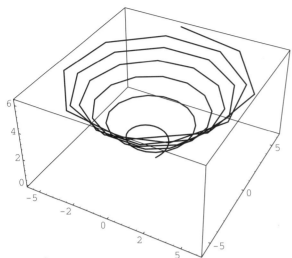

Figure 4.11a

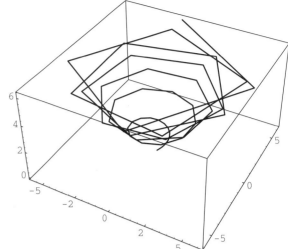

Figure 4.11b

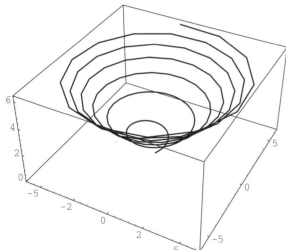

Figure 4.11c

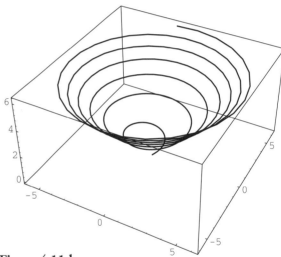

Figure 4.11d

Figure 4.11a

This series of images of curves in 3-space illustrate the power of parametric curves, as well as the caution that one must take in insuring that there is sufficient resolution to accurately compute the function. All of these functions are included in the 3-D Graphics Mathematica Notebook on the CD-ROM. This particular image was computed from the Mathematica command: **ParametricPlot3D[{t Cos[t^2], t Sin[t^2],t},{t,0,2Pi}, PlotPoints->100**. This resolution illustrates what the helix curve looks like at 50 points per π.

Figure 4.11c

At this resolution of 80 pts/Pi, although the curve appears far from continuous, there is enough resolution to discern the basic structure of the curve. The Mathematica command is: **ParametricPlot3D[{t Cos[t^2], t Sin[t^2],t},{t,0,4Pi,Pi/80}]**.

Figure 4.11b

Same as Figure 4.11a, but with 25 pts/Pi. Note how the structure of the curve breaks down entirely when Mathematica attempts to connect the nearest neighbor points.

Figure 4.11d

At 160 pts/Pi the curve appears to be fairly continuous.

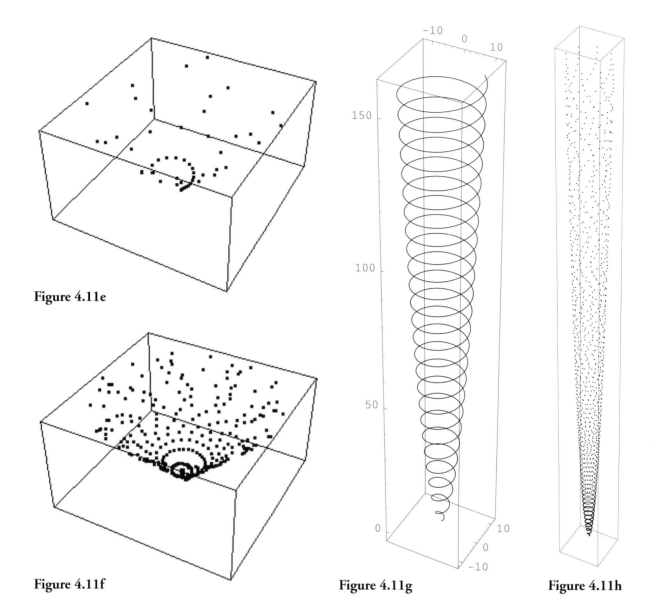

Figure 4.11e

Figure 4.11f

Figure 4.11g

Figure 4.11h

Figure 4.11e

A different approach to visualizing parametric curves plots individual points instead of connecting them. This can be an advantage in cases where the data is low-resolution, but can also be
visually confusing. In this image we plot the same helix as in
Figures 4.11a-d, but using individual points instead of connecting them. The resolution here is 25 pts/Pi. The Matheamtica
commands to produce this image are:
Table[{t Cos[t^2], t Sin[t^2],t}, {t,0,2Pi,Pi/25}];
ScatterPlot3D[testdata2c].

Figure 4.11f

At 80 pts/Pi we really don't get a good intuition of the structure
of this particular curve. but this is not necessarily the case for all
parametric curves. The Mathematica commands are:
Table[{t Cos[t^2], t Sin[t^2],t},{t,0,4Pi,Pi/80}];
ScatterPlot3D[testdata2b]

Figure 4.11g

This curve illustrates the difference between the continuous and
discrete methods of plotting a 3-D parametric curve at high resolution. In each case we plot the data at 200 pts/Pi. This particular image is generated by the Mathematica command:
ParametricPlot3D[{t Cos[t^2], t Sin[t^2],t^2}, {t,0,8Pi},
PlotPoints->1600].

Figure 4.11h

The same data as in Figure 4.11g, but generated by plotting
points with the Mathematica commands:
Table[{t Cos[t^2], t Sin[t^2],t^2}, {t,0,8Pi,Pi/200}];
ScatterPlot3D[testdata2]

In the next exercise we compute symmetric and nonsymmetric parametric functions $F\{x(t), y(t), z(t)\}$ in 3-space (Figures 4.12a and b). Notice how visually rich both images are. If you can get your data or equations into this sort of form, then parametric equations provide a number of advantages over simple $f\{x,y,z\}$. First, they are easier to understand since the equations can be viewed as vector components. Second, once the function is in this form it is straightforward to apply the machinery of differential geometry to establish relationships defining the geometric properties of the function—something which is much more difficult in the coordinate $f\{x,y,z\}$ representation. In this particular problem notice how a slight variation of the function produces a significant variation in properties of the surface. Specifically, notice that destroying the symmetry of the function introduces very sharp discontinuities in the 3-D surface. It is left as an exercise for the reader to compute the tangent, normal, and binormal vectors for this function. Another interesting exercise (although this will take a significant amount of compute time) is to compute different views of the object, thus highlighting different structural and geometric features.

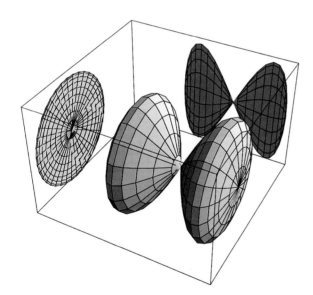

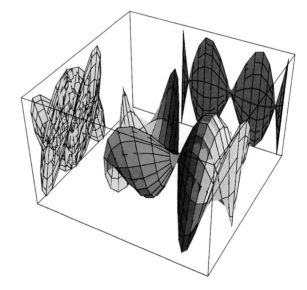

Figure 4.12a
This image shows a 3-D $F(u,v) = F\{x(u,v), y(u,v), z(u,v)\}$ with a "shadow" applied to two planes of the bounding box. The Mathematica command to generate this visualization is: **ParametricPlot3D[{Sin[u], Sin[2u] Sin[v], Sin[2u] Cos[v]}, {u,-Pi/2,Pi/2},{v,0,2Pi}, Ticks->None]**. It should be noted that, although projection is useful as an auxiliary aid in understanding a 3-D structure, one must be careful in interpreting the shadow. This is seen in Figure 4.12b, where we've altered the function slightly to produce a very different graphical object.

Figure 4.12b
This image was produced by the Mathematica command: **ParametricPlot3D[{Sin[u], Sin[2u] Sin[u], Sin[3u] Cos[2v]}, {u,-Pi/2,Pi/2}, {v,0,2Pi}, Ticks->None]** with shadowing turned on. Notice how the shadows reflect a symmetry in the object that really isn't there in 3-D.

Spheres and other Platonic geometric surfaces are particularly useful as teaching and presentation aids. We've already seen several examples of data sets mapped onto spheres. Later in this chapter we use spheres to represent molecules for molecular visualizations, and in Chapter 6 we use spheres to illustrate texture mapping and other fairly sophisticated computer graphics techniques that are available to do things like illustrate the astrophysics of planetary systems. Don't be intimidated by these Hollywood-type computer graphics: Powerful personal computers and high-quality commercial software have brought this power to the desktop level for any scientist or engineer with typical university-level funding. It's also easy to export Mathematica objects to universal 3-D data formats that can be read by a variety of rendering and animation packages on Unix and Macintosh systems. We discuss 3-D rendering and animation in more detail in Chapter 6.

CD 4.4

As far as spheres go, there are several ways of visualizing these fundamental objects. Figures 4.13a and b show two ways within Mathematica that one can do this, and they each have their advantages. One general suggestion is that users create a library of geometrical objects to use for presentations, publications, and creative play. This will save

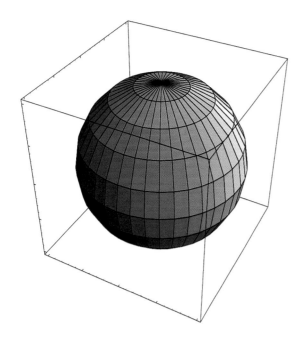

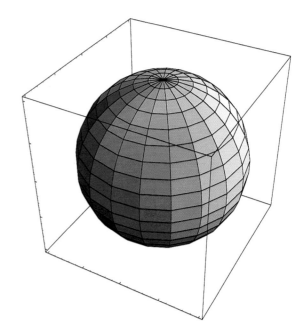

Figure 4.13a
This rendering of a sphere is computed in Mathematica with the command: **ParametricPlot3D[{Cos[u] Cos[v], Sin[u] Cos[v], Sin[v]}, {u,0,2Pi,Pi/20}, {v,-Pi/2, Pi/2, Pi/10}]**

Figure 4.13b
This image of a sphere is computed with the Mathematica command: **SphericalPlot3D[2,{theta,0,Pi}, {phi,0,2Pi}]**. Notice the difference in polygon structure between this figure and Figure 4.13a.

computing time and hunting around for files and commands. Since spheres are ubiquitous in scientific and engineering computing, our advice would be to compute several spheres at various resolutions. Different resolutions allow a trade-off between file size (and, hence, rendering time when importing a sphere into a rendering package) and aesthetics. This is an important consideration in all of these exercises. The researcher trying several configurations or views of a set of objects, for example, has a much lower requirement for image quality than when putting together a presentation for a funding officer. A function visualization that takes 10 seconds to evaluate and draw at a resolution of $20 \times 20 \times 20$ takes more than 100 times as long to compute at a resolution of $100 \times 100 \times 100$, not to mention the fact that there is more than 100 times as much data. In this regard, one could use the **PointParametricPlot3D** function to compute the sphere but with points instead of rendered polygons. This is useful, for example, to illustrate some relative features in the celestial sphere, or when placing specific structures inside the sphere so that they would be visible to the observer.

A variation on **ParametricPlot3D** is **SphericalPlot3D** and its coordinate-related cousin **CylindricalPlot3D**. These functions assume spherical and cylindrical coordinates, respectively, for the arguments and compute everything in terms of these. Notice that a sphere computed in **SphericalPlot3D** is somewhat different then a sphere computed with **ParametricPlot3D**. At first glance the objects appear the same, but closer inspection shows that the polygonal structure is different for each. For approximately the same resolution, the polygons for **ParametricPlot3D** are more elongated longitudinally than the more equant polygons of **SphericalPlot3D**. Examination of the PostScript code for each image confirms this, although it should be obvious already since the coordinate systems of each object are different. Nevertheless, even though the physical structure of each polygonal surface is different for the two spheres, for most scientific visualization applications this won't really make any difference.

Another useful visualization trick is to plot a 3-D visualization of a 2-D function. This is done by simply taking the 2-D function and creating a surface of revolution from it using the "**SurfaceOfRevolution**" command. Features that are small and apparently insignificant when viewed in 2-D can be quite visually apparent on a 3-D surface. Two simple examples illustrate this point (Figures 4.14, 4.15). In both cases the original curve is rotated around the z (vertical) axis. Thus, in the first case, $y = \sin x$, the surface of revolution turns out to be a sombrero-shape whereas the parametric curve in Figure 4.15 yields a cup shape.

CD 4.5

In both cases the 3-D rendering of the 2-D curve produces interesting, if not unexpected results. Variations on this theme include rotating around the *x* or *y* axes.

Beyond scalar parameters, researchers often are faced with visualizing vector fields. We've already mentioned 2-D contour and vector surfaces, which can be viewed as level curves and their corresponding tangent and normal vectors in a plane. 3-D contours can also be used as potential surfaces where the vector field can be derived as the gradient to some potential. Cases in point include electric fields or fluid velocity in an anelastic (incompressible) fluid. (3-D surfaces and 3-D contours are covered in more depth in Chapter 5 and **Tech Note 13**.) Another popular way to view vector fields is to assign a vector (magnitude and direction) to a subset of points in a 2-D or 3-D data set. In Figure 4.16a and b we illustrate the use of 3-D vector fields as a visualization tool. The Mathematica function **PlotVectorField3D** is the primary tool we use here to explore these functions. The advantage of this technique is that 3-D vector quantities are difficult to visualize any other way. However, there is a certain art in ensuring that the resolution is not too low, so that the structure of the field can be

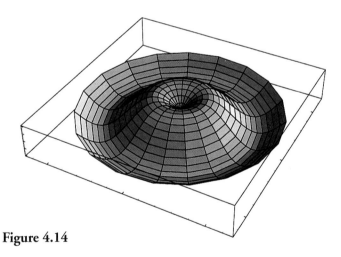

Figure 4.14

Figure 4.14
This image is computed by revolving sin x from $\{0, 2\pi\}$ around the point $x = \pi$. Surfaces of revolution are useful in a number of circumstances and can aid in visualizing features in functions of the form $y = f(x)$. The Mathematica command used to generate this image is:
SurfaceOfRevolution[Sin[x],{x,0,2Pi}, PlotPoints->{20,20}]

Figure 4.15
This surface of revolution is computed from a function $f(u,v)$ by rotating around the center of both coordinates. The Mathematica command to generate this image is: **SurfaceOfRevolution[{Sin[u],u^2},{u,0,3Pi/2}, BoxRatios-> {1,1,2}, PlotPoints->{20,20}]**

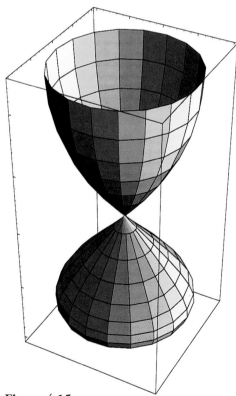

Figure 4.15

ascertained, but not so high as to obscure the features that one wants to bring out. Other parameters to note are the length of the vectors and the size of the arrowheads, although in most programs these parameters are generally automatically computed. In this image the vectors have no arrowheads so, although the general features of the function can be distinguished, it is hard to get a sense of direction of motion.

REAL-WORLD PROBLEMS

On the CD we apply some of these techniques to a couple of real-world problems to see how researchers might employ them in their daily work. The examples we've selected are typical of the sort of work that a graduate student or researcher in physics or astrophysics might be engaged in on any given day. The formulation time of any of these problems is fairly short, a few minutes once the problem is understood. The visualization time for each model is 2 to 10 minutes on a Mac IIfx with 32 MB RAM. One thing to watch in these sorts of computations is the resolution of the visualizations. Because high-resolution images take much longer to compute than low-resolution images, it is often tempting to conclude that a low-resolution graphic is properly represen-

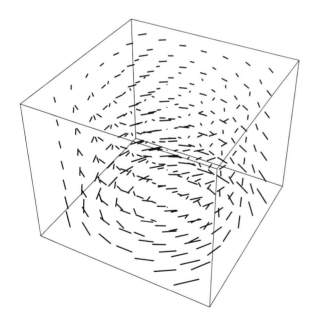

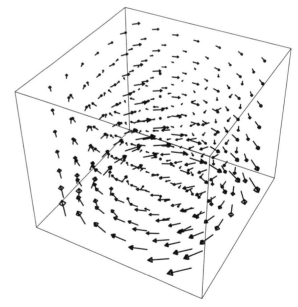

Figure 4.16a
This series of images illustrates the use of 3-D vector fields in visualizing analytical, computational, and empirical data sets. The Mathematica command for this visualization is: **PlotVectorField3D[{y, -x, 0}/z, {x,-1,1}, {y,-1,1}, {z,1,3}]**, where the components of each vector are, respectively, {y/z, -x/z, 0}.

Figure 4.16b
Arrowheads give definite direction and depth to the visualization. Howver, with only a finite (and usually small) amount of screen space, too many arrows can easily clutter up an image. The Mathematica command to produce this image is the same as the command to produce 4.16a but with VectorHeads set to "true".

111

tative of the solution, when in fact the function has not really been sampled sufficiently. One must carefully study each function or data set to be visualized to determine a resolution that is sufficient to demonstrate the structure of the function, yet computable in a reasonable amount of time. To learn this art simply takes a bit of practice on known analytic functions.

In this section we'll look at a simple classical physics problem: Kepler orbits of a point mass in a gravitational field. This problem is interesting in its own right, but affords some inside into different visualization techniques. A couple of other problems are included as Mathematica Notebooks on the CD-ROM, and the reader is encouraged to experiment with different ways of visualizing the functions described therein.

We first look at a couple of basic features of Kepler orbits. Specifically, the general solution for the equation of motion of a test particle in orbit around a gravitating body can be given by

$$r = a(1 - e^2) / (1 + e\cos(\theta)),$$

where a is the semimajor axis of the orbit, e is the eccentricity, defined in terms of the energy, mass, and angular momentum of the particle, and $\{r, \theta\}$ are the coordinates of the position of the particle at any point in the orbit. In the real world the particle could, for example, be a planet orbiting a star, or a spacecraft orbiting a planet. In Figure 4.17 we plot $r(\theta)$ for two cases: $e = \{-0.5, 0.5\}$ and θ ranging from zero to 2π. Figure 4.18a visualizes the general solution for the range $-0.5 \leq e \leq 1$. Notice the curvature of the surface and its peaks and valleys. This indicates that the particle would have very different motion for different values of $\{e, \theta\}$. In fact, depending upon the value of e, the orbit of the particle is either

Figure 4.17a
This simple graph of $r(\theta)$ for $e = -0.5$ is the most basic visualization of a continuous function. However, this is not the entire story, as Figure 4.17b shows.

Figure 4.17b
The same equation plotted with $e = +0.5$ shows a different functional dependence. Therefore, to understand the true functional dependence on e and θ we need to visualize the function in 3-D and with a contour plot.

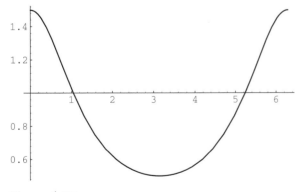

Figure 4.17a

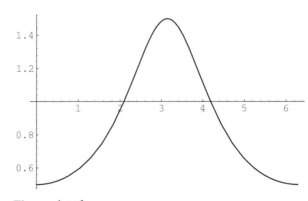

Figure 4.17b

elliptical, parabolic, or hyperbolic. In each case, $r(\theta)$ has a different functional form. Figure 4.18b shows $r(\theta)$ as a contour plot for comparison.

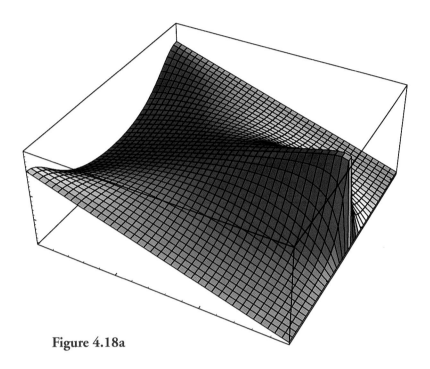

Figure 4.18a

Figure 4.18a
This visualization of $r(\theta,e)$ shows how Figures 4.17a and 4.17b can be computed as slices for $e = -0.5$ and $e = +0.5$. However, the 3-D structure could never have been inferred from the two plots shown in Figures 4.17.

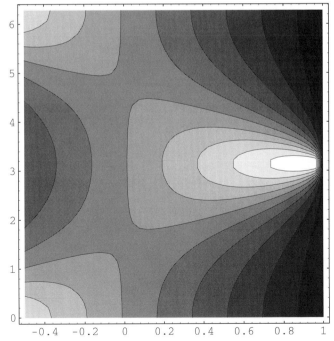

Figure 4.18b

Figure 4.18b
Contour plot of the function for comparison. Whereas Figure 4.18a provides dramatic structure to the function, there is more detail here than in the 3-D graph.

Molecular Visualization

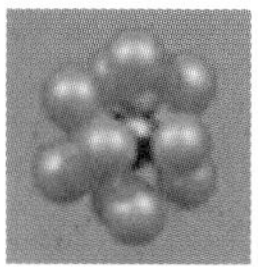

CD 4.6

Molecular biologists, chemists, and chemical engineers often need to know the structure and dynamics of existing or hypothetical molecules. In the past this data has been difficult to obtain. However, today software models of molecular structures and bonds have become mainstream on the chemical researcher's desktop. In this section we look at several of the interactive representations of molecules, and we examine the differences between the various kinds of displays. For our illustrations we shall use two molecules, a protein alpha helix and a buckminsterfullerene (buckyball) molecule. Both molecules have particular geometrical features that make them interesting to visualize—the helix since it can be used as a guide to visualizing the much larger DNA molecule, and the buckyball because of its spherical symmetry.

Researchers interested in molecular structure need to obtain a variety of different kinds of data about a given molecule, and an image

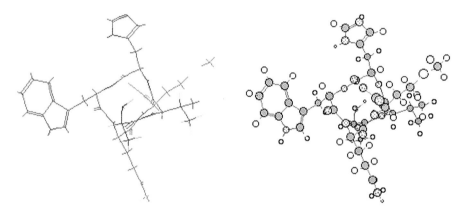

Figure 4.19a

Figure 4.19b

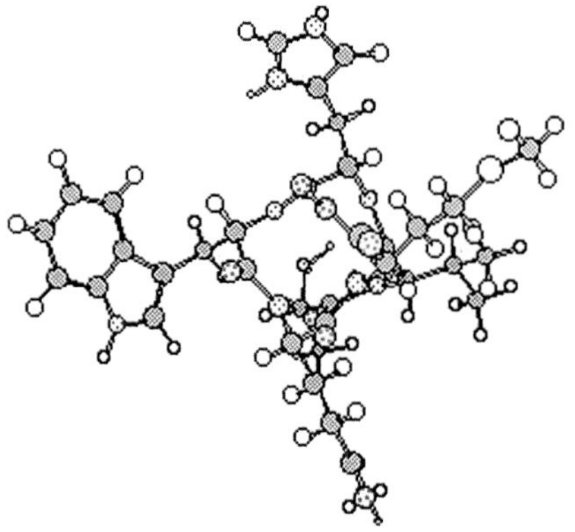

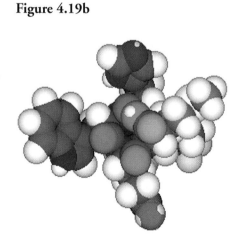

Figure 4.19c

Figure 4.19d

Figure 4.19a
Wireframe visualization of the protein alpha helix molecule.
(Courtesy Cambridge Scientific/Michael Schwartz)

Figure 4.19b
Ball-and-stick view of protein alpha helix.

Figure 4.19c
Cylindrical bond view of protein alpha helix.

Figure 4.19d
Space-filling view of protein alpha helix.

of its geometrical shape can be a good guide to the kind of interactions it might have with other molecules. Information such as atom and bond sizes and the dynamic characteristics of given bonds are critical for understanding the nature of a particular molecule. In this regard, one of the most important computing advances is the capability to interactively analyze and visualize the structure and dynamics of a molecule on a personal computer. One of the best software packages designed for interactive analysis and visualization is Chem3D, by Cambridge Scientific Computing, Inc. This package allows the researcher to, for example, manually rotate a molecule around a specified bond, or rotate the entire molecule around any axis. In addition, several views of any molecule are offered, such as wireframe, ball-and-stick, cylindrical bonds, and space-filling, and each of the views has various visualization options. The user can also easily specify parameters for animating a molecule, rotating about an axis or about a given bond. Raw data, images, and movies can be saved in a variety of formats. In Figures 4.19

CD 4.7

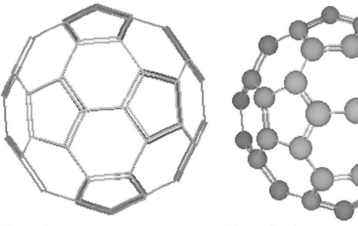

Figure 4.20a

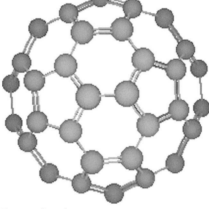

Figure 4.20b

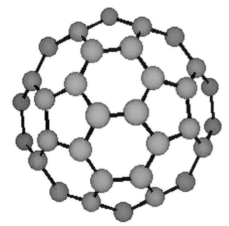

Figure 4.20c

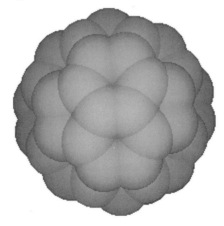

Figure 4.20d

Figure 4.20a
Wireframe view of buckyball.

Figure 4.20b
Ball-and-stick view of buckyball.

Figure 4.20c
Cylindrical bond view of buckyball.

Figure 4.20d
Space-filling view of buckyball.

and 4.20 we show views of the protein alpha helix and the buckyball, respectively. The first view of each molecule is wireframe, the second is ball-and-stick, the third is cylindrical bonds, and the fourth is space-filling.

Geophysics

An increasing number of experimental geophysicists are using visualization techniques as part of their daily data analysis activities. What makes these problems so interesting is the unique data collection environment that these researchers work in. One typical example is data collection from a borehole drilled several thousand feet into the ground to collect data on the structure and dynamics of the Earth's crust. To do this, researchers place a spinning ultrasonic transceiver in the hole which sends and receives signals at a rate of 600 pulses per rotation. The objective of the experiment—which drives the visualization method—is to locate and identify small structural features in the borehole. These features provide important geological history, as well as data on the structure and orientation of earthquake faults. Figures 4.21 and 4.22 show screen shots from software designed specifically to visualize and analyze these complex data structures. The software was

Figure 4.21
The "creatures from Dr. Who" are actually called "breakouts" which are best viewed in polar cross-section, and are the response of the borehole to high deviatoric stress. The intact rock is the orange and the blue-purple is the lower reflectivity break-outs , where rock has failed or fractured after the hole was drilled. This software was developed by Colleen Barton of Stanford University and Larry Tesler of Apple Computer, Inc. (Courtesy Colleen Barton, Stanford University Dept. of Geophysics)

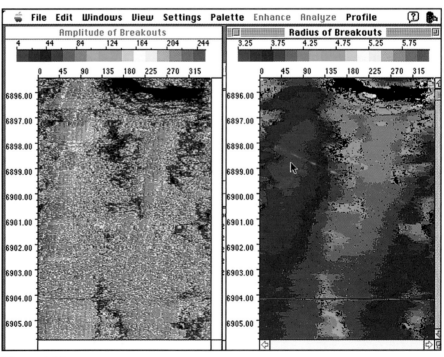

Figure 4.21

developed as a collaboration between Colleen Barton, a geophysisist at Stanford University, and Larry Tesler, chief scientist at Apple Computer.

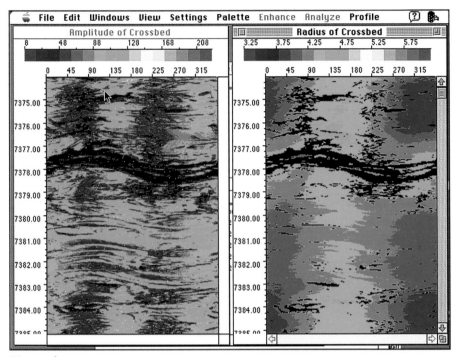

Figure 4.22a

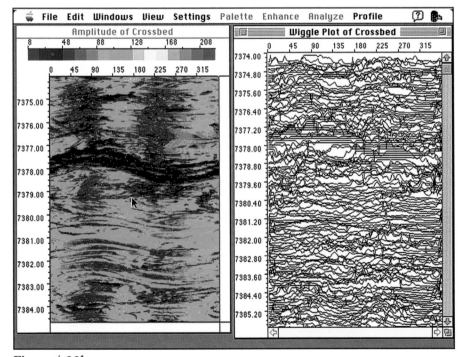

Figure 4.22b

Figure 4.22a and **b**
A spinning ultrasonic device in a borehole sends and receives signals at a rate of 600 pulses per rotation. Depth is in feet. Azimuth is in degrees. Amplitude is in arbitrary units. Radius is in inches. The big black sinusoid curve represents a fracture. The objective of this kind of visualization is to see small structural features in the borehole data. These features provide significant geological information, including the structure and orientation of the fracture. (Courtesy Colleen Barton, Stanford University)

CD 4.8

Planetary Astrophysics

In Chapter 2, Figures 2.20, we looked at a visualization of a magnetohydrodynamic (MHD) simulation of the solar wind interaction with Venus. There we found that, by using animation as an analysis tool Wolff and Norman were able to "trap" the short-lived phenomenon that they were looking for. However, the problem actually goes deeper than that if one asks what the relationship is between the various physical parameters such as magnetic field, pressure, and plasma density. We've already discussed several techniques for visualizing both individual and multiple parameters, such as contours and colors, streamlines and particles, and so on. However, in certain cases such as the Venus ionosphere simulation, we are looking for extremely subtle relationships between parameters. As such we need a visualization technique that's particularly sensitive to variations in the *relationships* between parameters. In 1987 Matt Arrott and Stephan Fangmeier of NCSA's

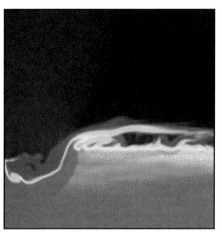
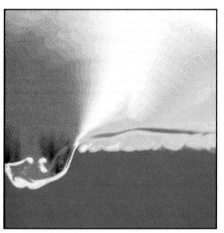

Figure 4.23a

Figure 4.23b

Figure 4.23
This set of images of a simulation of the solar wind interaction with Venus described in Chapter 2 shows, respectively, the density, magnetic field, and pressure of the plasma at an arbitrary point in time.

Figures 4.23a-c demonstrate the structural differences between the different parameters. This shows that a single parameter is often insufficient to describe the physics of a system.

Figure 4.23d shows how combining the parameters can yield correlative information by visual inspection. In this image shaded relief (height) represents density and color represents magnetic field strength, with blue equal to zero.

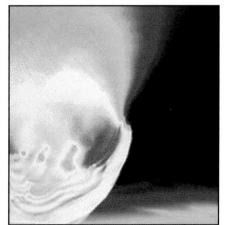
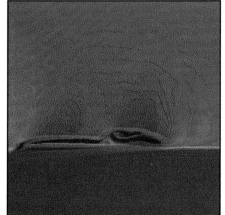

Figure 4.23c

Figure 4.23d

visualization group, working with Wolff and Norman, developed a technique to do just that. Figures 4.23 show a few frames from the Venus Plasma Cloud animation which illustrate the process. This visualization technique takes advantage of gradients in each of the variables and, as such, is particularly valuable for comparative data analysis. The single parameter images are shown in Figures 4.23a through c, while a multiparameter image is shown in Figure 4.23d.

Summary

In this chapter we've extended the metaphors developed in Chapters 1-3 to include the visualization of multiple parameters, as well as vector data sets, using commercial software. We also looked at the visualization of continuous functions, as well as molecular modeling, and we viewed numerous examples from different researchers. One topic that we did not address was tensor visualization. There has been some work in this area (for example, Haber, 1988), but at the present this is primarily a research topic. Most tensor variables are currently visualized by looking at their scalar or vector projections into some space. It's unclear if much more could be gained in this area unless a new visualization paradigm is developed. Animations for CD 4.9 through 4.12 illustrate some fascinating visualization of multiparameter systems.

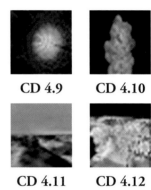

CD 4.9   CD 4.10

CD 4.11   CD 4.12

Suggested Reading

1. *Supercomputing and the Transformation of Science,*
   by William J. Kaufmann III and Larry L. Smarr,
   Scientific American Library, 1993.

2. *Scientific Visualization, Techniques and Applications,*
   K. W. Brooke et al., Springer-Verlag, 1992.

3. *Introduction to Scientific Visualization Tools and Techniques,*
   by Chuck Hanson, ACM SIGGRAPH '92,
   Course #1 Notes, 1992.

4. *Visualization Techniques in the Physical Sciences,*
   by Robert S. Wolff, ACM SIGGRAPH '88
   Course Notes #19, 1988.

5. *Application of Computer Graphics to Molecular Models,*
   by T. J. O'Donnell, ACM SIGGRAPH '92
   Course Notes #44, 1992.

Volume Visualization   5

So far we've dealt primarily with 2-D scalar or vector data, that is, data that can be expressed as $f(x,y)$, such as images, surface and wireframe plots, and contour plots. Visualization techniques that one uses in that domain form the mainstay of scientific data analysis and visualization to date. However, many data sets require more than a 2-D surface or a direct mapping to an image to visualize them. Examples are weather data (temperature and pressure as functions of longitude, latitude, and altitude), 3-D numerical simulations (all parameters are of the form $f(x,y,z)$), and medical imaging of the interior of the body. In addition, we can marry 3-D medical imaging technology with industrial design to create techniques for examining the interior of structures such as metals and building materials.

The first attempts at visualizing the interior of a system were medically based (Harris, 1978; Herman, 1979), and were specifically designed to work with tomographic data. However, the technology was directed at a specific medical application, required much more computing speed and memory than most researchers had available, and wasn't very generalizable. Thus, although the need had been around for some time, it is only since about 1988 that research scientists in a variety of fields and practicing physicians have exploited this technology on a wide scale. Before then, scientists wishing to study 3-D phenomena had to settle for, at best, a few slices taken along an axis, making it difficult to understand the 3-D nature of the structure under study. Time-dependent 3-D phenomena, likewise, were virtually impossible to visualize.

The vast improvement in computing hardware and visualization software over the past few years has made it possible for researchers, teachers, and students to begin to study the interiors of multidimensional systems on their desktops. In the mid-1980s the term *volume visualization* was coined to describe this discipline and exponentially increasing desktop computing capabilities spawned a cottage industry in volume visualization technologies.

In this chapter we will study both the applications of volume visualization software and the various visualization techniques that are used to produce images of the interiors of objects and data sets. Understanding different techniques is important to understand the nature of a particular volumetric image displayed on the screen. Moreover, different algorithms are effective for different types of problems, and each possesses different degrees of accuracy, dependent upon the type of data being visualized. Thus, for example, whereas it might be effective to employ nested, partially transparent surfaces for imaging the interior of a person's chest, that technique would not necessarily be useful for studying the 3-D structure of a thunderstorm.

The basic concept in all volume visualization paradigms is fairly straightforward. Consider a scalar data set $S(x,y,z)$ in a unit volume $\{0 \leq x \leq 1, 0 \leq y \leq 1, 0 \leq z \leq 1\}$. That data set could be the density or temperature of a gas, stress in a machine part, or the density of tissue or bone in a patient's body. At each point (x,y,z) in this volume we can define a value of the parameter. The fundamental issue is, then, how to map the physical parameters of a data set onto an image. This is where the various algorithms differ substantially.

Clearly the approach to the general problem needs to be different than that used to visualize 2-D data, or even data on a surface in space. In those instances the problem was fairly straightforward—no data was ever hidden from us behind other data. The worst case was with multiparameter data, where we needed to cleverly combine visualization techniques to visually determine the important features of the data set without making a visual mess of things.

In the volumetric case the problem is more complex, since we need to find a way to peer into the interior of the data. Moreover, given arbitrary interior structure of the data, we need to represent the structure so as to be visually meaningful. These requirements lead to certain kinds of problems, such as how to determine boundaries between different types of tissues from the data obtained in an MRI (magnetic resonance imaging) or CT (computed tomography) scan, or how to effectively compute a surface within a volume of data.

For example, let's assume that we need to visualize an MRI scan of a patient's head. At the minimum, there is a sharp boundary between the skull and the interior tissue, and within the brain itself there are several types of tissue boundaries. The data we have to work with are simply numbers that represent the effective density at a given point inside the patient's head. The boundary between the skull and the interior should be visible as a sharp density gradient. Given that fact, we should be able to define a contour surface that separates the skull from the interior data points. However, given that the data exists on a finite grid, and that the skull boundary will likely fall within some range of grid points, how do we effectively compute the contour surface? Moreover, once we have computed the surface, how do we display it?

This is very different from the problem where we have a smooth, continuous function $f(x,y,z) = C$ and we want to visualize f for various values of C. In this latter case we can use the mathematical properties of f to define well-behaved surfaces in the space under consideration. However, in the case of simulated or empirical data—"gridded data"—there may well be discontinuities, missing data, or, at the minimum, large derivatives between adjacent points in various parts of the data set. In these cases we need to be particularly careful how any kind of surface within the data volume is computed. As we shall see below, many of the algorithms developed by computer scientists in recent years are specifically designed to address this problem.

We will approach the general problem of volume visualization from a research scientist's perspective rather than the viewpoint of the computer scientist or computer graphicist. In that context, we will take a historical approach to volume visualization and study the 3-D analog of some problems examined in earlier chapters. We'll then look at several volume techniques and see how each can be applied to particular kinds of data sets. Finally, we'll discuss active research topics in this growing field of scientific visualization.

CD 5.1

CD 5.2

Historical Background

Three-dimensional data can be viewed as either existing at specific (x, y, z) locations, or grid points, or comprising a set of volume elements, called *voxels* (Figure 5.1). Both approaches have their strengths and weaknesses, especially with regard to rendering images of a scalar function with a wide range of values.

In an early attempt to solve this problem, Herman (1979) employed a technique wherein a threshold was established between two materials, and a voxel was classified as either containing or not containing a given material. If the voxel contained the material, it would be imaged in a particular color or gray scale, with the face of the voxel treated as a opaque square. This technique has problems with resolution as well as accuracy and does not allow the researcher to "see inside" the volume very well. A different approach was taken at about the same time by Harris (1978), computing an image by averaging intensities along parallel rays from the volume to the image plane. This has the effect of simulating X-rays, but again there is the difficulty of not really being able to see inside the volume.

In the mid-1980s Pixar, Inc. developed a powerful technique for rendering the interior of volumes containing multiple materials. Pixar's hardware and software became widely known in the computer graphics industry and achieved remarkable technical successes in medical imaging, though not in the scientific community at large, possibly because it was several years ahead of its time. In 1988 volume rendering exploded on the computer graphics scene, and the Pixar work was at the heart of this rapidly growing area of research. Drebin et al. (1988)

Figure 5.1

3-D data can be viewed as either existing on a grid or comprising a set of volume elements called voxels. In the grid view, the data retains its natural geometric structure, so that data on nonrectangular, nonuniform grids can be visualized. In the voxel view each voxel can easily be assigned a color and opacity.

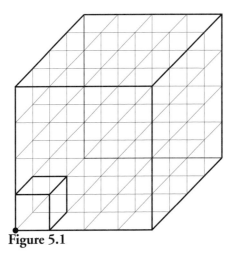 

Figure 5.1

described the landmark Pixar technique in a classic paper on volume rendering. Basically, their method consists of a shading model and a lighting model. The shading model allows both the interior of an object and the boundaries between various regions in the material to be visualized simultaneously, while the lighting model simulates the absorption of light along the ray path to the eye.

Pixar's technique set a new standard for volume rendering and spawned the explosion of work that has occurred over the past several years. The Drebin algorithm is described in **Tech Note 11**, and examples from the Pixar work in biomedical imaging are shown in Figure 5.2: a CT scan of a skull in Figure 5.2a, and a CT scan of a skeleton in Figure 5.2b. The different views of each object reflect different values of parameters in the volume renderer.

CD 5.3

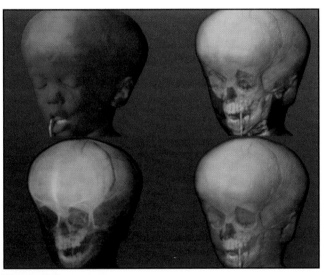

Figure 5.2a

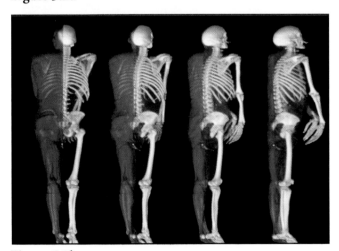

Figure 5.2b

Figure 5.2a
Rendered images from a 124 slice 256 × 256 CT study of a child illustrating the power of the volume visualization algorithm by Drebin et al. The different views reflect different values of parameters in the volume renderer. The CT study is by Franz Zonnefeld, Ph.D. (Courtesy Loren Carpenter, Pixar)

Figure 5.2b
Rendered images from a 650 slice 256 × 256 CT study of a man. A matte volume was used to apply different levels of translucency to the tissue on the left and right halves. The CT study was done by Elliot Fishman, M. D., and H. R. Hruban, M. D., Johns Hopkins Medical Institution. (Courtesy Loren Carpenter, Pixar)

From a purely scientific perspective, there are problems with many of the volume rendering methods used today. For example, Drebin et al. pointed out that surface rendering techniques, which compute polygonal surfaces within a volume, implicitly assume that a volume of data can be accurately modeled by a set of thin surfaces suspended in clear air. Unfortunately, local variations (clumps, bumps, discontinuities, and so on) within the clear volumes can be lost in surface models and thus may not be accurately visualized. By employing such a technique in visualizing complex volumetric data the researcher or clinician might assume that there were no local variations within the data and hence could easily miss critical structures. Adding more contour levels may solve this problem, but at considerable computational expense. This is very similar to the relationship between 2-D contour plots and shaded images that we discussed in Chapter 2.

The Drebin et al. approach is, however, more geared to medical imaging or cloud visualizations, where the data structure is fairly well known, since it implicitly assumes the density ranges and gradients of the various materials being imaged (see **Tech Note 11**). Other related volume-rendering methods have since been developed, such as volume ray-tracing (discussed later in this chapter and in **Tech Note 12**), that provide a fairly general solution to visualizing 3-D scalar fields of data. But those techniques have their difficulties as well. The bottom line seems to be that the best technique to use is very problem specific.

Volume Visualization as a Research Tool

HYDRODYNAMICS

As an example of the sorts of structures that one might find in a volume, consider the cosmic jet computed by Michael Norman of NCSA (Norman, 1990) that we examined in Chapter 2 (Figure 2.2). In the 2-D version the distinguishing characteristics were the bow shock out in front of the flow and the turbulence around the central jet. Let's now look at some results from the 3-D version of this simulation (Figure 5.3). Here the density is represented by $\rho(x,y,z)$. The main difference between the 2-D and 3-D versions of the computation is that the 3-D jet is also computed in z as well as x and y. Another notable difference is that, whereas in the 2-D simulation the x-y computational grid was 400×200, in the 3-D model the x-y grid is only 101×82. The z-dimension is calculated along a 64-cell grid. Using a smaller resolution is done strictly to conserve computational resources since, if the 400×200 resolution were actually maintained in the 3-D model (say, $400 \times 200 \times 200$) we'd

CD 5.4

CD 5.5

have 27 times as much data, and the calculation would take 27 times as long as the 2-D problem.

In Figure 5.3a we used Spyglass Dicer to slice the jet once perpendicular to each of the axes, while in Figure 5.3b we show isosurfaces (3-D contours) of the same jet computed with IDL. Figure 5.3c shows a volume of the jet rendered by a ray-tracing algorithm.

Figure 5.3a
This visualization of a gas jet shows how powerful the simple technique of "slicing and dicing" can be when it comes to bringing out essential feature of a volume data set. With Dicer the user has interactive control of the visible surfaces. However, this technique cannot identify individual 3-D surfaces. (Courtesy Michael Norman, NCSA)

Figure 5.3b
This visualization of a shock wave, computed in IDL, shows how individual surfaces can be identified with a 3-D contouring method. (Courtesy Hal Elgie, RSI Inc.)

Figure 5.3c
This visualization of the same jet shows how a ray-tracing technique can bring out fine structure features that surface-rendering and Dicer-like techniques cannot. (Courtesy Peter Hughes, Apple Computer)

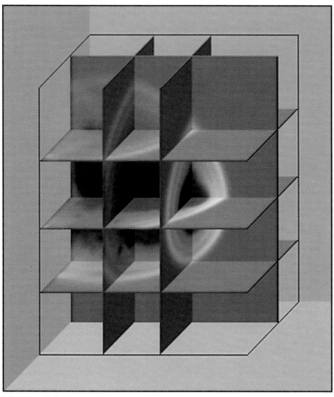

Figure 5.3a

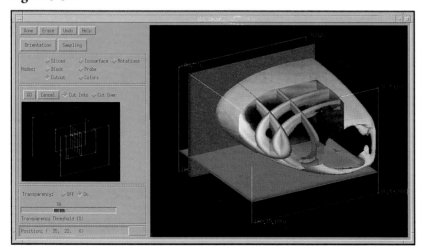

Figure 5.3b

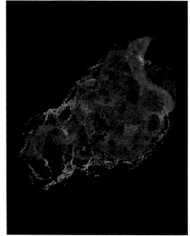

Figure 5.3c

Although each representation in Figure 5.3 provides some insight into the physics of the shock wave, none gives us enough 3-D information to thoroughly understand the 3-D structure in much detail. One can conclude that often several visual representations of a data set are necessary for full understanding of the structure and, if applicable, the dynamics of the system.

Other things we can do with the data are analogous to the kinds of manipulations performed in Chapters 1 and 2, such as image processing, varying the transfer function between floating point and voxel value, and varying the color structure of a palette. However, the very fact that we have a 3-D structure provides us with additional problems, such as how to determine the reality of structures within the volume, or how to search for a particular feature within the volume.

MEDICAL IMAGING

Much of the development of volume visualization algorithms comes from applications driven by the medical imaging community. In particular, volume visualization has strong roots in the need to be able to display 3-D imaging data from CT, MRI and PET (positron emission tomography) techniques. Each of these kinds of medical imaging technologies has its own specific requirements for volume rendering.

Traditional X-ray images are designed to detect large differences in density between soft tissue and bone. Additionally, because X-rays are shot from in front of the object of interest onto a photographic plate placed behind the object, the traditional X-ray image is simply the resultant projection of all of the absorbing material onto the film. Thus, for example, an X-ray image of a patient's skull is a flat projection on a plane of all of the bone matter lying between the exterior of the skull and the film plate. Obviously, this does not provide the doctor or the medical researcher with the tools to analyze either the 3-D structure of an object like a human skull or the various kinds of soft tissue inside it.

CD 5.6

CT overcomes these difficulties by effectively taking X-ray images of "slices" of a given structure. The images are obtained by directing narrow beams of X-rays through the body at various angles. The CT machine physically rotates around the body, shooting X-rays at one segment of the body at a time in a very narrow beam. The objective is to obtain a set of images of, say, a brain in a living organism that would be equivalent to physically slicing the brain into a number of parallel pieces.

Rather than recording the image on film, in a CT scan a digital image of the slice is obtained from the CT detector, which monitors the absorption of the X-rays. The data for each slice is a matrix of numbers indicating the intensity of the X-rays at each straight line through the tissue plane. Once the CT scanner has circled the patient for a single slice, it moves to the next slice, and so on until the entire image of the soft tissue is obtained. The pattern and intensity of the X-ray images of each section of a given slice are encoded as digital data, much like the spacecraft images we talked about in Chapter 1. However, the difference is that each slice in a CT represents specific data coordinates in 3-D space. The doctor or researcher typically has a sequence of images of different slices of the object laid out to analyze. Once a slice is obtained, the full spectrum of image processing technology can be applied to the image to bring out specific features. Furthermore, from the coordinates and orientation of each slice a computer can reconstruct a 3-D image of the region being imaged. This technique is often invaluable to the surgeon seeking to examine an organ before surgery, or in medical diagnostics where the condition of a bone is uncertain. Figure 5.4a, a CT scan of a child's head shows the slices that the CT imager took.

CD 5.7

Figure 5.4a

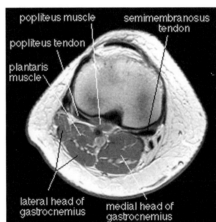

popliteus muscle   semimembranosus tendon
popliteus tendon
plantaris muscle
lateral head of gastrocnemius   medial head of gastrocnemius

Figure 5.4b

Figure 5.4a
This CT-scan of a child's head clearly shows different CT "slices".
(Courtesy NCSA)

Figure 5.4b
This detailed MR image of the region around the knee indicates how volume visualization can be a very valuable tool for teaching as well as research (Courtesy Michael L. Richardson, M.D., Deptartment of Radiology, University of Washington)

Figure 5.4c
This CT image of a Roman period Egyptian mummy was produced in View-It, a general purpose multidimensional image processing, analysis and visualization program created by Clinton S. Potter and Patrick J. Moran at NCSA. The principal investigators on this project were David P. Lawrence and Sara Wisseman. (Courtesy NCSA, Clinton S. Potter)

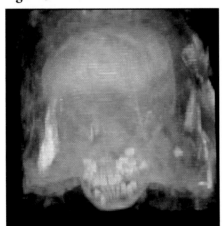

Figure 5.4c

CD 5.8

Figure 5.5a
An MR image of a human
head. The volume has been
rendered without color but
has been illuminated by a
lighting model. Using voxel
and gradient thresholding,
multiple transparent
internal surfaces are easily
distinguished from one
another. The image was
generated by using
VoxelView from Vital Images.
(Data courtesy Siemens AG.)

Figure 5.5b
The volume in Figure 5.5a
has been edited to reveal
internal structures and
anatomically pseudo-colored
with a custom color scheme.
The opacity has been
adjusted to enhance the
definition of fine structures
of the skin and surface
features. The image was
generated by using
VoxelView. (Data Courtesy
Siemens AG.)

Figure 5.5c
This image of an MR scan
of a brain illustrates the
complementary capabilities
of Dicer to a projection or
ray-tracing method like
VoxelView of View-It.
(Courtesy Spyglass, Inc.)

Many of the imaging and computer graphics concepts employed
in CT are also inherent in PET and MRI. The principal differences lie
in the physics of each technique and what physiological structure and
functions each technique can actually see, as well as their resolution and
sensitivity. Since CT is X-ray based, an image is formed by allowing the
X-rays to penetrate the entire object. Thus, the best that one can hope
for is to obtain an X-ray "optical depth" reading by assessing the amount
of X-radiation that has been absorbed by the object. It can discern bone
structures and anomalies quite well, but not the soft, X-ray-transparent
interior tissues of the body. A CT-scan of a mandible (Figure 5.4b)
shows how CT-imaging can be used to identify particular features in a
complex soft tissue region, while Figure 5.4c shows the CT-scan of an
ancient Egyptian mummy.

On the other hand, MRI takes advantage of the fact that the entire
human body (excluding bones) is primarily made up of water, and MRI
images use large magnetic fields and electromagnetic waves in the radio-

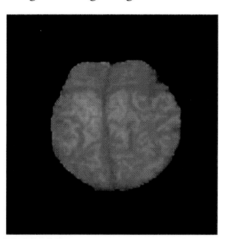
Figure 5.5a

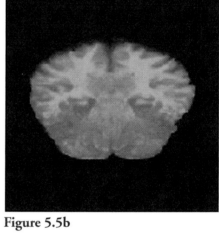
Figure 5.5b

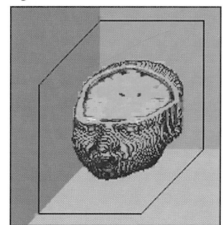
Figure 5.5c

frequency range to compute the distribution of hydrogen in the object under study. In fact, bones often do not show up at all in an MRI image. In Figures 5.5a and b, images from VoxelView, the entire skull structure is stripped away revealing the underlying cerebral structure. As it can measure radio waves from hydrogen in the interior of the body, MRI can resolve structures that are completely interior to the body. Since different kinds of tissues have different amounts of water, MRI can use this information to distinguish various regions of the body and to set density levels for a visualization. Figure 5.5c, obtained with Dicer, shows a rather novel way of visualizing sections of the brain. In Figure 5.6 are several MRI slices of a brain, each slice revealing different structural elements.

MRI can also resolve very small scale structures, on the order of one micrometer, and researchers at several universities have applied high-resolution MRI to such diverse areas as plant growth and the accumulation of toxic substances in the body. Researchers can monitor the progression of a disease or toxin in a single rat, something not

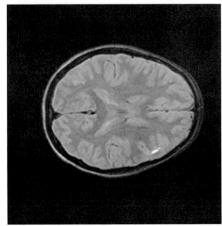

Figure 5.6a

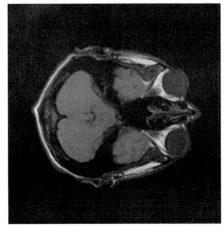

Figure 5.6b

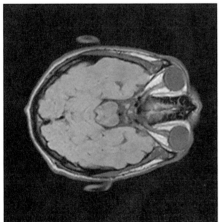

Figure 5.6c

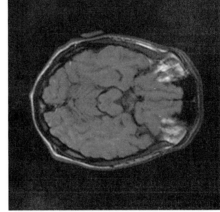

Figure 5.6d

Figure 5.6a-d
This sequence of four MR images of a brain shows the kind of clarity and resolution that projection techniques can provide to radiologists, doctors, and medical researchers. (Courtesy NCSA)

131

possible with invasive and destructive procedures. One can imagine that soon real-time volume visualization, coupled with high-resolution MRI, will be a widely used non-invasive technique for human medicine.

PET measures the emission of positrons from weakly radioactive substances injected into the body. These substances are generally short-lived radioactive isotopes of elements commonly found in the body. The isotopes emit relatively low-energy positrons, which travel for a couple of millimeters in the body until they collide with electrons. Positron-electron collisions produce gamma rays going in directions at nearly 180° from each other. Gamma-ray detectors placed around the body capture a relatively complete data set of emissions. By injecting these isotopes directly into the bloodstream, researchers and clinical physicians can examine how the body is metabolizing particular chemicals. In that context, in contrast to MRI and CT, PET is dynamic rather than static, and can discern time-dependent metabolic processes in different parts of the body, most usefully the brain.

Basic Techniques in Volume Visualization

Now that we have a general feel for the kinds of things that one can do with volume visualization, let's examine some of the most popular algorithms in a bit of detail. Following Foley et al. (1990), we consider two basic categories of volume visualization algorithms: *surface-based*, which compute surfaces within a given volume, and *direct volume renderers* (DVR), which display integral densities along imaginary rays passed between the viewer's eyes and the data set. Some researchers (such as Hanrahan, 1990, and Levoy, 1990) would further subdivide the DVR category into *binary voxel* (based on opaque cubes or their corresponding polygons) and *semitransparent volume rendering* (assigning transparency to a given voxel based on the value of the parameter being rendered) algorithms. For these purposes we shall stick with surface-based and DVR classifications.

Volume ray-tracing, a variant on a long-standing technique in computer graphics, is a particularly effective strategy for visualizing certain kinds of volumes. We discuss volume ray-tracing in more detail later in this chapter and in **Tech Notes 11** and **12**, but the basic concept is illustrated in Figure 5.7, where we show that the image the observer sees depends upon the color and the opacity of all of the objects in the line-of-sight.

VoxelView, from Vital Images, Inc., employs a sort of inverse, simplified ray-tracing (see **Tech Note 12**) where each data point is mapped into a single voxel, and each voxel into a single pixel in an orthogonal (nonperspective) view of the data. The result of the VoxelView approach is a very fast and accurate algorithm and, even on a personal computer like a Macintosh without hardware assist for 3-D graphics, one can use VoxelView to rotate a volumetric structure in essentially real time. VoxelView's inverse ray-tracing technique (this can be viewed as a type of projection technique) assumes that each data point falls on a grid point. Furthermore, the number of pixels is assigned to be equal to the x-y grid resolution, so that each grid point maps exactly to a single pixel. This eliminates all of the performance and data integrity problems associated with averaging data points, but it also introduces a difficulty for people who have data sets with x-y resolution smaller than a reasonably viewable image (less than 200×200 pixels). In Figure 5.8 we show two images from VoxelView, where transparency has been used to highlight specific regions within each structure. One critical feature in the software is user control over the

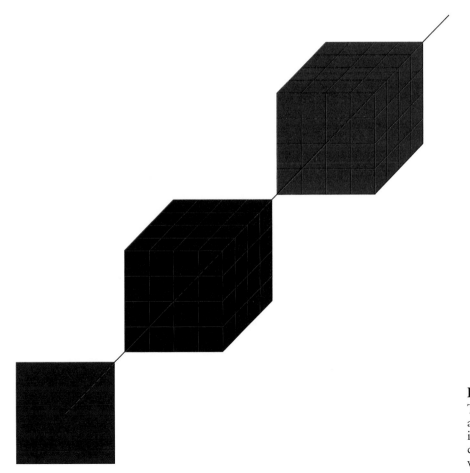

Figure 5.7
The color and opacity of a pixel in a ray-traced image is computed by adding the colors and opacities of all voxels along the ray.

133

thresholding for each of the surfaces. This allows the user to adjust different contour surfaces within the data set so as to align the visible contours with specific features or structures of interest.

Dicer operates on a data set differently than other techniques. Rather than attempting to compute isosurfaces, or ray-tracing through volumes, the user simply picks a particular plane through the data orthogonal to one of the coordinate axes and creates an image of the data on that plane. This is essentially the same as computing an image from 2-D floating-point data. The Dicer technique, while not sophisticated by computer graphic standards, enables the scientist to probe the 3-D

CD 5.9

Figure 5.8a
A single cell from the spinal cord of a lamprey eel. The data was obtained with a laser scan confocal microscope. A default voxel value threshold results in the elimination of voxels for tissue surrounding the cell. The opacity of the volume has been lowered and the image is illuminated. The image was generated by using VoxelView.
(Data courtesy P. Wallen, Karolinska Institute, Stockholm, Sweden)

Figure 5.8b
This image of an excised dog heart was scanned with an Imatron ultra-fast CT machine. The arteries were injected with a radio-opaque dye to improve their visibility. Software such as VoxelView and Voxelblast (by Vaytek, Inc. of Fairfield Iowa) allow the personal computer user to locate specific objects within a volume by interactively adjusting parameters while viewing the images.
(Data courtesy B. Knosp, R. Frank, M. Marcus, and R. Weiss, University of Iowa Image Analysis Facility and Department of Internal Medicine)

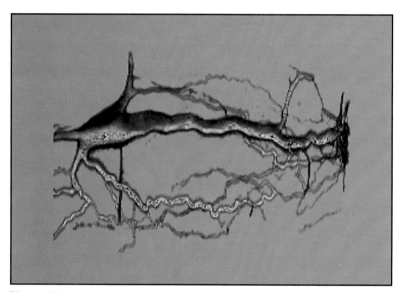

Figure 5.8a

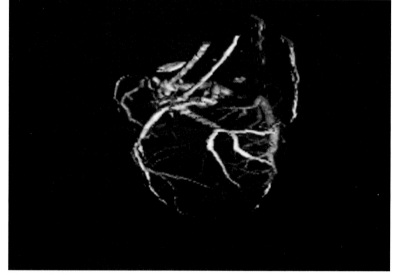

Figure 5.8b

structure of a body of data with accuracy identical to that of the computed data. Thus, programs such as Dicer and VoxelView can do the kind of volume visualization on a personal computer that was previously constrained to expensive, fast workstations.

Data Integrity Issues

There are some basic issues that must be explored to fully understand what the image that you're viewing actually represents. As we have discussed, there exists a wide array of rendering techniques, each specifically tuned to enhance performance, visual appearance, or numerical accuracy for particular styles of visualization. The principal question for scientific data is not how fast an algorithm is, or how pretty the final image looks, but whether or not the visualization is an accurate representation of the original data set.

To explore this issue let's examine a hypothetical cube of data, where at each point $\{x_i, y_i, z_i\}$ of the coordinate lattice there exists some value of a scalar parameter S_i. We saw in Chapter 2, and in **Tech Note 3**, that several types of errors can creep into the visualization process. In 2-D these problems can be annoying and time-consuming; however, in 3-D errors can be disastrous, since it is extremely difficult to work manually with a 3-D matrix. Nevertheless, the conceptual problems in 3-D are very similar to their counterparts in 2-D.

First, there is the question of whether or not to scale (logarithmically or otherwise) the data before or after averaging over grid points (in the case where the data resolution is greater than the desired image resolution). Second, the color transformation process itself can often lead to misinterpretations, depending upon how the data is mapped onto color space and whether discontinuities in actual data values are reflected in the color mapping employed. Third, depending on how the number of pixels compares to the number of data points, one must use an averaging process that either maps one data point onto several pixels or several data points onto one pixel. In the former case, a small feature can be made to appear much larger with respect to its immediate environment, while in the latter case a physically small, but critical feature such as, for example, a soliton in a simulation of a slightly turbulent flow, a hairline crack in a jet engine blade, or a small tumor in a human brain can accidentally be averaged away for the sake of a smooth display. It is up to the researcher to thoroughly understand the visualization method being used, the integrity of the data, and any transformations between "data space" and "color space."

As was discussed in **Tech Note 3**, it is also important to understand that averaging and color transformation do not necessarily commute. Consider the simple case of a 2-D array of data where the number of data points is larger than the number of pixels: we need to average the data to obtain an image. Let Figure 5.9a represent four data points in this matrix. If we do a simple average of these data and logarithmically transform to color space we get color = Transform[log(5)]. Alternatively, if we take the log of each point first we obtain color = Transform[2log(10)]. The color of all data points in the image would be different for the two cases, yet both represent the same data set. As we pointed out in Chapter 2, we could use a quadratic or some other

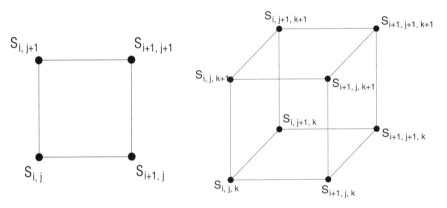

Figure 5.9a   **Figure 5.9b**

Figure 5.9a

In 2-D all reasonable averaging schemes invoke weighted averages of combinations of the four nearest neighbor points. Here we let $S_{i, j+1} = S_{i+1, j+1} = 10$ while $S_{i, j} = S_{i+1, j} = 0$.

Figure 5.9b, c

In the 3-D case things get a bit more complicated, and one must determine the best way of averaging neighboring points. Here we show two possible ways of averaging a cube of data. In Figure 5.9b the eight vertices of the cube are averaged to obtain a value at the center, whereas Figure 5.9c shows a method which averages the six neighboring axial points along with the center point.

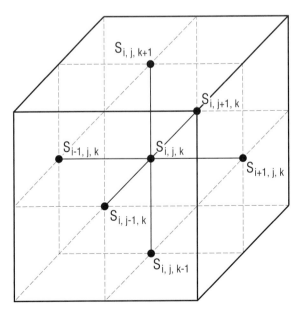

Figure 5.9c

interpolation scheme to derive an average, but we would be no better off for accuracy since we would have no additional real information.

In the 2-D case represented in Figure 5.9a it is relatively straight-forward to look at the data and determine if a particular visual feature is correct. A careful researcher can easily study the numbers and compare them to the actual image before drawing any conclusions. However, in 3-D the problem is much more difficult, since the relationships between neighboring data points are much more varied and complex (Figure 5.9b). This problem is further exacerbated since data averaging in three dimensions can take many forms, with each voxel being treated as an entity unto itself with its own color and opacity. Color transformations can also take many forms since we can transform either a particular plane of the data or the entire data set. Basic concepts, such as how to add data sets or volumetric images need to be developed in 3-D.

Algorithms

The basic concepts of each major class of algorithms, as well as their strengths and weaknesses, are discussed here so that the physical or biological scientist can determine which type of volume rendering is best for a given problem. For example, as we have already seen, physicians or researchers looking at MRI scans need to be able to see detailed structure within an object with which they are already very familiar, such as a brain or a heart. In that application it is important to be able to discern specific surfaces. It is also important to be able to section or "slice" the data along specified planes so as to correspond with actual physical sections that a surgeon might perform.

On the other hand, astrophysicists studying simulations of three-dimensional fluid flows have no real knowledge of the actual 3-D structure of the flow, so having nested transparent surfaces does not necessarily provide the most useful information. We've observed this in some sense in Figure 5.3. Moreover, since the computational astro-physicist is primarily concerned with the relative location of various flow-induced structures within the computational domain, it is usually not that important to be able to view individual contour surfaces in 3-space—in fact, it can be very disorienting. Similar requirements exist for engineers seeking to understand the interior structure and properties of a material or circuit under different thermal or physical conditions. These kinds of researchers are generally less concerned with morpholog-ical features than with numerical accuracy. What is of prime importance to them is to be able to "slice" the data along specific axes, and to look at images and contours of individual planes of data. This is most similar to 2-D data analysis and visualization, where the researcher would use a program like Spyglass Transform, Mathematica, or IDL to analyze an image of a plane of data taken from the volume.

Finally, consider a visualization of smog, clouds, or other amorphous structures. In these cases it can be important to see the full 3-D structure of the data, as well as the relative location of distinct features. However, for these sorts of data sets one often needs to be able to determine the opacity of the structure as a function of wavelength. Thus, for example, one might need to be able to accurately visualize a smoggy day in Los Angeles from a variety of perspectives. Below we examine the kinds of visualization schemes used in each of these types of applications.

SURFACE-BASED ALGORITHMS

Surface-based algorithms create surfaces within the (scalar) data volume cube. The fundamental concept for this class of volume visualization algorithms is that, given a scalar parameter or function $\phi(x,y,z)$, we want to determine surfaces of (approximately) constant ϕ that intersect the coordinate grid points. Thus, for example, given an MRI or CAT scan of a patient's brain, we would like to look at each particular tissue separately. Since each kind of tissue or bone has a particular density, these density values can be used to identify specific contour regions in the data set.

The basic idea is to construct level surfaces throughout the volume as best as possible (a level surface is defined herein as a continuous surface within the 3-D volume such that, at each point on the surface, the value of the data is the same). In practice, the level surfaces will consist of contiguous polygons. Nevertheless, one can make a reasonable approximation to a surface for relatively gradual changes in the parameter being visualized. To do this we note that at each coordinate point in the 3-D grid the data has a particular value. The actual surfaces that are constructed are developed as intersections of the level surfaces, for which f = constant, with the hypothetical edges connecting these grid points. Once the intersections are determined, a polygonal mesh can be defined that represents the iso-potential surface, which is then rendered using traditional polygonally based computer graphics techniques as described in the next chapter.

Surface-based algorithms are fairly well suited for medical imaging, since medical images need to be able to display multiple tissue densities and specific tissue boundaries. Each tissue boundary can be assigned a particular color and an effective opacity based upon its isodensity value. The actual structure and location of the surface, and its color and opacity, can then be determined from the thresholds for the surface contours defining each tissue type. Contours can be made visible to varying degrees by assigning opacities according to the order of the boundaries between the different tissues in the data set. An illustration of this technique is shown in Figure 5.9c. Note, in particular, how each density level is visually distinguished from its neighbors.

This general kind of surface-rendering technique is not limited to medical imaging; take for example the image of the water density in a severe storm simulation, shown in Figure 5.10. This image is part of a well-known visualization performed by the NCSA Visualization Group as part of a research project with meteorologists Robert Wilhelmson and Lou Wicker. Figure 5.11 shows surfaces of equal concentration in an argon-helium mixing flow simulation also done at NCSA, and Figure 5.12 shows some visualizations of gas concentrations computed in WaveFront's Visualizer software. In both of these instances we see that the use of isosurface contours to specify particular 3-D contour levels enables the researcher to examine particular regions in a continuously varying scalar function. These visualizations were created on a Silicon Graphics Iris VGX using custom software to produce the polygonal data set for the 3-D contours.

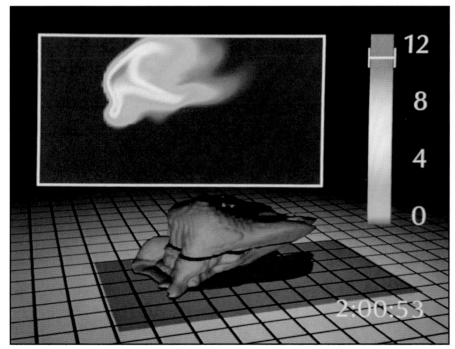

Figure 5.10

Figure 5.10
This image of the water vapor density of a simulated severe storm cloud illustrates how surface-based algorithms can provide insight into the large-scale structure of dynamic phenomena. (Courtesy Robert Wilhelmson and Lou Wicker, NCSA)

Despite the obvious utility of surface-based algorithms, they have some problems associated with the computation of the volumetric contours. First, there is an inherent potential for sampling errors, due to the fact that the surfaces are only created at prespecified contour levels.

CD 5.10

Figure 5.11
Ion concentration surfaces of a simulation of argon-helium mixing flow. The original data consists of a tomographic series of cross-sectional images. The image shows the contour surface for a particular argon-helium concentration. (Courtesy Kevin Wu, Sun Microsystems)

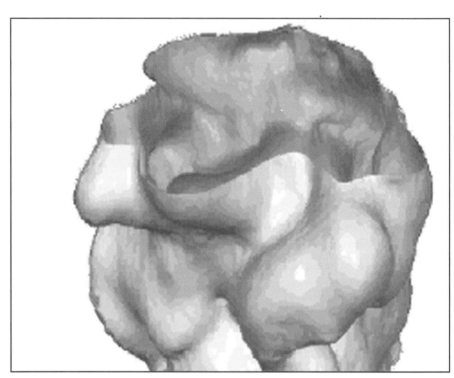

Figure 5.11

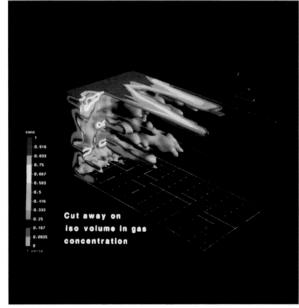

Figure 5.12a

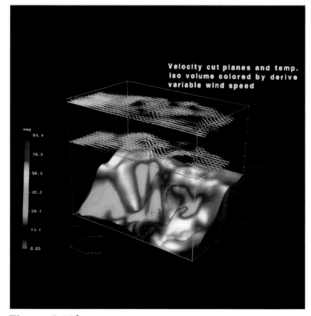

Figure 5.12b

As is the case with 2-D contouring, if the ranges of isolevels are poorly chosen, or sampling occurs at too low a frequency, then the visualization may be misleading. To avoid this problem, researchers can check the accuracy of their visualizations by recomputing the images for different sampling frequencies and looking for artifacts (much as computational fluid dynamicists must confirm numerical results by running simulations of known problems at multiple resolutions).

Second, the surface-generating techniques are all too happy to model any noise that might be present in the data, and their high-precision representation of such noise can be confusing or misleading to the eye. Such typically high-frequency information can also result in isolevel structures that are very computationally expensive to render (due to the many additional polygons that end up being generated to model the noise). While it might be possible to reduce this problem by simply smoothing the original data, one stands the obvious risk of smoothing away real features as well. This is more of a problem for empirically gathered data than for numerical simulations.

Perhaps the two best known surface-based techniques are Marching Cubes, first developed by Lorenson and Cline (1987), and Lorenson et al.'s (1988) subsequent algorithm, Dividing Cubes. Although both algorithms produce 3-D surface contours from volume data, Marching Cubes creates triangles as primitives whereas Dividing Cubes uses points with normals. In both techniques, users select the

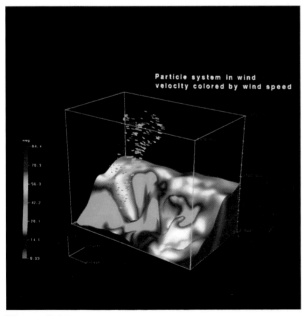

Figure 5.12c

Figure 5.12a
Cutaway volume visualization of the density of a gas jet.
(Courtesy Mike Wilson, Wavefront, Inc.)

Figure 5.12b
Velocity cut-planes and temperature isosurfaces.
(Courtesy Mike Wilson, Wavefront, Inc.)

Figure 5.12c
Particle visualization of 3-D volume over temperature isosurfaces.
(Courtesy Mike Wilson, Wavefront, Inc.)

desired surface by specifying a particular density value. However, Marching Cubes is designed to be used for data where the number of triangles is less than the number of pixels, whereas Dividing Cubes becomes important when the number of triangles approaches the number of pixels. The Marching Cubes algorithm is discussed in more detail in **Tech Note 13**.

DIRECT VOLUME RENDERING (DVR) TECHNIQUES

One of the main problems with surface-based techniques is that by introducing artificial surfaces within a volume one is implicitly introducing discontinuities in the data. These discontinuities are highly nonlinear and necessarily introduce artifacts in the final rendered image. Thus, a visible surface may, in fact, not correctly represent the actual data structure that the surface is modeled on. One way of getting around this problem is to forgo the surface rendering approach entirely and employ a technique that directly represents the data within a given voxel.

These kinds of techniques are referred to as direct volume rendering. The Drebin et al. (1988) method discussed earlier (also see **Tech Note 11**) assumes that the measured data consists of several different "materials" (for example, skin, bone, and muscle in a hand) and that at any point within the volume, the (scalar) data value represents the sum of the materials at that point (no more than two materials can occupy a single voxel in their model), so each voxel can readily be described by the percentage of each material within it. Color and opacity of each voxel can then be computed based upon the mix of materials present and the color and opacity control parameters for those materials. The method also explicitly computes certain boundaries between different materials within the volume based upon density gradients across voxel boundaries. Large gradients correspond to sharp transitions between materials. In this manner, both volumetric and surface color and opacity are modeled. Drebin et al.'s approach explicitly does *not* threshold the data, since thresholding produces unwanted artifacts. No surface geometry is ever explicitly represented as polygons.

One drawback of the Drebin approach is that it is necessary to provide as input all of the expected material densities. That means either that one has to be very familiar with the data or that there must be some pre-existing model that allows effective weights to be assigned, a priori, to each component of the voxel. Pre-existing models for the data are occasionally available for X-rays and CT scans, but they have not yet made their way successfully into the visualization mainstream. The method's assumption that only two constituent materials may ever be present in a single voxel may not always hold if the volume data is acquired at too low a resolution.

A different approach has been taken in a series of papers by Levoy (Levoy, 1988; 1989; 1990a; 1990b) and Upson and Keeler (1988) in which the authors use ray-tracing techniques to create a volumetric image (**Tech Note 12**). The basic concept in each of these is to assign a color (in terms of red-green-blue) and an opacity to each data point on the 3-D grid, and then to simply compute the color of a pixel defined by a ray emanating from the observer's eye through the image plane, and then penetrating the volume of data. Samples are taken at equally spaced distances along the ray (Figure 5.13), or at each intersected voxel. Some inverse ray-tracing ("projection") techniques essentially cast the rays from the voxels to the eye, and can be much more efficient when the data set resolution is lower than the pixel resolution. These are discussed briefly in **Tech Note 13**. The advantage of the ray-tracing techniques over the Drebin technique is that one does not need a density model of the data set to begin the computation. However, ray-tracing is, in general, very slow. Levoy (1990b) outlined several optimizing techniques to improve the efficiency of ray-traced computations.

CD 5.11

Figure 5.13
In ray-tracing samples are taken at equally spaced distances along the ray. The color and opacity of a given pixel in the resultant image is computed by summing the individual contributions of each sampled point.

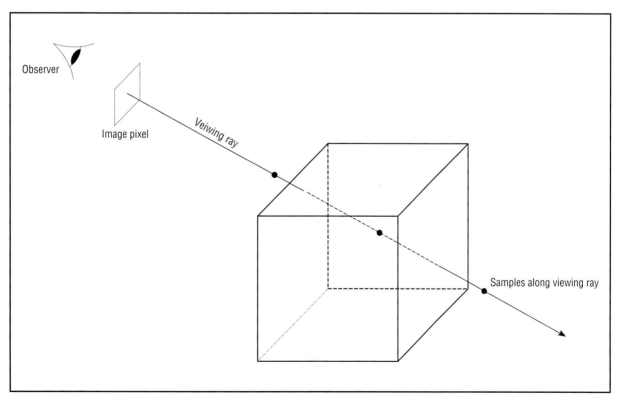

Figure 5.13

Summary

In this chapter we discuss a number of ways of visualizing the interior of 3-D scalar data structures, a class of techniques known as *volume visualization*. There are two classes of volume rendering: direct volume rendering and surfaced-based. Examples from a variety of fields were used to illustrate several contrasting approaches, including slicing and dicing along coordinate axes, surface rendering, and ray-tracing. Although the sheer variety of available volumetric visualization techniques can be bewildering to a scientist, each method has its advantages and disadvantages depending upon what information one might desire. A reasonable approach toward selecting a particular visualization scheme is to first study the data set you're interested in visualizing, determine the functionality that you need, and then find the best technique that matches your needs. This process is helped considerably by the available commercial software. Since we cannot do justice to this rapidly growing research field, we urge the serious investigator to read, or at least glance through, the "Suggested Reading" below for more detailed information.

CD 5.12

Suggested Reading

1. *Introduction to Volume Visualization*, by Marc Levoy, ACM SIGGRAPH '91 Course Notes #7, 1991.

2. *Introduction of Volume Visualization*, by Arie Kaufman ACM SIGGRAPH '92, Course Notes #8, 1992.

3. *State of the Art in Volume Visualization*, by Pat Hanrahan, ACM SIGGRAPH '93, Course Notes #8, 1993.

Modeling, Animation, and Rendering

6

When image analysis, traditional scientific graphics, or volume rendering alone satisfy a particular visualization need, the techniques discussed in the previous chapters should serve as a complete solution. However, some visualization tasks lend themselves better to other, *surface*-based (as opposed to volume-based) visualization tools. These tools derive from the more traditional modeling, animation, and rendering techniques associated with the graphics used in computer-aided design or the film and television industries. Although the techniques may be similar and may derive from the same theoretical framework, there are subtle but important differences. The entertainment objective in employing these technologies is to fool the viewer into believing that a particular effect is real. The scientist, on the other hand, uses these technologies to convey the meaning of data, regardless of the aesthetic appeal of the image, though aesthetics and information content do sometimes walk hand-in-hand. Perhaps the best example of this is the Voyager Saturn flyby simulations done by Jim Blinn at JPL. One of Blinn's main objectives was to realistically simulate light passing through Saturn's rings. For this he appealed to radiative transfer theory, and the results were spectacular (Figure 6.1).

In this chapter we look at the general technologies necessary to "realistically" visualize known, observable phenomena. We mean realistic from the perspective of the scientist rather than the filmmaker, although some artistry often needs to be applied to a visualization for

CD 6.1

Figure 6.1
This computer-generated image of Voyager as it passed close to Saturn's rings, done by Jim Blinn in 1981, is one of the earliest examples of using transparency to represent real natural phenomena. Here, Blinn used a physical model of the opacity of Saturn's rings as the basis for his computation, performed on a PDP-11/55 with 256K RAM. (Courtesy NASA/JPL)

educational or communicative purposes. For the most part realistic simulations render surfaces of objects in terms of large numbers of polygons, and we shall discuss both the techniques required to make a single frame, or image of an animation, as well as the animation techniques themselves that can add effective realism to any simulation. Surface-rendering and 3-D animation techniques that were once the tools of computer graphics specialists and a small circle of highly expert software engineers are now available as part of relatively low-cost commercial software packages on personal computers. These surface-rendering techniques are all based on surface-modeling primitives of some type, such as polygons or spline patches, some tool for animating the various models, and some method for determining which of the many model surfaces is visible and how they should be colored and lit. A rich history of research into these topics is available in the annual conference proceedings of SIGGRAPH and in the suggested reading list at the end of this chapter.

Figure 6.1

In this chapter we attempt to provide enough detail to develop an intuitive understanding of the basic methods of the field, and to couch it in a framework that will make it clear how these methods differ from and relate to each other. In so doing, we hope to make it easier for the reader to approach and use these types of visualization tools and to make informed decisions between various implementations of them. With the aid of the referenced Tech Notes, there should be enough groundwork laid to enable the interested reader to build custom tools with a minimum of additional research. To that end we also include some practical considerations not always addressed in more traditional, theoretical computer graphics references.

In this chapter we briefly outline the basic techniques of traditional, surface-based modeling, rendering, and animation. The reader unfamiliar with the terms and concepts described herein is encouraged to read the references at the end of the chapter. In the following sections we briefly describe the process of surface modeling, scene composition, animation, rendering, particle systems, and texture, reflection and bump mapping. Examples in this chapter are drawn from both the entertainment industry and the scientific visualization community.

Surface Modeling

The complex curvatures and topologies of the objects employed in visualization of scientific phenomena, and in the commercial world of film and television, are usually handled by the polygon- and spline-based primitives of surface modeling.

There are a variety of methods available for generating these models. For simpler objects, especially surfaces of revolution or extruded shapes, interactive software tools may permit the object to be modeled entirely in the computer. Mathematical formulas may be visually inspected by creating surface models and rendering them. For complex objects not easily represented by a mathematical equation, fairly detailed engineering-style drawings can be made (Figures 6.2) and then encoded, or digitized, one point at a time. Depending on the detail of the drawing and model, a small desktop graphics tablet may suffice, or more professional equipment may be called for, such as a Calcomp/Talos tablet with accuracies of 0.001 inch (Figure 6.3). In some instances, existing objects, or specially created sculptures may be used (Figures 6.4, 6.5). These can then be digitized either by a 3-D digitizer such as a Polhemus, with accuracies around 0.01 inch, or by using slit-aperture light sources (or a laser) and sophisticated software for analyzing the outlined contours of the object (Figure 6.6).

In scientific visualization, unlike entertainment applications, surface models are often generated algorithmically from the original (measured or simulated) scientific data. These models are almost always constructed from some form of 3-D contouring, very much like the methods discussed in Chapters 2 and 4 for generating 2-D contour plots, only carried out on the 3-D grid corresponding to the locations of the original data. The resulting isopotential contour surfaces can then be lit and shaded like any other computer graphic object (Figure 6.7).

Whichever modeling method is employed, the result is a specialized data structure that fully describes the 3-D object for the rendering and animation software. When dealing with very complex objects, it is common to also build low-detail versions of these objects, either by hand or algorithmically. These 3-D object data structures typically consist of a few counters that indicate how many elements of data are present, a set of (x, y, z) coordinate triples describing the location of the

CD 6.2

Figure 6.2a
Detailed engineering drawing of the Gunstar from *The Last Starfighter.* (Courtesy Digital Productions)

Figure 6.2a

points on the surface of the object, and a connectivity list describing the sequence of "connect-the-dots" line segments that will define the polygonal mesh composing the object. This is the minimum amount of information needed to describe the object's surface. Additional information is sometimes provided such as adjacent edges or faces, as in the *winged-edge* data structure, when it is useful for particular geometry manipulation tools or rendering software.

It may also be of value to provide a distinct set of information that relates the local coordinate systems of a group of objects to a higher, common coordinate system. This is especially true of complex objects that, for ease of modeling, have been broken up into a number of smaller parts. The person creating the models may also provide *scene* files that contain the coordinate transformations necessary to fit multiple parts together into complete, hierarchical structures. Scene files can be nested to provide various levels of organization, up to and including a global coordinate system for the entire scene.

Figure 6.2b
Computer graphic rendering of the model based on the drawing in Figure 6.2a. (Courtesy Digital Productions)

Figure 6.2a

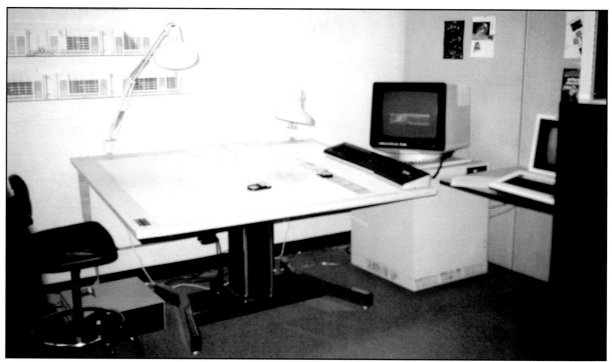

Figure 6.3

Figure 6.4

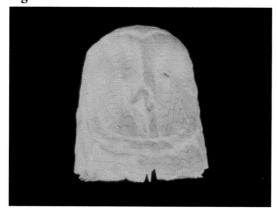

Figure 6.5

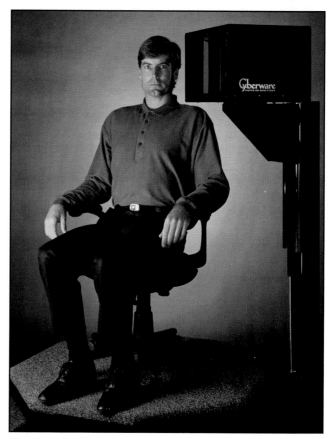

Figure 6.6

Though polygons are the most common modeling primitive, some modeling systems use splines to define the surfaces of objects. Non-Uniform Rational B-splines, or NURBs, have recently become the most common basis for such models. NURBs permit the modeling of complex curves by specifying a few control points rather than the many polygonal edges that would be needed to describe the curve in a piecewise linear fashion. However, many of the traditional rendering techniques ultimately require the NURBs to be decomposed into polygons before rendering anyway, thus reducing their value to some extent. They are also a great deal more computationally complex than polygonal models. Still, the power they have for compactly expressing complex shapes has made them more common in the last few years.

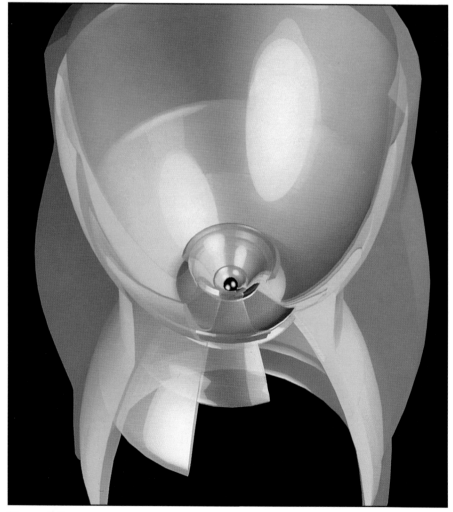

Figure 6.7

Figure 6.3
Professional computer graphics tablet and encoding station.

Figure 6.4
A photograph of the sculpted owl's head that was used in the creation of the computer model of an owl shown in the opening title sequence of the film *Labyrinth*. (Courtesy Bill Kroyer)

Figure 6.5
Computer graphic rendering of a model created from the real, sculpted object in Figure 6.4. (Courtesy Bill Kroyer and Digital Productions)

Figure 6.6
Cyberware 3-D scanning system. (Courtesy Cyberware)

Figure 6.7
3-D isopotential surfaces of density in the vicinity of a black hole. (Courtesy John Hawley and Digital Productions)

Scene Composition and Animation

In production graphics, the object models must be composed into some desired set of scenes, then animated. In scientific visualization the principal elements of scene composition and animation may come directly from the underlying physical processes being measured or simulated. However, even in the scientific realm, it is frequently desirable to combine hand-crafted object models with algorithmically generated and controlled models. Thus, tools for controlling the placement and movement of these objects are an important piece of a computer graphics system.

Scene composition and animation are best dealt with in a very interactive, real-time system. Though most people working in the field would like to be able to work with real-time shaded images, computational constraints are such that most animation is done using wireframe models. By sacrificing realistic imagery, it is possible for animation systems to focus on providing better interactive response time and accurate frame rates during animation—crucial attributes during the designing and animating of scenes.

Low-cost animation systems, including microprocessor-based systems, typically allow the user to control only two degrees of freedom at a time by means of a mouse or a joystick; selections of these degrees of freedom are made from an on-screen palette, a menu, or special function keys. More sophisticated workstations may have six or more control knobs that make it easier to directly manipulate x, y, z, roll, pitch, yaw, and possibly scale, object-to-object interpolations, and other animation control parameters. It may also be possible to use more than one layout of knob-to-parameter mappings to support less frequently accessed functions, such as x-, y-, and z-skew.

All these animation control parameters must ultimately be determined for each object of every frame of the scene. To facilitate this gargantuan task, all 3-D animation systems utilize *key-frames* and *in-betweening*. In this technique the various animation control parameters are specified in detail at certain important key-frames, along with an interpolation method for determining the values of these parameters at all the frames between key-frames. For example, in a 10-second animation for film, consisting of 240 frames, the animator might provide position specifications at frames 1, 120, and 240, as in Figure 6.8. A linear interpolation would provide values along the gray lines for the intermediate frames, while a more useful spline interpolation would provide values along the black curves in that figure. Thus the user need only set up the scene at a relatively small number of key-frames, depending upon the animation system to interpolate reasonable values for the control parameters at the intervening frames. Of course it's never quite that simple, and the user frequently needs to worry about the derivatives of the parameters (velocity, angular velocity, acceleration, angular acceleration, and so on), or else the animation ends up looking jerky and unnatural. Good animation packages at least support some type of *slow-in* and *slow-out* (or *ease-in* and *ease-out*) technique. These techniques give the user an easy way to force the object in question to accelerate and decelerate gracefully from a stationary state.

As discussed previously, scientific visualization efforts often use a model of a real physical process to control what might be thought of as the animation in a scene. The computer graphics community has also embraced simple physical models for the animation of some scene elements. These *physically based animation* techniques (often referred to as *physically based modeling*) vary in the degree of accuracy or completeness in the physics underlying their animations, but typically provide a more naturalistic motion than is attainable by hand, for much less effort. They can also provide animations that are essentially impossible to create by hand, such as Michael Kass and Gavin Miller's flowing water

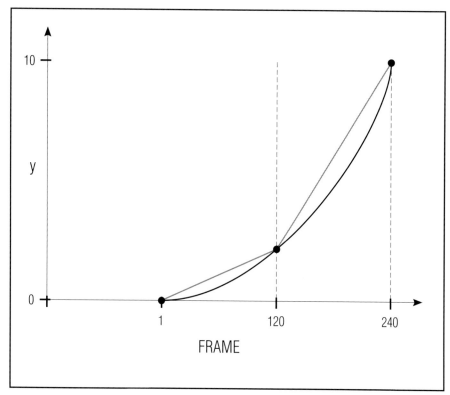

Figure 6.8

Figure 6.8
Plot of animation parameter (vertical axis) versus frame number (horizontal axis), showing key-frames at 1, 120, and 240, with both linear and spline-based interpolated parameter values at in-between frames.

CD 6.3

simulation (Figure 6.9) and the corresponding animation on the CD-ROM. This work (Kass and Miller, 1991) is particularly striking since it takes a velocity-depth regime of laminar flow (low-velocity, shallow water) for inviscid, incompressible fluids (such as water) and attempts to accurately model our perception of the entire process. From the entertainment industry, the visualization of the planet Jupiter in the film *2010* (discussed in Chapter 7) is another example of physically based animation.

Animation systems must compute the same matrix transformations that rendering systems do (see below) to position and move all of the objects in a scene. For reasons of speed, however, they do not typically compute the lighting and color information required to rasterize, or shade these objects.

The result of the animation process is a data file that captures the placement and the animation of all objects in the scene, so the scene can be repeated precisely, or modified, as many times as necessary. Such an animation file, sometimes called a *movie file*, is used to specify the same sequence of object positions to the rendering software, which produces realistic shaded images of each frame in the scene.

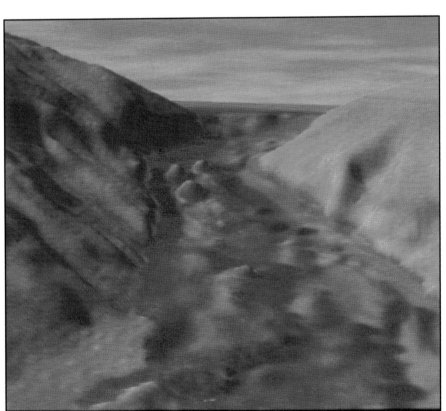

Figure 6.9
Computer-generated image of flowing water. (Courtesy Michael Kass, Gavin Miller and Apple Computer)

Figure 6.9

Rendering

The rendering process takes all of the object models, places them in the positions specified by the animation file, and produces a detailed color image of the scene. This requires two somewhat separable, major tasks: *hidden-surface removal* (or *visible-surface determination*) and *shading*. Renderers are typically classified according to their method of hidden surface removal, since most lighting and shading techniques can be coupled to any hidden-surface algorithm. In fact, multiple shading methods (sometimes including programmable shaders) are usually made available in a given renderer.

All rendering algorithms must fill in the color, usually in the form of an RGB triple—red, green, and blue color components—of each pixel in a window through which an observer is imagined to be looking. This window is said to be in the observer's *image plane*, and is specified by an angular field of view. The angular cone with four faces that is framed by the lines drawn from the observer's *eye-point* through the corners of this window is referred to as the *viewing frustum* or *viewing pyramid* (see Figure 6.10). All of the algorithms must have

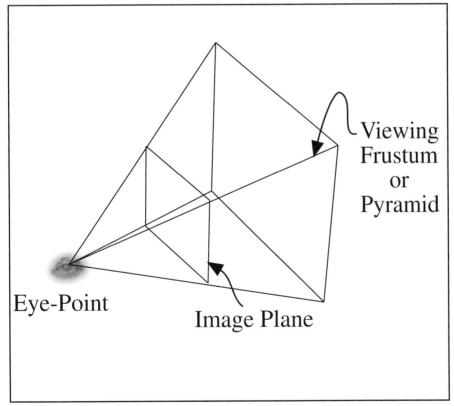

Viewing Frustum or Pyramid

Eye-Point

Image Plane

Figure 6.10

Figure 6.10
The observer's eyepoint and field of view determine the viewing frustum (or viewing pyramid).

some method for determining which objects are visible and which are not, from the observer's point of view; this is the functionality known as *hidden-surface removal* or *visible-surface determination*. And each must have a *shading* method for determining the color that the observer will see at a given point, whether it is simply the color of the object at that location or some more complex *illumination model*. An illumination model may compute the color at a point on an object as a function of that object's color, other objects' colors, light source colors and locations, surface properties of the object, and so on.

Although many rendering algorithms are being researched and tested today, most of the commercial footage produced to date for paying customers has been created with either a *scanline-sampling algorithm*, an *A-buffer* algorithm, or a *z-buffer* algorithm. A unique *bucket-sorted micro-polygon* rendering algorithm has been developed and used to excellent effect for in-house productions by Pixar, including "André and Wally B.," "Luxo, Jr.," and the Academy Award winning "Tin Toy" (Figure 6.11). Conceptually simpler ray-tracing algorithms are common research vehicles, but they suffer from being computationally expensive, and must sacrifice their conceptual simplicity in order to build appropriate space-partitioning data structures to be computa-

Figure 6.11
Image from "Tin Toy" rendered using the micropolygon technique. ©1988 Pixar. (Courtesy Pixar)

Figure 6.11

tionally tractable at all. Even more computationally expensive are a class of rendering algorithms that fall under the heading of *radiosity*. These algorithms are capable of modeling the diffuse light reflections among all objects in a scene, and can produce some startlingly realistic images, such as the "Virtual Museum" (Figure 6.12). If all objects in a scene to be simulated can be static, however, with only the point of view moving, many of the subtle light interactions can be precomputed, thus rendering the technique reasonably efficient.

An extensive review of rendering algorithms is beyond the scope of this book, but **Tech Notes 14** and **15** explain the basic operation of a few of the more common techniques currently in use for visible surface determination and for shading and illumination, respectively. Readers wishing to pursue the subject further should consult the suggested reading list at the end of this chapter.

CD 6.4

Figure 6.12
Soft, realistic lighting effects in a scene from Apple's "Virtual Museum," rendered using the radiosity technique. Notice the shadows on the floor and over the "Plants" and "Astronomy" signs. (Courtesy Apple Computer)

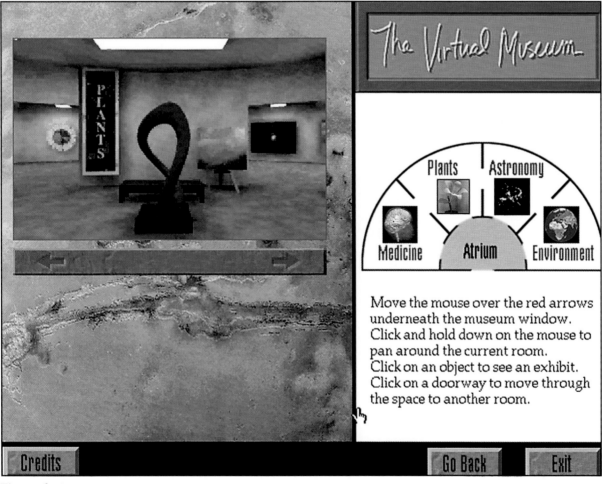

Figure 6.12

Special Topics

In this section we look at particle systems and various kinds of mapping techniques, special topics in computer graphics that have found their way into the world of scientific visualization. Although these techniques were not really developed with the scientist-user in mind, today they provide the researcher with additional tools to visualize complex, multivariate phenomena.

PARTICLE SYSTEMS

A very different form of renderer is used for *particle systems*, a technique sometimes used for visualizing flow fields, and used to great effect in the film *Star Trek II: The Wrath of Kahn*, to create the "Genesis Effect" (Figure 6.13 and Movie 6-5). A distinguishing feature of particle systems, and a principal reason for their invention, is a highly variable, usually algorithmically determined, model topology and animation. When applied to fluid flow visualization, computer graphic particle systems are conceptually similar to classic flow visualization techniques involving the injection of oil, smoke, or powders into a fluid in order to observe the resulting streamlines or particle paths. In the computer graphics field, particle systems are most commonly used to model natural phenomena such as fire, fireworks, atmospheric effects, trees, or grass.

Reeves (1983, 1985) described a number of different particle systems used for these various natural phenomena. Fire and fireworks are

Figure 6.13
Particle systems were used to model this birth of a planet's ecosystem in *Star Trek II: The Wrath of Kahn.*
©1982 Paramount Pictures Corporation. (Courtesy Pixar, and Paramount Pictures)

Figure 6.13

described mostly by their algorithmic particle paths. The actual rendering is somewhat simple, with the illumination due to all particles simply being summed into the affected pixels, clamping the pixel intensity to 1, with no attempt to provide for occlusion of particles by other particles. To integrate the particle systems with a more traditionally rendered planet for the "Genesis Effect," the particle systems that originate from the back side of the planet are rendered into one image, the planet is rendered into a second image, and the particle systems that originate on the front of the planet are rendered into a third image. These three images are then composited back to front, eliminating the need to store any z information with the rendered images of the particles. Slightly more complex methods were used for the trees and grass shown in Figure 6.14, from the "André & Wally B." animation mentioned earlier. Methods for probabilistically adding highlights, based on depth into the tree relative to the light source and shadowing by intervening trees, provided the dappled sunlight effects. A modified z-buffer approach, with all particles from a particular tree being assigned the single z value associated with that tree, was used for handling occlusion. Anomalies resulting from this simplified rendering were not particularly noticeable, perhaps due to the overall complexity of the scenes.

Yaeger et al. (1986) used a 2-D particle system as part of a physically based model of Jupiter for the film *2010: The Odyssey Continues* (Figure 6.15). Some of their methods are detailed in Chapter 7. The primary difference between their and Reeves's earlier rendering algo-

Figure 6.14

Figure 6.14
Forest scene from "André and Wally B." created with a complex particle system. ©1984 Pixar. (Courtesy Pixar)

rithm is that here it was assumed that there would almost always be multiple particles per pixel. A pixel's color was determined by averaging the colors of all particles contained in that pixel.

Sims (1990) devised a fairly general purpose set of motion algorithms for particles and used them produce one of the most beautiful computer graphic animations to date, "Particle Dreams" (Figures 6.16). Sims divided the operations used to move particles into four categories: those that set position, those that set velocity, those that alter position (or apply velocity), and those that alter velocity (or apply acceleration). He provided a comprehensive set of these operations for working in a continuum between detailed kinematic control, where an animator has control over the frame-to-frame position of every particle, and physically based animation, where an animator does little more than set proper initial conditions and start up the simulation. Sims's particles have specifiable radii, color, and opacity at both head and tail, and occupy a variable number of pixels depending on distance from the observer. His particle renderer takes advantage of the inherent massive parallelism of the Connection Machine on which it runs to do a proper antialiased, occluded, motion-blurred rendering of these particles. One of the

CD 6.5

Figure 6.15
Computer-generated image of the planet Jupiter. A simple particle system was used, in conjunction with realistic gas dynamic equations, to simulate the giant planet. Compare this image to the real images of Jupiter shown in Chapter 1. (Courtesy Digital Productions)

Figure 6.15

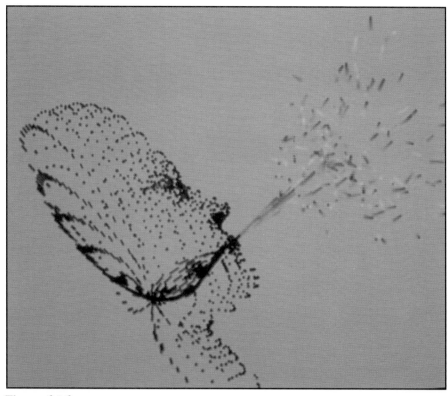

Figure 6.16a

Figure 6.16a
The "Self Breathing Head"
from Karl Sims's "Particle
Dreams" animation.
(Courtesy Karl Sims)

Figure 6.16b

Figure 6.16b
"Waterfall" from "Particle
Dreams." (Courtesy
Karl Sims)

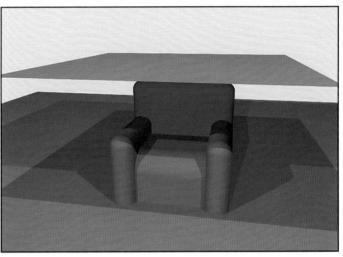

Figure 6.17a

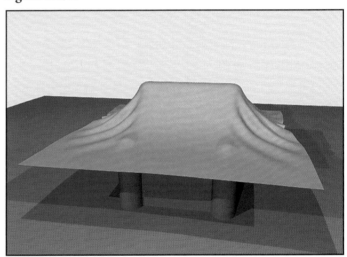

Figure 6.17b

CD 6.6

Figure 6.17
This sequence of images
shows how cloth can be
modeled with a particle
system designed to simulate
the physical properties of
complex materials. This
technique directly models
the microstructure of a
material, in this case the
interlaced threads.
(Courtesy David Breen,
Rensselaer Polytechnic
Institute).

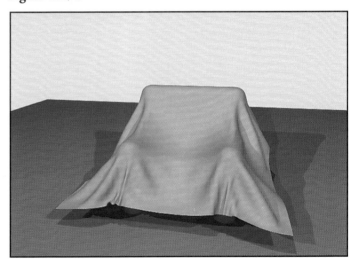

Figure 6.17c

primary technical challenges was simultaneously guaranteeing that the necessary data structures would not exceed the capacity of the machine yet would use the many processors efficiently. Sims used a *false position method* (Press et al., 1986) to determine a problem decomposition that would utilize the multiple processors effectively. He integrated more traditionally modeled surfaces with his particle systems by decomposing them into the same pixel fragments as are used for the particles, and executing the rendering algorithm on the combined fragments.

A new application of particle systems is taking place at the Design and Manufacturing Institute at Rensselaer Polytechnic Institute in Troy, N.Y. There, researchers are using physical models coupled with particle systems to model the draping of cloth as well as different kinds of biological systems (Breen et al., 1992) (Figure 6.17).

TEXTURE, REFLECTION, AND BUMP MAPPING

Two very useful methods for adding apparent detail to computer graphics models, without adding polygons and their associated computational expense, are texture and bump mapping. Texture mapping, first devised by Catmull (1974) and refined by Blinn and Newell (1976), is very much like applying a deformable layer of wallpaper over the surface of an object. Any amount of detail in the pattern of the texture appears to exist on the surface of the texture-mapped object. Thus texture mapping is also a handy method for mapping arbitrary 2-D arrays of scientific data onto arbitrarily shaped and oriented 3-D computer graphic objects.

Bump mapping, developed by Blinn (1978), is somewhat like applying a deformable layer of embossed wallpaper over the surface of an object. That is, rather than modifying the object surface's color, it perturbs the surface normal in such a way as to make that surface appear raised or lowered.

In texture mapping, the texture is just a picture that exists at its own resolution, the pixels of which are sometimes referred to as *texels* (to prevent confusion between the pixels in the texture map and the pixels in the final rendered image). To map the texture onto an object's surface, the texture image is usually considered to vary between (0,0) and (1,1), from, say, the upper left edge to the lower right edge. Coordinate pairs (u,v) may then be used to specify some location (some texel) within the texture map. Each vertex of the object that is to be texture-mapped will be assigned a (u,v) coordinate pair, which can be interpolated along edges and spans, just like the other shading parameters, to provide a (u,v) location for each pixel in the image being rendered. The shader can then look up the color of the texture map at the (u,v) location corresponding to each pixel and modify the surface color with the color of the texel in the texture map at that (u,v) location. Figures 6.18a and 6.18b show the different computer graphic models with the same texture map applied. In this case, the models were computed in Mathematica and then imported into Electric Image where the Arsia Mons texture used in Chapter 3 was then applied in each case.

Though the story given above captures the basic principles of texture mapping, in practice it isn't usually quite that simple. Potentially large discrepancies in the size of the destination image pixels and the source texture map's texels (which discrepancy can vary from frame to frame) means that aliasing artifacts can be very pronounced and highly objectionable without some form of antialiasing. A technique called MIP mapping, due to Williams (1983), uses an additional one-third the memory of the original texture map to store multiple averaged-down versions of the original map. The appropriate resolution map is selected based on the ratio of texel size to pixel size, thus providing an efficient means of determining appropriately antialiased color detail in the final image. An important extension to MIP mapping by Heckbert (1986) computes a weighted sum in a similarly chosen MIP-map level, based on an oval filter in the texture (u,v) space, that is derived from a transformed circular filter in the original image space. Heckbert's method is more accurate than simple MIP mapping, yet retains its efficiency relative to antialiasing schemes executed in the original texel space.

Reflection mapping also maps an image onto an object's surface. However, instead of using a (u,v) parametric mapping based purely on the object's geometry, the mapping is based on the direction of a *reflection vector* computed by reflecting the vector from the eye to the point on the object's surface about the surface normal at that point. Spherical reflections may utilize a specially warped image for this purpose, while a technique based on a reflection cube may use six standard images corresponding to each of the faces of a cube imagined to enclose the reflective object. Figure 6.19 shows a highly reflective automobile exterior rendered using this technique.

Bump mapping uses first derivatives of the values in an image to locally perturb surface normals. The same type of (u,v) parametric mapping used for texture mapping is used to map into the bump map image. The antialiasing schemes appropriate to texture mapping do not strictly apply to bump mapping, however, as they only smooth the resulting bumps rather than properly antialiasing the resulting illumination levels. This technique does not actually affect the position of points

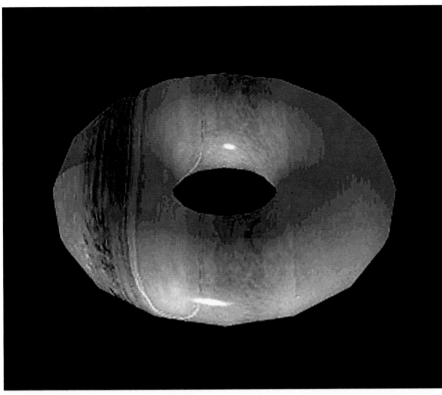

Figure 6.18a
Texture map of Arsia Mons
Mars image onto a torus
created in Mathematica.
Notice the highlights and
reflectivity of this image.

Figure 6.18a

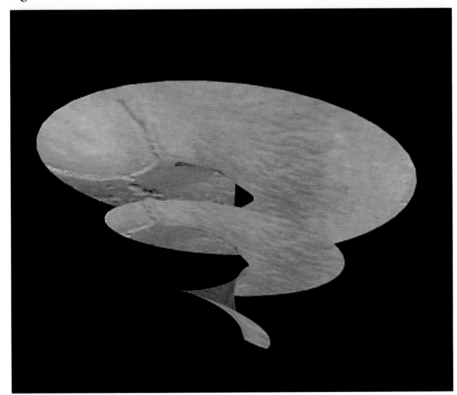

Figure 6.18b
The same mapping
technique is used to map
the Mars image onto a
helical "screw." Notice the
lack of any highlights or
reflectivity in this image.

Figure 6.18b

on the surface, so the effect is betrayed by non-bumpy edges in silhouette. The silhouette problem is not especially noticeable in most cases, however, so the technique offers a reasonably efficient means of adding apparent surface detail to objects. Figure 6.20 shows a transparent globe with a bump-mapped surface.

Figure 6.19
Computer graphic rendering of an automobile using a reflection map. (Courtesy Digital Productions)

Figure 6.19

Figure 6.20
Computer graphic rendering of a globe using a bump map. (Courtesy Digital Productions.)

Figure 6.20

Applying Surface Visualization Techniques

In this section we show a few scientific visualization examples of uses of the techniques discussed in this chapter. Figure 6.21, done by Jim Blinn and Robert Wolff, is a frame from the 1982 animation "Jupiter's Magnetosphere: The Movie" one of the first polygonally based visualizations done for research and analysis purposes. In the figures, the magnetic field lines, as well as the plasma sheet and the torus swept out by the Jovian moon Io, were represented by transparent tubes, a technique that Blinn developed specifically for this animation. Jupiter was produced by texture-mapping Voyager images onto a sphere. That particular project required nearly two years of work in a customized hardware environment with a Vax 11/780 with 8 MB of RAM and a couple of hundred MB hard disk space as a rendering engine (about equivalent to a Mac IIci), and with considerable investment in custom software written by Jim Blinn. In today's technological environment virtually all of the tools needed to create such an animation are available in commercial software packages, and desktop computing environments

CD 6.7

Figure 6.21
This image, from *Jupiter's Magnetosphere: The Movie* shows one of the first applications of 3-D rendering and animation techniques to research problems. (Courtesy NASA/JPL)

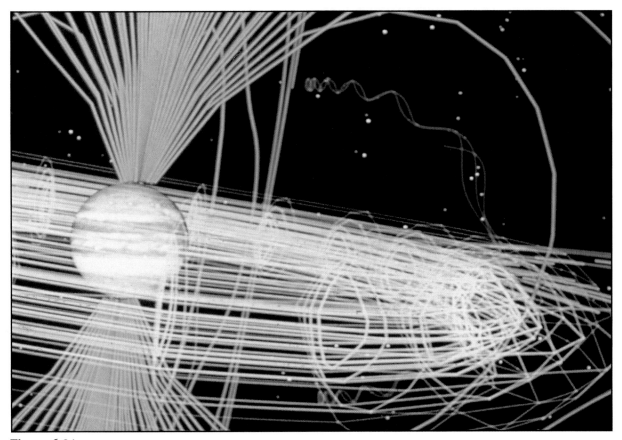

Figure 6.21

CD 6.8

CD 6.9

CD 6.10

are many times more powerful than the old Vax minicomputers. Mike Backes and Rob Wolff show the beginnings of a Mac-based *Jupiter's Magnetosphere* in Movie 6-8, done in 1991, with the entire sequence shown here being designed and computed in less than a day on a Mac II ci with 8MB RAM and an 80 MB hard disk.

Movie 6-9 and Figures 6.22a-e illustrate a visualization of the evolution of a cometary tail that Jeff Goldsmith and Rob Wolff did in 1985. The visualization technique borrowed from Blinn's transparent tubes used in the Jupiter magnetosphere visualization and also made use of some theorems on solid-body deformations developed by Al Barr for physically based animations (Barr, 1984). Figure 6.22f shows this same technique applied by Wolff and Goldsmith to the analysis of the 3-D structure of a twisted magnetic flux.

Movie 6-10 shows an early use of a commercial software package for solid-model visualizations. These frames were done by Peter Farson and Rob Wolff in 1986 using Wavefront software running on a Silicon Graphics Iris 3030. Here the Io torus is represented by a particle system, and real Voyager plasma data is coupled into the animation as an image of the plasma density of the Io torus. Another innovation in this animation was the use of an Alliant FX-80 as a *coarse-grained* parallel renderer. The parallel renderer was developed by Farson and Scott Stein (then of Wavefront). Interestingly, one of us (Yaeger) was also responsible for implementing a coarse-grained parallel renderer on Digital Productions' Cray X-MP in the early 1980s.

Figure 6.22a-d

Figures 6.22a-d show a sequence of images from a simulation of the evolution of the plasma tail of Halley's Comet in 1986, while Figure 6.22e shows an actual set of observations of a comet tail. In the simulation, the lines represent the interplanetary magnetic field being draped over the (conducting) ionosphere of the comet to form the plasma tail. The dust tail from Halley, 1910 is shown for reference.

Figure 6.22b

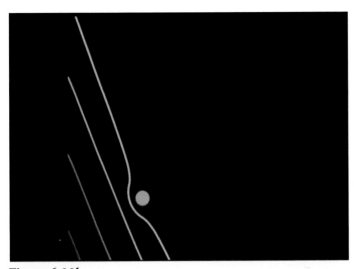

Figure 6.22b

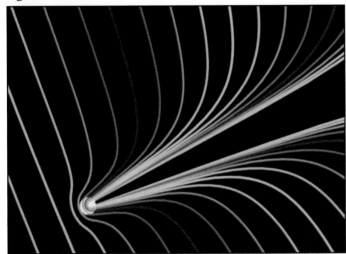

Figure 6.22c

Figure 6.22d

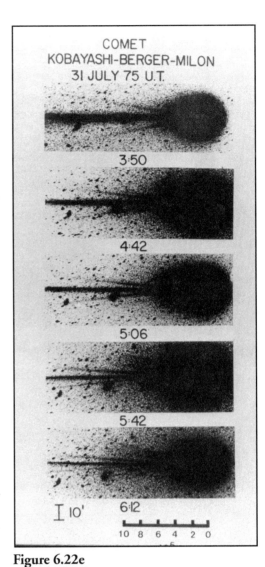

Figure 6.22e

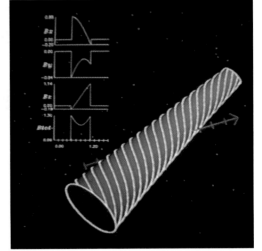

Figure 6.22f

CD 6.11

CD 6.12

Figure 6.23 and Movie 6-11 are from a series of visualizations done at NCSA using a combination of Wavefront software and NCSA's own custom visualization tools.

An unusual application of these techniques is shown in Figure 6.24 and Movie 6-12, created by one of the authors (Yaeger) to visualize an *Artificial Life* world called "PolyWorld." Here a group of polygonally based artificial creatures interact with each other and their environment

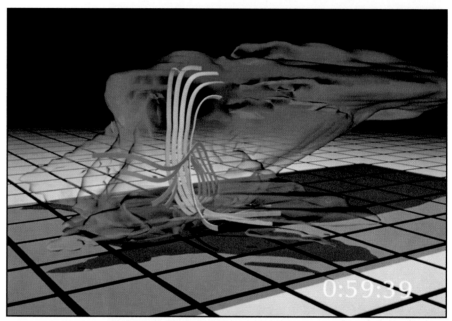

Figure 6.23a

Figure 6.23a,b
These images from the NCSA visualization of a severe storm illustrate how a variety of modeling and rendering techniques can be applied to show the basic science of very complex phenomena. (Courtesy Robert Wilhelmson, NCSA)

Figure 6.23b

under the control of evolved nervous systems consisting of artificial neural networks. Surface-based rendering techniques are used not only to display the world to the *ALife* researcher, but to give a form of vision to the organisms in the world. The scene is rendered from each organism's point of view, and the resulting pixel map is fed as input to the creature's neural network, like light falling on a retina. One of the principal outputs of this simulator is the *ethological* level behaviors of the organisms, phenomena which are only observable over time. Hence we see here an example of an application of computer animation techniques actually enabling a line of research. Without the ability to observe animated sequences of activity in this computational ecology, the characteristic behaviors of the organisms could not be understood. And those very behaviors are based on a visual perceptive mechanism that itself relies upon computer graphics.

Figure 6.24
An ecosystem in the computer, this Artificial Life simulator, Larry Yaeger's "PolyWorld," shows multi-colored organisms, bright green blocks of food, brown barriers that prohibit movement, and a dark green ground plane, where artificial organisms live, die, and evolve. The small group of images in the upper left show the point of view of each of the organisms in the world.

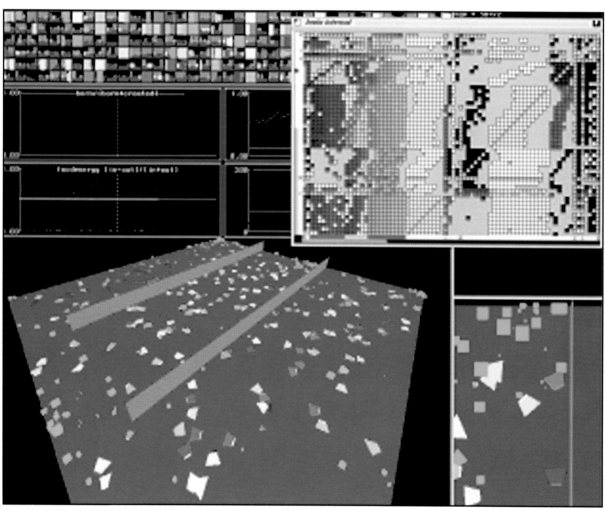

Figure 6.24

Summary

In this chapter we've explored some of the more complex techniques for visualizing data. The methods described here differ from those in previous chapters, in that they were not really developed for data analysis, but rather for realistic rendering of objects for artistic purposes. In addition, the user paradigm is different for these techniques as well. Whereas techniques like image processing and volume rendering are designed for interactive analysis, the polygonally based techniques described in this chapter are usually used to create presentations or stand-alone animations. Nevertheless, because of their sheer visual power, polygonally based renderings are increasingly finding their way into scientific visualizations as what was once custom software migrates down to easy-to-use commercial packages at the workstation and personal computer level.

In the next chapter we delve into the complex world of production computer graphics and the deadline-driven work that often produces breakthrough computer graphics technologies such as particle systems and morphing, the technique first seen in *Willow* and greatly popularized in *Terminator 2* and recent Michael Jackson videos. This treatment is interesting from two perspectives. First, from a strictly technical point of view, we can see how exciting new computer graphic techniques are developed under production conditions. Second, we can see something of how technology transfer takes place between the scientific computing community and the entertainment industry. This linkage seems to be most structured at the annual ACM SIGGRAPH meetings, where scientists and computer graphics researchers and developers gather from around the world.

Suggested Reading

1. *Tutorial: Computer Graphics*, second edition, by J. C. Beatty and K. S. Booth, IEEE Computer Society Press, 1982.

2. *Computer Graphics: Principles and Practice,* second edition, by J. D. Foley, Andries van Dam, S.K. Feiner, and J. F. Hughes, Addison-Wesley, 1990.

3. *Tutorial and Selected Readings in Interactive Computer Graphics*, by H. Freeman, IEEE Computer Society Press,, 1980.

4. *Principles of Interactive Computer Graphics*, second edition, by W. M. Newman and R. F. Sproull, McGraw-Hill, 1979.

5. IEEE's *Computer Graphics and Applications.*

6. ACM's *Transactions on Graphics.*

7. ACM's *Computer Graphics* Annual SIGGRAPH Proceedings.

Visualization in Film and Television

7

Though most of this book is devoted to the application of computer graphics visualization techniques to the worlds of mathematics and science, we would be remiss to ignore the domain where many of the techniques we have discussed were popularized and refined: the commercial computer graphics industry of film and television. If the fields of mathematics, medicine, and computer science were the crucible that forged computer graphics, the commercial production houses that produce the special effects for Hollywood's movies and television programming have been the hammer and anvil that reshaped and refined computer graphics into a hardened and mature tool. And the cross-fertilization has by no means abated. These two communities continue to borrow techniques (and researchers) from each other, to provide a truly natural feel to elements in a commercial production, or to provide greater visual impact and convey additional information in a scientific visualization.

In Chapter 6 we saw examples of particle-systems rendering in the "Genesis Sequence" in the film *Star Trek II: The Wrath of Kahn* and a visualization of Jupiter in the film *2010*. Most computer graphics used in the film and television industries, however, is based on the polygonal rendering techniques discussed in that chapter and **Tech Notes 14** and **15**. The now standard computer graphics production pipeline, consisting of *modeling*, *animation*, and *rendering*, as discussed in Chapter 6, is at the center of the commercial computer graphics process. Integrating the results of the computer graphics process with live-action filming is another important area of effort and investigation. And, of course, these technical production activities are interlaced with the realities of project funding, artistic design, film recording, editing, and so on.

A Brief History of Computer Graphics in Film

John Whitney, Sr., also known for the slit-scan technique that produced the visually powerful "into the monolith" imagery of *2001: A Space Odyssey*, is often credited with bringing computer graphics to the film industry. He experimented with war-surplus analog computer control mechanisms from antiaircraft weapons to control the motion of a camera in the late 1950s and 1960s and produced a number of short animations and television commercials. He continued his work with computer imagery, always seeking to create harmonic, algorithmic motions, producing some very attractive mandala-like imagery in a series of short animations through the 1970s and 1980s.

Ivan Sutherland's 1962 MIT thesis on an interactive computer graphics interface, called Sketchpad, demonstrated for the first time the power of computer graphics as a method for controlling and interacting with computers, and served as a great inspiration to other researchers. The University of Utah and the New York Institute of Technology fostered rich environments for this fledgling science, producing a crop of computer graphics researchers and techniques that have helped to shape the field.

The first feature film to use computer graphics imagery, rendered in the style used today, was the 1982 release *Tron*. The effects for *Tron* were created by a number of fledgling production facilities, Information International Incorporated ("Triple I"), Magi Synthavision, Digital Effects, and Robert Abel and Associates, most of which are no longer in business and none of which is currently involved in computer graphics production. All of these companies produced television commercials for a time during the 1980s as well as some unused and seldom seen but impressive test footage for *Star Wars* (from III).

In *Tron*, computer graphics was used to portray . . . computer graphics. But in 1984, Digital Productions created the first photorealistic images for a feature film, *The Last Starfighter*, using a Cray X-MP supercomputer. Here the computer images were integrated with live action as realistic scene elements, rather than as monitor graphics or computer-generated imagery. Instead of the traditional models and miniatures, computer graphics was used to create all the spaceships, planets, and high-tech hardware in the film. Digital Productions also created effects for the opening title sequence of *Labyrinth*, the planet Jupiter for *2010*, the animation for Mick Jagger's "Hard Woman" rock video, and a string of award-winning television commercials during the 1980s but is no longer in business. They also produced some impressive test footage for a few special projects, including *Dune* and *Star Trek: The Next Generation*.

Pixar, a LucasFilm spin-off, used a particle system to create the imagery depicting the birth of a planet as the result of the "Genesis Effect" for the film *Star Trek II: The Wrath of Kahn*, which was also used in the third film in that series. Pixar also produced the stained-glass-window-come-to-life effect for *Young Sherlock Holmes* using rendering and texture-mapping techniques. They are perhaps better known, however, for their John Lasseter–directed series of short subjects, including the Oscar-nominated "Luxo, Jr.," and the Oscar-winning "Tin Toy."

ILM/LucasFilm produced some unique special effects for *The Abyss* and *Terminator 2*. Though used quite differently in these two films, both sets of effects were based on traditional rendering techniques coupled with a method for dynamically warping the shapes of objects and images now known as *morphing* (ILM actually first showed its morphing techniques in the less commercially successful *Willow*). The firm has also created television commercials and music videos using these techniques.

Other computer graphics production for television commercials has been done by the now-defunct Cranston-Csuri Productions, its successor MetroLight Studios, the Robert Abel spinoff: Rhythm and Hues, and the oldest surviving (and still thriving) computer graphics production house: Pacific Data Images. DeGraf/Wahrman, a Digital Productions spinoff, produced effects for the film version of *The Jetsons*. In addition, the dropping prices of graphics workstations and the growing capabilities of microprocessor-based systems have given rise to smaller independent production houses such as Homer and Associates, and Kleiser-Walczak, as well as some in-house production at various film studios.

Computer graphics has also given a behind-the-scenes assist to traditional animation in most Disney films since *The Great Mouse Detective*, and in Kroyer Films' recent *FernGully: The Last Rainforest*. Disney brought computer graphics back in front of the camera to provide the ballroom interior scenes for *Beauty and the Beast*.

This is certainly not an exhaustive list of all computer graphics effects for film, but it does hit most of the early landmarks.

How Tough Is This Job?

Although Macintosh and other microprocessor-based computers are beginning to have the power and the software to produce some wonderful 2-D and even 3-D images, most high-quality rendered images for film and television are produced by high-powered graphics workstations, such as Silicon Graphics Irises, by powerful Unix or DEC/VMS minicomputers, or in a few fortunate cases by extremely powerful Cray supercomputers. Why is this the case?

Back-of-the-envelope calculations are sufficient to indicate the magnitude of the computational power problem. If it takes, say, 500 operations to calculate each of three colors for each pixel in a 2560 by 2048 image, then a single frame of film needs approximately 8×10^{10} operations to produce. There are 24 of these frames per second of film, so each one had better not take too long to compute! For a per-frame time of 2 minutes, it would be necessary to sustain a computational rate of about 66 MFLOPs (a MFLOP, or "megaflop," is 1 million FLOating Point operations per second; we are purposely blurring the distinction between computer instructions, operations, and floating-point

Figures 7.1a,b
Color storyboards for a television commercial graphically depict the objects, scene composition, and intended motion. The action flows across the top panels of 7.1a, then the top panels of 7.1b, then the respective bottom panels. (Courtesy Digital Productions)

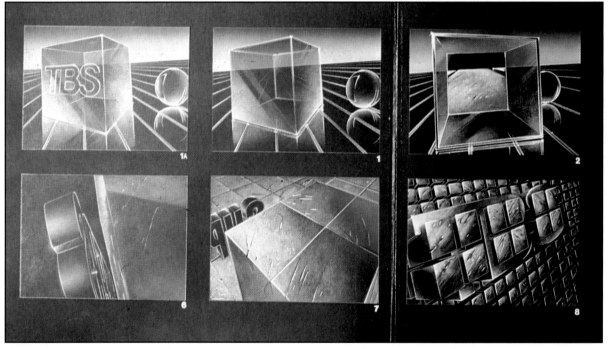

Figure 7.1a

operations to keep this simple). Though peak rates may be much higher, today's supercomputers typically deliver a few tens of MFLOPs in overall, sustained computation; hence, even the most powerful super-computers can be expected to labor heavily over significant computer graphics applications.

A Look at the Production Process

Most computer graphics effects produced for film or television are necessarily the result of a collaboration between the production facility and the film's director and effects supervisor, or the advertising agency representing the commercial client. In either case, the most common scenario is for the customer to have some idea as to the nature of the images desired, frequently including at least a rough *storyboard* of the commercial or film scene. An art director at the production facility then typically produces a refined storyboard to the satisfaction of the client. Figure 7.1 shows a particularly refined set of storyboards, created by Mario Kamberg, for a television ad for Turner Broadcasting (then WTBS). Not all storyboards are this detailed; simple black and white sketches often suffice. Figures 7.2 shows a close-up of one of the panels from these boards and a single frame from the final commercial that corresponds approximately to the drawn frame.

Figure 7.1b

If the job is perceived to present any technical challenges (which is often the case), the technical staff of the production house—programmers, digital modelers, technical directors, and technical management—also become involved in the design and bid process, to ensure feasibility of the project and to determine the best approach to

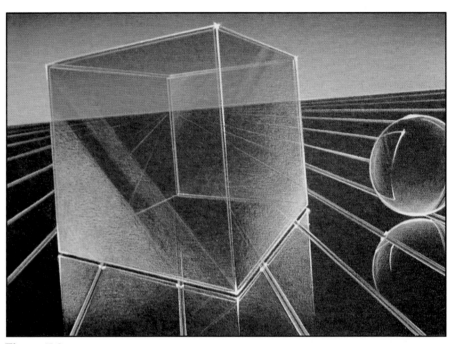

Figure 7.2a
Single panel detail from the full storyboard in Figure 7.1. (Courtesy Digital Productions)

Figure 7.2a

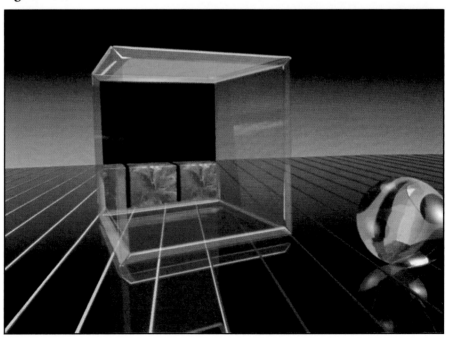

Figure 7.2b
Corresponding frame from the fully rendered commercial. (Courtesy Digital Productions)

Figure 7.2b

producing the desired images. Even the technical aspects of computer graphics are much more of an art than a science, especially as they relate to the production of a particular piece of animation.

Once the artistic design is settled upon, the process unique to the computer graphics industry begins. The computer graphic objects must be carefully designed and built. These models are then arranged and animated so as to compose the scenes called for in the storyboards. Color, light, and shading all must be specified for the objects in a series of test renderings. And finally the complete sequence of animation, with all of the shading parameters, must be rendered and recorded on film or video.

The resulting imagery may be used as is, edited together with other footage, and possibly even digitally or optically composited with live action to create the final product.

In some production houses, the same individual plays the roles of art director, modeler, animator, and technical director, carrying out every phase of the production from original idea and design to final rendering. In other establishments, people tend to specialize in one or two of these various aspects. People involved in the production process often find themselves writing their own software to algorithmically generate an object model, to control its motion, or to modify its appearance. So individual job descriptions vary and blur from place to place and time to time, though the basic steps in the overall process remain consistent.

Design and Modeling

The first stage is the design and construction of the models that will be employed in the scene composition, animation, and rendering stages. Sometimes this first stage is technically difficult, and sometimes it is merely labor-intensive. The construction of the components of a Sony Walkman model that fly through space and assemble themselves (Figure 7.3) is straightforward, though requiring a great deal of effort and time. The design and modeling of an owl for the opening title sequence in *Labyrinth* (see Figure 7.4) is considerably less straightforward: How should the wings and feathers be designed to fit seamlessly into the torso in all modes of flight, from all viewing angles?

As mentioned in Chapter 6, simple objects, such as surfaces of revolution and extruded shapes, can often be modeled entirely in the computer. More complex objects, however, usually require the drafting of fairly detailed engineering-style drawings. From these drawings,

181

individual points are encoded by hand into the computer. In Chapter 6 we saw one of the original engineering drawings used to encode the Gunstar—a complex spaceship designed by Ron Cobb for the film *The Last Starfighter*—along with a rendered image of that ship (Figure 6.2). Though designed and modeled almost a decade ago, this remains one of

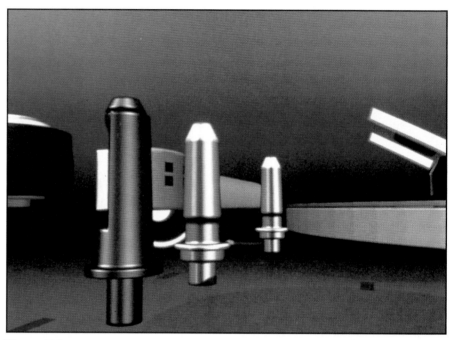

Figure 7.3a

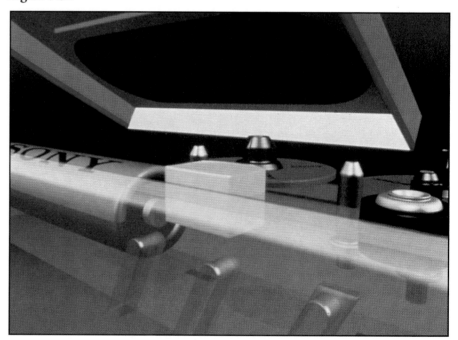

Figure 7.3a,b
Geometrically simple objects compose these scenes from a Sony Walkman commercial.
(Courtesy Digital Productions)

Figure 7.3b

the most ambitious, detailed computer graphic models built to date. In fact, a single instance of the Gunstar contained as many as 750,000 polygons, when shown with wing panels open to display its armament. When shown with the wing panels closed, and as much internal detail removed as possible, the Gunstar still comprised approximately half a million polygons. The scene from *The Last Starfighter* shown in Figure 7.5 and in Movie 7-1 on the CD-ROM, which shows six Gunstars lined up in a hangar, consists of approximately 3 million polygons, and probably still holds the world record for most complex computer graphic image.

Another approach to the creation of computer graphic models is to start with an existing, or specially constructed, real 3-D object. Points on the surface of this object can be entered into the computer by means of a 3-D or *three-space* digitizer, consisting of a sort of pen and a sensing device that can determine the location of the tip of the pen in a volume of space. Alternatively, the physical object can be illuminated by a thin slit of light, rotated in small, constant angular increments, and then reconstructed in the computer by software that analyzes the resulting sequence of projected 2-D contours. The head of the owl in Figure 7.4

Figure 7.4

Figure 7.4
Complex, organic objects compose this owl from the opening title sequence of *Labyrinth*. (Courtesy Digital Productions)

was created using such a technique (also refer to Figures 6.4 and 6.5).

These models are often built in pieces, each of which may be animated, lit, colored, and shaded very differently. The pieces, however, must fit together in a precise, predetermined fashion. Accordingly, it is a useful practice to have a separate level of abstraction—a *scene file*—that specifies the relation between a part's local coordinate system and the coordinate system of the assembled parts. These scene files make it possible to build up complex, hierarchical structures to describe compound objects. Since the person responsible for designing and encoding the models is bound to be the person who is most knowledgeable about the objects, the task of creating these first-level scene files usually falls to the model builder. Though it is possible to nest these scene files, to define higher and higher levels of organization up to a complete description of the desired scene, the final scene composition is usually determined in the animation stage, using software designed for that purpose.

Scene Composition and Animation

The second stage in the computer graphics process is animation, which includes scene composition. During this stage, computer animators take all the various objects that have been modeled, and place them into a sequence of scenes that correspond to the original storyboards.

Scene composition and animation require a highly interactive

CD 7.1

Figure 7.5
Approximately 3 million polygons compose this highly detailed scene of multiple Gunstars, from *The Last Starfighter*. (Courtesy Digital Productions)

Figure 7.5

environment during setup and accurate frame rates during playback. The first attribute facilitates the overall design of the scene, and the second permits a realistic assessment of the motion and "feeling" of the animation. Most animation systems, even high-end ones, use wireframe displays rather than shaded images.

Animation of simple, rigid objects is fairly straightforward, requiring little more than the positioning of the objects at a few points along their paths. Animation of complex, interlocking rigid objects, or flexible, organic objects—especially for *character* animation—can be very difficult indeed. Motor gears, pistons, and the like are often animated algorithmically, based upon mathematical descriptions of their rhythmic motions. Animated characters and flexible shapes call upon a variety of advanced techniques, including object and image interpolation (now called *morphing*), *physically based animation* (or *physically based modeling*), *squash and stretch*, *witness-point tracking* (or *rotoscoping*), and kinematic assists in hierarchical animation.

Many of the techniques used in traditional 2-D animation extend fairly directly to 3-D character animation. The artistic skills of traditional animators also transfer well to this new form of artistic expression. In fact, some of the most successful efforts to date come from traditional animators, like John Lasseter and Bill Kroyer, who have brought their traditional animation skills to bear on computer graphic animation. While working for Pixar, Lasseter has produced a string of

Figure 7.6
A scene from Pixar's Academy Award–nominated "Luxo, Jr." ©1986 Pixar. (Courtesy Pixar)

Figure 7.6

CD 7.2

wonderfully funny and warm animations—"André and Wally B.,"
"Luxo, Jr.," "Red's Dream," "Tin Toy," and "Knick Knack"—that have
set the pace for the industry and garnered him Oscar nominations and
awards (see Figure 7.6). Kroyer lent his animation and directorial skills
to computer graphics in the films *Tron*, *Labyrinth*, and the recent
FernGully: The Last Rain Forest (among others). Kroyer's animated owl
for the *Labyrinth* titles is one of the most realistic and naturalistic animations to date, and won the NCGA's animation award (Figure 7.2). His

Figure 7.7a

Figure 7.7
Images from Bill Kroyer's
"Technological Threat."
Notice the smooth integration of traditional animation
(the dog) with polygonally
based computer graphic
animation (the robot and
the environment).
(Courtesy Kroyer Films)

Figure 7.7b

hilarious, Oscar-nominated "Technological Threat" short subject combines computer graphics and traditional animation techniques, and echoes the zaniness of classic Warner Brothers cartoons (Figure 7.7).

CD 7.3

All animation systems must provide a method for the user to position the graphic objects in space, adjust their angular orientation, scale their size, and control the virtual camera's location and field of view. Since these and a variety of other animation control parameters must ultimately be specified for each and every frame, all useful animation systems provide some method for specifying these parameters at key-frames (as discussed in Chapter 6) and interpolating values for these parameters at intermediate frames. Since the key-frames represent transition points in the control parameters, it is easy for discontinuities in velocity and acceleration to arise that cause the resulting motion to appear jerky or unnatural. A key aspect of better animation systems (and animators) is their support for (and attention to) these derivatives of parameters at key-frames.

A good animation system also permits the animator to easily cut and paste, shrink and expand, and generally manipulate key-frames and ranges of frames. All of the animation sequences of the owl in *Labyrinth* are based upon a single 13-frame animation cycle depicting the basic wing motion during flight. This permitted the animator, Bill Kroyer, to focus a great deal of attention on this basic flight cycle, carefully tweaking x-, y-, and z-translations, roll, pitch, and yaw, plus multiple levels of interpolated shapes for every single feather in the model, as well as head, legs, and other wing structures. Kroyer was then able to craft all the different scenes by combining the basic motion of the bird's torso with properly manipulated (and only occasionally modified) portions of this full cycle of flight animation.

CD 7.4

In production work, the art director and a computer animator (or technical director) work closely together to determine the final scene layout and motion, based on the original designs in the storyboards. Routine commercial production can involve any or all of the above techniques, depending upon the design of the particular job. Since commercial clients are always in search of something new and different, the range of techniques continues to expand. Movie 7-5 shows a typical wireframe animation of the components of a (Clio award winning) Sony Walkman commercial, produced at Digital Productions. This Movie also contains some test renderings and a final rendering of the same commercial, to show how the original animation is used to guide the final filming. Pseudo-wireframe animation was used for the characters in a music video for Mick Jagger's "Hard Woman," also produced at

CD 7.5

CD 7.6

Digital Productions (Figure 7.8). Witness-point tracking, or roto-scoping, is a technique where the actions of a live model are interpreted by computer software from the dots placed on her bodysuit. Some recent character animation may be seen in Figure 7.9, from a Listerine commercial produced at Pixar. An example of 2-D and 3-D morphing produced at LucasFilm/ILM from the film *Terminator 2* is shown in Figure 7.10.

Figure 7.8

Figure 7.8
Pseudo-wireframe characters in a scene from Mick Jagger's "Hard Woman" rock video. (Courtesy Digital Productions)

Figure 7.9

Figure 7.9
Character animation is a central element in this well known Listerine commercial. ©1991 Pixar/Colossal Pictures. (Courtesy Pixar)

Figure 7.10

Figure 7.10
Image interpolation, or
morphing, plays a major
role in the creation of this
shape-shifting character from
Terminator 2: Judgment Day.
(Courtesy Carolco/ILM/
Lightstorm)

Rendering

As the animation is being finalized, it is common to begin working on the lighting and shading of a scene. Test rendering to a high-resolution monitor—typically 1280 (horizontal) by 1024 (vertical) resolution with 24 bits of color (8 bits each for red, green, and blue)—let the art director and the technical director decide on the final look of the scene. This process involves placement of the light sources in the scene, specifying the various control parameters for those lights (including color, distance and angular rolloff, and so on), determining the color and surface properties of the objects in the scene, and specifying any special texturing or surface-modifying parameters for those objects. The end result can be a *photorealistic* image, such as the castle interior in Figure 7.11, or it can be a fantastical image, such as Figure 7.12.

As was discussed in Chapter 6, a variety of rendering algorithms exist for the creation of these images. However, by far the most common rendering algorithms in use for actual commerical production are the scanline-sampling, a-buffer, and *z*-buffer algorithms. These

Figure 7.11
Computer-generated castle interior. (Courtesy Digital Productions)

Figure 7.11

algorithms provide a computationally efficient means for the depiction of fairly complex scenes. The typical number of polygons in a frame from an ordinary television commercial ranges from around 50,000 to 100,000 polygons, hence the need for a computationally efficient rendering solution.

The bulk of a technical director's time during this stage of production is spent defining the various parameters that control the lighting and shading of a scene. Each object must typically be assigned color and surface material properties that affect the manner in which light is reflected from that surface. If an object is to be partially transparent, then the parameters controlling its degree of transparency, and the manner in which that transparency is modulated by its orientation with respect to the eye, must be set. Additional detail may be added to an object by the specification of texture maps and bump maps. And the addition of a reflection map can make a reflective object appear realistically embedded in its surroundings.

Each light that serves as an illumination source for the scene must also be specified, in terms of its color, and its range of effectiveness and rolloff characteristics as a function of both distance and angle.

Figure 7.12
Computer-generated fantastical landscape. (Courtesy Digital Productions)

Figure 7.12

Color Calibration

Despite the best efforts of the manufacturers of computer graphics display monitors and film recorders, and of the engineers and technicians who maintain them, differences in the perceived color of rendered scenes on the various devices occur. These differences can sometimes be objectionable enough to warrant real concern. Hours spent tweaking light and surface colors and control parameters to obtain a look that is *just so* can be frustrated by subtle variations between the colors on a graphics monitor and the colors recorded on film or video. Little wonder, since display monitors create their images by exciting light emission in phosphors subjected to streams of electrons, while film images are created by the transmission of light through layers of materials that have been chemically altered by exposure to light. And the atrocities visited upon the color space by conversion to NTSC video are better relegated to a horror story than a technical discourse.

Color calibration of display devices is another topic that could easily fill an entire book, and is necessarily beyond the scope of this one. The difficulties inherent in the problem, including interdependencies between the multiple color components in different color regimes, make its solution a thorny one.

In practice, however, it is possible to go some distance in addressing this problem by first keeping the display devices as closely calibrated as possible (by monitoring and adjusting for film density in different regions of special color charts, and providing carefully constructed color calibration curves for the film recorder), and then by bracketing, or *wedging* shots in color space. Before committing the animation and rendering selections to final filming, it may be desirable to select a few representative frames and to record them using software filters that subtly adjust the color space and the overall film density. The art director and the commercial client can then examine the frames and select control parameters for these software filters that can be applied to every frame during the final filming process. This stage of the process also makes it possible for the art director to make last-minute decisions about whether the shot might look better if it was overall a bit brighter, or cooler, or warmer, and so on.

Final Filming

When all modeling, animation, rendering, lighting, and shading decisions have finally been made, the complete set of specifications is then submitted to some form of final filming queue. Depending upon the type of computer equipment available and the complexity of the particular job, this stage can take a few hours to a few weeks. Especially in the case of complex, lengthy jobs, it is usually desirable to first make a complete filming pass at a significantly lower resolution, to spot any unforeseen problems. Some commercial computer animation houses make it a routine policy to record these low-resolution test renderings for every job, to avoid expensive retakes of the final, high-resolution pass.

Integration with Live Action

In some cases, especially in the world of television advertising, the rendered images are the end product. But often, in both film and television, the computer graphic images need to be combined with live-action footage. Sometimes a real actor needs to be placed into a computer-generated environment. Sometimes a computer image is just one component of a complex scene also involving live action and traditional special effects. A number of techniques have evolved to facilitate this integration.

COMPOSITING WITH MATTES

A common method of combining computer graphics with live-action film is that of *holdout mattes*. The use of mattes to composite multiple elements of a scene is a standard tool of the traditional live-action film effects world. The technique can be applied to models and miniatures, or to special hand-painted scenes called *matte paintings*. With physical objects like models, the method typically involves photographing them against a dark background, and then creating a moving matte by pushing the film to create a special high-contrast version of the actual effects footage that is white, or clear, where the model is located, but black, or dense, everywhere else. This moving matte and its negative reversal are used to optically composite the model shot with live-action footage on an optical compositing bench. An optical compositing bench is basically just a well-aligned, well-calibrated projector-camera pair on a very stable platform. The projector projects light from any previously exposed and developed film source through a set of lenses onto the fresh film in the camera mounted opposite it. By first exposing a new film negative to the live-action imagery, but using the moving matte to hold out or block the light where the model should be, rewinding, and then re-exposing the same negative to just the model imagery, an effective composite scene can be created that appears to contain both live action and the model.

With matte paintings, the painting may occupy a major portion of the frame, with live-action elements merely superimposed. Frequently, they are used to provide views of an imaginary city or planet—without the expense of building an entire set or the impracticality of shooting on location—by dovetailing the painting with structural elements of the live-action footage. Whole environments can be created or modified to provide a unique setting for a film.

Some classic special-effects films using traditional methods, such as *Blade Runner*, have been known to composite more than a dozen layers to create the special visual imagery the director wished to create. Films employing computer graphics effects have also taken advantage of this technique. In fact, computer effects are particularly well suited for compositing, since the same software that produces the full-color effects images can produce absolutely identical scene composition and motion, but with pure white backgrounds and pure black objects, or vice versa, thus guaranteeing perfectly matched effects and holdout mattes. This can produce crisp edges on objects composited into scenes, or, as in the case of the computer graphics Jupiter used in *2010* (discussed below), to provide a deliberately soft atmospheric haze.

Today, the computer effects and the live-action footage are likely to be composited digitally rather than optically. Given fast, high-resolution, color-accurate scanners and film recorders, the individual frames from the various source materials can be read into the computer, composited based on color, density, or whatever, and then recorded back to film. The process is very similar to that of optical compositing, but with the degree of flexibility and control associated with the computer.

The video world has analogs of these processes, and makes use of much the same techniques. Video switchers have been able to composite multiple video image sources for years, usually on the basis of color. Also, since the video signal is already electronic, and of lower resolution than film, the conversion to digital format is easier and more direct. A variety of manufacturers provide equipment for converting the signal to digital video and for performing compositing based on color, density, and so on, as well as directly manipulating the images on a frame-by-frame basis. Here again, computer effects can provide flawless mattes, or perfectly uniform color background keys for video compositing.

WITNESS-POINT TRACKING

Compositing usually requires that there be little or no camera motion; most often the camera is *locked down* for composite shots. Camera motion is almost impossible to duplicate during the photographing of the various elements of the scene, and almost any discrepancy in the camera motion between multiple elements in a scene will produce a disquieting, unnatural feeling in the resulting composite imagery that can completely destroy the intended illusion. One method for freeing the camera from its moorings, *witness-point tracking*, is to provide visual cues at carefully measured locations directly within the live-action scene, which can later be interpreted by computer software to determine the precise position, orientation, and lens characteristics of the original camera. There are many difficulties in this approach, including the occasional obscuring of the witness points by actors and other elements of the scene. Also, to reliably track the various witness points it may be necessary for the computer to get a human assist, by having people digitally encode the witness point locations within a number of frames, akin to the labor-intensive process of rotoscoped animation. However, the method permits the direct integration of live-action and computer graphics effects footage without the need for a locked-down camera. Once the software determines the position of the real, physical camera, it can place its virtual camera in the same position relative to the virtual objects, and the resulting imagery composites accurately and gracefully with the original footage.

The Planet Jupiter in *2010*

The processes described above are common to nearly all computer graphics production. Many jobs, however, bring special challenges, unique to the constraints and artistic design of the particular piece of work. Following is one example demonstrating the types of problems encountered and solutions devised for a real project. This particular project is also, perhaps, the one Hollywood production that is closest in form and function to the application of these techniques to the realm of scientific visualization. Indeed, one of the principals on this project, Craig Upson, went on to lead the efforts in scientific visualization at the same company, Digital Productions, as well as taking those ideas and techniques to the National Center for Supercomputer Applications, now famous for the world's most effective and attractive scientific visualization.

Early discussions between the film's director, Peter Hyams,

special effects director, Richard Edlund, JPL scientific advisor, Richard Terrile, and representatives from Digital Productions, including one of us (Yaeger), centered on the Voyager spacecraft images of Jupiter and how these might be used to provide realistic animations of the planet for backgrounds in the film. One technique considered was a 2-D interpolation or morphing technique to provide animated sequences of frames between actual spacecraft photos, using *tie points* to provide a means of mapping features in one frame to the same features in subsequent frames. Another technique considered was the creation of a fractal-based, Jupiter-like image, whose fractal control parameters could be modified over time to provide animated sequences. Unfortunately, the first approach suffered from the problem that the original spacecraft data was acquired at too low a resolution to provide the sharp, detailed images needed for large-screen projection, coupled with the fact that there were too many undesirable artifacts in the original data, including large gaps, and the occasional unwanted moon in the way. The second approach suffered from the fact that it could only produce a Jupiter-*like* image, and, by now, thanks especially to the Pioneer and Voyager spacecraft, everyone knew quite well what Jupiter really looks like; it was also unclear whether the range of controls provided by the fractal generation parameters could provide useful animated atmospheric flows.

A unique solution to the problem came from Yaeger's combined computational fluid dynamics and computer graphics backgrounds. He felt that some realistic, if not completely accurate, fluid dynamic equations could be solved—reasonably quickly—for the atmospheric flow fields and used to push around literally millions of small particles that carried along the colors of the planetary gases. These millions of particles could be rendered into an image by straightforward particle rendering techniques. And the resulting 2-D image could be mapped onto a sphere and rendered with traditional 3-D computer graphics imaging methods, thus providing the illusion of a true, 3-D atmospheric flow field, based on actual photographs of the planet Jupiter. Thus, the recognizable visual characteristics of Jupiter could be provided, along with a very naturalistic fluid motion for its atmosphere.

To bring this vision to fruition, Yaeger hired Craig Upson away from Lawrence Livermore National Laboratory, who brought with him a similar background in computer fluids and visualization techniques, and contracted with Robert Myers, a former cohort of Yaeger's from the computational fluids world, to write the fluid dynamics engine. This team rapidly built the tools and techniques needed to produce a test animation that won Digital Productions the job. This first test animation used an original Voyager spacecraft image to provide the particles' colors and distributions, a flow field based on hundreds of hand-marked and encoded vortical features, and a simple cylindrical mapping of the resulting texture maps onto a full sphere.

Besides the obvious tasks of defining and implementing the appropriate fluid dynamics model (always envisioned as a 2-D plus time, stream function-vorticity, pseudospectral technique, and discussed in more detail in Yaeger et al., 1986), and developing the particle-rendering algorithm and software, a number of other tricky issues presented themselves, among the most difficult of which were the specification of the initial flow field and its registration, or alignment, with the image-derived particles. Upson devised a technique for taking a collection of hand-marked and encoded vortex locations and sizes, and then, together with Yaeger, deriving a vorticity and fluid velocity field that corresponded to these features. An image based on this derived flow field could then be visually superimposed on the planetary image to obtain a set of registration parameters allowing the flow field to correctly line up with the corresponding atmospheric features. Figure 7.13 shows the marked-up spacecraft photo, and Figure 7.14 shows Upson and Yaeger together with the encoding station used to capture these vortical features for the computer. Figure 7.15 shows a simple color-map visualization of the resulting vorticity field.

This early test animation was just 25 seconds in length, but it completely convinced the film's director to go with the technique. Director Peter Hyams wrote the following to his collaborator Arthur C. Clarke (Clarke, 1984), who was also author of the original *2001*, following a screening of one of the early tests: "There is an outside chance that this silly film may actually work. I just saw the second Jupiter test from [Digital Productions president John] Whitney. It is an enhanced image of Jupiter . . . with elevation added to the cloud formations. It is astonishing. I looked at it . . . and told them it needed a good deal of work . . . and there were problems with color . . . however, I thought it had possibilities. I lied through my pointy teeth. It is amazing. I simply don't want them to know how excited I am."

Despite Hyams's enthusiasm, budget constraints meant that only about 2 minutes of final footage could be ordered from Digital Productions, which would have to suffice for approximately 35 minutes of on-screen time. So Upson and Yaeger worked with Edlund and his artists to design seven different shots of the "digital Jupiter" that could be rotated, flipped, cropped, and lit in a variety of ways to satisfy the various storyboarded scenes of the film. Accordingly, one unusual

197

constraint on the footage created by the Digital Productions team was the necessity to light the computer graphics models in an almost nondirectional fashion. Unfortunately, this resulted in a flatter, less three-dimensional appearance for the models than would have been the case if they could have been more appropriately lit for each scene.

As is frequently the case with a Hollywood production, concerns

Figure 7.13
Original Voyager "snakeskin" image of Jupiter, with atmospheric vortical features hand-marked for encoding. (Courtesy Digital Productions)

Figure 7.13

Figure 7.14
Craig Upson and Larry Yaeger at a typical encoding station used to input the flow-field features to the computer. (Courtesy Digital Productions)

Figure 7.14

about visual aesthetics overrode issues of physical realism. In particular, an observer orbiting Jupiter would not actually be able to observe the winds rotating and flowing as they are shown in these images. The actual appearance would change noticeably over time, but more on the order of hours, rather then the seconds of real time in the movie simulation. However, everyone involved in the production felt that a slow, but perceptible motion to the planet's atmosphere would give Jupiter a much more powerful, more dramatic presence. Accordingly, the software "knobs" were adjusted to provide the desirable rate of atmospheric flow, without regard for their technical correctness. In fact, Myers came up with a slight modification to the flow equations that permitted two separate knobs to be able to control the banded, equatorial flows independently of the rotational, vortical flows. This allowed the optimal selection of both the overall planetary wind speeds and the rotational rates of smaller atmospheric features.

As was mentioned earlier, the original Voyager spacecraft images were not sufficiently resolved to provide the level of detail needed for the final 70-mm projections. To obtain this additional detail, a large 8-foot blowup was made of the original Voyager photograph, and then detailed and enhanced by artist Ron Gress at Boss Films. Working directly on top of the original photograph, and using more detailed closeups of Jupiter and other vortex flows, Gress airbrushed a beautifully detailed and very accurate approximation to the planet's atmosphere. Figure 7.16 shows a portion of this artistically enhanced "snakeskin" (the name given to these cylindrical maps of the planet's atmosphere by the scientists at JPL); note the tremendous additional detail relative to the marked-up snakeskin of Figure 7.13.

Figure 7.15
Color-coded vorticity field resulting from the hand-marked vortical features. (Courtesy Digital Productions)

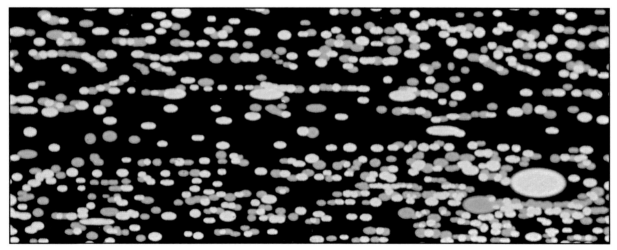

Figure 7.15

This image was then carefully photographed in a sequence of overlapping photographic tiles (to provide maximum resolution), and then scanned into the computer back at Digital Productions. Using image manipulation and blending software written by Yaeger, Upson recombined these overlapping tiles into a single very large, very detailed digital map of Jupiter's atmosphere. The same software was used to excerpt portions of this master image to provide the sections of atmospheric image needed to serve as texture maps in each of the specially designed scenes. Figure 7.17 shows one of these excerpted details of Jupiter's surface before it has been mapped onto the spherical planet.

Upson then wrote software to explode these texture maps into particles. Typically there were 5 to 10 million particles for a particular scene's texture map, each carrying a slightly dithered version of the color of the pixel from which it originated. It was these particles that were then blown around, or advected, by Myers's flow field simulation. Frame by frame, computational step by step, the flow-field was updated, the positions of all the particles were updated, and then the particles were rendered to create an updated atmospheric texture map. The particle rendering was done according to a scheme suggested by Yaeger, wherein the color of each pixel in the resulting texture image was simply the incrementally computed average of the color of all particles falling within that pixel.

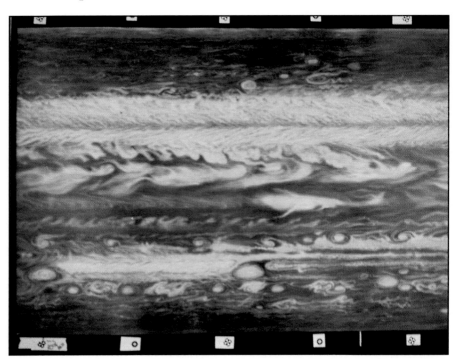

Figure 7.16
Artist-enhanced snakeskin image of Jupiter. (Courtesy Digital Productions)

Figure 7.16

200

Even with millions of particles to model Jupiter's atmosphere, the possibility existed that small holes might develop in the image of the atmosphere, as the particles were advected around by the simulated winds, naturally clumping and dispersing. Upson devised an elegantly simple solution to this problem, which was to use the previous frame's image as a backdrop for the current frame. Thus any pixel in the new image that was devoid of particles would determine its color from the corresponding pixel in the previous frame's image. At least for simulations as brief as these, this (coupled with the sheer number of particles) was completely sufficient to guarantee an apparently continuous and smooth image, rather than looking like a collection of dots, or a smooth pattern peppered with holes.

Figure 7.17
Excerpt from the artist-enhanced Jupiter snakeskin. (Courtesy Digital Productions)

Figure 7.17

To retain maximum possible resolution in these texture maps, Yaeger devised a method of *nonlinear texture mapping* that took advantage of the foreshortening at the edges of the planet, thus reducing the amount of detail that needed to be stored near these edges, and permitting maximum resolution to be retained in the large central sections of the planet. The result was similar in effect to MIP mapping (discussed in Chapter 6), but required much less memory, since large portions of the texture map were stored only at a reduced resolution. This technique only works, however, for a fixed relationship between the observer and the object; the vantage points that comprised the carefully chosen set of scenes for this job happily admitted to such a unique optimization. This type of nonlinear texture mapping also shares something in spirit with the arbitrary texture-mapping functions used in today's morphing techniques. Figure 7.18 shows one of the views of Jupiter used in the film which benefited from this technique.

Another single-frame photograph of Gress's version of Jupiter had its vortical features marked up and encoded by Upson in the same manner as in the original test (Figure 7.19). This provided the initial flow field for the computer model of the planet's atmosphere. With this flow field, the full, high-resolution map of Jupiter, and the various tools and techniques they had built in hand, Upson was able to launch into construction of the final versions of the individual scenes. Besides cutting out planetary textures and flow fields, and setting up the

Figure 7.18
Limb of the computer-generated Jupiter, demonstrating the foreshortening that permitted nonlinear texture mapping. (Courtesy Digital Productions)

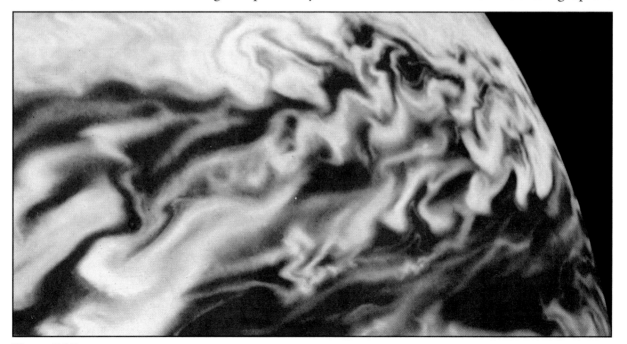

Figure 7.18

nonlinear texture mapping parameters, this even included adding a dent in the planet and superimposing a velocity sink on the flow field for special scenes involving the transformation of Jupiter (Figure 7.20).

Meanwhile, Gary Demos, David Ruhoff, and David Keller mounted a 65-mm film camera on the III film recorders then in use at Digital Productions (normally used to record 35-mm film), and integrated control over it into the final film-queue's software. And Yaeger and co-worker Mitch Wade moved the most time-consuming code—the nonlinear texture generating particle renderer—into assembly language, for speed. With this effort, and a method designed by Yaeger for simultaneously utilizing both processors of their Cray X-MP, the per-frame computation time, including the flow-field calculations, the particle rendering, and the 3-D texture-mapped imaging, was reduced to just 2 minutes per frame. Since this almost exactly matched the amount of time needed by the film recorder to paint the 4096 by 3072 pixels onto the 65-mm film, the group had achieved a well-balanced system, and no further special optimizations of the software were required.

CD 7.7

Figure 7.21 shows the digital rendering of the planet Jupiter, and a close-up view of a side of the monolith that was never afforded in the film. Movie 7-7 contains images of the planet in motion, as they were delivered to Boss Films, before integration into the film, while Movie 7-8 presents an interview with Craig Upson and Larry Yaeger discussing the techniques employed in creating the "Digital Jupiter" effect.

CD 7.8

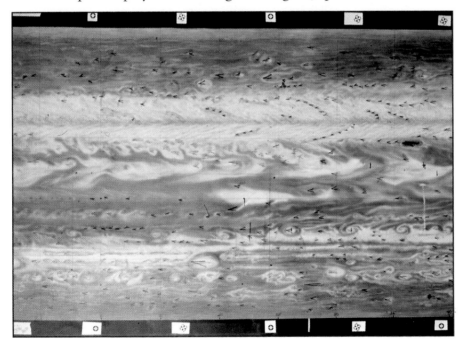

Figure 7.19

Figure 7.19
Artist-enhanced Jupiter snakeskin, with atmospheric vortical features hand-marked for encoding. (Courtesy Digital Productions)

Figure 7.20
Computer-generated Jupiter
with dent and velocity sink
to simulate the monolith-
induced implosion.
(Courtesy Digital
Productions)

Figure 7.20

Figure 7.21
Unusual view of the
monolith in orbit around
Jupiter. (Courtesy Digital
Productions)

Figure 7.21

Finally, whereas most computer animations used in film and TV have traditionally been created with high-performance Silicon Graphics machines and supercomputers, powerful personal computers are being used more and more. A very dramatic example of a particle simulation was done in *Terminator 2* using Macintoshes running *Electric Image* rendering and animation software. This is shown in Movie 7-9.

CD 7.9

Summary

Hollywood certainly has benefited from the scientific community that researched computer graphics imaging techniques over the years. But the scientific community has, likewise, benefited from the maturation of those techniques in the economic market of Hollywood. The visual aesthetics of artists in the film community have also had a positive influence on the attractiveness, and, it can be argued, to even, the information content of scientific computer graphics.

Following the work on *2010*, Digital Productions entered into a series of arrangements between the National Science Foundation, through its National Supercomputer Initiative, and individual scientists throughout the nation. These arrangements brought together a specialist from any of a variety of fields, including numerical astrophysics, radio astronomy, and meteorology, with a computer graphics specialist. Working together, they devised suitable means of visualizing the measured or simulated data captured by the scientist. Then the graphics specialist used existing tools or implemented new ones, as appropriate, to render high-quality film images of the scientist's data. This arrangement worked well, exploiting the strengths of each researcher, without requiring either to spend a lifetime mastering the other's field, and produced some striking footage of black holes, galaxies, fluids and storm weather patterns (see Figures 7.22 through 7.24, and Movies 7-10 through 7-12).

Through Digital Productions alumni—Craig Upson, Nancy St. John, Stefen Fangmeier, Matthew Arrott, and others—this approach was exported to the National Center for Supercomputer Applications (NCSA) in Champaign-Urbana, Illinois. Here explicit affiliations were set up between Larry Smarr's Art Department at the University of Illinois and the scientific visualization group at NCSA. The work that has come out of this group of people has been phenomenal, both in terms of its ability to communicate the fundamental physical processes being measured or modeled, and in terms of the beauty of those communications.

CD 7.10

CD 7.11

CD 7.12

The visualization techniques that evolved from these collaborations helped fuel an entire subfield in computer graphics: volume rendering. And as scientific visualization has grown into its own

Figure 7.22
Density contours in the vicinity of a black hole (this is essentially a detail view of Figure 6.6). (Courtesy John Hawley and Digital Productions)

Figure 7.22

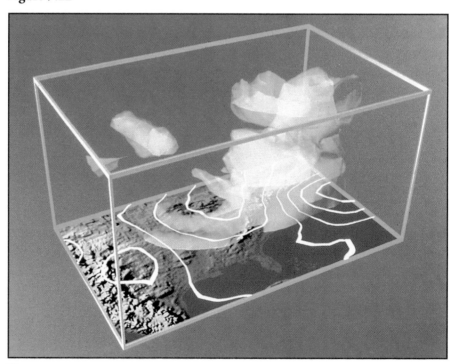

Figure 7.23
Storm wind and water-density patterns. (Courtesy Digital Productions)

Figure 7.23

domain, certain common techniques, such as volume rendering, 3-D contouring, particle rendering, color mapping, and so on, have recurred with enough frequency that standardized tools and visualization environments could begin to be considered, designed, and built.

Thus it is that tools and techniques from the scientific world coupled with a valuable filtering through the demands and aesthetics of Hollywood, gave rise to today's sophisticated levels of computer visualization of natural phenomena.

Suggested Reading

1. *Special Effects: Creating Movie Magic*, by Christopher Finch, Abbeville Press, 1984.

2. *Industrial Light & Magic, The Art of Special Effects*, by Thomas G. Smith, Ballantine Books, 1986.

3. *Enchanted Drawings: The History of Animation*, by Charles Solomon, Knopf, 1989.

4. *Cinefex*, Edited and Published by Don Shay.

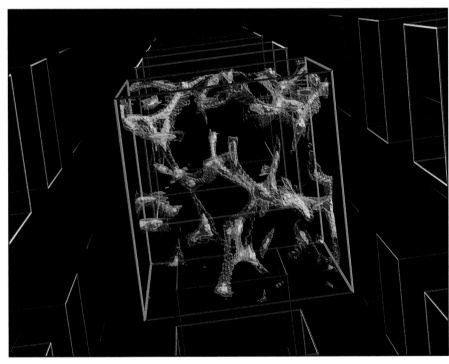

Figure 7.24
Intergalactic density contours. (Courtesy Joan Centrella and Digital Productions)

Figure 7.24

Tech Note 1

COLOR

This Tech Note explains how researchers can apply color theory to image display and the visualization of scientific data. The intent here is to convey enough information to enable scientists to use color intelligently and consistently in their data analysis, presentations, and publications. There are continual complaints by scientists about how their beautiful image of a galaxy, molecule, or simulation was ruined when they sent it in for publication or put it onto videotape. Some of this problem lies with journals that use outdated color processing technologies and procedures, or whoever produced the video for the researcher. However, the researcher can mitigate much of the difficulty by simply applying a few basic principles at the outset of the process. In principle, then, researchers should be able to produce a color image of their data on an RGB monitor, record that image to videotape, send the image to a journal for publication, and have all three versions look nearly identical under the same lighting conditions.

The Needs of the Scientist

At scientific meetings it often happens that a researcher shows a 35-mm slide transparency or a video of a particular phenomenon to make a particular point, only to have members of the audience respond, "Based on the data you just showed us, I don't see where you have much of an effect at all." An argument ensues that eventually must be broken up by the session chair. In fact, both people are probably correct, a point that usually gets lost on the audience listening to the debate. The problem is that the researcher presenting the data simply could not control the various transformations that color images undergo between media, hence an effect clearly present in the data (and probably clearly visible in the original visualization) was rendered nearly invisible by the media conversion process. In addition, depending upon things like

209

room lighting, the projection media, and the color sensitivity of the eyes of each observer, a given image could very well look entirely different in different media, even to different people in the same room.

In practice, producing a consistent image across different media is an art that takes a fair amount of knowledge and experience to do well. For the scientist, however, the process is generally a nightmare. What usually happens is that the scientist creates an image on the screen, and then either (1) shoots a 35-mm slide of it directly off the screen—either by pointing a camera directly at the monitor or using an attached screen-recording camera—or (2) creates an electronic file of the image and sends that off to a slide service (which simply creates a 35-mm slide), and then sends the slide off to the journal, or (3) sends the electronic image directly to the journal on a floppy disk or a Syquest cartridge. In the video world, the researcher generally uses whatever facilities are available (usually something jury-rigged by local lab "video-gurus") to create a video from a sequence of images. The 35-mm slide, the published image, and the video all look different from the original RGB image on the scientist's monitor and, what's worse, they all look different from each other.

To solve this problem for any environment, we need to develop some basic understanding of color theory. To begin with, color theory was designed largely for print publications of artwork, where inks and paper vary widely. Computer-generated images were an afterthought, at best. Since about 1987 (the year the Mac II was born) the desktop publishing industry has taken off, and many commercial artists now produce their work on computers. This has led to a considerable refinement (some might term it a revolution) of the entire color printing process. Thus, for example, Adobe Inc.'s Photoshop, perhaps the most popular image painting and image processing programs, has specific tables for various standard inks and papers that can be calibrated along with an image during the process of color separation (where the image is separated into its component colors for hard-copy output). This gives an author substantial control over the paper reproduction of a computer image. Photoshop also provides calibration settings that enable the artist to adjust the computer monitor for room lighting conditions—all to provide a constant color model of the image across all print and display media.

However, the scientist has very different needs than the artist. Images of scientific data are almost always tied to a specific numerical data base: a matrix of numbers, either integers or floating- point. These numbers are precise representations of data and are immutable. Thus, the scientist cares very little about monitor calibration, or the effects on the image of room lighting, so long as the significant features in the visualized data are readily discernible. The computer artist, on the other hand, is entirely tied to the visual representation of color and has little interest in the numerical values of the colors. The artist only cares that the image "looks right" both on the screen and in print.

Another problem that scientists face is the effect of the eye's nonlinearity on the perception of the relationship between data points (pixels) in an image of a data set. Thus, for example, a highly nonlinear function, or a small region of large numerical fluctuations in a data set, could get mapped into a color range—say, violet—that appears narrow to the eye. Conversely, a relatively uninteresting region in a data set could get mapped onto a wildly varying region of color space—say, orange. Hence, choosing the proper color mapping is critical to the efficacy of the data visualization.

Color Basics: Physics and Physiology

As visualization technology becomes more and more integrated with everyday research and teaching, it is important for scientists to understand the nature of images and computer graphics. Based on a fundamental grasp of the perception of color and light. In this regard, we can immediately separate out chromatic light (colored light) from achromatic light (gray-scale images). Achromatic light only has one parameter, intensity or luminance, essentially the magnitude of the flux density (photons/cm^2/s), which is a scalar quantity. The intensity is what we generally refer to as "gray-scale levels," where 0 is defined as black and 1 is defined as white. Gray-scale levels are usually discussed here in terms of number of bits deep and integer intensity levels: an 8-bit gray scale contains 256 intensity levels, for example, and a 1-bit bit-map contains two intensity levels (black and white). An 8-bit gray-scale representation of a data set must therefore assign a mapping from data space to the 256 gray-scale levels.

Another term often used is brightness. Brightness generally refers to "perceived" intensity, which is important to keep in mind when developing a mapping from data space to image space. Typically, 8 bits of gray-scale information is enough to provide the appearance of continuous tone images to the eye. However, as we mentioned in Chapter 1, many doctors and radiologists would like 12- or 16-bit gray-scale images of X-ray, CAT, and MRI scans since that is the actual dynamic range of the data. Even though 8 bits may be enough to create a continuous appearance when applied to the entire data range, when the data is scaled up to reveal artifacts in a subset of the full data range, finding subtle discontinuities in intensity or color may be a problem if the original data isn't saved at sufficient resolution. To be precise, the term brightness refers specifically to self-luminous objects, whereas the term lightness is generally applied to reflecting objects, though the distinction is not rigorously adhered to.

In traditional discussions of color, two other quantities, *hue* and *saturation*, are usually considered in addition to brightness or lightness. Hue effectively determines the dominant wavelength of the reflected or transmitted light from the object or image. Saturation refers to the difference between a given color and a gray of equal intensity. A completely saturated color consists of 100 percent of the dominant wavelength, and a partially saturated color contains some white light. White or gray light has no single dominant wavelength but is instead composed of all visible wavelengths at equal magnitudes, and hence is considered to be 0 percent saturated. Figure T1.1 shows the relationship between various concepts used in color theory.

Images produced by scientific instruments or by simulations are usually of the (R,G,B) flavor. This is somewhat of a historical accident but a major convenience for scientists, since all color computer monitors and all TV monitors have R, G, and B electron guns that excite the red, green, and blue phosphors on the display screen. The red, green, and blue emphasis derives from the *tristimulus theory* of color perception, which is based on the observation that there are three kinds of color sensors in the eye, called cones, with peak sensitivities at 440, 545, and 580 nanometers. The 440-nm peak lies in the blue range of the spectrum, and the latter two peaks are in the yellow range. Since human eyes have a peak sensitivity in the 550-nm range due to the structure of

Figure T1.1
This triangle shows the various relationships between the different terms used in color theory. Between the vertices, along each side of the triangle is a continuum—grays, color shades, and tints—while interior to the triangle are "mixes" of gray, tints, and shades of pure color.

Figure T1.2
Precise numerical relationships between different colors can be understood through this "color cube" where each vertex represents a specific color. All RGB colors can be computed from this model.

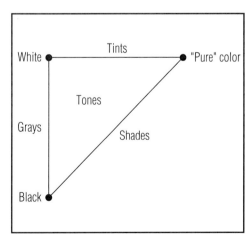

Figure T1.1

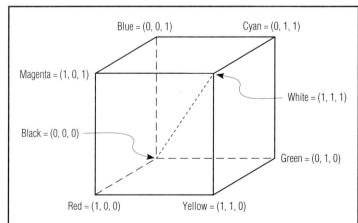

Figure T1.2

the solar spectrum, the eye's response to blue is much less than its response to red and green as defined in this manner.

This fact also means that, due to the nonlinear spectral response of the eye, certain colors cannot be made from superpositions of the three primaries. This means that certain colors that we can see in nature cannot be displayed on an RGB monitor. While this may not affect data from simulations or certain experiments very much, it is certainly conceivable that a geologist, for example, could observe a certain colorimetric phenomenon in a rock formation or volcanic lava flow and not be able to accurately reproduce it electronically.

Today color theory, and its application to print, display, and broadcast media, is a well-developed science, with many color models designed for very specific theoretical or practical purposes. Scientists need know about only three such models, all of which can be represented as a Cartesian cube. The RGB model deals with the additive primaries and is used exclusively in color computer monitors. The CMYK model (Cyan, Magenta, Yellow, blacK), essentially the complement of the RGB model, is used almost exclusively in the four-color printing process. The YIQ model, used in U.S. commercial broadcasting, restricts the range of RGB colors to those acceptable for videotape reproduction.

For monitors, RGB triples are defined in terms of the *chromaticities*, which are strictly functions of the dominant wavelength and saturation of the color and are independent of luminous energy (see Foley et al., 1990). The chromaticities are derived from the three standard primaries developed by the Commission Internationale de l'Eclairage (CIE) to match the complete range of visible colors. The CIE system allows, for example, conversion of colors between cathode-ray tubes using different phosphors with different response functions.

From the RGB space we can define the relationship between CMY and RGB as

$$\begin{bmatrix} C \\ M \\ Y \end{bmatrix} = \begin{bmatrix} 1 \\ 1 \\ 1 \end{bmatrix} - \begin{bmatrix} R \\ G \\ B \end{bmatrix},$$

$$\begin{bmatrix} R \\ G \\ B \end{bmatrix} = \begin{bmatrix} 1 \\ 1 \\ 1 \end{bmatrix} - \begin{bmatrix} C \\ M \\ Y \end{bmatrix}$$

where the unit column vector is the RGB representation of white and the CMY representation of black. Given CMY, we can then use black in place of equal amounts of C, M, and Y, according to the model

$$K = \min(C, M, Y)$$
$$C = C - K$$
$$M = M - K$$
$$Y = Y - K$$

The relationship RGB-to-CMYK is shown in the cube in Figure T1.2. It should be noted that since CMYK is designed for print media, the characteristics of the paper and the inks used to print the image must be taken into account in the transformations.

In transferring images to videotape the problem is somewhat more restricted, so the YIQ system was developed to prevent oversaturated colors from bleeding across television scan lines (for example, a set of very fine bright red flow lines on a computer monitor may end up videotaped as a red smudge across a TV screen). The RGB-to-YIQ mapping is defined as

$$\begin{bmatrix} Y \\ I \\ Q \end{bmatrix} = \begin{bmatrix} 0.299 & 0.587 & 0.144 \\ 0.596 & -0.275 & -0.321 \\ 0.212 & -0.528 & 0.311 \end{bmatrix} \begin{bmatrix} R \\ G \\ B \end{bmatrix}$$

The transformation from YIQ to RGB is given by the inverse of the previous transformation,

$$\begin{bmatrix} R \\ G \\ B \end{bmatrix} = \begin{bmatrix} 1.000 & 0.9557 & 0.6199 \\ 1.000 & -0.2716 & -0.6469 \\ 1.000 & -1.1082 & 1.7051 \end{bmatrix} \begin{bmatrix} Y \\ I \\ Q \end{bmatrix}$$

For a more detailed discussion of this problem see Foley et al. (1991), and references cited therein, or Winkler (1992).

Media Conversion Rules

In summary, unlike the artist, to whom colors are more subjective impressions than objective numerical values, the scientist usually deals with functionally defined RGB data on a computer monitor. There are some general rules to follow that will help ensure high-quality, faithful representation and reproduction of the data in any medium.

1. Make sure that your color range, as defined by the mapping of your data values to color space, visually represents the qualitative features of your data. Proper choices of dynamic ranges in the color

space, and possibly superimposed contour levels or distinct color bands corresponding to critical contour levels can help make your point. Chapter 2 and Tech Note 3 discuss some other issues relating to the imaging of floating-point data that can affect the choice of an optimal color map for displaying data.

2. For transfer to printed media, remember that your RGB data is going to be transformed to CMYK space, and that the characteristics of the ink, paper, and publication process are going to influence this transformation and the final appearance of your images. Generally the publisher will do this. However, it is possible for you to create the CMYK separations yourself in a simple one-step process with a program such as Adobe Photoshop.

3. For transfer to video, remember that your RGB data will necessarily be transformed to YIQ space. Some applications allow you to limit the saturations and hues to those displayable in NTSC/YIQ-based video. Designing your original layouts within these constraints will avoid trouble down the line.

4. Always demand test proofs of slides, prints, articles, or video before the image is published. With the current state of color calibration systems, neither you nor your publisher can possibly be aware of all the possible direct and indirect influences on image color between your original data display and its published form. But if you get a chance to see the end result of the process, and your publisher is willing to listen, it isn't difficult to say, "this is too red," "too dark," or whatever.

Tech Note 2

FUNDAMENTALS OF IMAGE PROCESSING

CD T.1

In this Tech Note we discuss the mathematics of image processing and how these techniques can be applied to images for both artistic and scientific purposes. Much of the discussion centers around discrete two-dimensional Fourier transforms and their applications, since in image processing one often manipulates not only the original array of pixels that form the image, but its spectral representation as well.

When we discuss *spatial domain*, we refer to the actual matrix of pixels composing an image that you would normally view on your monitor. All image-processing operations in the spatial domain are necessarily performed on the actual array of pixels. The term *frequency domain* refers to the matrix of numbers making up the Fourier-transformed image, and operations within that domain occur on that matrix. However, to truly understand the effect of a given transformation in Fourier space one needs to convert back to image space using the appropriate 2-D inverse transform. In commercial programs like Photoshop this conversion is done automatically and is transparent to the user.

Image Processing in the Spatial Domain

As discussed in Chapter 1, image transformations are generally referred to as filters. Because images tend to vary considerably from one region to the next, these filters are usually not conceived of as operations performed on the entire image at once. Rather, most image processing filters are constructed as small $m \times n$ matrices (m would equal n in the square-array case), called *masks* or *kernels*, that operate on a neighborhood of pixels around a given pixel with location (i,j). This neighborhood is usually referred to as a *subimage*, and the image processing proceeds by moving the transforming mask from pixel to pixel throughout the entire image. The values or weights of the mask determine the type of filter (low-pass, high-pass, bandpass, and so on). We discuss this in more detail after introducing 2-D discrete Fourier transforms.

Given a subimage of pixels,

$$I_{ij} = \begin{bmatrix} p_{11} & p_{12} & p_{13} \\ p_{21} & p_{22} & p_{23} \\ p_{31} & p_{32} & p_{33} \end{bmatrix}$$

and a 3×3 mask,

$$M_{ij} = \begin{bmatrix} m_{11} & m_{12} & m_{13} \\ m_{21} & m_{22} & m_{23} \\ m_{31} & m_{32} & m_{33} \end{bmatrix}$$

operating on pixel p_{22}, the new value of p_{22} becomes

$$p_{22}' = m_{11}p_{11} + m_{12}p_{12} + \ldots m_{32}p_{32} + m_{33}p_{33}$$

This dot-product-like computation over the area of the filter kernel is referred to as *convolution* of the kernel with the image. Though somewhat computationally expensive to apply to an entire image, it is a common method for providing a variety of image filtering tools. Shortcuts are possible in Fourier space, and some of these are discussed later in this Tech Note.

Gray-Scale Transformations

The simplest spatial transformation is obviously a 1×1 filter. In this case the transformation only depends upon the pixel being operated on and hence is by definition a gray-level or color transformation only (sometimes referred to as *point processing*). Typical gray-level transformations would be of the form

$$g' = R(g), \ g \le v$$

$$g' = S(g), \ g < v$$

where v is a particular gray-level and R and S are arbitrary functions. Such transformations would be used for effects like creating negatives (as in medical imaging) or *contrast enhancement* or *stretching*, where, for example, pixels with values below v would be darkened while those with values of v or higher would be brightened. To create a negative of an image, one simply reverses black and white. Thus, given, say, an 8-bit image ($0 \leq g \leq 255$), the negative would be formed by letting

$$g' = 255 - g.$$

Examples of negative transformations and contrast enhancement are shown in Figures T2.1 and T2.2, respectively, using Viking Orbiter images to show the dramatic effects that simple image processing can have. The image used in these examples is from Volume 5 of the Viking Planetary Data System CD-ROM, depicting the Arabia Terra region of Mars with resolution roughly 1/256 degree per pixel, or about 231 m per pixel. The original images were roughly 300×300 pixels. The imaging transformations were performed in Photoshop on a Mac IIci with 20 MB RAM and a cache card and each one took roughly a second to do. The speed of the transformation reflects the elementary calculations that gray-level transformations require. However, as we shall discover, many image processing functions can be quite computationally intensive. Figure T2.1a shows the original Viking Orbiter image, while Figure T2.1b shows the negative of that image. Notice, in particular, the difference in the crater outlines between the two images. Figure T2.1b is actually a *positive* image.

Another important aspect of an image is the distribution of pixels across gray-levels, that is, the number of pixels p that have a particular gray-level g. This discrete distribution, $p_i(g_i)$, is called a histogram, and one can view the histogram as giving an overall indication of the darkness or brightness of an image. We briefly discussed histograms in Chapter 1, where we observed that altering the contrast of an image is the same as stretching out the pixel distribution across gray-levels. Some operations on histograms, like uniform brightening or darkening, can be carried out by single-pixel spatial transformations.

An image's histogram can provide important information about that image. An image with a histogram weighted toward high gray-levels appears light whereas an image with a histogram centered around low gray-levels is dark. The width of a histogram also tells us something about an image. A narrow histogram means that there is not much dynamic range in the data. This means that there is not much contrast (difference between the lightest and darkest parts) in the image. On the other hand, a wide histogram means a large dynamic range and a fair amount of contrast in the image. In Figure T2.1c we've adjusted the

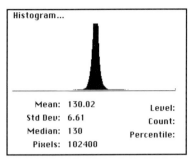

Figure T2.2a

Figure T2.1a

Figure T2.1a

An original single-channel Viking image shows faint features such as craters and possibly ancient rivers. Observe that the craters appear to be raised somewhat from the surface, indicating that this image is actually a negative. The faintness of the image is due to the small dynamic range of the data.

Figure T2.2a

This figure is the histogram of the image in Figure T2.1a. Notice how narrow the distribution is, reflecting the small dynamic range in pixel value (brightness). The numbers are the statistical attributes of the distribution of pixel values in the image.

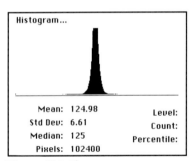

Figure T2.2b

Figure T2.1b

The negative of this image is actually the "positive" of the image. Here the craters actually appear to be depressions in the surface.

Figure T2.2b

This histogram is similar to Figure T2.2a because of the narrow dynamic range of the data. However, the histogram statistics reveal some important differences in the two images.

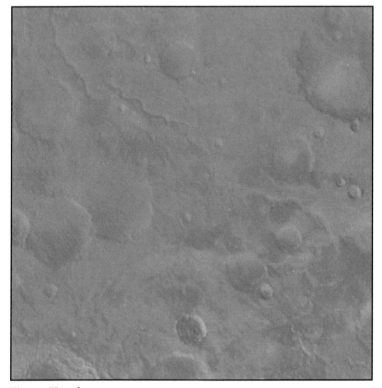

Figure T2.1b

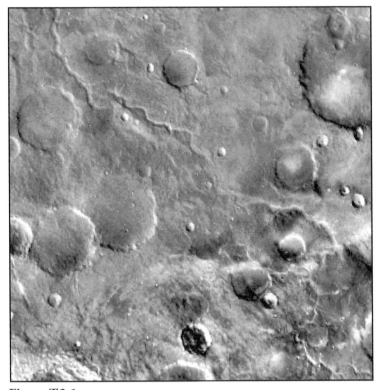

Figure T2.1c

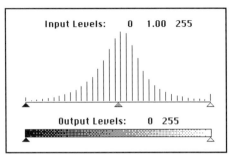

Figure T2.2c

Figure T2.1c

In this image we've adjusted the dynamic range of the image to bring out more detail in the image by distributing the gray-levels of the image.

Figure T2.2c

Histogram of Figure T2.1c. Notice how much more spread out the pixel distribution is than in Figures T2.1a,b.

Figure T2.1d

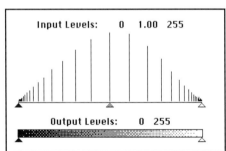

Figure T2.2d

Figure T2.1d

In this image we've applied histogram equalization to distribute the pixels more evenly across brightness values.

Figure T2.2d

This image of the histogram of Figure T2.1d shows what happens to an image under histogram equalization.

dynamic range of the image to bring out more detail in the image by distributing the gray-levels of the image, while in Figure T2.1d we've performed a histogram equalization to Figure T2.1a. Figures T2.2a–d are the respective histograms of Figures T2.1a–d.

In Figures T2.1 and T2.2 we saw that histogram equalization is an effective technique for bringing out features in an image. By definition a histogram equalization is simply a transformation of the original distribution of pixels such that the resulting histogram is more evenly distributed from black to white. In an ideal case, given an analytical, continuous distribution of the number of pixels as a function of gray level, one could define an equalization function that produced a perfectly flat histogram in which the number of pixels for each brightness level was the same. In practice, the discrete, nonanalytical nature of an image histogram means that, first, a mapping that would produce a perfectly flat histogram is difficult if not impossible to define, and, second, there are really a variety of possible mappings rather than one single obviously best mapping.

The simplest method for performing histogram equalization is based on the fact that the summation over the number of gray-levels of the number of pixels at each gray-level must equal the total number of pixels. Hence partial sums over a subset of the total number of gray-levels are naturally normalized by the total number of pixels to fall conveniently between 0 and 1. Formally, we define a scale factor s_i to be used to multiplicatively scale the brightness of all the pixels initially at gray-level i as

$$s_i = \frac{1}{n}\sum_{j=0}^{i} n_j$$

where n is the total number of pixels and n_j is the number of pixels at gray-level j. Applying s_i to all gray-levels automatically distributes pixel brightnesses over the full range of possible intensities. Histogram equalization has an effect somewhat similar to contrast stretching, but the automatic nature of histogram equalization (versus the necessity of hand-picking the point about which the stretching is to occur) makes it an attractive technique.

In practice, methods for targeting the equalization to a specified histogram and for applying the equalization subject to local constraints are used to provide even more powerful and effective image enhancement tools. For more detailed descriptions of these techniques, we refer the reader to Gonzalez and Woods's *Digital Image Processing* (1992).

2-D Discrete Fourier Transforms

One of the most powerful techniques in image processing is the use of 2-D discrete Fourier transforms to separate out information according to spatial frequencies, or the length-scales of features in an image. Frequency information is used to discern features such as discontinuities or structures (small scale, or high frequency) or gradual parameter gradients (large scale or low frequency) or background shading. Frequency, as used within the image-processing context, refers to *spatial frequency* $k = 2\pi/\lambda$, where λ is the *wavelength* of the feature. As in most analyses of waves or periodic functions, k is traditionally referred to as the *wavenumber*. In an image model, the wavenumber k actually refers to features in the image of roughly size $2\pi/k$. The basic relationship between an image and its representation in terms of frequency components is the Fourier transform. However, the Fourier transform is generally treated as a property of continuous functions. Since an image deals with discrete data, we need to look at a version of the Fourier transform that operates on discrete data. In this part of the Tech Note we outline the mathematical foundation for Fourier transforms and develop a few image-processing filters from the general theory.

To understand discrete Fourier transforms we first consider the 1-D Fourier transform of a continuous function $f(x)$, defined by the relations

$$F(k) = \int\limits_{-\infty}^{+\infty} f(x)e^{ikx}dx$$

$$f(x) = \int\limits_{-\infty}^{+\infty} F(k)e^{-ikx}dk$$

where x is a spatial variable and k is the spatial frequency or wavenumber (inverse wavelength) variable (Press et al., 1988, p. 398). The function $f(x)$ must be an integrable function, where the integral of $f(x)$ converges. $F(k)$ is by definition the Fourier transform of $f(x)$, and $f(x)$ is the inverse Fourier transform of $F(k)$. For convenience and clarity, we will adopt a shorthand notation and denote the forward Fourier transform of a function by the symbol $\Im$ and the inverse Fourier transform by $\Im^{-1}$. Thus the previous equations may also be written as

$$F(k) = \Im f(x)$$

$$f(x) = \Im^{-1}F(k)$$

Below we list some elementary properties of Fourier transforms that the reader can use for reference. In all of these, $f(x)$ is the original function and $F(k)$ is its Fourier transform, and the symbol $\Leftrightarrow$ denotes a reciprocal "implies."

$$f(x) = f(-x) \Leftrightarrow F(k) = F(-k) \qquad \text{"symmetry preservation"}$$

$$f(x) = -f(-x) \Leftrightarrow F(k) = -F(-k) \qquad \text{"anti-symmetry preservation"}$$

$$f(ax) = \Im^{-1} \frac{1}{|a|} F\left(\frac{k}{a}\right) \qquad \text{"spatial scaling"}$$

$$F(ak) = \Im \; \frac{1}{|a|} f\left(\frac{x}{a}\right) \qquad \text{"frequency scaling"}$$

$$f(x - x_o) = \Im^{-1} F(k) e^{2\pi i k x_o} \qquad \text{"spatial shifting"}$$

$$F(k - k_o) = \Im \; f(x) e^{-2\pi i k_o x} \qquad \text{"frequency shifting"}$$

The *total power* in a signal is the same whether it is computed in the time (or spatial) domain or in the frequency domain. This is called *Parseval's Theorem*, and expressed in terms of the real numbers associated with image processing can be written:

$$P = \int_{-\infty}^{+\infty} f^2(x)\, dx = \int_{-\infty}^{+\infty} F^2(k)\, dk$$

For positive frequencies and real functions $f(t)$, the power per unit

Figure T2.3a

3-D plot of $F(k,l)$ for $\{k,l\} = \{1,1\}$ illustrating the structure of the 2-D Fourier transform.

Figure T2.3b

Image of $F(k,l)$ for $\{k,l\} = \{1,1\}$

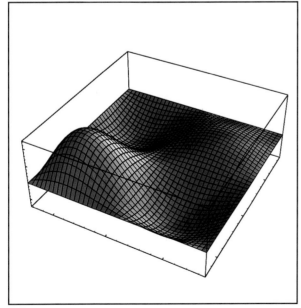

Figure T2.3a

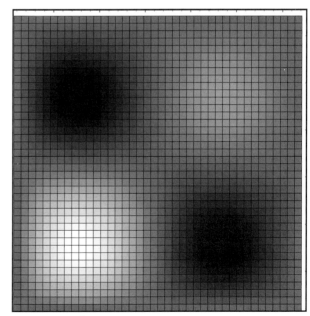

Figure T2.3b

frequency (called the power *spectral density*) is given by

$$P_f(k) = F^2(k)$$

This last equation needs to be kept in mind when we consider *aliasing* as a phenomenon in sampling theory.

For dealing with images, however, we generally need a 2-D Fourier transform, since images are best represented by matrices. Given a continuous and integrable function $f(x, y)$, the 2-D Fourier transform can be understood from the previous equations as

$$F(k, l) = \int\limits_{-\infty}^{+\infty} \int\limits_{-\infty}^{+\infty} f(x, y) e^{i(kx + ly)} dx dy$$

where k is the wavenumber in the x-direction and l is the wavenumber in the y-direction.

The 2-D Fourier transform operates over the plane the same way that the 1-D Fourier transform operates over the line, and Fourier transforms of separable functions are simply products of the Fourier transforms of the individual functions. Thus, for example, whereas the 1-D Fourier transform of a step function along the x-axis is proportional to $\sin(\pi kx)/\pi kx$ the 2-D transform of a "box" function is proportional to

$$\frac{\sin(\pi kx)}{\pi kx} \frac{\sin(\pi ly)}{\pi ly}$$

Figure T2.4a
3-D plot of $F(k, l)$ for $\{k, l\} = \{3, 3\}$

Figure T2.4b
Image of $F(k, l)$ for $\{k, l\} = \{3, 3\}$

Figures T2.3 and T2.4 show 3-D plots and images of the Fourier

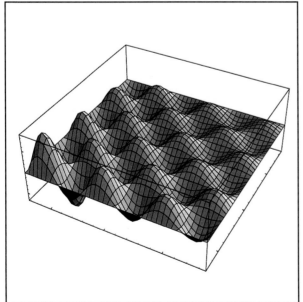

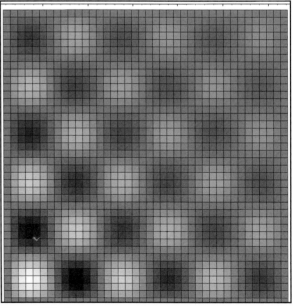

Figure T2.4a

Figure T2.4b

transform of a box function for $(k,l) = (1,1)$ and $(3,3)$. The (x,y) range is from π to 3π.

Whereas 2-D Fourier transforms are a powerful tool for analysis of the structure and periodicity of two-dimensional continuous functions, in image processing we are dealing with matrices of discrete pixels. To apply this machinery to images we need to employ the *discrete Fourier transform*, defined by

$$F(k) = \frac{1}{N}\sum_{k=0}^{N-1} f(x)e^{(ikx/N)}$$

for $k = (0, N-1)$, and

$$f(x) = \sum_{k=0}^{N-1} F(k)e^{(-ikx/N)}$$

for $x = (0, N-1)$ (Gonzalez and Woods, 1991, p. 88). The values of k in the discrete Fourier transform correspond to samples of the continuous transform at values 0, Δk, $2\Delta k$,...,$(N-1)\Delta k$, while discrete values of x simply correspond to the various sample points in our image data. In Figure T2.5 we show an approximation to a square wave obtained by successive approximations of its Fourier transform.

In the case of a matrix I_{mn}, the 2-D discrete Fourier transform pair is

$$F(k,l) = \frac{1}{MN}\sum_{k=0}^{M-1}\sum_{l=0}^{N-1} f(x,y)e^{i(kx/M+ly/N)}$$

$$f(x,y) = \sum_{k=0}^{M-1}\sum_{l=0}^{N-1} F(k,l)e^{-i(kx/M+ly/N)}$$

Figure T2.5a

Successive approximations to a square wave. Notice how each image gets closer to a square wave. Here, the single sine wave, represented by the Mathematica command: "Plot[Sin[x],{x,0,10Pi}, PlotPoints->100]" indicates the first plot of the series.

Figure T2.5b

In this plot we've added another component to the expansion, and we see the beginnings of a square wave structure. The Mathematica command to generate this is: Plot[Sin[x] + Sin[3*x]/3, {x,0,10Pi}, PlotPoints->100]

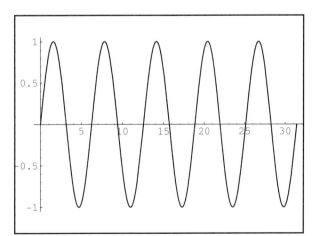

Figure T2.5a

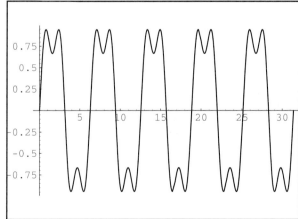

Figure T2.5b

In the same manner as the 1-D case, sampling of $f(x,y)$ occurs along a (uniform) grid at intervals of $(\Delta x, \Delta y)$. 2-D Fourier transforms have all the algebraic properties that you would expect, including distributivity, translation, rotation, scaling, and periodicity.

Finally, since derivatives are widely used in image processing as another way of highlighting small-scale features, for reference we take the 2-D Laplacian of $f(x,y)$,

$$\nabla^2 f = \frac{\partial^2}{\partial x^2} + \frac{\partial^2}{\partial y^2} f$$

and show its Fourier transform:

$$F[\nabla^2 f(x,y)] = -(2\pi)^2(k^2 + l^2)F(k,l)$$

where $F(k,l)$ is the Fourier transform of $f(x,y)$.

2-D Mask-Based Spatial Transformations

As we mentioned earlier, small filters or masks applied to neighborhoods of individual pixels are perhaps the most often used tools in standard image processing. Programs like Photoshop, for example, allow the user to specify masks of any size with complete freedom in choosing the individual mask elements, and then instantly apply them to a given image. The masks can be used as filters to highlight specific small-scale features in an image by simply selecting the feature and applying the mask. They can also be used to smooth out regions of an image where there are undesirable small-scale artifacts. Moreover, they are easy to use and require no understanding of spatial frequencies on the user's part.

Figure T2.5c
In this plot we add four more terms to the expansion with the command:
Plot[Sin[x] + Sin[3*x]/3 + Sin[5*x]/5 + Sin[7*x]/7 + Sin[9*x]/9 + Sin[11*x]/11, {x,0,5Pi}, PlotPoints->200]

Figure T2.5d
Finally, we get much closer to the square wave by computing 15 terms with the command:
Plot[Sin[x] + Sin[3*x]/3 + Sin[5*x]/5 + Sin[7*x]/7 + Sin[9*x]/9 + Sin[11*x]/11 + Sin[13*x]/13 + Sin[15*x]/15 + Sin[17*x]/17 + Sin[19*x]/19 + Sin[21*x]/21 + Sin[23*x]/23 + Sin[25*x]/25 + Sin[27*x]/27 + Sin[29*x]/29, {x,0,5Pi}, PlotPoints->400]

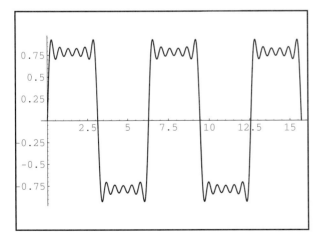

Figure T2.5c

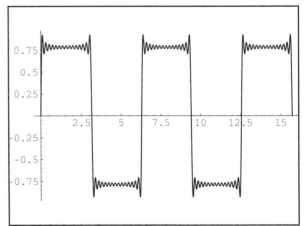

Figure T2.5d

From another perspective, however, the spatial masks actually act as filters in the frequency domain by either filtering out or enhancing high-frequency (small-scale) structures. Even though the user is not explicitly working with the Fourier components of the image, the net effect is to operate on certain frequency domains. In that regard it is instructive to understand the basic nature of filters, and the relationship between different kinds of spatial masks and the corresponding filters in the frequency domain. As a general rule, we can divide frequency filters into *low-pass*, *high-pass*, and *bandpass filters*. Each type of filter corresponds to the range of wavenumbers or frequencies that are allowed to pass through it. A low-pass filter suppresses all frequencies above a certain value, letting the low-frequency components pass, whereas a high-pass filter suppresses all frequencies below a certain value. A band-pass filter allows only a certain range (a band) of frequencies to pass through. Each of these filters is illustrated in Figure T2.6.

Let's now examine how different kinds of spatial masks correspond to the different bandpass filters. For a low-pass filter we need to construct a spatial mask to average neighboring pixels, since the process of averaging smooths out pixel-to-pixel variations (high-frequency components). Obviously, the smoothest variation will be when all elements of the mask have the same value, since then equal weights are assigned to both the pixel being recomputed and all of its neighbors. A

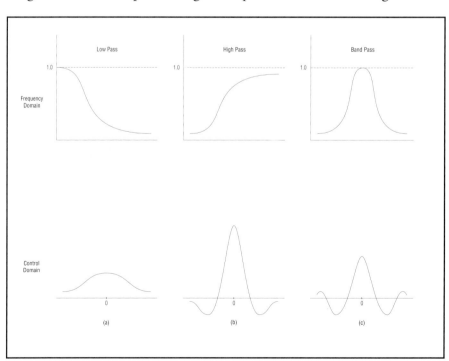

Figure T2.6
Low-pass, high-pass, and bandpass filters and their corresponding Fourier transforms.

Figure T2.6

typical low-pass filter would have all ones as the matrix elements:

$$M = \begin{bmatrix} 1 & 1 & 1 \\ 1 & 1 & 1 \\ 1 & 1 & 1 \end{bmatrix}$$

Figure T2.7 shows this filter applied to an image of vertical velocity from a numerical simulation of a severe storm. The original image is shown in Figure T2.7a, while the transformed image is shown in Figure T2.7b . Notice how the filter has effectively eliminated all small-scale structure from the image. So, for example, if we took a gray-scale image with purely local variations in contrast, a low-pass filter would simply average the entire image to a single shade of gray. One can adjust the numbers in the matrix, but the averaging process is quite powerful; for example, even if one puts zeroes in the corner elements of the matrix, not much would be different in the resulting image. The velocity image was created in Spyglass Transform from the original floating-point data and then simply copied and pasted into Photoshop via the Macintosh clipboard.

High-pass filters are designed to accentuate small-scale structures such as edges. From the previous discussion we can conjecture that to produce a high-pass frequency filter, we need to have a large difference between the matrix elements of the mask. That is, we want a mask that accentuates the differences between neighboring pixels. This is best accomplished by having negative contributions from pixels surrounding the central pixel under the mask as the mask moves pixel-by-pixel through the image. We can test this simple hypothesis by applying a high-pass filter to Figure T2.7a of the form

$$M = \begin{bmatrix} -1 & -1 & -1 \\ -1 & 8 & -1 \\ -1 & -1 & -1 \end{bmatrix}$$

Clearly, each bright pixel gets substantially enhanced over its neighbors as one moves the mask through the image. This is shown in Figure T2.7c, while Figure T2.7d shows the same filter applied to the earlier Viking Orbiter image. Notice how the contours of the velocity field are all that's visible, while in the Mars image the filter enables us to easily pick out the craters from the background.

As a final word on spatial filtering, we consider the problem of noise in an image. Noise can be from any source of bad data, and usually appears as lots of small bright spots, that is, large-amplitude, high-frequency data. One generally wants to get rid of the noise somewhere during the early phases of image processing without destroying any of the major features of the data. Obviously high-pass or bandpass

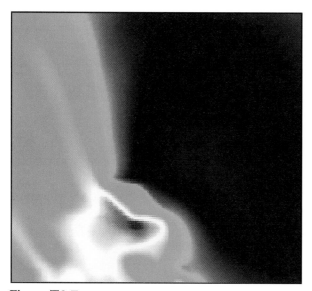

Figure T2.7a

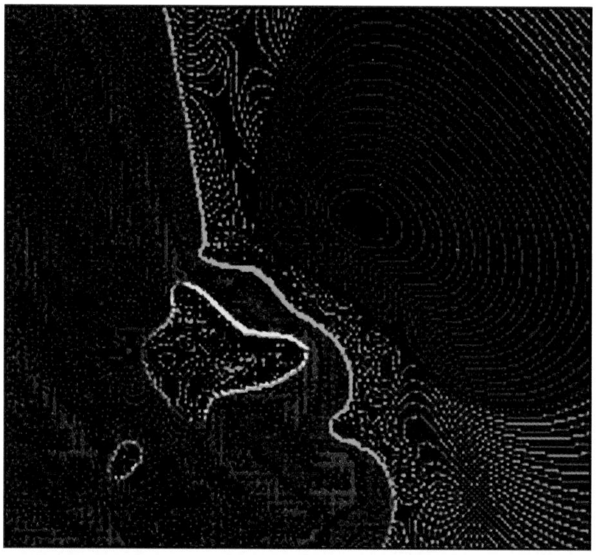

Figure T2.7c

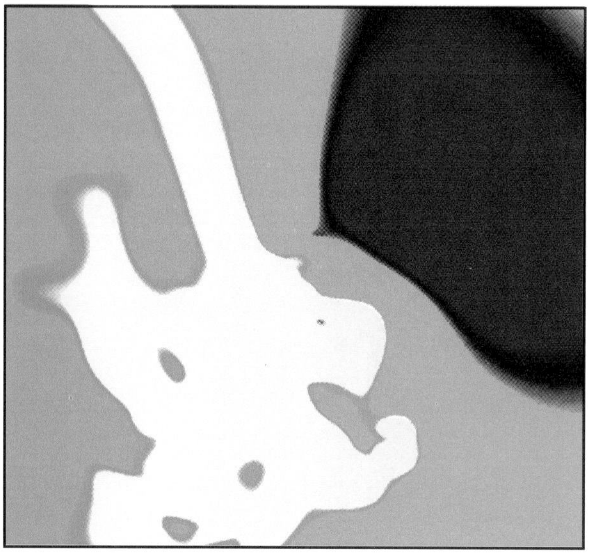

Figure T2.7b

Figure T2.7d

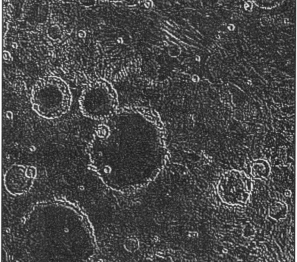

Figure T2.7a
An image of vertical velocity from a numerical simulation of a severe storm. (Courtesy Lou Wicker/NCSA)

Figure T2.7b
The same image after the low-pass mask has been applied. This type of filter has the effect of eliminating all small-scale structure from the image.

Figure T2.7c
A high-pass filter operating on Figure T2.7a. Only outlines of the main features remain visible.

Figure T2.7d
The same high-pass filter applied to the Viking Orbiter image from Figures T2.1. Only the outlines of craters remain.

filters won't do, since they would only enhance the spurious bright spots. Low-pass filters would seem, at first glance, to make sense except, as we have learned, they tend to blur sharp features rather than simply remove the noise.

One popular spatial technique for noise reduction is called a *median filter*, which replaces each pixel value with the median of the pixel values in a defined neighborhood of that pixel. In Figure T2.8 we show what happens when a median filter is applied to a noisy image. The image we chose is the Jupiter Great Red Spot image from Figure 1.2a in Chapter 1. In Figure T2.8a we added some Gaussian noise to the original image (the Gaussian simply defines the distribution of color values of the noise), while in Figure T2.8b we apply a median filter which effectively removes the noise by using values from the neighboring pixels. However, the final image will always look a bit out of focus, since we also lose edge sharpness with this approach. The user needs to be aware of the trade-offs in this context.

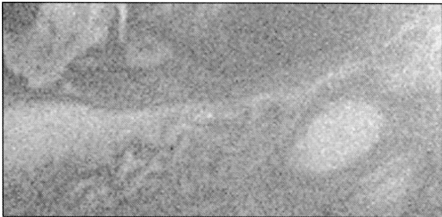

Figure T2.8a

Figure T2.8a
Gaussian noise added to the image of Jupiter's Great Red Spot in Figure 1.2a.

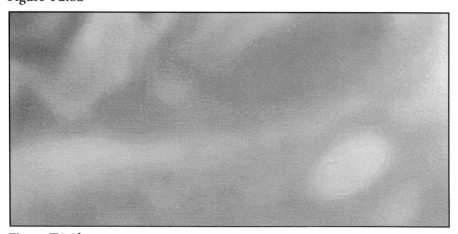

Figure T2.8b

Figure T2.8b
A median filter applied to Figure T2.6a removes the noise but also blurs the image.

Convolution

From the algebraic properties of Fourier transforms discussed previously, we can define an important relationship, convolution, which is of critical importance in image processing and data analysis. Classically, the *convolution* of two functions $f(x)$ and $g(x)$, denoted as $f(x)*g(x)$, is defined by

$$f(x)*g(x) = \int_{-\infty}^{+\infty} f(\tau)g(x-\tau)d\tau$$

where τ is an integration parameter. If we think of $f(x)$ as the signal and $g(x)$ as a filter in space, then conceptually this equation tells us that the value of the convolution at each point, x, is the integral of the product $f(x)$ with the filter $g(x)$ shifted so that its origin is at x; that is, we are applying a spatial filter to a function by moving the filter throughout the range of that function. In imaging this is the kind of spatial filtering operation that we discussed in the previous section, where the filter "slides around" the image. From the algebraic properties of the Fourier transforms of f and g we obtain $f(x)*g(x) = g(x)*f(x)$. However, the more interesting result is that $f(x)*g(x) = \Im^{-1}F(k)G(k)$; that is, the convolution of f and g can be evaluated by simply computing the product of the individual Fourier transforms of f and g. Correspondingly, taking the convolution of two Fourier transforms in the frequency domain corresponds to multiplying their inverse Fourier transforms in the spatial domain.

In this case, the filter function is generally termed the *convolution kernel*. Together these results constitute the *convolution theorem*:

$$f(x)^*g(x) = \Im^{-1}F(k)G(k)$$

$$F(k)^*G(k) = \Im\, f(x)g(x)$$

In the two-dimensional case the convolution of $f(x,y)$ and $g(x,y)$ is given by

$$f(x,y)*g(x,y) = \int_{-\infty}^{+\infty} \int_{-\infty}^{\infty} f(k,l)g(x-k,y-l)dkdl$$

and the convolution theorem in two dimensions is given by

$$f(x,y)^*g(x,y) = \Im^{-1}F(k,l)\,G(k,l)$$

$$F(k,l)^*G(k,l) = \Im\;f(x,y)\,g(x,y)$$

For image processing we use discrete convolutions, which can be written as

$$f(x,y)*g(x,y) = \sum_{k=0}^{M-1}\sum_{l=0}^{N-1}f(k,l)g(x-k,y-l)$$

where M and N are the number of points in the x- and y-directions, respectively.

Convolutions are an important aspect of image processing for a couple of reasons. First, it is often easier to develop filters in the frequency domain, and we can achieve results very easily by multiplying the filter with the Fourier transform of the image. Second, whereas the summation given above can be very computationally expensive, the convolution theorem allows us to avoid the numerical integration altogether by simply multiplying together the Fourier transforms of f and g. The trick is to get the Fourier transform calculation fast enough to be useful. Toward that objective we note that calculation is of order N^2, where N is the number of points, for ordinary Fourier transforms. However, Fourier transforms can be computed rapidly with what is known as a *Fast Fourier Transform* or FFT (Press et al., 1988, p. 386–392). FFTs vary as $N\log N$, and thus can reduce the computation time for Fourier transforms by several orders of magnitude, depending upon the size of the arrays to be transformed. Thus, for example, a normal Fourier transform computation on a 1000×1000 image would be on the order of 10^{12} computations, whereas an FFT would perform roughly 6×10^6 computations. For a 1 MFLOP computer—the kind of performance that is commonplace in today's personal computers—the FFT would take roughly 6 seconds rather than 12 hours for the normal Fourier transform.

Sampling Theory

Discrete Fourier transforms and convolution naturally lead to the concept of how a data set samples real phenomena. This is a fairly important topic, since all digitally based data analysis requires samples to be taken at (generally regular) intervals. Sampling theory also comes into play in volume visualization, as discussed in Chapter 5 and **Tech Note 11**.

In the simplest example of sampling, we can just take several measurements of a time-varying signal, $f(t)$, at regular intervals in time. Sampling in one dimension should be very familiar to most people, since modern compact disks (CDs) are based on the premise that a large enough number of measurements of an analog signal should describe the signal well enough that a listener cannot tell the difference between the original analog source and the digitally recorded tracks. In the audio domain, CD sampling rates are 44.1 kHz at 16 bits, where the first number refers to the sampling frequency while the second refers to the dynamic range of each sampled point. We explore this concept further in Chapter 4 and **Tech Note 9** when we examine sound as a data analysis tool. Since both sound and images can be described in terms of their Fourier transforms, the same principles that apply to sound sampling apply to image processing as well.

If we are given a function $q(x)$, a *sampled representation* of $q(x)$ is achieved by simply multiplying $q(x)$ by a *sampling function* $s(x)$, yielding a composite function,

$$g(x) = s(x)q(x)$$

The composite function is then used as the input data set in the convolution calculations described previously.

A sampling function is typically a discrete function with impulses occurring at regular intervals throughout the sampled function's domain and each impulse having unit amplitude. If Δx is the

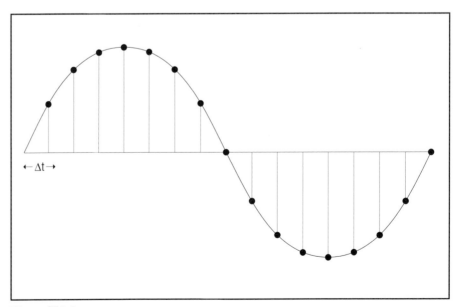

Figure T2.9
A sampled function needs to be sampled at a frequency greater than the Nyquist frequency. Here we show a typical sine wave with many samples over its wavelength.

Figure T2.9

sampling interval, the quantity $f = 1/\Delta x$ is called the *sampling frequency*. Thus, for example, if

$$q(x) = \sin\lambda x, \ (0 \le x \le X)$$

and

$$s(x) = \begin{cases} 1, & x = i\Delta x \\ 0, & elsewhere \end{cases} \quad \text{where } i = 0,1,2,...,X/\Delta x$$

then the sampled sine wave, $g(x)$, would be a discrete function with $X/\Delta x + 1$ points (Figure T2.9).

 If we consider the general case of sampling of an arbitrary function $q(x)$, it is natural to ask if there is a minimum sampling rate above which $q(x)$ is completely determined. Since any function $f(x)$ can be Fourier analyzed (decomposed in terms of sine waves), another way of looking at this issue is to sample a sine wave at different frequencies until we find a critical sampling frequency, below which the sampled sine wave does not resemble the original function. When we do these experiments, a critical frequency, the *Nyquist frequency*, arises that is defined as

$$f_N = \frac{1}{2\lambda}$$

which basically says that the critical sampling rate of a sine wave is two samples per cycle (Press et al., 1988, p. 386). If a continuous function $q(x)$ is sampled in an interval X, and is bandwidth limited to frequencies lower than f_N, then $q(x)$ is completely determined by its samples.

 This is called the *Sampling Theorem*, and it shows that the information content of a bandwidth-limited function is considerably smaller than that of a more general continuous function. On the other hand, if there are frequencies greater than f_N, that is, if the function is not bandwidth-limited to less than the Nyquist frequency, the power spectral density that lies outside of the range $-f_N < f < f_N$ is spuriously moved into this range (Press et al., 1988 p. 401). This phenomenon is called *aliasing*, and it is difficult to impossible to remove this misrepresented data from the sampled function (short of carrying out the bandwidth limiting before sampling).

 The 2-D analog of 1-D sampling follows the discussion already presented for the difference between 2-D and 1-D convolutions, except that one must remember that there are two length scales, one in the x-direction and one in the y-direction. Thus, in sampling a 2-D function or an image, Δx and Δy are determined by

$$\Delta x = \frac{L_x}{N}$$

$$\Delta y = \frac{L_y}{M}$$

where L_x and L_y are the ranges in the x- and y-directions, and N and M are the number of intervals (pixels) in the x- and y-directions. For such an image, then, the Nyquist frequencies will be given by

$$f_{N_x} = \frac{1}{2\Delta x}$$

$$f_{N_y} = \frac{1}{2\Delta y}$$

Thus when we go to produce visualizations of our scientific data, any frequencies (wavelengths) in the original data that are greater (shorter) than f_{N_x} ($2\Delta x$) in the x-dimension or f_{N_y} ($2\Delta y$) in the y-dimension will produce aliasing artifacts in the resulting image.

Tech Note 3

VISUALIZATION OF FLOATING-POINT DATA

CD T.2

In this Tech Note we discuss a rather important issue in the visualization of floating-point data: the question of the physical relevance of the resulting image. A few years ago this wasn't really a problem, since hardly anyone was visualizing their floating-point data beyond simple graphs and 2-D contour plots. However, with the rapid advances in desktop visualization technologies researchers now have tools that are considerably more powerful than mainframe-based graphics packages of a few years ago. And, as with any new technology, there's a certain danger associated with its misuse. A pretty image can be seductive to a researcher eager to publish. As a result, all too often a generally careful researcher neglects to check the *numerical* accuracy of the image to be published if it "looks" OK.

This is not always a problem since often a researcher employs a visualization technique to illustrate a particularly large effect. However, in many instances—especially when dealing with large numbers of images—"visual errors" can lead to serious misinterpretations of data. For example, the same floating point array $f(x,y)$ viewed as an 8-bit image looks different depending upon both the color table (gray-scale or RGB?) and the transform function (linear or logarithmic?) employed to map it onto color space.

Another perspective is to view the imaging of floating-point data as a fancy method of curve-fitting. Just as you would check the algorithm used to draw a straight line or a "best-fit" curve through a bunch of points, you should ascertain the validity of the visual representation of your complex data sets. This question is central to the entire visualization metaphor, but it is frequently ignored by users as well as by commercial and public-domain software developers.

The best way to illustrate this issue is by example. All the examples to follow were done with Spyglass Transform version 2.1 on the

Macintosh. Transform uses a linear scaling equation as its default color transform:

$$datarange = datamax - datamin$$
$$colorrange = colormax - colormin$$
$$colorvalue = colormin + colorrange$$
$$* (datavalue - datamin)/datarange$$

(You can transform the floating-point data within the program to effect any mapping scheme that you desire using a variety of built-in functions.) For interpolated images, where the number of datapoints does not equal the number of pixels, the color of each pixel is determined by calculating a "smoothed" data value using a bilinear interpolation method.

Figure T3.1a
An 8-bit gray-scale image of the data set in Table T3.1 with the attached palette using the default linear transform algorithm described in the text. An eight-level contour of the original floating-point data is overlaid for quantitative comparison. (Courtesy Robert Wilhelmson and Lou Wicker/NCSA)

Figure T3.1b
This image is the same floating point data, but displayed in "banded" gray-scale.

Table T3.1 Original floating-point data

-0.310	-0.300	-0.300	-0.300	-0.300
-0.290	-0.280	-0.280	-0.280	-0.270
-0.280	-0.270	-0.260	-0.260	-0.250
-0.240	-0.230	-0.220	-0.220	-0.210
-0.160	-0.140	-0.120	-0.120	-0.120
-0.050	-0.040	-0.020	-0.030	-0.040
0.000	0.010	0.020	0.010	-0.010
0.010	0.010	0.010	0.000	-0.020

Table T3.1 shows some floating-point data $\xi(x,y)$ from a simulation of vorticity by Bob Wilhelmson and Lou Wicker of NCSA. Note

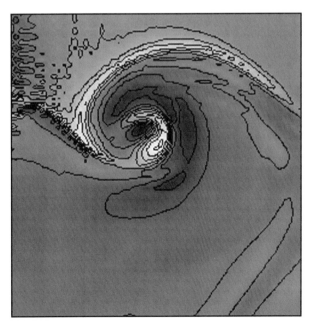

Figure T3.1a

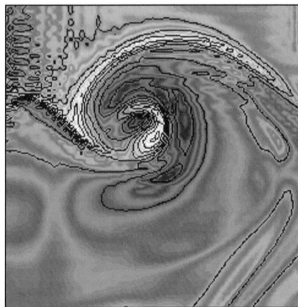

Figure T3.1b

in particular the point-to-point variation of ξ in the region shown. Figure T3.1a shows an 8-bit gray-scale image of this data set with the attached palette using the default linear transform algorithm described above. On this and all subsequent images in this example we've overlayed an 8-level contour of the original floating-point data for numerical comparison Figure T3.1b is the same floating-point data, but displayed in "banded" grayscale, while in Figure T3.1c the same data is shown transformed into a different color space.

Table T3.2 Log-transformed data

-0.509	-0.523	-0.523	-0.523	-0.523
-0.538	-0.553	-0.553	-0.553	-0.569
-0.553	-0.569	-0.585	-0.585	-0.602
-0.620	-0.638	-0.658	-0.658	-0.678
-0.796	-0.854	-0.921	-0.921	-0.921
-1.301	-1.398	-1.699	-1.523	-1.398
-INF	-2.000	-1.699	-2.000	-2.000
-2.000	-2.000	-2.000	-INF	-1.699

Table T3.2 shows the original data set transformed by log10, which allows us to study a log-transform into color space. The algorithm avoids the problem of taking the log of negative numbers:

$$\text{Newdata} = \log10(\text{abs}(\text{olddata}))$$

Figure T3.1c

Figure T3.1c
The same data shown transformed into a different color space.

Figures T3.2a and b show the corresponding banded gray-scale and color images of the new data set, respectively.

From these images and their contour overlays, the problem becomes clear: reasonably constructed images of data can yield very different interpretations of the data, depending upon how the data is transformed and displayed in color or grayscale space.

Furthermore, notice certain critical assumptions about the way that the color transform algorithm works in all of these examples:

1. *The matrix of pixels is assumed to be isomorphic to the matrix of floating-point data.* Otherwise we must invoke the interpolation function; see below for discussion on averaging.

2. *The array of floating-point data is assumed to be on a regular grid.* If the data is irregularly spaced, the image must still be a regular array of pixels, and it will usually be difficult to determine any spatial aliasing from simply studying the image. Moreover, the averaging scheme itself must reflect the nature of the grid; for example, if the grid is on some sort of affine space, the mapping must reflect the structure of that space to be meaningful.

3. *Pixel intensity or color round-off is done to the nearest integer.* This may or may not produce problems depending upon the values of the data just before the color transform occurs; for example, a linear transform of data within a narrow range will be less affected by round-off errors than a logarithmic transform of data with a large range of values.

Figure T3.2a
The banded gray-scale image of the data set formed from the transformation "Newdata = log10(abs(old-data))".

Figure T3.2b
The color image of the data set formed from the transformation "Newdata = log10(abs(old-data))".

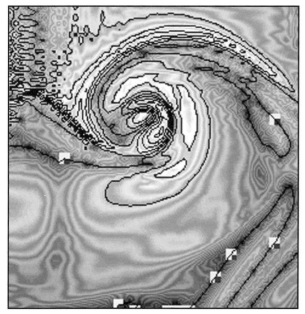

Figure T3.2a

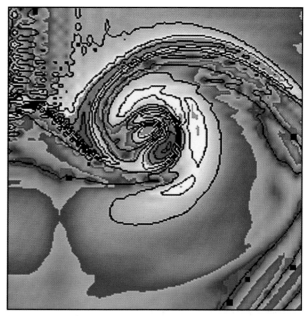

Figure T3.2b

4. *There is no automatic way of dealing with bad data values.* Thus the image could be skewed by a bad floating-point datum. This is relatively easy to deal with if the bad data value is at an extremum, but if it's stuck in the middle of your array somewhere, you'll have to explicitly determine a mechanism for handling the error.

Averaging Schemes

Let's address the question of averaging schemes in a bit more detail. Imagine a situation where the floating-point grid, $a(i,j)$, is twice as large in each dimension as the pixel grid $c(i,j)$. Thus, to produce an image we must average four floating-point numbers to produce each pixel. In the simple case of a uniform square grid, the effective grid value of the floating-point data is determined by four points.

Now, this may appear to be a simple problem, but the averaging process itself can be tricky. There are several choices, and it's not entirely obvious which one is the best for a given problem. Consider the following methods, for example, each of which makes sense by itself, but none of which commutes with any of the others. In each of these examples we use the term "effective grid point" to indicate the average of the data on the "real" grid points (the grid points on which the actual floating-point numbers were originally computed or measured) such that an effective grid point is isomorphic to a pixel.

Method 1: Average, Take Log, then Convert to Color

Define

$$\langle a \rangle(i,j) = 1/4\,[a_{11}(i,j) + a_{12}((i,j) + a_{13}(i,j) + a_{14}(i,j)]$$

$\langle a \rangle(i,j)$ is the value at the $P(i,j)$ effective grid point, formed by averaging the value of each of the four surrounding real grid points. This value is the one used to compute the color of the corresponding pixel.

$$b(i,j) = \log\langle a \rangle(i,j)$$

$$c(i,j) = \text{Color transform of } b(i,j)$$

Method 2: Take Log, Average, then Convert to Color

Define $b(i,j) = \log a(i,j)$

$$\langle b \rangle(i,j) = 1/4[b_{11}(i,j) + b_{12}(i,j) + b_{13}(i,j) + b_{14}(i,j)]$$

$$c(i,j) = \text{Color transform of } b(i,j)$$

Method 3: Take Log, Convert to Color, then Average

Define $b(i,j) = \log a(i,j)$

$c(i,j)$ = Color transform of $b(i,j)$

$\langle c \rangle(i,j) = 1/4[c_{11}(i,j) + c_{12}(i,j) + c_{13}(i,j)) + c_{14}(i,j)]$

Note that methods 2 and 3 will be the same for a linear color transform, but different for a nonlinear color transform. There is no one right way to do the averaging and color conversion, even for the simple case of a uniform grid and a gray-scale color mapping. Different software packages could use different algorithms (and different color palettes) that would produce different images from the same data set. This means that you and your collaborator across the country might reach entirely different conclusions from the same data.

This exercise should teach you to be extremely careful when publishing (or presenting) images of floating-point data. Know the numbers behind the images and arrange for the color scheme and the display, print, or projection device to accurately represent what it is that you are trying to get across. Furthermore, to back up your statements about the data you should always publish the corresponding floating-point data. Finally, if you use a commercial image display and analysis package, you should obtain the color transform algorithm from the manufacturer if you have not derived it yourself.

Tech Note 4

SINGLE-FRAME ANIMATION

This Tech Note is based upon work that Scott Stein, of Apple Computer, did in 1989–90 as part of Apple's Scientist's Workbench Project (Wolff, 1990). Here we discuss single-frame animation from the perspective of the working scientist rather than the professional video or special-effects producer. The requirements are different, both in quality and cost, and one must be careful not to "overbuy" when configuring a system for a lab or office setup. As you will see, a good system need not be very expensive.

CD T.3

The Video Mac

There are boards for personal computers that put out NTSC composite signals, allowing you to make real-time videotapes of what appears on your monitor screen. However, a researcher may have hundreds or thousands of images in a folder or directory somewhere on a hard disk. Depending upon their size, each of these images could take several seconds to display in real time, and they may or may not be time-sequences of simulations or empirical data. The researcher often needs to show the data to colleagues at other research facilities or at professional meetings. Also, some images, titles, or figures with captions may need to be displayed for several seconds. Any real-time video system is largely inadequate for this task. To videotape these data using one of the "real-time" systems involves an enormous amount of manual labor, and the results may not yield a smooth animation of the data. This problem is worsened with the increasing capabilities of researchers doing 3-D rendered animations, where each frame could take several minutes or even hours to compute.

The solution to the problem is a single-frame animation system. It is now possible to get a complete Hi-8 mm or SVHS-based single-frame animation system for less than $10,000. This Tech Note describes a low-cost single-frame animation system that has been installed and in production as a desktop animation system in a distributed computing environment at a number of sites around the United States. For a more detailed analysis of the system see Scott Stein's sidebar "Bootleg Video Project" in Wolff (1990).

The generic system, referred to as "Video Mac," consists of a Macintosh II-type or Quadra computer, a 24-bit frame buffer, a NuBus-based animation controller card, a low-end encoder/transcoder for conversion from RGB to NTSC rate video, an NTSC monitor, a local area network interface card (optional, if needed), and a low-cost SVHS or Hi-8 mm VTR system capable of doing "insert edits" (for single-frame animation). The components are not restricted to any one manufacturer (except the Mac, but obviously other computers could be used, providing there exists software and hardware for them).

One of the beauties of this system, aside from its low cost and ease of use, is that in today's commercial video market there is a great deal of flexibility allowed in choosing the brands and models of the actual component equipment used. The entire system is controlled from the Mac with an interface developed by Diaquest, Inc. This system is also scalable from a low-cost desktop system, all the way to a high-end, broadcast quality production environment. In fact, a high-end version of this system, using a Sony LVR-5000 WORM (Write-Once-Read-Many times) laserdisk recorder was used to produce *Mars Navigator* (see **Tech Note 8**). The basic Video Mac as described in the 1990 article is configured as follows:

- 1 Mac II-type or Quadra with at least 8 MB of RAM
- 1 TruVision Vista card (configured with 4 MB of RAM)
- 1 Diaquest animation controller card
- 1 TruVision VIDI/O encoder with S-VHS video I/O
- 1 JVC BRS-811U insert edit VHS/S-VHS VTR
- 1 Sony PVM 2030B monitor (with S-VHS capabilities)

Figure T4.1 is a diagram of the system, showing where the analog video and digital computer wires begin and terminate. The system is designed to support NCSA's HDF (Hierarchical Data Format) file format, as well as PICT, Targa, and raw RGB files. HDF has been adopted by NASA as the standard file format for data analysis on the Earth Observing System (EOS) Mission, which will produce about 10^{15} bits per year beginning around 1997. NCSA is using the Video Mac as a desktop animation system connected to a Convex mini-supercomputer. The bottom line is that the Video Mac system is easy to assemble and is designed to be used by the average scientist who is not expert in video technology, but needs to make videos of data for analysis, for use at scientific meetings or for teaching. Diaquest has also released QuickTime-based software that uses the Diaquest controller to read time-coded videotapes one frame at a time and digitize them (with an appropriate board) into QuickTime movies. This has the advantage of giving the best possible QuickTime movies from old videos, but at the cost of taking nearly 30 seconds per frame to digitize them.

The Single-Frame Process

The computer graphics industry has been creating animations in the form of frame sequences for many years. These sequences were always rendered one at a time and either stored on a hard disk of sufficient size or recorded directly to film or videotape. The majority of affordable computers available today cannot display 24 (or 32) bit deep images at a frame rate acceptable to give good quality full-motion video. Moreover, since the general medium of exchange is videotape, one needs to find a way of creating video from the digital images. To be able to see these images as a video at 30 frames per second, one must record each

Figure T4.1
Basic diagram of the desktop video system used for single-frame animation. The system is scalable to very high-end systems but can be configured for a very nominal price. The Macintosh controls all elements of the system and can integrate individual slides with the animated data.

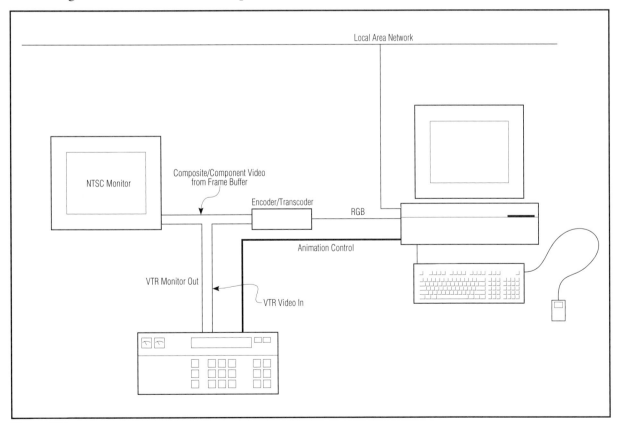

Figure T4.1

245

frame one at a time on a special video recorder. Once the master has been created, the video can be reproduced on any videocassette recorder.

In the actual process of single-frame animation, a single frame is placed on a videotape in the exact location needed to play back at proper speed. To do this, the tape must be running at 30 frames per second (30 fps). As the computer has a hard time displaying images at 30 fps, the recorder must stop after it has recorded a single image, then rewind to a point before the next frame. This is called pre-roll, and the point to which it rewinds is called the pre-roll position. During the pre-roll the next image is displayed on the frame buffer and the recorder starts forward, comes up to speed, and records the image at the next position on the tape. Most video recorders have a pre-roll of about 5 seconds to allow the tape to be at the proper speed. Over a period of time this process wears down even the most robust tape deck, so periodic maintenance and adjustment is recommended. Recently, Sony and other companies have created WORM laserdisk recorders that are capable of recording as many as 50,000 frames, each randomly addressable. Since the recording is electronic and not mechanical, these devices are many times faster as well as mechanically more robust. And the medium is not subject to wear upon playing. Hence, if the budget will permit it, such units are well recommended.

Tech Note 5

PRODUCING QUICKTIME MOOVs
by Scott Stein, Apple Computer, Inc.

CD T.4

One of the least understood parts of Apple's QuickTime architecture is the actual construction of a QuickTime movie. There are many ways this may be done, depending on what quality you are after. Also, the source material used to make the movie may come from many different formats and quality, and can greatly affect the outcome. A movie used in a published document or shown to a large audience warrants better quality. On the other hand, applications such as video mail can probably get by with considerably worse characteristics. Quality should be decided by the user based on the quality of the source, what use the movie will have, and what the target audience needs to see. Available storage space may also influence the quality used.

Making a digital movie from standard video sources is essentially the reverse of the single-frame animation process. Analog images must be grabbed one frame at a time, digitized, and placed in a file. The computer must process the current information in the frame buffer, possibly compressing the information, and store the resulting digital image on a hard disk. Depending on the "format" of the target animation file, the individual images are collected together along with display information. If the image is created by the computer itself, each image can be collected directly into the file. With QuickTime, the digitized frames need not be collected in order. The QuickTime movie format uses a system of pointers that allow interleaving for use in many interesting ways. Basic QuickTime commands allow the file to be "flattened" (put in order) for efficiency, if so required. Some frame buffers and frame-grabbing software take longer to digitize a frame than others do. Depending on the quality needed, many different methods are available to the user. The user should consider whether motion, size, or image quality may be a dominant factor.

Acceptable quality is usually determined by experimenting with settings provided by most QuickTime recording applications. QuickTime has over 100 internal settings that can vary characteristics of a digital movie. Most are for the experienced user, and require an expert understanding of the QuickTime architecture. To help the typical user, QuickTime recording applications choose optimal values for most of the parameters. The variables most often offered to the user are general image quality level, frame rate, and compression method. Each of these variables affects other parameters within QuickTime. For example, a user who finds that a movie is not playing smoothly may choose to increase the frame rate. The movie might then smooth out, but the storage required to save it to disk would likely increase. To compensate, the user might try to increase the amount of compression, but this would decrease the quality of the animation. Another example might be for the user to keep the original setting and choose a different codec (compressor-decompressor). Different compression algorithms have different quality and storage requirements. Choosing a different compression standard may not always be possible and depends on the target for the movie. There are many cases in which the user might even want to use a lossless compression method. Lossless provides the least compression and requires the greatest disk space, but provides the best quality (especially when changing to a new format without recourse to the original images) and better supports certain effects, such as scaling the movie window size.

Quality

The quality of a video recording has always depended on the type of equipment used, especially in the analog domain. Since most digital video still originates in the analog format, it is reasonable to assume that the better the equipment used, the better the QuickTime movie. We can define four basic quality levels associated with producing movies; *uncomfortable*, *acceptable*, *good*, and *best*. We will ignore the lowest level here.

An acceptable movie shows no signs of motion degradation and is clear enough for the viewer to discern all of the objects within it. There are commercially available products that simply plug into a NuBus slot of a Macintosh and do a "quick" digitization, sometimes directly into QuickTime. This method has obvious advantages in that it's simple to use and only requires a composite video signal. A camcorder, video-cassette recorder, or laserdisk can provide easy input to this type of device without any special training. On the other side of the coin, the technology required to do this type of "real time" digitization (with store) is in its infancy. Sometime frames are only partially captured and the playback unit's freeze-frame may not show an entire frame. This can be truly frustrating when trying to simply grab a single, random frame to paste into a document or some other non-QuickTime application. Moreover, the quality of the video frame itself may not be very good if the display resolution and color characteristics of the playback unit are inferior. Finally, the compression algorithm may introduce unwanted artifacts into the stored image. The extent of this problem depends on the type of codec used to process the movie; at the time of this writing, most of these fast, real-time devices use software codecs because of the high cost and limited availability of hardware-based compressors.

This method is best used for such applications as video mail, quick visualization of data, and motion previews for high-quality animations. It can also be effective for teaching and research purposes, as well as for demonstrations to colleagues and management. QuickTime movies can also be integrated into word processing documents and presentations, as well as Mathematica Notebooks and Hypercard stacks, so that you can annotate (even with voice) any animation that you've digitized. Recording live video sources through a camera is very similar to recording from a videocassette recorder and requires the real-time method in order to process the information fast enough. However, the user should be aware that a single minute of uncompressed 160×120 QuickTime video at 24-bit color at 30 fps will take over 10 MB of disk space—without sound.

Today, premium quality QuickTime movies come at higher price in both time and money. Also required is a prerecorded segment of video. The recording can be on standard videotape or any of the broadcast standards, although carrying out such higher quality digitization based on a VHS source, in particular, is probably not worth the effort. In many cases these tapes are required to have SMPTE time code, which allows the frame grabber to be synchronized with the boundaries of each frame. In fact, there are some cases where each field of a frame may be considered. Once you have this information, a precise frame grab (capture of a single frame from a video) can be made and inserted into a movie. When you are finished, you have a collection of high-quality digital images that can be compressed and manipulated for most applications.

Applications such as Apple's Grab Guy (available from Apple on the QuickTime Developer CD) create what is called a QuickTime MooV (pronounced "movie") file from a SMPTE striped source on a single-frame video recorder. Grab Guy asks the user for the start point (inpoint), finish (endpoint), quality, and play frame rate. The number of frames that need to be digitized, along with the locations on tape, are calculated. The tape deck is configured and the recording begins. The tape deck must be able to be advanced by exactly one frame. With some tape decks this can be done with a simple advance command; others must come up to speed (pre-roll) as was explained above. Using this method, the time required to digitize and process a QuickTime movie is comparable to single-frame animation, except in this case you are grabbing instead of recording. New devices such as optical WORM (Write-Once-Read-Many times) drives only require a frame advance command. Built-in digital frame buffers help to store the frame very quickly. Since the disk is always spinning, there is no pre-roll required and the laser head can seek storage tracks in the same way an audio compact disk operates. The storage of most component video WORM laserdisks can exceed 44,000 frames. The time to advance to the next frame is approximately one second. This type of device has major time-saving advantages.

So after using this single-frame method you have a fully aligned, genlocked, and synchronized digital movie that is free from the imperfections caused by misaligned or missed frames and the necessarily lower quality codecs (due to speed requirements) of realtime digitizing frame buffers. A QuickTime movie generally will not play every frame of a movie. Along the same line, not every frame needs to be recorded. A movie that is being digitized at a frame rate of 12 fps will generally only require the capturing of every second or third frame in the sequence. During display, if QuickTime finds that it is ready for the next frame and the CPU is not able to process it, a frame will be skipped. Also, if the CPU has already processed a frame and QuickTime is not ready to present the next one, that frame is displayed again. In reality, the frame is not updated, thereby allowing the QuickTime codec to catch up. This characteristic is essential to using scaleable digital video over emerging communication architectures such as ATM (Asynchronous Transfer Mode).

The next step in the quality ladder is to utilize pre- and post-processors on the video signals. With the technique described above (where the frames are fully synchronized), we may still have quality problems from the camera used to grab the video, a poor tape deck, or something else. One thing for sure is that if you put garbage in, you get garbage out. Even given a high-quality BetaCam tape, digitizing from the composite video output can produce poor results without a properly matched video-capture device. The BetaCam uses a type of component format, known as Y-R, that is unique to Sony devices. SVHS and Hi-8 mm decks use a format known as Y/C 3.58, and 3/4-inch (U-Matic SP) decks use Y/C 688. Depending on the exact model deck, you may have a choice of using RGB. Most digital computers, editing devices, switchers, and special-effects equipment have an option of using some form of component video. When composite video merges the components into one signal, there is some permanent loss of information. It follows that a composite source gives you less information than if you had used the component signal in the first place. A *transcoder* is a device that converts between formats. A *decoder* can be used to go between RGB and composite. Many transcoders have an encoder and decoder for NTSC composite video. Most digitizing frame buffers have an input for component sources. If you are considering consumer products, you might find Y/C 3.58; as you move toward more professional equipment you will have the option of most component formats. Of course, you can expect a substantial increase in cost for this expanded capability.

Suggested Reading

1. *Video Technology for Computer Graphics,* by Dean Winkler,
   ACM SIGGRAPH '92, Course Note #4, 1992.

2. *Apple's QuickTime Programmer's Manual,*
   Apple Computer, 1991.

Tech Note 6

NETWORK-BASED VISUALIZATION

by Scott Stein, Apple Computer, Inc.

Networks have become a way of life for most computer users. The scientist has been using networks to view images created on larger machines for many years. Computer-generated images have been sent to recording devices and other computers for well over a decade via basic file transfers. With compression, it is now possible to have a digital video signal whose bandwidth requirements allow real-time transport by some local area networks. The frames of the digital video are put in packets, along with information about such things as destination address, payload length, and routes. Some protocols require information used to detect errors. Packetizing video data causes additional overhead, making it harder to display. A network with a large bandwidth is not enough to produce a reasonable display at the destination if the characteristics of the network are not suitable for displaying the video in real time. The video can become jerky, and the viewer's software may be forced to drop frames and play catch-up at some later time. This is most apparent when the movie is played over a communications network that is based on CSMA (Collision Sense Multiple Access) or token rings, where the media access control layer properties prevent any use of adaptive bandwidth control.

Network Models

In a CSMA network, a server begins transmitting packets and looks for packet collisions from other sources. If a collision occurs, both transmitters must back off and try again. A unique "seed" is used in each of the network interfaces to try to balance the network retransmit times. Since it is not possible to determine when any foreign device may transmit, it is hard to guarantee the performance required to transmit time-based data. Studies have shown that it is possible to play

QuickTime videos over a quiescent 10-Mb/s Ethernet. But as the network becomes more congested, the performance of this type of network can vary dramatically.

Token ring based networks such as Fiber Distributed Data Interface (FDDI) do a better job of handling multimedia data, but only slightly. A token ring network uses a "token" to govern which of the attached nodes will transmit. When the node has finished, the token is passed to the next node. The length of time a node is permitted to keep the token is a value decided collectively by all the nodes. If a node has not finished sending all of the source data, the token must be given up anyway. In an FDDI 100-Mb/s network, the token returns relatively soon. Multimedia applications have a better chance of success mainly because of the possible order-of-magnitude increase in bandwidth. The total bandwidth used by any node is an aggregate value based on how many times the token is received and for what length of time. If an application is sensitive to the delay between transmit times (receiving the token), adding additional nodes to the ring will require the application to make adjustments (if it can). In fact, as nodes come and go, the network must be rebalanced each time. Though QuickTime MooVs do much better on this type of network, the basic problem of being able to predict and adapt to bandwidth is not solved.

One type of network that is showing great promise in moving multimedia data is Broadband Integrated Services Digital Network (B-ISDN) which defines an asynchronous transfer mode (ATM) that uses fixed "cells." The cells circulate at high speed through an ATM switch that has private channels to each node. Networks are expected to begin with 150-Mb/s bandwidth connections. It is not expected that a node will use the 150 Mb/s to run a single application; instead, many lower speed connections will be used to communicate. Since all of the cells are the same size and are circulating at the same speed, applications know exactly when the next segment of data needs to be delivered to the network interface. Before a connection to another machine is allowed, the application must make a request for a virtual circuit of sufficient bandwidth. The network figures out the virtual path and checks to see if the destination node, along with all network elements in between, can support the requirement.

Assuming the request is approved, there is a guarantee of bandwidth, and predictable performance is achieved. The application needs only to send out a "probe" to check latency, and then it can begin to place data in the cells. Other requests for service are handled on a request-by-request basis. If there is not sufficient resource to satisfy the request, the virtual circuit is not allowed. The network is therefore responsible for preventing congestion, and it disallows connections that would cause the cells to block. If the application or the network service provider permits, data can also be buffered on the receiving end during periods of network quiescence, thus further optimizing the use of network bandwidth.

Servers

The network is not the only limiting factor in the high-speed transport of multimedia data. The device that actually places the data on the network (the server) must be able to keep up with the demands of the application. Any network node has the potential to become a server. If a user creates a multimedia file that will be played directly off the user's machine, that machine becomes a server. A machine that can transmit many simultaneous multimedia files to remote clients needs to understand the characteristics of the network and must know how to recover from potential network congestion. This type of server needs large amounts of disk storage and must also have a very high speed interface to the network. It is anticipated that there will be very large servers that contain thousands of hours worth of media information. This information may come from places such as the Smithsonian Institution, large museums and libraries, or from your local elementary school. If the server is not capable of supporting its clients, it does not matter how much bandwidth is available on the network.

Server technology is seen as an important piece of the emerging multimedia delivery business. Research and development is just now beginning within the industry. Multimedia conference servers are looked at as being the most complex to develop. It is believed that for a many-to-many relationship between conference participants, some sort of composite connection must be created to reduce network traffic. Specifically, the participants would send data streams to a server. The server would then produce a single composite data stream and send it back to the participants. The server could also manage the integration of additional multimedia events such as a visualization occurring on a supercomputer located somewhere on the network. The server would need to handle delays and requests from each of the participants. At the same time, the server needs to be aware of network traffic as well as other conferences taking place on its other channels.

Tech Note 7

DETERMINING HEIGHT FROM STEREO PAIR IMAGES

In this Tech Note we show an example of how to determine the height of an object from spacecraft images, assuming only that the spacecraft's location is known exactly and that the images overlap the region of interest. The technique discussed here is a specialized solution of a more general problem and is used to illustrate the general kinds of techniques that one uses to determine this information. This general technique is particularly valuable for those cases where there is a lot of imaging data but no direct (altimeter) data.

The algorithm itself is fairly straightforward, and requires few assumptions beyond what is clearly known, although it does depend upon accurate measurements of spacecraft–target angles. The one constraining assumption, for this derivation, is that all triangles in the figures below lie in the same plane. This is not correct in the general case, but the derivation suffices to illustrate the general principle.

The key to the concept is that spacecraft positions and velocities are well known at all times through ground-station tracking. This is different from, say, an airplane flight where the plane's position is neither accurately kept nor recorded. Figure T7.1 shows the general problem, where the spacecraft positions at the times of the images are at P_1 and P_2. Note the three-dimensional nature of the problem; under the assumptions for our simplified derivation, Q_1, Q_2, P_1, and P_2 all lie in a plane (Figure T7.2). The object in question has unknown height h; however, angles ϕ_1, ϕ_2 and θ_1, θ_2 are known, since these are the angles of a normal to the camera lens that the images are taken from, as is the distance d between the spacecraft observation points.

Given these data it is relatively straightforward to develop the appropriate trigonometric relationships between the various angles shown in Figure T7.2. The derivation is given below, where the objective is to find h as a function of d and θ_k and ϕ_k.

To begin with we use Figure T7.2 to define

$$\tau = \phi_1 + \phi_2 + \theta_1 + \theta_2$$

which leads to

$$\gamma = \pi - \tau - \beta$$

We also have

$$\delta_{1a} = \frac{\pi}{2} - \phi_1; \ \delta_{1b} = \frac{\pi}{2} - \gamma; \ \delta_{2a} = \frac{\pi}{2} - \theta_1; \ \delta_{2b} = \frac{\pi}{2} - \beta$$

and $\alpha = \pi - \theta_2 - \phi_2$

From the figure we find the elementary relations

$$\frac{\sin \theta_2}{b} = \frac{\sin \phi_2}{a}, \ \frac{\sin \gamma}{b} = \frac{\sin \phi_1}{h},$$

and $\dfrac{\sin \beta}{a} = \dfrac{\sin \theta_1}{h}, \ \dfrac{\sin \alpha}{d} = \dfrac{\sin \phi_2}{a}$

which leads to

$$h = a \frac{\sin \phi_1}{\sin \gamma} \frac{\sin \theta_2}{\sin \phi_2} \text{ and } a = d \frac{\sin \phi_2}{\sin \alpha}$$

After a few substitutions we find

$$h = -d \left[\frac{\sin \phi_1 \sin \theta_2}{\sin(\theta_2 + \phi_2) \sin \gamma} \right]$$

where γ is given by

$$\gamma = \cot^{-1} \left[-\cot \tau - \frac{1}{\sin \tau} \left(\frac{\sin \phi_2 \sin \theta_1}{\sin \theta_2 \sin \phi_1} \right) \right]$$

and $\tau = \phi_1 + \phi_2 + \theta_1 + \theta_2$.

This special case illustrates the approach to computing the height of an object from overlapping images. In real applications of this technique, a similar computation would be performed at each pixel in the image pair, thus producing a terrain database at the same resolution as the original images.

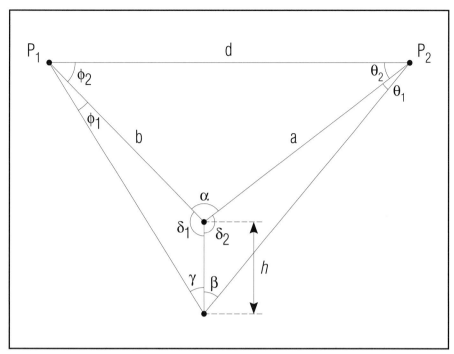

Figure T7.1

Figure T7.1
The general problem of determining height from a pair of stereo images, where the spacecraft positions at the times of the images are at P_1 and P_2. Note the 3-D nature of the problem. See text for definition of angles.

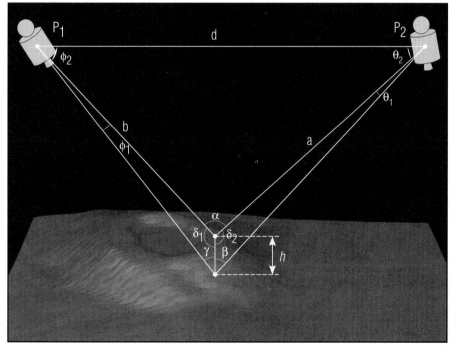

Figure T7.2

Figure T7.2
This image, adapted from Figure 3.6, illustrates the degenerate case when the top and bottom of the object under study and the spacecraft all lie in a plane.

Tech Note 8

TERRAIN RENDERER FOR MARS NAVIGATOR

by Peter Hughes, Apple Computer, Inc.

In recent times, large terrain databases have become more and more commonplace. Researchers funded by NASA and USGS deal regularly with databases in the size of hundreds of megabytes. The Earth Observing System (EOS) will send down thousands of terabytes of images and altitude data. It is important to develop tools for rapidly visualizing these large datasets. *Mars Navigator* is an interactive videodisk tour of the planet Mars sponsored by Apple Computer, which is currently on permanent display at the Technology Center of Silicon Valley in San Jose, California. The dataset used in *Mars Navigator* takes up 250 megabytes and comprises over 30 million sample points, translating to approximately 70 million polygons when triangulated.

The specialized terrain renderer, written by the author for the project is named the Barsoom renderer, after the fictional name for the planet Mars in the novels of Edgar Rice Burroughs. It is designed to produce frames for animations involving flying over terrain, and thus has several requirements to assure reasonable rendering time, image quality, and animation quality. The speed of rendering must be maximized without decreasing image quality. This isn't so critical if there are only a few frames to compute, but if there are thousands of frames, like in *Mars Navigator*, then the difference of a factor of two or four can make the difference between a few days vs. a few weeks of rendering time. Some steps taken are the use of clipping (not rendering portions of the terrain that are out of view) and adaptive subsampling (rendering more distant terrain at a lower resolution). To assure the quality of the images, several samples per pixel must be averaged together. Appropriate filtering of the images produced is required to avoid "sparkle" during an animation, and care must be taken to see that the adaptive subsampling does not cause "pops," or sudden changes in resolution.

Data Structure

To accomplish sampling based on the distance from the viewpoint, a special data structure is used called the "exponential pyramid" (Tanimoto and Pavlidis, 1975). This data structure has as its "base" a square array of data that is some power of 2 on a side. The next level of the pyramid is the same image filtered down to one-fourth the original size; that is, each level of the pyramid is one-half the dimensions of the previous level. This is shown in Figure T8.1. The data for *Mars Navigator* is divided into 256 by 256 sections called "submaps," each of which forms the base of an exponential pyramid.

Williams (1981, 1983) named the technique of adaptive subsampling "mip-mapping." Williams suggested that, besides the two texture parameters U and V, a third parameter D should be used, representing the level of resolution. D is a noninteger parameter, allowing smooth interpolation between levels. The integer part of D can be considered to be the level being accessed, while its mantissa can be considered to be a linear interpolation constant between this level and the next higher level. To extract a sample from a mip-map, bilinear

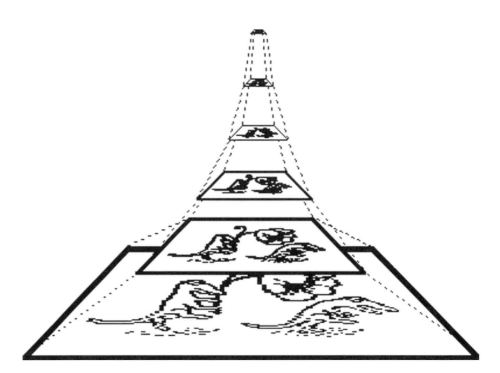

Figure T8.1
The exponential pyramid.

interpolation is used at each level to determine the sample value at the location of each sample point. The values for the levels are then linearly interpolated on the basis of D:

$$D = \log_2 \left[\frac{w}{dap} \right]$$

where w is the sample spacing at lowest level, d is the distance to submap, a is the angular width of the pixel, and p is the polygons-per-pixel parameter.

The parameter p is specified beforehand as a control on the level of precision at which the image will be drawn. Higher p specifies a higher resolution for the image. The angular size of a pixel can be approximated by dividing the image's field of view by its resolution. This careful use of interpolation thus prevents sudden changes of resolution during animation.

Filtering

To produce the higher levels of the exponential pyramid, a method of filtering must be used to convert large sections of the original data into smaller submaps. This can be done by making the value at each point in the submap (downsampled map) equal to a weighted average of a region of the original data. The weights used in this average are basically a convolution kernel. Turkowski (1988) presented a frequency-domain analysis of different filters. In a carry-over from image processing, a filter with a sharp-edged kernel produces greater high-frequency leakage, which can lead to "sparkle" in animations. In *Mars Navigator*, a trapezoidal filter was used. Other convolution kernels, such as gaussian and sine functions, produce less leakage.

Clipping

Clipping is done by comparing the coordinates of each submap to the region visible in a particular frame. If no portion of the submap falls in the visible region, the submap is not rendered. Figure T8.2 shows how clipping and adaptive subsampling might be used to render a terrain map. The figure shows a grid of submaps with the eye-point positioned near the upper left-hand corner. The visible region is between the two lines converging on the eye. For the purposes of this illustration, submaps at the lowest level of the exponential pyramid are rendered with 8 by 8 polygons. The four submaps nearest the eye are rendered at this resolution, depicted by dashed lines. Farther from the eye, the resolution falls off, thus the submaps are drawn with fewer polygons.

During the rendering of the *Mars Navigator* animations, savings from clipping and adaptive subsampling amounted to as much as 95 percent in the total amount of data required for each frame.

Fitting Submaps Together

Certain corrections are made for edge and corner points to make submaps at different levels of resolution fit together properly. This is done by forcing the edges and corners to be calculated at the lowest resolution of adjacent submaps. Consider adjacent submaps A and B shown in Figure T8.3. Submap A is at a higher resolution than submap B. Points on the edge of A will have values identical to corresponding points on submap B. These points are called "aligned edge points."

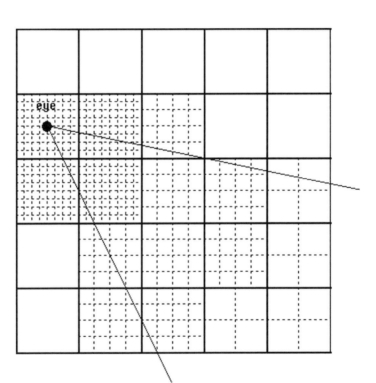

Figure T8.2
An example of clipping and adaptive subsampling.

Points on the edge of A that fall between points on B ("nonaligned edge points") will have elevation and color values interpolated between the nearest aligned edge points. Corner points are given the value appropriate to the lowest resolution submap of the four adjacent submaps (the greatest D value).

Rendering the Surface

Once the elevation and color values are calculated for every point in the submap, the height field is converted to a triangulated mesh and rendered using the Silicon Graphics GL graphics library. The polygons produced are Gouraud-shaded for smoothness and z-buffered for hidden surface removal (see Chapter 6 and **Tech Notes 14** and **15** for definitions). A lighting model can be used to shade the terrain produced. For the Mars terrain data, a lighting model is not required,

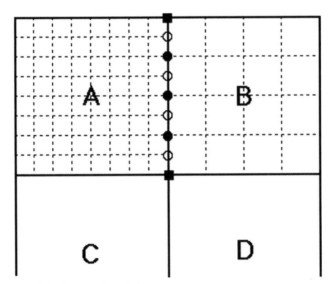

- Interior sample points
- Aligned edge points
- Non-aligned edge points
- Corner points

Figure T8.3
How the Barsoom renderer classifies points on the edge of submaps.

since the data are obtained photographically and already contain lighting information.

Efficiency

Rendering every polygon in the terrain would imply an algorithm of order n^2, where n is the number of samples in one dimension (and the terrain is square). The Barsoom renderer also uses an algorithm of this order since for an enormous terrain, the most distant submaps would be subsampled to their lowest resolution. Despite this performance in the asymptotic case, the performance of the Barsoom renderer is effectively order $\log n$ in the range of terrain sizes expected today, and far beyond (Hughes, 1991). This is because the renderer downsamples terrain by a factor proportional to the square of the logarithm of the distance from the camera.

Rendering Details

The Mars terrain was rendered at a resolution of 1280×972, then postfiltered to 640×486 (video resolution), using a Gaussian filter. This method provided effectively four samples per pixel. Rendering time for the terrain (not including postfiltering) was about one minute per frame using a Silicon Graphics VGX machine. A terrain image of western Valles Marinaris for *Mars Navigator* created with the Barsoom renderer is shown in Figure T8.4. The image perspective is looking westward toward Tharsis Montes.

Figure T8.5 takes this concept a bit further, showing a fictional, terraformed Mars with a planetwide ocean 1 km deep. The ocean is colored blue, while most of the rest of the planet is colored green except for the high mountains and volcanoes, which retain their natural reddish color.

Figure T8.4

Figure T8.4
The Mars terrain was rendered at a resolution of 1280 × 972, then postfiltered to 640 × 486 (video resolution), using a Gaussian filter. This method provided effectively four samples per pixel. The terrain image of Western Valles Marinaris for Mars Navigator created with the Barsoom renderer is shown here. The image perspective is looking westward toward Tharsis Montes.

Figure T8.5

CD T.5

Figure T8.5
This image uses the rendered terrain to show a fictional, "terra-formed" Mars with a 1-km deep planetwide ocean.

Tech Note 9

SPLINES AND KEY-FRAME ANIMATION

In this Tech Note we briefly describe the nature of splines and how this mathematical technique is used in determining a smooth 3-D animation from a set of key-frames. A 3-D animation generally consists of one or more structures along with a single camera through which the viewer is looking and one or more light sources. All of these entities are free to rotate and translate in space. As a general rule, for scientific visualization purposes we like to keep moving things to a minimum. This means that (1) all light sources are fixed in space, (2) all objects move in predictable trajectories, and (3) the camera is either fixed or moves with one of the objects (such as a simulated spacecraft). These simplifications reflect the axiom that *the objective of most visualizations is to communicate information, not to dazzle the viewer.* For motion picture special effects, however, the objective is often to dazzle the viewer, so it is often the case that the more moving objects the merrier.

Splines are a way of smoothly fitting a curve to a fixed number of points in 2-, 3-, or *n*-dimensional space. There are two general kinds of splines: that those that actually touch all of the control points and those which use the control points as a polygonal approximation of the curve. When splines are used to animate objects, the control points are the key-frames of the animation, and the general problem that splines attempt to solve is to create smooth motion between the points. In addition, splines can be used to create smooth surfaces over a polygonal mesh, as well as to simulate gradual deformations of solid bodies (see Chapter 6 and **Tech Note 14**). Because of their general utility in a variety of applications, the literature on splines is extensive, going back more than 50 years (see Foley et al., 1990; pp. 478–531; Bartels et al., 1987, and references cited therein; also, see ACM SIGGRAPH course notes in any year). A brief, but particularly well-written discussion of splines is in Rogers and Adams's *Mathematical Elements for Computer Graphics* (1990, pp. 247–378).

For our purposes we only need to briefly describe the basic concepts of splines. Moreover, with the growing sophistication of animation software, for most scientific applications all splining is transparent to the user. The user simply sets key-frames to specify the overall flow of movement in the animation, and then the computer fills in the "in-between" frames as we described in Chapter 3 (Figure T9.1). An exception to this technique is needed for objects that are driven by simulation results or empirical measurements. Their animation needs to bypass or override the spline-based key-frame animation system by specifying the object positions at each frame. In some animation systems it may be necessary to kludge an override by specifying a key-frame at every frame.

In a simple model where we have key-frames at points P_1 and P_2 (Figure T9.1), we can obviously draw a straight line between them. However, to go to point P_3 we'd have to make a sharp turn. This is not acceptable since it induces a discontinuity in the motion. What we do, instead, is construct a spline curve that smoothly interpolates between the points, creating the effect of smooth motion. Originally, splines were flexible design tools used by boatbuilders to help them create complex boat hull shapes.

Splines are actually parametric curves, and we can understand the basic theory by considering a parametric function in 3-space, $Q(t) = [x(t), y(t), z(t)]$. From a geometric perspective, one can define the tangent, normal, and binormal vectors based on the parametric representation, and from there develop curvature and other differential geometric properties of the system. In the context of the key-frame problem, we actually have curve *segments* between each pair of

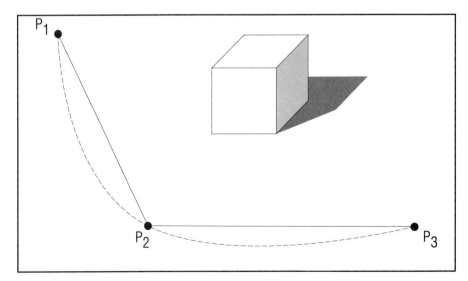

Figure T9.1
A simple model of a spline around an object where we have key-frames at points P_1 and P_2. To get to point P_3 smoothly we need to create a curve (spline) that avoids sharp turns.

key-frames. Mathematically, then, for each curve segment, constraints can be placed on the values of the endpoints of the segment, its tangent, normal and bi-normal vectors (the binormal is defined from the cross-product of the tangent and normal vectors), and the continuity (the derivatives at the endpoints) between adjoining segments. Each key-frame can be considered to be a *control point* of the curve (Figure T9.2).

Splines between key-frames are continuous in their first and second derivatives at the points where they join, although they do not have to actually intersect the key-frames. Types of splines talked about in the general literature are uniform B-splines, nonuniform B-splines, and β-splines. Other curves often used in computer graphic literature are *Hermite* curves, defined by constraints on the two endpoints of the curve and the corresponding tangent vectors; and Bezier curves, which are defined by the endpoints and two other control points not on the curve.

The advantage of using splines in key-frame animation is that they are based on connecting curve segments, rather than attempting to define a continuous curve through space. Thus, they allow one to smoothly connect key-frames to form a smooth animation. However, if a camera or object moves too abruptly in a particular direction, the spline can "break" and the in-between frames lose their sense of continuity. This often leads to rather chaotic animation sequences, where objects spin out of control or suddenly speed up to warp factor 8. In the 3-D animations supplied with this text, some are flawless, but others have errors in the motion splines of either the subject of the animation or the camera. See if you can spot any (Hint: look at the movement of the "creatures" in *Tourists*).

CD T.6

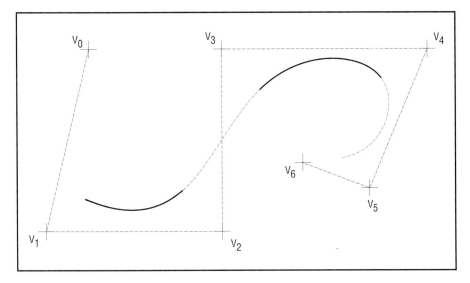

Figure T9.2
A 2-D spline connecting several key-frames together. Each of the key-frames can be considered to be a control point of the curve, and the resultant motion of the object is interpolated between the key-frames.

Tech Note 10

SONIFICATION

As we discussed in Chapter 4, one problem that researchers constantly face in attempting to visualize complex systems is that they run out of visualization techniques since there are generally many more parameters than there are distinct ways of collectively showing the data. As an example, consider a time-dependent 2-D gasdynamic or atmospheric data set. Typical parameters to be visualized simultaneously include density (scalar), pressure (treated as scalar), and velocity (vector). We could use color for density, contours for pressure, and vectors for velocity (Figure T10.1). Time-dependence can easily be handled through animation. This is fine so far, but consider what to do if we were interested in, say, composition in a multispecies fluid. We could possibly use height or transparency, but the visual image is already too

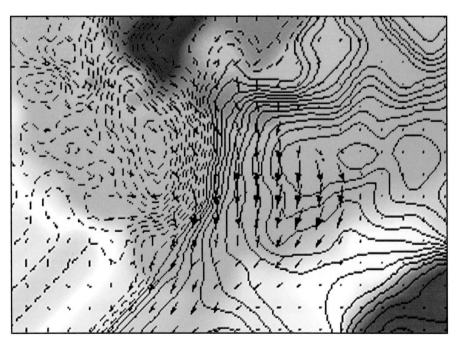

Figure T10.1
This image of velocity (arrows), temperature (color) and pressure (contours) shows the general problem of attempting to visualize too many different types of data on a single image. Sound can be a useful and interactive way of exploring a multiple parameter data set. (Courtesy Brand Fortner, Spyglass, Inc.)

cluttered for the eye to pick out specific features. Any more visual information would do more to confuse than to elucidate the problem. An interesting solution that has appeared recently is the use of sound as an exploratory "visualization" tool.

Although a number of people have studied sound as an analysis tool for over a decade (Bly, 1982; Buxton, 1989; Lunney and Morrison, 1981; Mezrich et al., 1984; Yeung, 1980), only within the last couple of years has the technology evolved to the point where it could be considered useful for scientific data analysis. One of the first examples of using sound as an analysis tool was in 1979, when Fred Scarf of TRW, principal investigator of the Voyager Plasma Wave Experiment, used an 8-bit, 8-channel synthesizer attached to an Apple II computer to translate the 8-channel plasma wave data into audible sounds. Since the frequencies of the AC electric fields were in the audio range, it was straightforward to map each spectral channel to a particular synthesized frequency range. The results were extremely enlightening, and certain types of wave structures, such as ion-cyclotron waves, whistlers and electron plasma waves, had definite audio signatures that could be easily picked out from the general background noise. Moreover, well-defined events, such as the crossing of the Earth's bowshock (the boundary region that separates space dominated by the Earth's magnetic field from

Figure T10.2

This is a frequency-time spectrogram (image) of a sound, where frequency band is on the *y*-axis and time is on the *x*-axis. Gray-level represents intensity, with darker being more intense. Notice how certain features are apparent in the image.

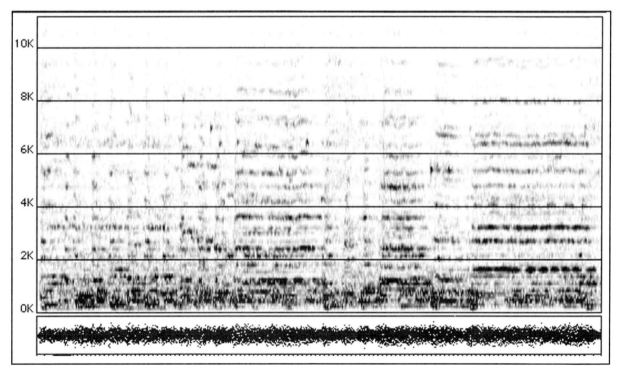

Figure T10.2

that dominated by the solar wind), could be picked out by their distinct audio signatures.

Frequency-Time Spectrograms

Frequency-time spectrograms are standard analysis tools today for analog signal data, and in Figure T10.2 we show a typical frequency-time spectrogram from sampled sound. The data was obtained by digitizing an analog sound source at 22 kHz (that is, 22,000 samples per second) at 8-bit resolution. The y-axis of the spectrogram represents frequency and ranges from zero to 11 kHz. At each point in time a given frequency has a particular amplitude which is represented by a gray-level from zero to 255. As with other time-series data, Nyquist criteria and dynamic range affect the accuracy of the digital representation of the analog data.

Although the Voyager data was very popular at press briefings and presentations, the plasma wave audio analysis remained primarily a curiosity and was not really used for mainstream data analysis. The one exception to this perhaps is the 1981 analysis of the Voyager 2 crossing of the Saturn ring-plane. At the time there was a general concern about the possibility that the dense micrometeoroid (micron-sized meteoroids) environment close to the planet could damage the spacecraft as it moved through Saturn's ring-plane at a relative velocity of several tens of kilometers per second.

During this period there were some strange events observed, but nothing that specifically pinpointed micrometeoroids as the culprits, until Scarf and co-workers listened to the plasma waves. Theory indicated that micrometeoroids inside the main ring structure were charged negatively due to the plasma embedded in Saturn's magnetosphere. The number of electrons per particle, depending upon the radius and the conductivity of the micrometeoroid, was in the range of several hundred to several thousand electrons per particle. If a micrometeoroid with these properties hit the spacecraft, it seemed reasonable that the electrons would splatter, emitting copious electromagnetic waves in the process. Unfortunately there was so much noise in the visual data that nothing could be ascertained. However, when Scarf played the audio data a very clear "machine-gun" sound could be heard that was precisely correlated with the few seconds that the spacecraft spent in the region of greatest dust concentration.

Despite this success, sonification of data never really took hold in the space sciences community, most likely because of the general difficulty of putting together a production-level system. Another issue, perhaps more fundamental, was that sound seemed to be applicable only to time-series data such as the plasma wave data from Voyager. And, for the most part, time-series data is more efficiently analyzed by studying a single image of all of the data in a frequency-time spectrogram, rather than by listening serially to a sonic representation of the data over a period of time, especially when that period of time could be hours.

MIDI, Electronic Music, and Scientific Computing

In 1986 electronic music had begun to take hold, and the Musical Instrument Digital Interface (MIDI) specification that had been developed a couple of years earlier to allow performance data to be transferred between different manufacturers' instruments was suddenly being used for all sorts of strange music-computing activities. In essence, MIDI allows a Postscript-like code to represent certain attributes of a particular sound as it is played on a MIDI-equipped musical instrument. With MIDI, an individual can sit at a keyboard and compose a piece of music, recording the precise sequence of all the sound characteristics of a variety of electronic instruments (timbre), as well as keystrokes, pressure, velocity, and nuances of the performance data, and have nearly the precise piece played back anytime later by a computer or dedicated MIDI hardware sequencer attached to the system. MIDI has proved to be a major advance in music technology and is now a standard in music performance and production.

The MIDI concept seemed to have potential for interactive data analysis, especially since personal computers could interface to MIDI instruments. Moreover, in contrast to the sampled data problem, where significant computation is required to digitize and play a data set, MIDI allowed many sounds to be played at once. Within this context one could imagine using MIDI-based sound as an "exploratory" tool to study multispectral data. The idea is, basically, that one could employ a mouse or other gesture-device to roam over a multispectral image-based data set that had mineralogical data embedded under an image or a terrain-rendering of a particular region, much the same as a doctor uses a stethoscope to listen for abnormal sounds in a patient's body. Under this "multispectral audiolization" scheme, each mineral would have its own unique acoustic signature, with timbre, amplitude, and pitch indicating relative abundance. The acoustic signature would be isomorphically mapped to the mineral's spectral signature. In this scenario the researcher would act as sort of an explorer, poking at different pixels or regions of pixels with a mouse or cursor and evoking various sounds, depending upon the characteristics of the underlying data. The same method could obviously be used with digitized sound as with Scarf's plasma wave data. However, for real-time interaction with multiple sounds one needs considerably more computing power than is available in today's desktop computers.

Currently there are a number of efforts underway to use sound as a visualization and analysis tool. Two such environments are discussed below, one being developed by Theo Gray at Wolfram Research as part of his work on digitized sound in Mathematica 2.x (Wolfram, 1991) and the other, based on MIDI, being researched by Stuart Smith and Georges G. Grinstein in the Computer Science Department at University of Lowell, in Lowell, Mass.

Sound in Mathematica

Gray's work evolved out of an interest to provide richer capabilities to Mathematica-produced Postscript graphics. The first version, released with the Mathematica 2.x front-end for the Mac and NeXT, allowed one to aurally encode data or mathematical expressions in a manner very similar to the spectrogram-style linear sound structure shown in Figure T10.2. To audiolize a function $f(t)$, users type in a brief Mathematica command of the form "**Play[f, {t, tmin, tmax}]**", and on evaluation, Mathematica plays a sound whose amplitude is given by f as a function of time in seconds between "tmin" and "tmax." This command also produces a graphic that displays an approximation of the sound's waveform. When Mathematica actually plays a sound, its amplitude is sampled a certain number of times per second and then output through the sound hardware and the digital-to-analog converters on the computer. Recall that the Nyquist theorem requires roughly a $2f$ sampling rate to sample a frequency f so, for example, if we wanted to play a 10-kHz tone we would have to sample the signal at a minimum of 20 kHz. Obvious applications of this approach to sonification include data analysis and mathematics for visually impaired people, and general mathematics education in the high-school and university environments. Just for fun, in Figure T10.3 we've computed a "futuristic" sound in Mathematica with the command:
"**Play[Sin[1000*t*(1+0.1*Exp[-5*t] *Sin[1234*t])], {t,0,2}]**".
To play a list of data (rather than a function) the Mathematica command is "**ListPlay**" instead of "**Play**."

Gray is currently working on extending this metaphor to arbitrary-dimensional data, wherein one could aurally encode information to specific visual properties of the data. However, limitations in real-world applications of this technique include CPU speed and memory, as well as the number of sounds, or timbres per pixel, that one could practically accommodate. Right now each pixel, or Postscript polygon, can generate a single tone. This is fine for a single nonvisible parameter assigned to a given pixel. However, in the general case one would need a multitimbral sound output capability. This requires a more elaborate hardware setup that is unlikely to be available on a mass scale for some time. Nevertheless, the advantages of this simple system are that one could encode data with aural information, include it in a compound document (one containing text, data, images, animations, and sound), and put it on a file server for colleagues or students—and do it all with standard hardware in a Macintosh or NeXT environment. A Mathematica notebook on sound is included on the CD, where we've computed a variety of sounds in one dimension, as well as a couple of 2-D test cases from Gray's work.

Exvis

A completely different approach to sonification is being taken by Stuart Smith, Georges Grinstein, and co-workers at the University of Lowell (Smith et al., 1990) as part of the *Exploratory Visualization* (Exvis) project, a multidisciplinary effort to develop new ways to explore

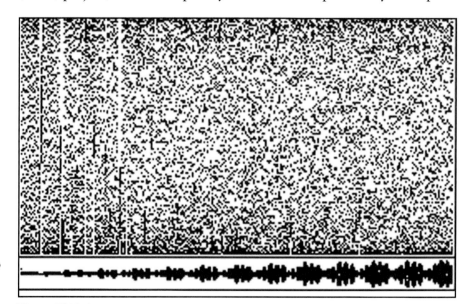

Figure T10.3
A Mathematica generated sound, with the command:
Play[Sin[1000*t*(1+0.1*Exp[-5*t] *Sin[1234*t])],
{t,0,2}].

Figure T10.3

and analyze multidimensional data. (The general Exvis project was briefly described in Chapter 4.) The Lowell effort in sonification solves the multitimbral problem by using external sound generation MIDI boxes. The Lowell effort is geared toward studying the psychophysical basis of using sound as a medium to present data, an approach that has strong human-interface considerations as well. Within this context one can explore those properties of sound that would be of value as data attributes. Smith's group discovered that, in addition to pitch and amplitude, other sound attributes that can be manipulated independently are the attack and decay rates. The human ear is particularly sensitive to attack rates, and short-attack-rate instruments such as the piano are perceived entirely differently than long-attack-rate instruments such as the violin. By employing MIDI devices rather than relying on the internal sound-generation capabilities of a particular computer, the Lowell researchers are able to map complex data variations into a multi-timbral aural space, and thus maintain a rich relationship between the properties of a given data set and their corresponding sonic representations. To go this route, one must have external MIDI sound-generation hardware, as well as some expertise in this rather arcane medium.

Tech Note 11

RENDERING IMAGES OF VOLUMES OF COMPOSITE MATERIALS

This Tech Note outlines a method, first described by Drebin et al. (1988), for rendering images of volumes containing a mixture of known materials. Such a method is particularly useful in medical imaging applications, where there are large gradients between the different substances of the patient's body and where the properties of different tissues are well known. In this approach, one first quantifies the original data set according to the percentage of each substance present in a given volume element, or *voxel*. The method then assigns each substance an averaged material density, color, and opacity value, which are subsequently used to determine volumetric density gradients and shading properties of each voxel. This yields highly accurate visualizations of heterogeneous materials in biomedical and physical systems. Other methods of volume visualization are discussed in **Tech Notes 12** and **13**.

Since the assignation of materials to voxels is not completely deterministic, a probabilistic method for estimating these parameters is used that relies on certain assumptions about the signatures of the different possible materials in the sample. This is conceptually very similar to a multispectral geological image where the observer has detailed observations of the entire spectrum, but there is no knowledge of the relative composition of the surface soil and rock.

Discussion of the Method

In the following discussion we employ notation consistent with Drebin et al. (1988). In the general case where the precise composition of a given voxel is unknown, one makes certain assumptions in order to obtain an approximate distribution of materials. When presented with this problem the choices are basically two:

1. Assume a binary classification for each substance in a given voxel based on the value of the voxel; that is, either a voxel is composed entirely of a given substance or there is none of the substance present.

2. Compute the best estimate of the percentage of each substance within the voxel and recognize that there will be unavoidable error with this method.

To solve this problem, Drebin et al. used a probabilistic classifier,

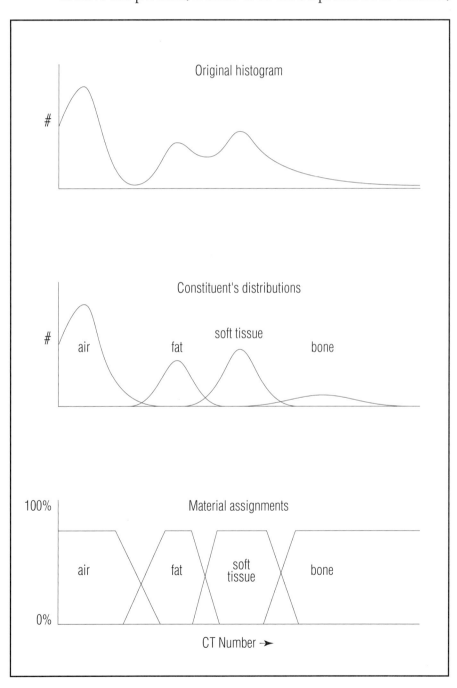

Figure T11.1
The distribution of materials across CT-number (after Drebin et al., 1988). (Courtesy Robert Drebin and Pixar, Inc.)

which assumes a mixture of materials to model the percentages of different substances that make up a histogram. The critical notion here is that, for nearly all biomedical data sets, a given voxel will contain at most two substances, provided the volumetric data samples are acquired with sufficient resolution. Moreover, if we then consider that different materials are of distinctly different densities, we can apply that knowledge to the probabilistic classifier to estimate material percentages. Once material percentages are available, volume data corresponding to other properties can be easily computed. This is shown in Figure T11.1, where the distribution across computer tomography number can be represented by

$$P(I) = \sum_{i=1}^{n} p_i P_i(I)$$

where n is the number of materials present in the volume, p_i is the percentage of material i in a given voxel, and $P_i(I)$ is the probability that material i has the value I. The total material density of a voxel can thus be written as

$$D = \sum_{i=1}^{n} p_i \rho_i$$

where D is the total density of a voxel, and ρ_i is the density assigned to material i.

Prior to rendering the image, the surface structure within the volume of voxels needs to be calculated. A surface exists within the volume when two materials meet at an interface. A surface has both a normal vector and a tangent plane at the point where the normal vector intersects the surface. The three components of the surface normal vector are computed from

$$N_x = \nabla_x D$$
$$N_y = \nabla_y D$$
$$N_z = \nabla_z D$$

A surface *strength* is also defined by both the magnitude of the gradient and the thickness of the transition region between materials. The larger the gradient and the sharper the transition, the greater the surface strength.

CD T.7

Application of the Method

Figures T11.2 to T11.6 illustrate the different steps in the complete algorithm for CT data. The same basic idea can be applied to other volumetric data sets.

1. Figure T11.2 takes the histogram of the original data set and decomposes it into its basic components of fat, tissue, and bone according to the (estimated) value of the CT data. This is somewhat arbitrary, based on a priori assumptions of the composition of the data. This process is termed the *material mapping*.

2. Next, the material mapping is converted to the *voxel properties* color and opacity (Figure T11.3) and actual density. The color and opacity are found from

$$C = \sum_{i=1}^{n} p_i C_i$$

where C_i is the effective color associated with material i (actually the product of color and opacity), and the p_i are defined, as before, as the percentage of the ith material in a given voxel.

3. The density is then used to compute the gradients to the data (Figure T11.4), while the color and opacity are used to calculate the shading of each voxel.

4. Figure T11.5 takes the density mapping and further separates it into gradient and surface magnitude.

5. Figure T11.5 also takes color/opacity, gradient, and surface magnitude and combines them to make a shaded volume.

6. Finally, in Figure T11.6, the shaded volume is rotated and projected and the image computed.

Figure T11.2

One first takes the histogram of the original data set and decomposes it into its basic components of fat (bottom right), tissue (bottom center) and bone (bottom left) according to the (estimated) value of the CT data. (Courtesy Robert Drebin and Pixar, Inc.)

Figure T11.3

The material mapping is then converted to the voxel properties color and opacity (bottom left image) and actual density (bottom right image). (Courtesy Robert Drebin and Pixar, Inc.)

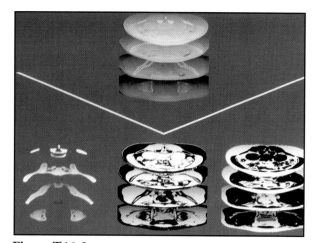

Figure T11.2

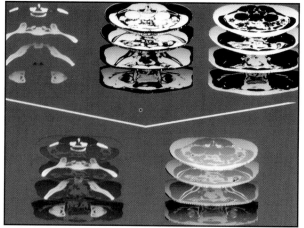

Figure T11.3

An added step may be needed, based on the fact that the integrity of the visualization depends strongly on the gradient vector at all points in the volume. As we saw in **Tech Note 2**, derivatives tend to be high-pass filters. Consequently, if the data set consists of a lot of noise, the normal vectors could be significantly distorted. In this case, a reasonable approach would be to first put the data through a low-pass filter to damp out the noise, then compute the normal vectors throughout the volume.

CD T.8

After the densities are computed it is important to consider lighting models for the data. Any self-consistent lighting model will do, the critical considerations of a lighting model being that a given material may be

- Translucent, thus partially absorbing incoming light
- Luminescent, thus emitting light
- Reflective, thus partially scattering or reflecting light.

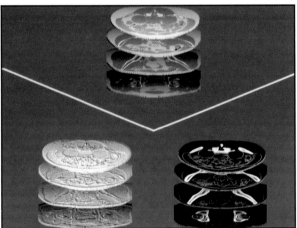

Figure T11.4

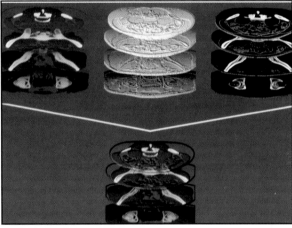

Figure T11.5

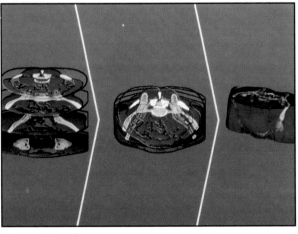

Figure T11.6

Figure T11.4
Next, the density is then used to compute the gradients to the data (lower left), while the color and opacity are used to calculate the shading of each voxel (lower right). (Courtesy Robert Drebin and Pixar, Inc.)

Figure T11.5
In this step, one takes color/opacity (top left), gradient (top center) and surface magnitude (top right) and combines them to make a shaded volume (bottom). (Courtesy Robert Drebin and Pixar, Inc.)

Figure T11.6
In the last step, the shaded volume (left image) is rotated and projected and the final image computed (right image). (Courtesy Robert Drebin and Pixar, Inc.)

Although the method described here is independent of lighting model, different lighting models will produce visually different images of the same data. In recent years a variety of lighting mechanisms have been developed by a number of researchers. This is discussed in some depth in Chapter 6 and **Tech Notes 14** and **15**, and for further reading the interested reader can examine the SIGGRAPH proceedings from 1984 to present.

Tech Note 12

RAY-TRACING OF VOLUME DATA

In Chapter 5 we discuss the general approach to visualizing a 3-D volume of data, and in **Tech Note 11** we delve into one particular approach to volume visualization used primarily in the medical community. In this Tech Note we examine another more widely used volume visualization method, *ray-tracing*[1], in some detail. However, rather than take a strict computer graphics view of ray-tracing as producing an image from a volume of colors and opacities, our approach will be a mixture of physics and computer graphics. The physics comes in at the problem definition stage, where we consider the question of what it means to render an image of a cloud of gas or dust. The computer graphics enters in the problem solution stage, where we look at different ray-tracing techniques for rendering an image.

Basically, in ray-tracing, linear rays are sent out from the observer through the data volume, first intersecting a pixel on the screen, and then sampling the data along regular intervals as it passes through the volume. Each ray only passes through a single pixel. The actual color of a given pixel is computed from the color and opacity of the individual voxels that it passes through (Figure T12.1). Herein lies all of the difficulty and all of the potential sources of error. This is also where all of the different computer graphic algorithms differ.

We will examine ray-tracing from different points of view. First we consider a physical argument that takes a geometrical optics approach to the problem. This approach illustrates the scientific

---

[1]Though similar to the common computer graphics rendering algorithm of the same name, when applied to volume rendering, rays penetrate near-continuous volumes without reflection rather than bouncing off of solid object surfaces, and lighting and shading are determined from integrated volumetric data rather than from models of surface reflection of light. Ray-tracing is sometimes used synonymously with ray-casting. In the polygonal rendering regime ray-casting is subtly distinguished from ray-tracing by implying that rays are terminated after their first encounter with an (opaque) object rather than being reflected (to possibly encounter other objects that might influence the shading of the first). Hence we see that, as applied to volume rendering, this technique is, in fact, more like ray-casting, despite the more common usage of the term ray-tracing.

objective of ray tracing, which is to accurately develop a graphical representation of a volume of data. The geometrical optics approach gives us the ideal version of this representation, but it is not practical. We then detail a couple of the more popular algorithms in use today. We also look at variations of the ray-tracing method. Finally, we look at problems that ray-tracing algorithms introduce in visual data analysis, and some of the possible solutions that researchers are currently exploring.

Geometrical Optics

From a physics perspective, we tend to look at a ray in a geometrical optics fashion: the ray is a continuous line passing through a volume of material with a particular density and absorption cross-section[2], and a photon is treated as a point particle (that is, with a

---

[2]Absorption cross-section refers to the light-scattering region around a particle, and may be thought of as a circle (a cross-section of a sphere) of a particular radius, and as having units of square centimeters.

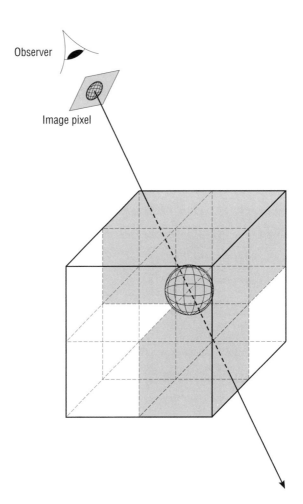

Figure T12.1
The color of a pixel in the image plane is determined by integrating the color and opacity of all of the voxels along the ray. (Courtesy NASA/JPL)

wavelength much smaller than any length-scale of the material). The question then becomes how to visualize the interior structure of the data. In addition, we need to determine how to map our physical understanding of optical depth into a computer graphic model of color and transparency.

Jim Blinn was the first person to actually consider some of the physical aspects of the visualization of light interacting with nearly transparent dusty or gaseous matter in his pioneering work on the simulation of Saturn's rings (Blinn, 1982), a frame of which is shown in Figure T12.2. However, Blinn only considered single scattering of particles, which limits his model to the optically thin case. Kajiya (1984) extended and refined Blinn's work somewhat by considering multiple-scattering models which allow for a reasonable model of the extremes of optically thick dust or gas. Kajiya took a radiative transfer approach which essentially follows Chandrasekhar's (1950) classic work on the subject. By taking this approach Kajiya was able to solve the extrema of both the optically thin and thick cases, but not the general solution for

Figure T12.2
This image, from the 1981 Voyager 2 Saturn Encounter simulation, by James F. Blinn and Charles E. Kohlhase, shows one of the first applications of transparency in computer graphics. Here, Blinn's realistic model of Saturn's ring system allows starlight to shine through. (Courtesy NASA/JPL)

Figure T12.2

arbitrary optical depth. However, in neither approach were spectral characteristics of the interaction of light with matter explicitly taken into account. Nevertheless, these efforts were the first to attempt to incorporate realistic physical properties into a computer graphic rendering of such a scattering phenomenon, and were an important step towards present day work.

Taking a physics approach, a very simple solution can be obtained to the ray-tracing problem by starting with the concept of optical depth: the degree of reduction in intensity that radiation undergoes while passing through a material. Consider a cube of semitransparent material of arbitrary optical depth, with a light source behind it and an observer in front. We would like to gain some information on the structure of the material by viewing the light after it has passed through the cube. To compute this, we know that the light follows some path through the material, depending upon the index of refraction of the substance. The path can be described by the general parametric equation of a curve in 3-space:

$$\mathbf{r}(s) = \mathbf{r}_0 + x(s)\hat{e}_x + y(s)\hat{e}_y + z(s)\hat{e}_z$$

where s is an arbitrary parameter along the curve, $\mathbf{r}_0 = \mathbf{r}(s = 0)$, the $\hat{e}_i$ are the Cartesian coordinate basis vectors, and $(x(s), y(s), z(s))$ are well-behaved functions of s. As was the case with splines (see **Tech Note 9**), this structure can be used to define the gradient, normal, and binormal of the curve at any point along the curve, which can then be used to compute geometric structure. For a light ray, $s = t$ (time), and we can write the trajectory of a photon as

$$\mathbf{r}(t) = \mathbf{r}_0 + ct\left(\frac{\hat{e}_x}{n_x} + \frac{\hat{e}_y}{n_y} + \frac{\hat{e}_z}{n_z}\right)$$

where c is the speed of light and the n_k are the indices of refraction along the coordinate axes. If the material is isotropic and the index of refraction is close enough to 1, the path of the photon is essentially a straight line. By equating the path of the photon with the computer graphic concept of a light ray, we can use this analogy to understand the traversal of a "virtual ray" (in computer graphics parlance) through a volume of material. Note that employing non-isotropic indices of refraction allows an important flexibility in developing ray-tracing algorithms for data sets with a lot of structure.

Optical Depth and Ray-Tracing

Consider a ray passing through a slab of gaseous material $\Phi(\mathbf{r})$ of particle density n (cm^{-3}), thickness Δz (cm), and absorption cross-section (at wavenumber k) σ_k (cm^2), as shown in Figure T12.3. Optical depth is usually denoted as τ_k, and takes into account the (wavelength dependent) absorption cross-section as well as the density of the material. For a given wavenumber k the change in optical depth due to a slab of thickness Δz is defined as $\Delta \tau_k = n \sigma_k \Delta z$. Thus, if light at the top of the slab has an intensity I_0, then intensity of the light at the bottom of the slab, I_k, is given by (now dropping the wavenumber k subscript for clarity, but remembering that σ, τ, and I are wavelength dependent)

$$I = I_0(1 - \rho \sigma \Delta z) = I_0(1 - \Delta \tau)$$

Hence the change in I across the slab, ΔI, is just given by

$$\Delta I = I - I_0 = -I_0 \Delta \tau$$

In the limit, then, one can write

$$\frac{dI}{I_0} = -d\tau$$

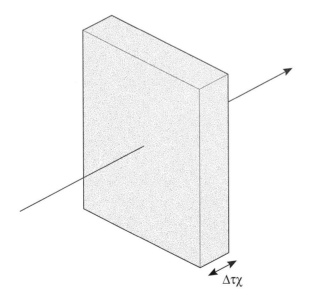

$$\Delta \tau = n\sigma \Delta \chi$$

Figure T12.3
This figure shows the basic concept of ray-tracing from a physical perspective, wherein a ray passes through a cloud of gas or dust. Here τ is optical depth, z is physical depth, Δz is the thickness of the slab, σ is the (wavelength-dependent) absorption cross-section of the gas, and n is the number density of particles in the slab.

which, after integration and exponentiation, yields

$$I = I_0 \exp(-\tau)$$

From this equation we see that an optical depth of 1 means that the intensity at that wavelength is reduced by $1/e$. By convention this is generally taken to mean that the cumulative material is sufficiently opaque that the numerical integration can be stopped.

The optical depth can be used to compute the extinction of a ray as it traverses the volume, passing through voxels with different densities. The intensity of the ray is decreased as it passes through each voxel by the opacity of the voxel. Each voxel contributes both color and opacity to the final color of the pixel that the ray ultimately passes through. We can stop integration along the ray path when the optical depth reaches unity or any set opacity.

In computer graphics terminology, the optical depth is associated with the opacity of a given volume, while the color—hue, saturation, and brightness—can be strictly related to the floating-point value of $\Phi(\mathbf{r})$ through some transform function. The issues then resolve to the following:

• How is the data value of a voxel determined from the data values on the gridpoints?

• How many voxels are sampled along the ray?

• How are the color and opacity of a voxel determined from a given data value?

Each of these problems must be addressed if we expect a successful visualization of any real data set. In the next section we examine these issues and outline a couple of algorithms that are currently in use by researchers and software developers.

Ray-Tracing Algorithms

The basic idea of ray-tracing techniques is to assign a color and a partial opacity to each voxel, independent of how the voxel itself is constructed. The color of each pixel in the image plane is determined from a blending of the color and opacity of all of the voxels that fall in a line that passes through the observer's eye and the pixel under consideration. As in other visualization techniques, it is the mapping from data space to color and opacity that determines the accuracy of the technique for a given data set. Thus, while the physical approach as described in the previous section is aesthetically pleasing, it suffers from a number of practical shortcomings:

• It assumes a continuous distribution of $\Phi(\mathbf{r})$, with no defined gridded structure for the data, and integrating through every voxel can be extremely (computationally) expensive.

• No algorithm is defined for averaging data points in the volume as a prior step to building voxels.

• No algorithm is defined for transforming the original data to color and opacity so that the inherent meaning of the data is retained when the data is imaged.

To get around these problems, computer graphics researchers have developed techniques to improve performance and accuracy of volume rendering. Below, we briefly look at a couple of them.

For a ray-traced image we can define two generic approaches to data transformations, assuming that the data exists on a rectangular grid. Both ways of computing the image have their merits, and one needs to do adequate testing to determine which method is best. In the first case, we take point samples at equal distances along a ray. This method was first employed by Levoy (1988) and is fairly inexpensive and straightforward for data on a regular grid (Figure T12.4). One simply samples the ray at regular intervals along the path, determines what voxel the sample lies in, estimates the value of the color and transparency, then adds the color and opacity of the contributions of all of the voxels sampled. The accuracy of the algorithm clearly depends upon the number of samples along the ray. In the case of sharp discontinuities in the data being sampled, such as the density in a shocked gas, regular samples designed to produce a fast image might miss the shock structure entirely. Some workers simply sample every voxel along a ray, but these techniques tend

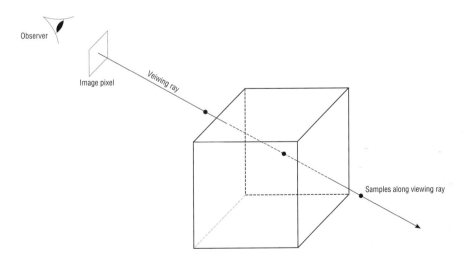

Figure T12.4
In the most basic ray-tacing method, one simply samples the ray at regular intervals along the path, determines what voxel the sample lies in, estimates the value of the color and transparency, then adds the color and opacity of the contributions of all of the voxels sampled.

to be fairly expensive (Snyder and Barr, 1987; Wilhelms and Van Gelder, 1991). Several variations on the general method simply look for those points where the ray enters and exits each voxel and assign some interpolation scheme to determine the value of the data in between (Max, 1986; Upson and Keeler, 1988; Wilhelms, 1991).

Ray-tracing provides a very powerful vehicle for studying the interior structures of any 3-D scalar fields. However, implementations of ray-tracing tend to have problems associated with sufficient sampling along the ray path, as well as the general problem of mapping from data space to color space. One therefore has to be extremely careful when interpreting results of ray-tracing visualizations. This is especially true if the data set is known to have small-scale structures in a single dimension, such as shock waves or defects in a material.

The other way of doing things is to use *projection methods*, wherein each voxel is projected onto a pixel or pixels, and its contribution to each pixel is computed, in a sort of inverse-ray-tracing approach (casting the rays from the voxels to the pixels rather than from the pixels to the voxels). Projection methods have a couple of distinct advantages over simple ray-tracing methods from the user's perspective. First, projection methods tend to be faster, since they don't have to sample very voxel between the projective plane and the screen. As a result of this, they don't exhibit the sampling problems that ordinary ray-tracing does. Second, since projection methods draw from back to front, the user can observe the image unfolding, layer by layer, rather than viewing

Figure T12.5a

This visualization of a 3-D jet was done by Peter Hughes of Apple Computer. The data came from a simulation by Michael Norman of NCSA. Image data is sampled randomly along each ray, thus enabling the detection of small-scale features that would ordinarily go undetected by uniform sampling along the ray. (Courtesy of Peter Hughes, Apple Computer)

Figure T12.5b

This image of a neuron is from a laser confocal microscope scan of a neuron from a lamprey eel computed by Vital Images' VoxelView volume visualization software. VoxelView actually uses an object-based splatting projective. (Courtesy Vital Images and P. Wallen, Karolinska Institute, Stockholm)

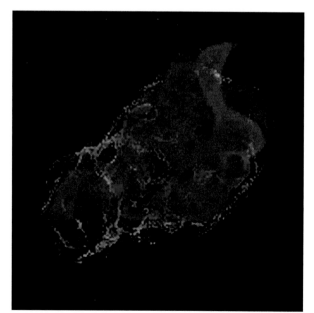

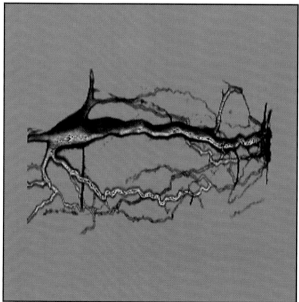

Figure T12.5a

Figure T12.5b

the single composite image that results from the addition of color and opacity values in a ray-traced image. This leads to the ability to interactively control the display of an image, depending upon what structures the user is interested in. Vital Images' VoxelView software uses this approach, and the result is a fast, powerful, interactive volume rendering technique.

Projection methods and ray-tracing are often referred to as *direct volume rendering*, as opposed to techniques that extract isosurfaces from the data, which are discussed in **Tech Note 13**. However, they are somewhat more difficult to implement because one has to keep good track of individual voxels. The interested reader is referred to papers by Wilhelms and Van Gelder (1990a) and Laur and Hanrahan (1991). The latter paper introduces a concept called *hierarchical splatting*, which employs an octree data structure combined with projection. Figure T12.5 shows two examples of DVR images. Note the distinctive gel-like look of the images.

CD T.9

Tech Note 13

MARCHING CUBES ALGORITHM FOR POLYGONALLY BASED VOLUME RENDERING

This Tech Note summarizes the classic *Marching Cubes* algorithm developed by Lorenson and Cline (1987) for rendering biomedical volume data. Marching Cubes is a type of surface-rendering technique and, hence, is fundamentally different from the direct volume rendering methods discussed in **Tech Note 12**. Whereas ray-tracing methods sample the volume of data along a ray cast from the observer through the material, the Marching Cubes technique divides a volume into a polygonal mesh based on the coordinates and scalar values of the original data points, in essence finding the 3-D contour surfaces in much the same way that traditional plotting packages find 2-D contours. Once the polygonal mesh is constructed, then one can use rendering techniques to create an image of that surface.

The surface of interest is determined as a 3-D contour of a particular value of the (scalar) data within the volume, with the resulting polygonal mesh serving as a model of that surface at the value of interest. Since the surface to be rendered is polygonally based, one can apply the vast machinery of polygonally based rendering techniques to produce well-defined images of the object of interest. To enhance the information content of these images, Lorenson and Cline computed surface normals at each vertex from the original scalar data. This information can be used by many polygonal renderers to guide the lighting and shading calculations more accurately than would be possible if normals were computed by the renderer from the polygonal mesh description.

While surfaces created in this manner can retain and display a significant amount of detail, they may also appear artificial or jagged if the polygonal mesh (or the original data volume) is too coarse, though this is usually not a problem with medical imaging data. In addition, errors or noise in the data can easily lead to surface artifacts; if the original data resolution is adequate, however, averaging it down to a lower resolution can quite effectively low-pass filter the data and help eliminate some of these artifacts. Finally, to compute a surface one has to know the data value of the surface to be computed, and that requires a priori knowledge of the data. Thus, for example, to compute the surface of a tumor in a brain from an MRI scan, one would have to know the density of the normal brain tissue relative to the tumor tissue and then use that knowledge in determining where to set the thresholds of the algorithm.

Despite these problems, surface-based techniques such as marching cubes can provide outstanding images of specific structures and thus have become a major research tool in medical imaging and volume visualization (some of the most striking visualizations of fluid flows from Digital Productions and NCSA were produced in a similar manner). A number of variations on this approach exist, each with its own strengths and weaknesses. In that context, marching cubes is simply representative of a general class of polygonally based volume-rendering processes.

Outline of the Algorithm

The Marching Cubes process basically works as follows. We first slice the data space along one axis into n slices, where n represents the number of data points in a given direction. From each two adjacent layers, we then form cubes as shown in Figure T13.1. An appropriate surface value (contour level) is then selected, according to the data analysis requirements of the problem. This contour level is used to compute the shape of the surface to be imaged.

The algorithm computes the surface's shape by marching from one cube to the next, performing a binary classification of each vertex. This consists of assigning a 1 to each vertex at which the data value exceeds (or equals) the selected contour value, and a 0 to each vertex at which the data value is less than the selected contour value. A vertex is said to be inside (or on) the surface being defined in the first case (a 1 was assigned) and outside the surface in the second case (a 0 was assigned). Thus we see that the surface intersects those cube edges where one vertex is outside (1) and the other vertex is inside (0) (Figure T13.2), and the intersection of the surface with that edge may be determined by some form of interpolation between its two vertices (Lorenson and Cline stated that a simple linear interpolation is sufficient).

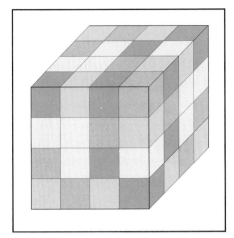

Figure T13.1a

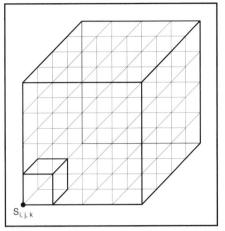

Figure T13.1b

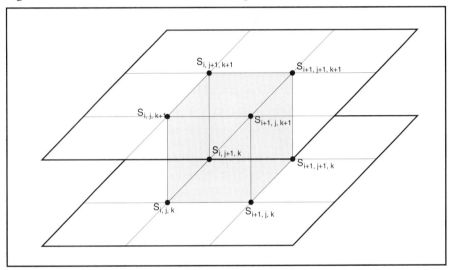

Figure T13.1c

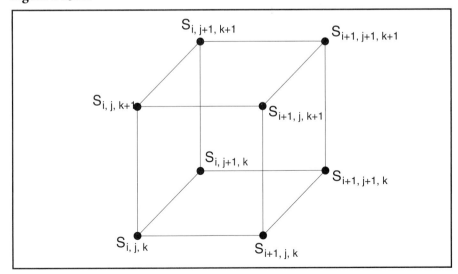

Figure T13.1d

Figure T13.1a-d
Developing a 3-D contour visualization of a volume data set. Figure T13.1a shows the actual volume composed of different shaded voxels. Figure T13.1b is the underlying polygonal structure, with the cube in the lower left-hand corner highlighted. Figure T13.1c isolates that cube as being formed by two adjacent planes. Figure T13.1d shows the individual cube structure.

Since there are eight vertices in a cube, and two possible states for each vertex, there are $2^8 = 256$ possible ways that a surface can intersect the cube. However, using the symmetry of the cube, one can show that there are only 14 unique cases, with one to four triangles per cube being generated by the intersection of the surface with the cube. Lorenson and Cline used an 8-bit look-up table (based on the binary classification of each cube's vertices) to determine which of the 14 cases is to be computed, calculates the appropriate new triangles and edges, and adds them to the surface's data-structure. For efficiency's sake, they only computed new edge crossings, using cube-to-cube coherency to simply look up surface-edge intersection information from the previous, adjacent cube.

Once the surface triangles are determined, Lorenson and Cline's method uses central differences to compute an effective surface normal at each vertex of the data cube, and then interpolates that normal to the point on the edge at which it intersects the surface being constructed. This retains maximum information about the surface's orientation at each point.

Lorenson and Cline have gone on to implement a solid-based renderer for their data-structures that easily allows them to display cutaway views and cross-sections through the resulting contour surfaces. The surface data-structures, however, can be rendered and shaded by

Figure T13.2
This image shows the surface of interest intersecting a cube of data. A value of "1" indicates that the data value is equal to or greater than the value of the surface at that point, while a value of "0" indicates that the data value is less than the value of the surface at that point.

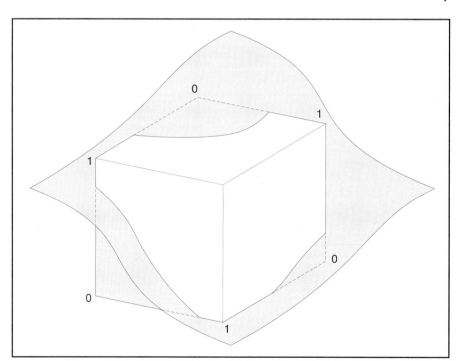

Figure T13.2

any surface renderer (such as those discussed in Chapter 6 and **Tech Notes 14** and **15**).

It is, of course, possible to produce surfaces at more than one contour level. Nesting such contour surfaces, and using either cutaway

Figure T13.3a

Figure T13.3a
This image from a simulation of a severe storm shows how polygonally based methods can be used to isolate a specific 3-D contour. (Courtesy Robert Wilhelmson and the NCSA Visualization Group)

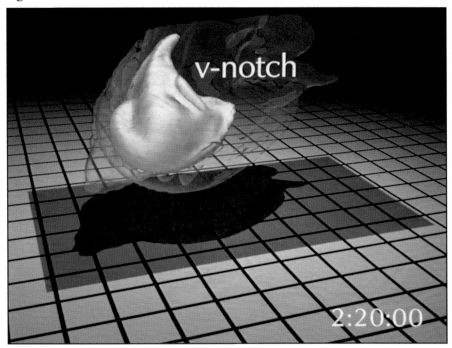

Figure T13.3b

Figure T13.3b
Here transparency is used in conjunction with a polygonally based renderer to illustrate specific nested surfaces within a storm structure. Note that, in contrast to ray-traced methods where the entire volume is generally visualized, in polygonally based methods individual contours can be isolated for analysis. (Courtesy Robert Wilhelmson and the NCSA Visualization Group)

views or translucent surfaces to permit their simultaneous viewing, can provide a lot of information about the structure of 3-D volumetric data (though inappropriate choices of level values, number of levels, or other imaging parameters can also cause such displays to become hopelessly muddled).

By first creating a polygonal surface data-structure and then rendering that surface, Marching Cubes differs significantly from either the Drebin et al. approach (**Tech Note 11**) or the direct volume-rendering approaches (**Tech Note 12**). A polygonally-based approach's strengths are the extreme amount of detail and the clarity of that detail in the resulting visualization. Its weaknesses are that it is computationally complex—creating the surfaces can take longer than the actual rendering, which may itself be expensive due to the great amount of detail (large number of polygons) in the surface models—and that hand-picking the appropriate contour levels and method for their display can present difficulties, depending on the nature of the data and a priori knowledge about that data. Figure T13.3 shows two examples from NCSA of polygonally based volume rendering. Notice how, in contrast to DVR methods, the desired surface in a polygonally based scheme can be isolated and rendered.

Tech Note 14

ALGORITHMS FOR VISIBLE SURFACE DETERMINATION

Rendering algorithms are the pen and pencil of computer graphic art. They are responsible for actually creating, for rendering, the synthesized images. In order to do so, they must provide a translation from the geometrical description of an object to the visual representation of that object. They do so by first determining just which objects are visible from the observer's point of view, and then assigning an appropriately shaded color at each visible point on those objects. In this Tech Note, we discuss a few of the most common algorithms used in the first stage of rendering: visible surface determination.

Ray Tracing

Ray-tracing algorithms, in their most basic form, are almost trivially simple. Imagine an observer's eye-point, an image window or plane that is divided into an array of pixels, and some collection of objects on the other side of the image plane from the observer (Figure T14.1). By tracing a line, or ray, from the eye-point through each pixel in the image plane, and following it until it either hits one of the objects or passes entirely beyond all the objects, we can determine just what the observer will see in each pixel in the image plane. Coloring in each pixel according to either the color of the object that the ray intersected, or the background color when no object is intersected, will produce an image of the scene from the observer's point of view.

The image can be made more realistic if the color that is recorded at an intersection is determined not just by the object's color, but also by its surface material properties (shiny, dull, and so forth), and by the location and color of any lights in the scene. Mirrorlike objects can be modeled by *reflecting* the ray off of the object, and following it to see what other objects it might hit. Glasslike objects can be modeled by *refracting* the ray through the object, and tracing it to see what else it might hit.

There are two main problems with the simple story told above. The first is the tremendous amount of computation that can be required to search through a large number of objects, and the polygonal facets of each of those objects, for each and every ray/pixel in the image. This is greatly compounded when rays are reflected from those objects, thus forcing yet another search through the object list. Much of the research effort in ray-tracing has been devoted to finding the most appropriate data-structures for partitioning the space inhabited by the objects so as to speed up the intersection search and calculation.

The second problem is that sending only a single ray through each pixel results in a sampling problem known as *aliasing*. Since an extremely small variation in the angle of the ray relative to the eye can produce large variations in the locations traversed by the ray as it recedes farther and farther from the eye, objects can easily be intersected or not in adjacent pixels. Large changes in the color of adjacent pixels that result from these sampling artifacts can cause the edges of objects to have a *jaggy* appearance in the resulting images, producing a stairstep representation of what should be a smooth edge. And as objects or the observer move over time, the resulting changes in these artifacts can cause a

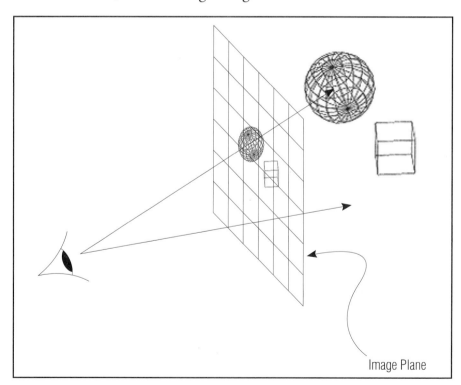

Figure T14.1

The ray-tracing rendering algorithm casts rays from the observer's eyepoint through an image plane into the scene, and colors the image plane according to what those rays intersect.

Image Plane

sparkling effect along object edges that can be quite objectionable.

The other major area of research in ray-tracing, then, has been to attempt to address the aliasing problem. Simply casting more rays can help, but the jaggies just reappear at a finer scale. *Stochastic* or *distributed ray tracing* (Cook, 1984) attempts to solve this problem by sending more rays, but randomly dithering their positions within the pixels. The same *jittering* of rays, but in other dimensions, can produce some other useful and attractive effects. Jittering them in time can produce a very effective motion blurring effect (Figure T14.2). Jittering the rays within the area of the effective camera lens can produce depth-of-field effects, further mimicking real optical systems. Of course, these additional rays only exacerbate the computational resource problem.

There have also been efforts to cast thick *cones*, *pencils*, and *beams* rather than rays in an effort to address the aliasing problem. These have met with some success, but with a corresponding increase in algorithmic complexity (even though the use of coherence in some of these approaches can actually improve overall performance relative to ordinary ray-tracing), and, in some cases, a limit on the types of geometric models that can be supported. In fact, ray-traced images can be recognized almost immediately by the limited geometric models they employ— typically, just spheres and planes, with the occasional cube, cylinder, or,

Figure T14.2
Stochastic ray-tracing was used to obtain the motion blur seen in this famous image from Pixar's 1984, a computer simulation of moving billiard balls in which the program is given the starting position of the balls, the initial velocity of the cue ball, and the location of the camera. (Courtesy Pixar)

in particularly advanced ray-tracers, ovoids. To their benefit, however, their images are frequently strikingly beautiful due to their more or less accurate modeling of the reflection and refraction of light.

Z-Buffer

The *z*-buffer rendering algorithm is the most common choice for hardware rendering solutions, and is also common in rendering software. As with ray-tracing, the basic algorithm is fairly straightforward. The technique in outline form is this:

1. Clear the frame buffer; that is, store the background color and some maximum z (depth) value in every pixel of the screen.

2. Transform the vertices (and thus the polygons) of an object into the coordinates of the image plane, or screen. This special *homogeneous* coordinate transformation is based on the relative positions of the object and the eye-point, and results in the *x*- and *y*-coordinates being aligned with *screen space*, and the *z*-coordinate being a measure of distance from the eye-point.

3. Take each polygon in the object, and starting at one vertex (typically the topmost), decompose the polygon into the scan-lines and the pixels that it overlaps. This means that we now know an RGB color triple and a z, or depth, value for each pixel that the polygon covers.

4. If and only if the z value at each pixel for this polygon is less than the value of z already stored at that pixel, then store this polygon's color and z at that pixel. The pixel's color and z remain untouched if the polygon's z is greater than the existing value of z; that is, if it extends beyond the "back of the screen" or is behind a nearer object.

5. Go back to step 1 and repeat the process until we have *scanned out* all polygons of all objects.

This repeated sequence of operations will result in the objects that are closest to the eye properly obscuring the objects that are farther from the eye.

In practice, steps 3 and 4 are actually combined, so there is no need to store the intermediate pixel colors and depths of step 3. Rather, as each polygon is scanned out, it is immediately either written to the color- and *z*-buffers or not.

With this basic method, it could easily happen that polygons will be scanned out that are not visible; this includes all of the polygons on the back side of the visible objects, as well as the polygons of objects that are occluded. A common speed-up technique referred to as *back-facing* polygon removal, or *back-face culling* (Figure T14.3) is based on the homogeneous coordinate transformation of step 2. From this step it is easy to ascertain which direction a polygon is facing. The cross-product of any two (non-colinear) edges of a polygon will produce a vector normal to the surface of that polygon. The sign of the dot product between that normal vector and a vector from the eye to any point on the polygon will determine whether that polygon is facing toward or away from the eye. In fact, after the transformation into screen space, the projection vector from the eye is just $(0,0,-1)$, so the back-face test reduces to simply determining the sign of the z component of that surface normal. Though it varies, the more common convention is that the "right-hand rule" applies in computing the normal vector from the edges, and that normal vectors whose z component is negative face away from the eye (corresponding to a positive dot product with the projection vector from the eye).

As straightforward as back-facing polygon removal may seem, of course nothing is ever quite that easy, at least not for complex objects and scenes. Not all polygons are planar, as they should be. In fact, unless generated algorithmically (and there can be precision-related

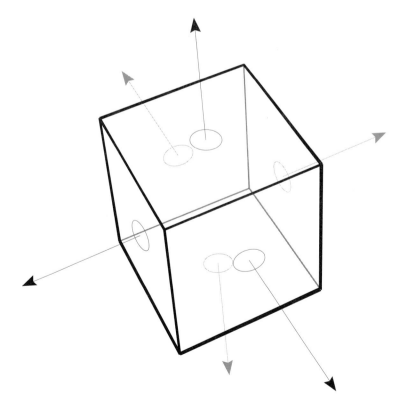

Figure T14.3
The faces of this cube lined in the lighter gray lines do not need to be rendered since they are not visible from this point of view, and are normally eliminated by the process of *back-face culling*.

problems even then), almost *no* polygons are completely planar, except for triangles (which cannot fail to be planar). As a result of small deviations from planarity, polygons at the edges of objects can sometimes be incorrectly removed before they are actually completely obscured. This results in small gaps along the silhouetted edges of objects if not dealt with properly. In animated sequences of frames, these disappearing and reappearing polygons can cause a quite annoying visual effect, sometimes known as *poly-popping*. Usually, simply requiring the z-component of the polygon's normal vector to be both negative and of a magnitude that is greater than some small threshold is sufficient to eliminate the problem. Yet, somehow, the problem can still be noticed in modern commercial animations from time to time.

As with ray-tracing, aliasing is also a problem for z-buffer algorithms. Except for *supersampling* (computing at a higher resolution than is actually displayed and then averaging down to the display resolution), there are no known solutions for this problem. In addition, z-buffer algorithms do not handle transparency well, unless the polygons are presorted and presented exclusively back-to-front or front-to-back, which greatly increases the amount of computation needed. To quickly visualize why, consider an opaque blue square at some distance from the

Figure T14.4a,b
Translucency problems inherent to standard z-buffer algorithms are demonstrated here; though a single, simple overlap can be computed by color averaging (the purple region in **a**), more complicated overlaps (the orange region in **b**) cannot be computed without significant extensions to the algorithm.

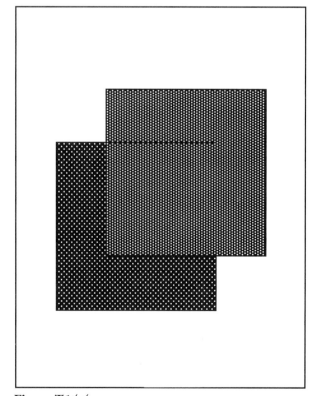

Figure T14.4a

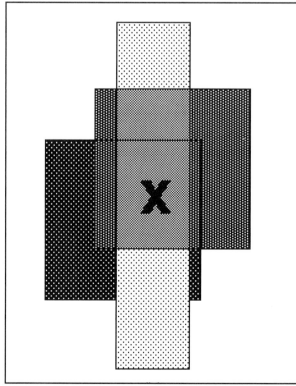

Figure T14.4b

eye. Then imagine a translucent red square interposed between the blue square and the eye. So far so good. One could imagine just averaging the red and blue colors based on how transparent the red square was, and seeing purple in the regions of overlap (Figure T14.4a). But suppose the next polygon to come along is a yellow square that lies between the red and blue squares (Figure T14.4b). Since it is behind the red one, its test on the value in the z-buffer will cause it to be discarded, rather than somehow visualized as behind the red square. Furthermore, no heuristic of any sort can possibly help us figure out that we ought to just go ahead and average the yellow and red colors now, since we no longer even know the original color of red; in the previous color-averaging step, we retained only the color that resulted from that averaging. Techniques involving multiple buffers or lists of all color and z values for each pixel can extend the algorithm to support transparency, but only at the price of significant additional memory and computational complexity.

Despite its shortcomings, z-buffer algorithms continue to be the mainstay of hardware rendering systems. This is principally because little more than a lot of memory and enough circuitry to decide whether or not a new value of z is greater than an old one is required to implement this form of hidden surface removal. Z-buffer algorithms also lend themselves well to rendering nonpolygonal surface primitives, unlike the next rendering technique.

Scanline Sampling

One of the most common rendering algorithms is known as scanline sampling. This technique is a little bit more complex conceptually than the previously described rendering methods, but it has the advantage of being computationally efficient (in software implementations). The algorithm may be thought of as consisting of four principal steps:

1. Transformation: conversion of the object's vertices into screen-space. This is the same homogeneous coordinate transformation as is used in the z-buffer algorithm above.
2. Clipping: elimination of all objects and portions of objects that lie outside of the viewing frustum (the observer's field of view). This is straightforward, except that care must be taken in determining the appropriate replacement vertex locations, vertex connectivity, and any accompanying per-vertex information when a polygon's edge is only partially clipped by the viewing frustum.

3. Hidden surface removal: determination of which surfaces are closest to the eye of the observer. This is the most complex step of the method, and is what gives the algorithm its name. It is discussed in more detail below.

4. Shading: assigning a color to each pixel based on the visible objects' colors, lighting, surface properties, and any special shading information such as texture-maps, bump-maps, reflection-maps, and so on. This step is common to most renderers, though the order in which the shading information is accessed is somewhat dependent on the algorithm.

With a reasonably efficient implementation of the hidden surface removal step, the final, shading step is usually the most compute-intensive part of a scanline-sampling renderer, representing approximately 80 percent of the processing time on a scalar machine (vector processors can reduce this fraction significantly since shading yields fairly readily to vectorization). This is due principally to the fact that these calculations must be carried out for every pixel of the image that is occupied by an object. On the other hand, this is the stage of rendering that is shared by all algorithms. With scanline sampling the other steps need not represent major

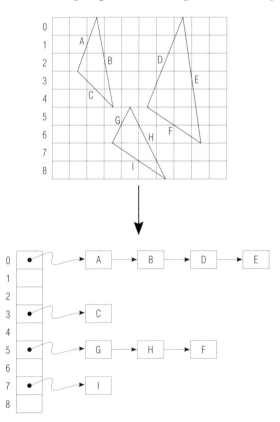

Figure T14.5

Creation of an *entering edge list*; a list of polygon edges is created that sorts those edges by the scanline on which they first appear (and secondarily sorts them by *x*-position and slope).

additional overhead, unlike ray-tracing. Also, scanline-sampling algorithms usually visit each pixel only once, as opposed to z-buffer methods that, in the process of scanning out every polygon, may make multiple computations per pixel. To exploit this efficiency, however, care must be taken in the implementation of the hidden surface removal step, which is usually the second most compute-intensive part of the overall method.

Hidden surface removal, or perhaps more aptly, visible surface determination may be thought of in terms of three main steps:

1. Create an *entering edge list*. That is, cycle through all of the edges of all the polygons of all the objects in the scene, building a data structure that keeps a list of all the edges that enter (whose topmost point appears in) each scanline of the image (Figure T14.5). The result is a data structure that can provide a list of all the edges that begin on any given scanline. For each edge, store its vertical extent (the scanline on which it terminates), the starting value (at the topmost vertex) and the rate of change of the value (per scanline) for the edge's position in x and all relevant shading parameters (color, surface normal, parametric texture map coordinates, and so on), plus the polygon number to which the edge belongs. For efficiency, sort each scanline's entering edges based on their horizontal position, x, and on their slope when their x values are equal.

2. Cycle through all scanlines, creating and maintaining an *active edge list*, which is sorted on horizontal edge position x (Figure T14.6). That is, to start things off, just add those

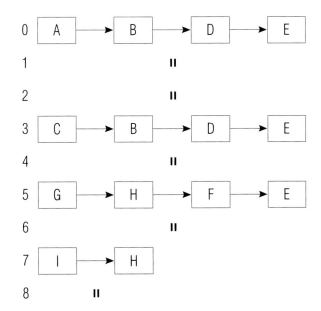

Figure T14.6
Creating and updating an *active edge list*; as the scanline-sampling algorithm advances one scanline at a time, a list is maintained of all polygonal edges that are visible on that scanline.

311

edges from the (already sorted) entering edge list that begin on the first scanline. Then cycle through the remaining scanlines, removing edges once they have run their full vertical length, and adding new edges as appropriate from the entering edge list. The values of all the shading parameters at these edges can be computed and updated incrementally by just adding the per-scanline rate of change to the value at the previous scanline.

3. Scan out the frontmost *spans*. That is, on each scanline, start with the leftmost active edge (if more than one edge exists at this precise x position, choose the frontmost). Then use the shade of the polygon corresponding to this frontmost active edge until either the polygon ends or another active edge appears that is closer to the eye. This check for frontmost active edge (and therefore, frontmost polygon) must be performed at the x locations of all active edges on this scanline. An appropriate shader should be invoked for each pixel in the horizontal runs between these active edges. The values of the shading parameters at each pixel are now determined by interpolating between the values at the left and right edges of the spans.

This decomposition into an entering edge list, an active edge list, and spans defines the heart of the scanline-sampling algorithm. In practice, however, there are complications. First of all, determining the frontmost span is *not* always straightforward as polygons may intersect, necessitating the introduction of additional edges to model the line of intersection; this condition may be detected by looking for adjacent frontmost edges that are not from the same polygon. If translucent polygons are to be supported, it becomes necessary to maintain a full z-sorted list of these spans at the edge locations and to be able to scan out multiple spans per pixel. Though this involves significant additional computational overhead, many scenes require transparency to seem realistic, or simply to convey the necessary information. Figure T14.7 shows a version of the object seen back in Chapter 6, Figure 6.2, with all polygons made semitransparent.

As noted above, almost all of these data-structures must be maintained in a sorted condition. The entering edges must first be sorted by scanline, or y, and then by horizontal position, or x. The scanline ordering is best obtained by a *bucket sort*, since the number of target categories into which the sorted edges must fall is limited and known in advance. Since we need to access these edge lists as a function of scanline, an array of pointers to the heads of the individual scanline lists makes an appropriate set of buckets for our initial y-sort. Thus, as each new entering edge is sorted, it is simply added to the head of the list associated with the appropriate scanline (the one at which the new edge begins). Another pass through our new data-structure then allows us to carry out a sort on the x-direction for the edges in each scanline's bucket. A QuickSort (Knuth, 1973) is a reasonable selection for this x-sort on the entering edges, since there is little chance that the unsorted lists will have any particular (or pathological) order before the sort (at least for any objects and scenes of sufficient complexity to cause concern about efficiency in the first place). Since a given vertex usually produces two entering edges, multiple edges with the exact same value for x can be expected to appear in these lists. It is important to modify the sort algorithm to also subsort edges based on their slope, when they enter at precisely the same x. This ensures that they will be in the correct order in all subsequent scanlines. Foley et al. (1990) recommended that this type of algorithm sort entirely on slope (within the buckets); but it is useful to sort first on x, so that the active edge list need only be traversed once when entering edges are being merged into it.

The active edge list must also be maintained in a properly x-sorted condition. Besides edges expiring and entering, they may also cross each other with or without their associated polygons actually intersecting. Accordingly, the active edge list is typically resorted at the end

CD T.10

CD T.11

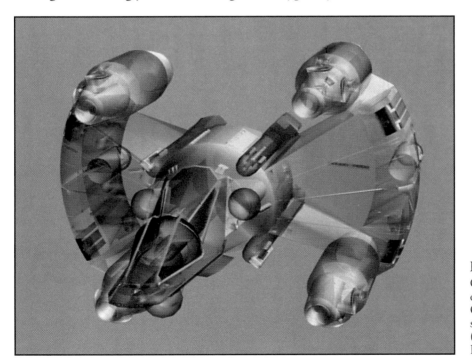

Figure T14.7
Computer-generated image of a glassy, translucent Gunstar, using a scanline-sampling algorithm. (Courtesy Digital Productions)

of each scanline's processing. This list is best treated a little differently, since it is usually almost entirely sorted, with only a small percentage of the edges having exchanged relative positions, before the resort. Misordered edges are also usually adjacent, rather than at arbitrary locations in the list. Hence, a technique that merely walks the list of active edges until a misordering is discovered, removes the misordered edge from the list, backtracks until the misordered edge can be reinserted, and then picks up from where the edge was originally removed, is quite efficient. Though similar to the *list insertion* sorting algorithm (Knuth, 1973), which is known to be inefficient (order N^2) for a random initial ordering, this method is of order N when the list is already presorted, and varies only slightly from N when the deviations from a presorted condition are few and local.

The z-sorting of spans, needed to properly handle transparency, is also relatively coherent from one position to the next and can similarly benefit from a sorting method that takes advantage of this coherency.

As with the other rendering techniques, scanline-sampling algorithms benefit from back-face culling and suffer from aliasing artifacts. The culling simply reduces the number of edges that must be maintained and sorted in the data structures. Aliasing is usually addressed by the brute force method of supersampling and averaging down, though using subpixel accuracy of edge positions in computing just the first and last pixels of spans can yield a computationally efficient, partially effective form of antialiasing.

Tech Note 15

SHADING AND ILLUMINATION MODELS

If rendering algorithms are the pen and pencil of computer graphics art, shaders are the ink and graphite that provide the actual color of the rendered image. Once a renderer has determined which portions of which surfaces are visible, shading and illumination models provide the mathematical description of how all the available light sources interact with those surfaces to reflect light toward the eye of the observer.

Shading

Once a visible surface has been detected, all rendering algorithms need a method for determining the color at the visible points along that surface. The methods for determining the appropriate surface color to display are known as *shading* methods. All shading methods, or *shaders*, except the most trivially simple, take into account the position of the observer, the position and color of any illumination sources, the relative orientation of the object's surface, and some measure of the reflective properties of the surface material, in addition to the intrinsic color of the object. Most shaders consider multiple lighting components, or sources of illumination. Some *programmable shaders* even leave the final form of the function that relates these parameters to the displayed color in the hands of the user (Cook, 1984; Perlin, 1985).

Foley et al. (1990) made a useful distinction between a *shading* model and an *illumination* model. The illumination model determines the relevant parameters and the mathematical relations among those parameters that determine the visible color at a point. The shading model determines how those relevant parameters are themselves to be calculated. For example, the simple *Lambertian* illumination model discussed below can be applied either in the *Gouraud* fashion—

computed using normals at vertices only, and interpolating color along edges and spans—or in the *Phong* fashion—computed using normals interpolated at each pixel in the span.

Illumination Models

Ultimately, all illumination models can be reduced to a function that relates the light falling on a point on a surface to the light that is reflected from that point toward the observer. The most common illumination models supported by modern graphics packages are *intrinsic*, *ambient*, *diffuse reflection* (or *Lambertian*), and *specular reflection* (usually *Phong highlights*). Actually, intrinsic illumination can be mimicked by appropriate settings of the ambient lighting parameters, and so is sometimes not explicitly included, though keeping it distinct from ambient lighting can be useful should the user of the software desire to reduce overall ambient lighting without affecting self-luminous objects. Though very widely used, all of these illumination models are empirical rather than theoretically sound, physically accurate lighting models. Some more sophisticated renderers may support the more physically based *Torrance-Sparrow* (or *Blinn*) or *Cook-Torrance* illumination models for specular reflections. These models, based on a theory of *microfacets* in an object's surface, were developed by physicists Torrance and Sparrow (Torrance et al., 1966; Torrance and Sparrow, 1967), introduced to the computer graphics community by Blinn (1977) and refined by Cook and Torrance (1982). They do a much better job of modeling highlights from shallow lighting angles, such as occur with backlighting, and produce a more convincing simulation of metal surfaces than do the simpler ad hoc illumination models.

For the purposes of our discussion here, we will adopt mostly the variable nomenclature chosen by Foley et al. (1990) in order to foster consistency in the field (not a particularly widespread phenomenon), and to ease the motivated reader's task in digging deeper into the subject matter.

The first and simplest illumination model is one that ignores even the light falling on an object, with brightness or color being determined solely by what might be thought of as a self-luminous, intrinsic color of the object:

$$I = k_i \qquad (1)$$

where I is the intensity of illumination perceived at a point and k_i is the intrinsic intensity of the object on which the point lies. Intrinsic illumination alone does not produce a very realistic simulated image, but it is a convenient way to simulate certain types of light-giving, self-luminous objects in a scene such as automobile taillights, console lights, power indicators, and so on. Since the light from objects lit in this fashion only affects the pixels the objects actually occupy, without shedding any light on surrounding objects, this technique is only suitable for objects of low to moderate brightness, or objects that are supposed to be at a considerable distance from the viewer and any foreground objects.

Note that equation 1 may be a scalar equation, in which case I and k_i correspond to monochromatic intensities. It may also be treated as a vector equation for red, green, and blue color components (or, indeed, any discrete spectral bands), in which case I and k_i may be thought of as vector color intensities, the usual (r,g,b) triples. This will be the case for all of the equations governing illumination models in this note. Foley and Van Dam point out that it is a useful convenience to consider the object's color components separately from its *material* properties. That is, it is useful to think about, and write software to model, $k\, O_\lambda$, rather than k_λ, where k is one of the illumination or reflection coefficients associated with the surface *material* of the object (k_i in equation 1, k_a in equation 2 below, and so on), the subscript lambda (λ) denotes a particular color component or wavelength of light, and O_λ is just the object's intensity for that color component. This allows one to easily adjust the reflective properties of the object's surface material without affecting its color components. A similar, useful abstraction may be applied to intensity versus the color of lights. However, we will not use the λ, color-denoting subscript in writing the various illumination equations here, partly to make the equations easier to read, and partly because even parameters that are *not* normally thought of as color- or wavelength-dependent, such as the various rolloff exponents below, *could* be different for each color component (producing some attractive, if not physically meaningful, lighting effects). In practice, keeping the surface material properties distinct from the object's intrinsic color is indeed useful, though for reasons of efficiency—so as not to recompute the $k\, O_\lambda$ product at each pixel—it is best to store the precomputed product along with the raw parameters, and use this precomputed product when actually doing the shading calculations.

All of the parameters of these equations may be thought of as varying between zero and 1, and are typically input and computed as such. In 24-bit, "true color" systems, there are eight bits per color, and thus the final light intensity components will be mapped onto the range 0 to 255.

Now, if we consider the perceived light at the point to originate not from the self-luminous quality of the object itself, but as a result of the reflection of a very diffuse, nondirectional light source, we have the next simplest illumination model: *ambient* lighting. Another name for this model, *diffuse shading*, can result in unnecessary confusion with other illumination models, so we will avoid it. Though somewhat approximated by the lighting experienced on the floor of a dense forest, or on an extremely cloudy day, ambient lighting is almost never found as the exclusive light source in normal experience, and simulated scenes lit only by an ambient lighting model do not seem very realistic. For example, a sphere lit only by ambient light would be visually indistinguishable from a disk. Ambient lighting, however, is a useful model for one component of lighting in real life and in computer-generated scenes. The ambient light reflected to the eye from a point may be expressed by

$$I = I_a \, k_a \tag{2}$$

where I_a is the ambient illumination level falling on the entire scene and k_a is the *ambient-reflection coefficient* of the surface at that point. Note that while I_a is a property of the light source, k_a is a *material* property of the object's surface.

The next lighting component that most shaders include is known as *diffuse reflection*, or *Lambert shading*. To avoid confusion with "diffuse shading," we will use the latter term here, although in deference to the variable nomenclature of Foley and Van Dam, we will retain the "d" (for diffuse) subscript on the Lambertian reflection coefficient. Lambert shading is associated with a directional effect of illumination from specific light sources, and is based on Lambert's law, which states that the energy of light falling on an object's surface is proportional to the cosine of the angle of incidence of that light. Basically, a surface oriented toward a light receives a lot of energy, and a surface oriented away from a light receives little, and the rate of modulation of this energy is determined by the cosine of the angle between the vector normal to the surface and the vector from a point on the surface to the light source (in Figure T15.1, this is the angle between vectors **N** and **L**). So the Lambert component of light may be expressed by

$$I = I_p \, k_d \cos \theta \tag{3}$$

where I_p is the intensity of a point light source, k_d is the *diffuse-reflection coefficient* or *Lambertian coefficient*, and θ is the angle between the surface normal and a vector from a point on the object to the light. In theory, θ is treated as varying only from 0 to 90 degrees, and surfaces facing away from the light are considered to be *self-occluded*, and thus not illuminated by the light. For *open* (as opposed to *closed*) objects, the absolute value of cos θ is often used to effectively invert the surface normals for surfaces facing away from the light, thus causing them to be lit in the same manner as surfaces facing the light.

A more useful form of equation 3 may be given as

$$I = I_p \, k_d \, (\mathbf{N} \bullet \mathbf{L}) \tag{4}$$

if vectors **N** and **L** (Figure T15.1) are normalized, unit vectors. Light sources are sometimes referred to as being *at infinity*, which means that all light arriving from that source is parallel, and thus **L** is a constant for all points on the object. A *local* light source must be specified by its location in the scene, and **L** must be computed at each point on the object. Lambertian lighting produces a gently graded ring of brightness, the center and brightest spot of which is oriented toward the light source. Though not strictly Lambertian, it is possible, and sometimes useful, to provide a control over the extent of this ring of light by introducing an exponent on the cos θ or (**N** • **L**) term to yield

$$I = I_p \, k_d \, (\mathbf{N} \bullet \mathbf{L})^{n_d} \tag{5}$$

where n_d is the *diffuse-reflection exponent* or *Lambertian exponent*. A value of one for n_d thus yields standard Lambert lighting, while a number less than one yields a wider, more diffuse ring of light, and a number greater

Figure T15.1

Schematic of the principal vectors used in illumination and shading.

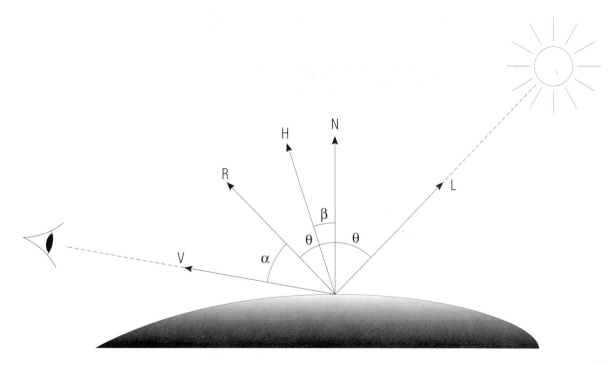

than one yields a smaller, more concentrated ring of light. Lambert lighting gives the appearance of a matte finish to an object.

A shinier surface material effect may be obtained by the next illumination model: *specular reflection*. Specular reflections, or *highlights*, are essentially the light reflected toward the eye by the object surface acting more or less like a mirror. In Figure T15.1, the vector **R** is just the mirrorlike reflection of the light vector **L** about the surface normal **N**. The vector **H** is the *halfway vector*, defined to be exactly halfway between the light vector **L** and the vector to the viewer **V**. Note that if the surface, the light, and the viewer were rearranged slightly so that **H** aligned perfectly with **N**, then **V** would also align with **R**. In this condition, the light would be reflected directly into the eye of the viewer, which is why **H** is also known as the direction of maximum highlights. So one form of specular reflection is given by

$$I = I_p \, k_s \, (\mathbf{N} \bullet \mathbf{H})^{n_s} \tag{6}$$

where I_p is the same point light source intensity as before, k_s is the *specular-reflection coefficient*, and n_s is the *specular-reflection exponent*. Here, n_s plays the same contracting or expanding role on the specular highlight as n_d did on the Lambert ring of light. Smaller values of n_s yield broader, more diffuse highlights, while larger values yield smaller, sharper highlights. Generally, larger values of n_s produce the appearance of shinier objects.

Specular reflections are typically computed to be in the color of the light, not the color of the object (in contrast to diffuse reflection). This corresponds well to the actual lighting observed on plastics but not very well to the lighting observed on metal, or velvet, whose highlights also tend to be in the color of the object. This is one reason why the objects in many computer graphics images look as if they are made of plastic (unless they are *reflection mapped*, in which case they look like the ubiquitous computer graphics chrome). The Cook-Torrance illumination model incorporates parameters that determine the color of highlights from surface material properties, and can yield considerably more convincing metal surfaces. A less computationally expensive method for approximating such phenomena in the simpler illumination models is to provide a single parameter that interpolates between object color and light color for the highlights, and let the user thus determine the appropriate final appearance.

A typical 3-D rendering package provides the ability to control the various parameters of equations 1, 2, 5, and 6 and sums these different illumination models to produce the total illumination at each point. In addition, these terms may be produced and summed for multiple light sources. Since the sum of all these contributions may exceed the maximum brightness of 1.0, it is necessary to either clamp (limit) the color brightnesses to 1.0, or to perform a more sophisticated scaling operation to keep all of the colors within a valid range.

A wide variety of other lighting effects exist, including *depth cueing* (modulating the perceived color toward some uniform background color as a function of depth), *light attenuation* (causing light to fall off as a function of distance), and *directional lights* (whose light does not radiate uniformly in all directions). All of these may be used to improve the apparent realism of a scene. There are also the much more sophisticated, physically based models of illumination mentioned earlier. The interested reader can pursue these topics at considerable length in Foley et al. (1990), the many references given there, and in the annual SIGGRAPH proceedings.

Shading Models

The illumination models given by equations 5 and 6 above depend upon knowledge of the surface normal **N**, the relative location of the viewer **V**, and the relative location of the light source **L** at each point on an object's surface. For polygonal objects, simple shading models may assume these vectors to be constant across the entire polygon and produce quick, but very unsmooth, faceted images of the objects. More sophisticated shaders take into account the variations in these vectors either at polygon edges or at each pixel.

The simplest shading model for polygons is known alternatively as *flat shading*, *faceted shading*, or *constant shading*. This model computes and displays a single color for an entire polygon. The surface normal **N** is assumed to be uniform across the polygon. The vector to the viewer **V** is assumed to be constant, either for the scene (which corresponds to a viewpoint at infinity), or per polygon (determined at a single point on that polygon, such as the polygon's center or its topmost point). The vector to the light source **L** is treated similarly. Thus the halfway vector **H** will also be constant for a given polygon, as will the computed color due to all illumination models.

A common, slightly more sophisticated shading model is named after its originator: *Gouraud* shading. Gouraud (1971) suggested averaging the normals from all polygons sharing a vertex to produce an effective normal at each vertex (Figure T15.2). The color intensities at each vertex may then be computed using whatever illumination models are desired. These color intensities are then linearly interpolated along the edges between vertices for the value at each scanline, and then, at each scanline, linearly interpolated again along the spans between edges for the value at each pixel. This results in a much smoother appearance than with flat shading. However, even though Gouraud shading provides a continuous change in color across polygonal edges (as opposed to the discontinuous color changes at edges in flat shading), it permits discontinuous changes in the first derivative of color intensity at these boundaries. By what is referred to as the *Mach-banding* effect, the human eye picks up these discontinuities, and perceives bright ridges at polygonal boundaries, breaking up the illusion of smoothness. Gouraud shading also tends to smear highlights over much larger areas than would a more accurate lighting model (due to its linear interpolation versus the more rapid fall-off associated with the n_s specular-reflection exponent) and may even miss highlights altogether if their area of peak intensity occurs entirely within the interior of a polygon.

All of these shortcomings are addressed, albeit at considerable additional computational expense, by the more sophisticated *Phong* shading model. Phong (Bui-Tuong, 1975) suggested interpolating not color, but surface normals along edges and spans. The illumination model is then recomputed at each pixel, using these interpolated normals (Figure T15.3). In addition to the expense of applying the illumination model at each pixel (rather than at each vertex as with Gouraud shading), the interpolated normals must also be renormalized

Figure T15.2

Surface normals from all adjacent polygonal faces are averaged to produce the surface normal at the shared vertex.

Figure T15.3

While Gouraud shading would compute the colors C_1 and C_2 from normals N_1 and N_2 and then interpolate for colors C_a, C_b, and C_c between C_1 and C_2, Phong shading would interpolate and renormalize the vectors N_a, N_b, and N_c from N_1 and N_2, and compute the colors C_a, C_b, and C_c directly from each interpolated normal.

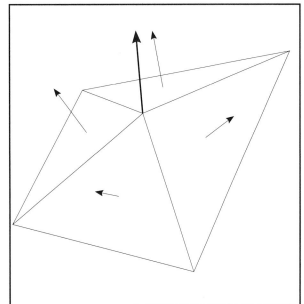

Figure T15.2

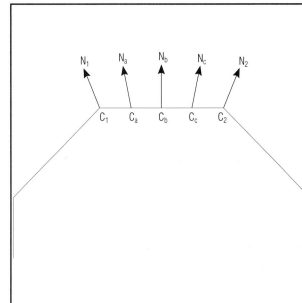

Figure T15.3

at each pixel. In return for this added computation, however, Mach-banding problems are usually eliminated, and specular reflections are much more appropriately modeled.

All shaders that rely on interpolation suffer from a number of subtle problems. Among these are perspective distortion, orientation dependence, unshared vertices, and unrepresentative vertex normals.

Perspective distortion arises due to the fact that the interpolations are being carried out in screen space rather than object space. Foreshortening effects cause the shading parameters linearly interpolated in screen space to diverge from their correct values if interpolated in object space. These effects vary with motion of the object or the viewer, and they can be quite disconcerting in animations involving low-detail objects (especially those that have been texture-mapped; see below). A more detailed model with smaller polygons can reduce this effect, by effectively sampling the correct values at vertices more frequently.

CD T.12

Orientation dependence of the interpolated shading parameters can cause the same polygon to shade differently when rotated. This effect is the result of the same point being computed from a different set of vertices in one orientation than in another. Decomposing the polygons into triangles eliminates this problem, at the expense of the decomposition process and the processing of the additional edges during rendering. In practice this is usually not a severe problem if objects are modeled with reasonable precision.

Unshared vertices along the edge of a pair of adjacent polygons can produce artifacts associated with the new interpolation range introduced into the shading of one polygon but not the other. The best solution to this problem is to simply not build models with unshared vertices; anytime two polygons share an edge, just make sure that they also share all vertices along that edge.

Unrepresentative vertex normals are caused by the process of averaging adjacent polygon normals that is used to compute the vertex normals, and tend to occur in low-detail models with sharp angles between adjacent polygons. The usually desirable smoothing effect that the averaged vertex normal provides results in a shaded image that appears too smooth, failing to capture the sharp changes in shading that should be present when adjacent polygons abut at sharp angles. Subdividing the polygons to produce a more detailed model can help solve this problem. Intelligent subdivision, through the use of special *coplanar* polygons (Figure T15.4) near the edges can greatly reduce the problem, at the expense of additional edges and polygons to process.

Figure T15.4

Coplanars are a form of intelligent subdivision of polygons that can be used to provide sharper edges (for the illumination model) on otherwise low-detail objects.

Figure T15.5

Creases are an alternate, algorithmic method of providing sharper edges on low-detail objects; here, surface normals at points 2 through 5 would be computed by averaging adjacent polygonal surface normals, while points 1 and 6 would maintain discontinuous normals based on the two abutting polygons.

An alternate approach that has never been published, but was implemented by Gary Demos at Digital Productions, is to compute separate normals along shared edges when polygons abut at relative angles greater than some specifiable *crease* angle threshold (typically 30 degrees or so; see Figure T15.5).

Regardless of the type of shader used, polygonal models with insufficient detail will always show their nonsmooth edges in profile. But despite the problems inherent in rendering and shading polygonal models, their rendering is sufficiently faster (and easier) than models based on splines or other curved surfaces that polygon-based rendering systems remain by far the most common surface visualization tool.

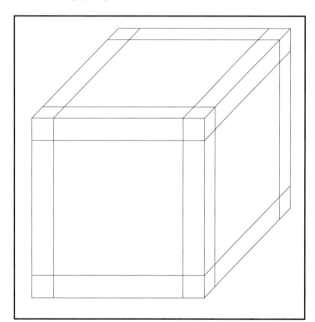

Figure T15.4

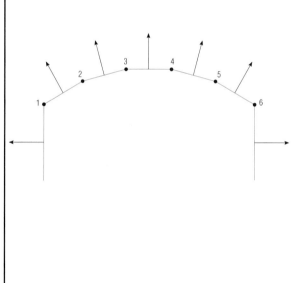

Figure T15.5

Appendix A
THE MAKING OF VNP

In this appendix we describe the trials, tribulations, and processes that we went through to produce this project. We do this for several reasons. First, as a historical record for ourselves, lest we forget the pain of childbirth, so to speak. Second, so that others with similar ideas and ambitions may have a realistic assessment of just what is required—with today's technologies—to produce a project as extensive as VNP. Third, so that we may improve on the process the next time around. We also hope that, by documenting the process, we'll provide some insight to multimedia hardware and software developers at Apple and elsewhere on the good, the bad, and the ugly in "the real world" of content developers.

We'd like to say, up front, that this project would not have been possible without the generous support of Apple Computer, both in terms of letting us use hardware and facilities, and the advice and help from a number of researchers in Apple's Advanced Technology Group (ATG). Putting this project together required a lot of resources at the cutting edge of multimedia computing. In what follows we describe all of the aspects of the project, from its inception to the development and testing of the CD-ROM—at least up until this section goes to press. We deal with the word processing and formatting issues, hardware and software environments, long-distance collaboration, the creation of and data management problems of the more than 300 drawings and images in the text, the making of the over 100 QuickTime animations that are on the CD, and the actual page layout production process itself.

As it turned out, we were really riding the edge of the technology-wave in a number of areas. The text could not have been written in a timely manner without Microsoft Word 5.0—with its built-in equation editor and its support for 32-bit PICT files. MS-Word 5.0 had just come out when we began the project, and we were able to standardize on this with our publisher and producer for a fairly low cost.

The images could not have been managed without Claris's Filemaker Pro 2.0, which came out in the summer of 1992 and which enabled us to develop an image management system. We could not have digitized videos with sound with good quality in a reasonable amount of time without Radius's loan of a Video Vision system, which had just come out in the spring of 1992. We could not have made QuickTime animations fast enough for CD production with high enough quality without QuickTime 1.5, and the Apple Compact Video codec, which came out in October 1992. And we needed the performance of a Quadra 950 to compress the animations fast enough (four times faster than a Mac IIfx) in the Apple Compact Video format.

TEXT

Creating the text for VNP was the easiest part technologically, but the most difficult content-wise. Obviously, with an enormous amount of computer graphics and visualization literature and software in the world, we needed to decide on the subset that would be the most useful and interesting to our target audience. This took a few iterations, but eventually we put together what we feel is a good, comprehensive text with sufficient references so that the reader who is interested in a particular topic can pursue it on his or her own.

Technologically, the "word processing" problem was somewhat harder, but we muddled through to an acceptable solution. One of the main requirements was compatibility with our publisher as well as with the production end of the operation, that is, what word processor did our editors and page layout people use. This actually turned out to be less of an issue than we initially thought, since most word processor documents can be easily imported into the two leading page layout programs, Aldus PageMaker and QuarkXPress. However, we felt that we should probably stick to the most popular word processors, just to be safe.

Microsoft Word 5.0, which had just been released, has an integrated equation processor—one of our major requirements. MS Word also enabled us to work with the two premier Macintosh equation editors—Expressionist, from Prescience, Inc., and MathType, by Design Science. It should be noted that there are several other fine word processors on the market, each of which has their strengths, and that it is not clear that we would make the same decision today, although the requirement of an equation editor narrowed the choice considerably. We would probably look very hard at this problem at the outset today. As it turned out, however, MS Word 5.0 was acceptable, although it is missing a number of important features such as a "compare documents" function, simpler and more flexible page numbering and printing options, and a true glossary creation capability, so that we could simply select a given word and have it appear as an entry in a glossary list in a way that would enable us to add its definition later. An indexing function that transferred data to page layout programs would also be helpful, as would some general intelligence that would allow you to search for items *in context*.

FIGURES

One issue that we identified early on was the problem of creating drawings and dealing with the sheer volume of images that we were going to have. In this section we'll look at these issues in some depth and try to use our "hindsight glasses" to try to develop a model that would work better than the way that we had done it originally. The figures in the text are delineated into two categories: *images* and *drawings*. Images are further divided into hardcopy images—those images which were provided to us in the form of 35-mm slides, 8×10 prints or 4×5 transparencies—and computer-generated images. Nearly all hardcopy images were scanned in at Robert Meyers Studio in Pasadena on a high-resolution (4000 dpi) Howtek D4000 drum scanner. Since there were well over 100 such images, this ended up costing quite a bit.

Once the images were scanned in we had the additional problem of handling them for analysis and page layout, since many of the images were 15 to 30 MB in size. This was handled in two phases. First Jan Benes (our production manager) in Oakland needed to have all of the images for page-layout and prepress work. This meant that we had to create 8-bit low-res images of all scanned and computed images and send them to him on a Syquest cartridge. Due to the iterative nature of publishing a work as complex as this, we ended up doing this several times. Second, at Bob Meyers Studio we needed to have all images in the right place for final page layout and film production. Fortunately, QuarkXPress automatically makes a low-res image linked to the corresponding high-res image, and you simply work with the low-res image in the final page-layout and color separation phase of the operation.

No matter what their source, all images were eventually processed by the authors in Adobe Photoshop, which we used as our all-purpose image processing, data translation, compositing and display software. The sheer size of each of the images meant that not only did we need huge amounts of disk space for the aggregate collection of images, but we were constrained to having to wait as long as 15 minutes for a given image to open up. To solve this problem we ended up making smaller versions, as well as 8-bit versions (in indexed color) of each of the images. For review, page layout and design purposes we also had to print out the images—sometimes in color and sometimes in gray-scale. For that we used Photoshop to create, by hand, composites of 3 to 6 images, which saved printing time and cost, but at the penalty of having to build the composites. In this process, computer-generated images were easier to deal with than hardcopy images since they weren't nearly as large. A typical computer-generated image was 100 to 300K, compared to many MB for a high-resolution scanned-in image.

Unfortunately, all of the images tended to breed, so to speak—there ended up being a lot of different versions of many of the images. Thus, for example, a data set might have first been created in Mathematica, or from raw data, then imported into Spyglass Transform for more analysis, or perhaps for a different color mapping, then into Photoshop for final layout. Each step along the way often generated images in two or three different formats, color schemes, and resolutions. In addition, some of the images used in Chapter 1 and Tech Note 2 had to be processed several times in Photoshop, with each version saved as a separate figure. Moreover, for the image processing sections, because Photoshop puts out histograms as dialog boxes, we had to take screen shots of the dialog boxes and then carve out the histograms from the larger screen using the bitmap tools in Photoshop. The bottom line is that we ended up with literally thousands of images, in many different formats, each of which had a particular reason for its existence. The problem was that the entire collection wreaked absolute havoc with any simple means of managing our image data base. Given that we were changing, adding, and renumbering images up until the day before we went to press, the problem rapidly got out of control, both in terms of the sheer volume of images, as well as the actual numbering of each image.

We also had a class of figures which we call "drawings." These were done by Ming Chen of the Art Center College of Design, and were basically line drawings or schematics of various processes mentioned throughout the book. These figures tended to have several versions, since there were corrections on most of them which needed to be addressed before any given image could be considered complete. Thus, there ended up being several versions of each figure floating around at any given time. In addition, these figures were done in Adobe Illustrator 3.1, a "professional level" illustration program that has its own set of problems—the most annoying of which is that not all images generated in Adobe Illustrator are able to be read by Adobe Photoshop.

Also, the PostScript™ vs. TrueType™ font problem which plagued us throughout the entire process seemed to be most severe in Adobe Illustrator.

The solution to many of these problems was to build an image data base. That way, each individual issue could be handled one-at-a-time. However, as was the case with much of the development of VNP, there wasn't any good software to do this when we started. But, as luck would have it, just as things seemed hopeless, help arrived. In the summer of 1992, Claris released Filemaker Pro 2.0, which enabled us to build a custom image data base, complete with data about each figure, such as its number, permissions status, author, location of original and/or high-resolution image, as well as the caption. We also provided a space for special notes on the image, and a set of "check boxes" for various aspects of each image. Jim Knighton of JPL, who had considerable experience with Filemaker Pro 1.1, built the first prototype for us to test the software and the general concept of using Filemaker to build an image data base, since earlier versions of Filemaker had several bugs that made the software unreliable for image data base management. After Knighton's prototype proved viable RSW developed the final data base which we used throughout the rest of the project. The image data base allowed us to rapidly progress from raw manuscript to final product, and probably saved a couple of months in the final production, since it provided us with an organized way of managing the increasing number of figures that we had.

All figures were stored on two FWB Hammer drives (1.4 GB and 1.0 GB, respectively) as well as several 600 MB optical disks, and about two dozen 44 MB Syquest cartridges. Bob Meyers also had copies of all of the scanned-in images, which we then used in production. In general, we tried to keep working 8-bit images in the top level folders of a single 1.4 GB Hammer drive. All of the images were backed up with 8-mm data-quality tape on a PCPC Jetstream drive using Netstream 2.1.1 backup software. For security, the backup tapes were kept in a location that was physically separate from the drives.

PAGE LAYOUT AND PRODUCTION

The page layout was done in QuarkXPress by Jim Predny at Black Hole Productions in Oakland. The QuarkXPress files were then sent to Robert Meyers Studio in Pasadena where the actual production of the films took place. First all of the original hi-res images were linked to the low-res images in the layout. All of the images were then run through SpectrePrint Professional, professional color separation software, for the final color separations. The low-resolution master files from SpectrePrint were then placed into the QuarkXPress files from Black Hole. Using this technique, the low-res master is then automatically linked to the hi-res file. In Meyers' studio we then sent the hi-res image files down over Ethernet to a Linotronic L330 Imagesetter. The files were then imaged on the Linotronic L330 at a resolution of 3386 dpi at a line-screen of 200. The L330 then imaged the files to composite film at 200 linescreen. The L330 puts out each of the four CMYK films, which are then processed and sent off to the printer.

BUILDING THE CD-ROM

Developing the CD-ROM was another massive task. Our objective was to have over 100 animations on the CD, with as many as possible having a sound track. One of us (Wolff) had made a CD-ROM in 1989 (the Apple Science CD), and so had some experience in development, production and testing of CD's. That experience turned out to be quite useful and helped prevent a few fatal mistakes, like insufficient testing, and attempting to make the CD cross-platform. Unfortunately, the reality is that animations—especially those with sound—only work decently on a Macintosh today. However, this will likely change over the next couple of years, as QuickTime for Microsoft Windows and Unix develops sufficiently. One problem that must be faced for the cross-platform environment is that, since all graphical environments are different, interfaces need to be developed in platform-specific environments. It's probably a good bet that, whatever happens over the next few years, developers will still have to do specific tweaking for the graphics, display, and audio environments of each platform.

The CD-ROM has several interesting features that we intended from the outset to build in: (1) an easy-to-use interface to all of the animations, (2) a folder of neat software and data sets for you to experiment with, (3) thoughts (videos) from several experts in computer graphics and data visualization, and (4) reference "pointers" between the book and the CD.

The animations themselves consist of three types: (1) Digitized video, such as the NASA animations where the animations were either real-time video directly off of the screen, or pre-computed as single-frame computer-generated animations and then digitized into QuickTime movies from their final videotape form. The objective there was to play with the various QuickTime compression parameters to maximize image quality, image size, and frame rate in both 8-bit as well as 24-bit graphics environments. (2) Computer-generated animations, where we simply made the QuickTime movie from the original data, such as the volume visualizations from VoxelView, and Mike Norman's animations of gas jets. Here the objectives were pretty much the same as in the case with the digitized videos. (3) Talking heads of the graphics and visualization experts, where the trick here was to try to sync up the audio with the lip movements of the researchers. This is somewhat difficult when the frame rates are constrained to below 20 fps on the CD because of many CD players' maximum data transfer rate (<150 KB per second).

The interface to the animations was programmed in Macromedia Director 3.1.1 by Ming Chen, our "man behind the scenes." Ming also spent innumerable hours creating the look and feel of the interface as well as each of the 100 icons that appear both in the interface and in the text. The icons were created from resized frames from each of the videos such that they would better resemble the original frames than the resized images.

A major difficulty that we had was to find a suitable development environment within which to build the interface. We did the original prototype in Supercard 1.6. Although the actual development would have been easier in Supercard than in Director, Supercard's future is uncertain, and we could not receive either the technical support nor the product development support to help us with some of the QuickTime and 24-bit color related issues that we had. Another constraint on the interface was the determination of a minimum screen size. We determined that, although there were a fair number of Apple 12-inch monitors being sold to LC users, the majority of color monitors currently in our primary market are Apple 13-inch RGB monitors. Thus, we designed the interface to work within the 13-inch environment. As a final word on the interface development, moving to Director cost us a couple of months of development time, and it has its own set of technical problems, but the end result proved to be a workable, though far from perfect environment. Thus, even though Director's rather arcane interface is a bit confusing—it does not treat QuickTime in a very graceful way and it is somewhat quirky when working with large numbers of objects and QuickTime movies—we were able to struggle through to achieve a pretty reasonable interface.

The actual CD-development environment is shown in Figure A.1, powered by a 32 MB Mac IIfx with a 160 MB internal drive and a SuperMac 24-bit accelerated graphics card. This photograph of the CD-production environment shows all of the components necessary to build a CD-ROM. Note that the specific components used here are only indicative of the generic kinds of components needed. From right to left (excluding keyboard and mouse) are an Apple 13-inch RGB monitor which we used as the target display; an Apple 21-inch monochrome monitor used for development of the Macromind Director interface; the Mac IIfx (standing behind the monitor); a Pinnacle Recordable CD (RCD) drive; a PLI 44/88 MB Syquest drive (top of drive stack); an FWB Hammer 600 MB drive (middle), used for the actual CD prototyping; an FWB Hammer 1 GB drive used for data management and immediate backup; and a Pinnacle REO-650 magneto-optical drive used for immediate random access backup. Not shown is the PCPC 8-mm Exabyte drive used for permanent archiving. Note that we have two monitors and five external SCSI drives attached to the FX. By componentizing the system this way we gain maximum flexibility at the expense of physical space on the desktop. This flexibility strongly contributes to efficiency in the development environment and is, in a number of ways, more efficient than partitioning a single large disk into multiple volumes. Moreover, although a Quadra 800 or 950 would have been desirable here, it was not necessary since there was not much computation involved, and the only available Quadra was much more valuable in the QuickTime system (Figure A.2).

Actually making the QuickTime movies (or QuickTime MooVs—"Moo-Vees," as they are properly referred to) proved an interesting challenge in itself. Animations came in several varieties—

Figure A.1
This photograph of the CD-production environment shows all of the components necessary to build a CD-ROM. From right to left (excluding keyboard and mouse) are two Apple monitors, a Mac IIfx (standing behind the larger monitor), a Pinnacle Recordable CD (RCD) drive, a PLI 44/88 MB Syquest cartridge drive (top of drive stack), two FWB Hammer drives, and a Pinnacle REO-650 magneto-optical drive. The dark bars in the monitors are due to video roll.

Figure A.1

existing Quicktime MooVs, PICS files, a series of PICT files (from which PICS files are then made), sequences of raw (RGB or gray-scale) image files, sequences of floating-point files, sequences of Mathematica images and, of course, videos—lots of them—in all sorts of formats: VHS, SVHS, U-Matic, U-Matic SP, 8mm, Hi-8mm, and laserdisk. If you look at Figure A.2 you'll see the QuickTime production system that we used to digitize videos and make the MooVs. The different video players are controlled by a simple composite audio/video switcher. A Quadra 950 with a 400 MB internal hard disk and 68 MB RAM controls the entire system. The input into the Quadra is through a Radius Video Vision and Adobe Premier 2.0 running on top of QuickTime 1.5. The actual video digitization process was controlled through Adobe Premier 2.0.

Digitizing a video is fairly simple in this environment. You simply select the video source and hit "Record" in Adobe Premiere. Various recording parameters (such as the size of the movie, whether or not it is compressed while digitizing, etc.) are set through dialog boxes in Premiere. Once the video is digitized, then it must be compressed to a reasonable size (< 10 MB per minute) and a reasonable frame rate so that it will play back from the (relatively slow) CD-ROM drive. To help achieve that frame rate one also needs to choose an appropriate image quality. This becomes kind of a black art that one must simply experience in order to understand.

Figure A.2
This photograph of the QuickTime production system shows the minimum necessary components to be able to create QuickTime MooVs from a variety of video formats. From right to left (on the desktop) are a Sony 20-inch video monitor, a PLI 44/88 MB Syquest cartridge drive, a PCPC 8mm tape backup drive, a 1.4 GB FWB Hammer drive, an Apple 16-inch color monitor, a Radius Video Vision multi-input interface box, a composite (consumer-level) video switcher, a Sony SVHS deck, and a Sony BVU-950 U-Matic SP deck. Not shown are the Hi-8mm deck and the Pioneer 4200 laserdisk. Below are the Quadra 950 CPU and the Apple 13-inch RGB monitor (necessary for the Radius Video Vision display).

Figure A.2

Although Premiere is good at recording and editing several video and audio tracks, it is not good at compressing video. This is best done through Apple's Movieshop software, written by George Cossey of IT Makers, where, it is *strongly* suggested in the documentation, you should select Apple's *Compact Video* compressor to compress the MooVs for CD production. The Compact Video codec is designed to allow the user to keep the data rate under a "magic limit," such as 100 K/s, which is roughly the bandwidth of the data transfer between the CD-ROM and the CPU. However, each video has its own problems, and one needs to look carefully at the different choices for compressing a video in order to get the best quality for each one. Moreover, each video can take as much as 2 hours per minute on a Quadra 950 to compress, so you want to be right more often than wrong. The Quadra 950 turned out to be about 4 times faster than a Mac IIfx for compressing images and animations. In other words, when we first began this project we were taking as much as 24 hours to compress a 3-minute MooV. Quicktime 1.5 is also a significant improvement over QuickTime 1.0, which we used at first (see Eric Hoffert's discussion of QuickTime on the CD-ROM). The videos themselves were digitized by RSW and Ming Chen in Pasadena over a period of a few months in late 1992 to early 1993.

The process is not cookbook by a long shot, and often Movieshop would run into an unsolvable problem while compressing, and we would be forced to start the compression process over again— even if the compression was 95% completed. Also, sometimes the completed compressed MooV would look just awful, and we would have to go back to the beginning and select new compression parameters. Getting up to speed in all of these technologies took a while to learn.

Testing the CD was another interesting experience. The prototypes and the final master were all done on desktop CD-mastering machines, with the majority of work done on a Pinnacle Recordable CD machine (RCD) which is a very small, easy to use system that creates a direct image of the source disk and puts it on the (writeable) CD-ROM. That CD-ROM can then be used as the master for the CD-pressing. We went through a number of prototypes (CD mastering is not for the faint of heart) testing for things like performance (both in the interface and in the QuickTime movies), video and sound sync, interface functionality, and correct data pathways to all of the animations. The original plan was to build a *test matrix*, which is a matrix of functionality that has testable features on the x-axis and Machine/Operating System configuration on the y-axis. Testing then consists of testing the software for each element of the matrix. This is what we did with the Science CD in 1989. However, back then Apple only had three color machines (original Mac II, Mac IIx, and the Mac IIcx—the Mac IIci had not been released yet), and there was only 8-bit color at the time.

Unfortunately, there are currently several dozen color Macintosh hardware configurations, as well as at least three 7.x operating system configurations at the time of this writing—we're currently only guaranteeing that the CD will run under System 7. This made the traditional testing matrix essentially impossible to use. So we had to substitute the "representative sample" method, wherein we test the CD on select systems and extrapolate to other environments. In our case, we tested the system on a Mac LC with 10 MB RAM; a Mac LC with 6 MB RAM—both with 8-bit graphics on a 13-inch monitor; several Mac IIfx configurations, a couple of Mac IIci configurations, and a Quadra 950 with a 13-inch and a 16-inch monitor. The four existing CD-ROM drives that Apple made at the time of production— the CDSC, the CDSC-Plus, the CD-150, and the CD-300—were each tested as well with each of the systems, as were various system configurations.

Once we successfully completed the CD testing, and we had a good master CD, we then went to a few CD manufacturers to price the CD production and artwork. Although at the time this text went to press we had not selected a vendor, this is the easiest part of the process. We simply ship the master CD to the vendor, along with the artwork for the label, and the vendor makes the number of copies that we ask for. The CDs are then sent to the book–binding company for incorporation with the text.

LOGISTICS

Two authors working on a project of this magnitude is a difficult enough task if they are co-located. However, we were 350 miles apart and, since each of us had significant Apple responsibilities for our regular jobs, sitting down for extended "togetherness sessions" was essentially impossible. Enter again Apple's technology—this time in the form of Apple's Appleshare-based Engineering Network, and AppleTalk Remote Access system, which allowed us to interactively, and visually view and work with the same files from home or the office. Since both of us are fairly technologically literate we were able to minimize any problems by simply keeping compatible. As it turned out, we were often on the phone at 2 or 3 a.m. looking at images and text over the network at 9600 baud and editing each other's work while we manipulated images and animations. Federal Express also did well in this operation since the two of us (Wolff and Yaeger) and Jan Benes were constantly sending disks, Syquest cartridges, and magneto-optical disks around California. Thus, with these tools, and less than a half-dozen meetings, we were able to develop, write, review, and edit the entire project long distance. However, we wouldn't recommend this process for everyone. It is definitely a bit intense—especially if you wish to maintain your sanity. Fortunately, both authors are a bit eccentric and are used to working "on-the-edge," so everything worked out well. Otherwise you wouldn't be reading this.

List of Visualization Software and Vendors Used in VNP

Adobe Systems, Inc.
1585 Charleston Rd.
Mountain View, CA 94039-7900
Photoshop
Illustrator
Premiere

Apple Computer, Inc.
20525 Mariani Ave.
Cupertino, CA 95014
408-996-1010
QuickTime
MovieShop

**Cambridge Scientific
Computing, Inc.**
875 Massachusetts Avenue, Suite 61
Cambridge, MA 02139
617-491-6862
Chem3D

Electric Image, Inc.
117 East Colorado Blvd.
Pasadena, CA 91105
818-577-1627
Electric Image Software

FWB Software, Inc.
2722 Gough Street
San Francisco, CA 94123
415-474-8055
Hammer 1000, 1400 Hard Drives

MacroMedia (MacroMind), Inc.
600 Townsend Street
San Francisco, CA 94103
415-442-0200
Director

**National Center for Super-
computing Applications (NCSA)**
405 North Matthews Ave.
Urbana, IL 61801
217-244-2909
NCSA Image

Pinnacle Micro, Inc.
19 Technology
Irvine, CA 92718
714-727-3300
RCD-202 Recordable CD-ROM

Radius, Inc.
1710 Fortune Drive
San Jose, CA 95131
408-434-1010
VideoVision

Spyglass, Inc.
701 Devonshire Drive
Champaign, IL 61820
217-355-6000
Spyglass Transform
Spyglass Dicer

SuperMac Technology
215 Moffet Park Drive
Sunnyvale, CA 94089
408-541-6100
Video Spigot

Synergy Software
2457 Perkiomen Ave.
Reading, PA 19606
215-779-0522
KaleidaGraph

Vital Images, Inc.
505 North 4th Street
Fairfield, IA 52556
515-472-7726
VoxelView

Wolfram Research, Inc.
100 Trade Center Drive
Champaign, IL 61820-7237
217-398-0700
Mathematica

337

Appendix B
GLOSSARY

a-buffer: A computer graphics rendering algorithm that utilizes a coverage mask at each pixel to allow subpixel coverage determination, thus reducing aliasing artifacts.

aliasing: In signal processing, undersampling of a continuous function which produces artifacts resulting from misrepresentation of frequencies higher than one-half the sampling frequency. In image processing, the finite number of pixels yields a limiting representation of an image that produces "jaggies" or "staircasing."

alpha channel: An extra 8-bit image channel (in addition to RGB) used primarily for transparency or graphic overlays.

angular roll-off: The modulation of light intensity as a function of angle measured from the principal light direction.

anti-aliasing: In imaging, applying gradation in intensity of neighboring pixels in an effort to correct aliasing artifacts.

Betacam SP: A half-inch, component-based videotape and recording format used mostly by the professional broadcast industry.

binary voxel: In certain types of volume visualization algorithms, a surface is classed as either passing through or not passing through a given voxel. In this sense, the voxel is treated as binary.

bi-normal: The vector formed by the vector product of the tangent and normal to a curve.

bit depth: In an image, the number of bits of dynamic range in an image. In sampling theory, bit-depth refers to the number of bits used in each sample. Thus, 8 bits gives 256 levels of dynamic range, whereas 16 bits gives 65,536 levels.

bow shock: The leading shock wave set up when an object moves supersonically through a gas.

bump map: An image or texture that is used to perturb an object's surface normals during the lighting and shading stage of the computer graphics rendering process, thus producing the appearance of a rough or bumpy surface. A parametric mapping, specified at the object's vertices, is used to generate the appropriate mapping to the object's surface.

cathode ray tube: The common display mechanism used in most television and computer monitors, involving the use of an electron gun to stimulate phosphors on a screen to create light and color.

CD-ROM: Compact Disk Read-Only Memory, a small laserdisk capable of holding 600 MB of data.

CMYK: A color model using cyan, magenta, yellow, and black as the primary colors from which all other colors can be constructed. This model is generally used in color printers using a variety of printing technologies.

codec: Compression-decompression algorithms used in many types of data image compression in QuickTime.

color channel: Generally defined as one of the 8-bit red, green, blue, or alpha channels.

color space: Some portion of the visible color spectrum. The color representation used to best visualize an image.

color transformation: The mapping of the original data to a particular color palette.

component video: A method of recording images onto videotape where separate components of color and brightness (chrominance and luminance) are laid down on the tape. This technique gives substantially better quality than composite video, since there is more information in the signal, but at a significantly higher cost.

composite video: A method of recording images onto videotape where brightness and color are laid down as a single signal on the tape. This technique has less information than in the case of component video, but is considerably cheaper.

compression: Techniques employed to reduce the amount of data needed to describe an image, animation or data file. Compression techniques can be lossy (information is lost in the compression) or loss-less (information is not lost in the compression). Compression plays an important part in QuickTime technology.

contour plots: A technique for plotting scalar data of the form $f(x, y)$ by constructing closed (level) curves of equal values of f.

control points: Special points that define the shape of a curve.

CRT: Cathode ray tube.

CT: Computed tomography, where the intensity of a point in an image reflects the density of the object. CT scans are generally performed with X-rays.

digital elevation data: In a geographical or planetary image, a data set where for each $\{x, y\}$ a value of z, or height, is assigned.

digitize: The process of converting an analog signal to a digital data set by taking samples of the amplitude at (generally regular) intervals.

direct volume rendering: The class of volume rendering techniques characterized by sampling data along a ray through the volume.

DVR: Direct volume rendering.

dynamic range: The difference between the largest and smallest amplitudes of a data set. For example. the dynamic range of a 256-level gray-scale image is 8 bits.

ease-in: A method for gradually accelerating an object, usually from a resting state, to provide a more realistic look to an animated sequence.

ease-out: A method for gradually decelerating an object, usually to a resting state, to provide a more realistic look to an animated sequence.

8-bit color: A false color scheme where all colors of an image are mapped into 8 bits (256 values).

Ethernet: A network standard that allows computers to transfer data reliably at data rates of roughly 10 Mbits/s.

eyepoint: The location from which a scene is observed.

false color: A technique for displaying images in some other scheme than natural color.

false image: An image of a data set which uses a subset of 24-bit RGBcolor space to display or accent specific features of the data set.

flat shading: One of the simplest methods for shading a computer graphics object, in which color is constant across the entire face of any given polygon.

fps: Frames per second.

frame: An individual image in an animation or video.

frame buffer: The hardware system in a computer where an image is stored before being displayed. Frame buffers are referred to by the number of bits per pixel and the maximum number of horizontal and vertical pixels.

frame-differencing: A technique for compressing data by computing only the difference in pixels between consecutive frames.

frame-rate: The number of frames per second (fps) in an animation. This concept is important in digitizing video for a QuickTime movie.

gamma correction: A look-up table used to relate the desired, perceived pixel brightness to a value which is actually used to control the electron gun in a CRT, taking into account the display properties of that particular CRT and, sometimes, the logarithmic response properties of the human visual system.

GB: Gigabyte (10^9 bytes).

Gouraud shading: A method for providing smooth shading of adjacent polygons, appropriate to diffuse lighting conditions and smooth objects. In this technique, surface normals are computed only at polygonal vertices, and the resulting colors are interpolated along polygonal edges and spans (contrast to Phong shading).

gray-level: The intensity of a monochromatic image at a given point, or pixel.

gray-scale: The dynamic range of gray-levels in a monochromatic image.

gridded data: Data that is defined on the vertices of a coordinate grid.

HDF: Hierarchical Data Format, a data standard developed by NCSA and used by researchers and developers worldwide for archiving as well as for interactive visualization and analysis.

hidden line: A line that is obscured by another line or surface in a wireframe image.

hidden surface: A surface that is obscured by another surface in a 3-D image.

Hi-8 mm: A component videotape format that uses two components, chrominance and luminance, to represent the video signal. Image quality and image resolution are higher than for the original 8 mm composite video format and most consumer video formats.

hold-out mattes: An image used to separate foreground and background elements, permitting a multiple exposure to be made which incorporates disparate elements into a single scene.

iconographic: A technique for using attributes of icons, or small figures, to represent variables in a multiparameter visualization.

image: At its simplest level a digital image is just an array of data. The array need not be square. Each datum in an image, called a pixel, represents a color.

image plane: A fictitious plane within the cone of vision and perpendicular to the field of view of the image.

image processing: Manipulating image color and dynamic range to bring out specific features that are not visible to the eye at first.

Imagetool: The first personal computer software developed specifically for imaging floating-point data.

in-betweening: The process of constructing frames between key-frames in an animation.

ionize: The process of removing an electron from an atom or molecule. Ionization usually occurs from collision with electrons or UV photons.

ionosphere: That region of a planetary atmosphere where ionization from solar UV radiation produces a stable ionized layer.

IR: Infrared, the portion of the electromagnetic spectrum just below the longest visible wavelengths (red). Frequently used to image heat content. Also used as the basis of most remote control devices.

isosurfaces: Surfaces within a volume that have the same parameter value (see level surface).

key-frames: Special frames in an animation at which object positions are specified, in order to define the full motion path of each object.

level curves: The set of all points on a surface with a given scalar value.

level surfaces: The set of all points in a volume with a given scalar value.

lighting model: Any of a number of algorithms used to define the perceived coloration of objects in a scene. A method for computing the perceived color of an object from its shape, its position relative to the observer, and the location of any and all light sources.

lossless compression: Compression techniques where information is not lost during the compression/decompression process. This type of compression can usually reduce the amount of data in an image by about a factor of 2 (less in very complex, naturalistic scenes, more in simpler scenes with uniformly shaded backgrounds and objects).

lossy compression: Compression techniques where information is lost during the compression/decompression process, while still retaining the essential features of the image. This type of compression can reduce the amount of data in an image by a factor of 10 to 100.

Mach bands: A visual artifact associated with Gouraud rendering, resulting from the human perceptual system's sensitivity to discontinuities in the first derivative of brightness. These discontinuities result from different linear interpolations being used to shade the polygons on either side of a shared edge. Because of the eye's sensitivity to these discontinuities, light and dark bands are perceived along the edges of polygons, even though their computed brightness is continuous across these edges.

magnetosphere: That region of space surrounding a planet that is dominated by the planet's magnetic field, which shields most of the solar wind from the planet's atmosphere or surface.

Marching Cubes: A method of visualizing 3-D data structures by looking for level surfaces in a 3-space comprised of a lattice of points. In contrast to DVR methods, where one can see the entire structure, marching cubes only allows a single surface to be rendered.

matte painting: A common special-effects technique in the movie business, a matte painting is an artist's depiction of a scene that is more or less seamlessly combined with other photographic materials to produce a desired setting, without the expense of building a set or shooting on location.

MB: Megabyte, or one million bytes.

MHD: Magnetohydrodynamics, a field of physics which describes magnetized fluids in astrophysics and plasma physics.

modeling: A generic term that in the field of computer graphics means the design and construction of computer models of objects to be used in scene composition, animation, and rendering.

morphing: Morphological transformation of images or objects. Usually this refers to various methods for interpolating images from one 2D shape to another, though it is sometimes used to refer to 3D object interpolation.

mosaic: A single image composed of smaller images "tiled" together.

MRI: Magnetic resonance imaging, a powerful type of magnetically based volume imaging technology used primarily to study interior tissues.

multimedia: The general term used to describe the collective use of sound, images, and text as a presentation or learning tool. Interactive computer graphics, computer animation, video and sound (either analog or digital), and textual materials are controlled by a computer to provide a rich experience. The large amounts of data involved in multimedia systems has made the CD-ROM format an attractive delivery medium.

multiparameter plots: Visualization techniques wherein more than one (scalar or vector) variable is displayed.

multisync: Used to refer to display monitors that are capable of synchronizing to more than one frame rate.

NCSA: National Center for Supercomputing Applications, in Champaign-Urbana, Illinois, where pioneering efforts in scientific visualization and scientific computing have gone on since 1985.

normal: In differential geometry, the normal is defined as a vector perpendicular to the tangent to the curve. In polygonally based modeling, surface normals are defined in terms of the vectors perpendicular to the planes of the polygons.

NTSC: National Television System Committee, a standard developed for television image display in the United States which displays video in composite format. The display resolution for NTSC is 512×486.

NURBs: Non-Uniform Rational B-splines. A family of curves sometimes used to model computer graphic objects and their animation paths.

Nyquist frequency: The lower limit of sampling rate, the Nyquist frequency is defined as twice the highest frequency in the original analog signal.

object models: A geometric and topological description of an object for computer graphics rendering purposes, usually in terms of polygons or spline curves.

opacity: The decrease in intensity of a light beam as it passes through an atmosphere or other transparent medium. Opacity is generally strongly wavelength dependent.

opaque: An opaque substance is one which does not permit any light to pass through it. A substance can be opaque at one wavelength but transparent at others.

optical depth: A dimensionless quantity used to measure the distance that light travels through a substance. An optical depth of unity means that the intensity of radiation has dropped off by a factor of $1/e$ as it passed through the substance. Optical depth is usually wavelength dependent.

optically thin: Generally taken to mean an optical depth near zero.

optically thick: Generally taken to mean an optical depth near one.

palette: The collection of allowable colors that can be used to display a given image.

particle systems: The use of trace particles to represent parameters in a visualization. Particles could be used to represent anything from stars in galaxies to fluid elements in dynamical flow.

PET: Positron Emission Tomography, a type of medical imaging technique that images the interior of an object or patient.

Phong shading: A method for providing smooth shading of adjacent polygons, capable of modeling both diffuse and specular lighting. In this technique, surface normals are computed at polygonal vertices, and then interpolated along polygonal edges and spans, with color being determined on a per-pixel basis from these interpolated normals (contrast to Gouraud shading).

photorealistic: Often viewed as the Holy Grail of computer graphics, photorealistic rendering is the attempt to create an image of an object or scene that looks as real as a photograph.

physically based animation: Computer graphics methods for controlling the animation of objects by simulating physical processes.

physically based modeling: See physically based animation.

pixel: Equivalently, picture element, a pixel is the smallest unit of a computer image and is assigned a unique color after rendering.

point plots: The most basic form of data graphing or visualization, point plots are simply the display of a dot at each $f(x)$.

polygon: A planar, connected sequence of straight line segments or edges. In computer graphics, a polygon is usually the simplest geometrical structure, often a triangle or quadrangle, which can be rendered.

polygonal mesh: A contiguous "net" of polygons, the geometric approximation to the actual object to be rendered. Construction of a polygonal mesh is a necessary first step in rendering, prior to constructing normals or computing lighting or shading models.

pre-roll: This is a short (typically 5 to 8 seconds) period of time that a videotape is required to roll before the point at which a recording is to be made, in order to allow the videotape machine's mechanism to reach a stable state so as to ensure the accuracy of the edit.

primitives: In computer graphics primitives are the most elemental objects from which all other objects are constructed.

projection techniques: A subset of DVR techniques which assumes that the image is being projected on a back plane.

QuickTime: Apple's time-based media standard which deals with animation, digitized video, compression, and sound.

radar altimetry: The technique used by spacecraft to obtain altitude data of a planetary surface from reflected radar signals.

radiosity: In computer graphics, the rate at which light energy leaves a surface, which includes transmission and reflection. Rendering techniques which compute the radiosity of all surfaces in a scene have been termed radiosity methods.

rasterize: Convert to a pixel array or raster.

ray-tracing: The general technique of computing an image by projecting rays into a scene and using their interactions with the contents of that scene to determine pixel colors. In surface-rendering methods, rays are intersected and possibly reflected or refracted by objects in the scene to determine visible colors. Ray-tracing is also used in volume visualization and is a type of DVR.

real-time: Acquiring data as it is being generated, in a single pass. When recording computer output to another medium, this would imply recording data at 30 fps off of a computer monitor, either by attaching a "video-out" board to the computer, which "streams" the data to the videotape, or by videotaping the screen with a video camera. When using a computer to digitally record input from some video source, this would imply acquiring, and usually compressing, that input by the use of a special video-digitizer board.

reflection map: An image mapped onto a (reflective) computer graphics object to provide the sense that the object is embedded in its environment. The technique for doing this is related to texture mapping and bump mapping, but uses reflection vectors to look up color values in the reflection map rather than a parametric mapping specified at the object's vertices.

relief map: A height-map of a region which appears to have height when viewed. Complementary to a contour map.

render: The process of converting the polygonal or data specification of an image to the image itself, including color and opacity information.

renderer: A software algorithm which renders an image, calculating a color at each pixel based on object visibility and lighting and shading models.

resolution: In an image, resolution is defined as the number of points in the x- and y-directions. In an n-dimensional data set, resolution is defined as the number of data points in each of the n directions.

RGB: Red-green-blue, the color standard employed by most computer manufacturers and which roughly corresponds, in frequency, to the three bands of color sensitivity of the human eye.

rotoscoping: Tracing live-action figures to provide realistic motion for animated figures.

sampling rate: In sampling theory, the frequency at which samples are taken of continuous data.

sampling theory: For an analog function, sampling theory refers to the general theory of constructing a digital representation of the data. Key parameters are sampling rate and bit-depth per sample.

SAR: Synthetic aperture radar, the modern terminology for SLAR.

scanline-sampling: A rendering algorithm used to determine which surfaces in a scene are actually visible from the observer's point of view. This method decomposes objects based on the scanlines they occupy, and then determines which are visible along those scanlines.

scatter plots: A simple graphical technique for data sets $y = f(x)$, where each data point is displayed as a dot in the x-y plane.

scene files: One method for organizing the positioning information for various objects and their constituent parts which compose a scene.

scientific visualization: This concept generally refers to any graphical or image representation of data. More generally, scientific visualization seeks to establish a general set of principles for visually representing complex data structures.

SCSI: Small Computer System Interface, a standard used to connect peripheral devices such as disk drives and scanners to personal computers and certain Unix computers. SCSI devices are an important component in modern personal computing by allowing easy expansion and customization.

SCSI-2: A newer SCSI standard whith higher data transfer speed than the original SCSI standard.

shaders: Software components or algorithms that determine how light is reflected from an object's surface, and thus how that object appears to an observer.

shading model: One of a variety of algorithms used in a shader.

shadow map: A technique for providing the appearance of shadows in a computer graphics scene, where an image (the shadow map) is created, typically by rendering the scene from the point of view of the light, and then using this shadow map to modulate the light's influence on other objects in the scene.

shadow plots: A visualization technique whereby a 3-D object is projected onto a coordinate plane. The projection is called a shadow and is useful to visually determine properties of the hidden portion of the object.

single-frame animation: A process whereby a videotape of a sequence of images is produced by transferring the images one-by-one to a pre-roll recorder or laserdisk machine. In contrast to real-time video, this process takes 15 to 30 seconds per frame, but produces the highest quality video possible. An inverse process, whereby each video frame is digitized via QuickTime, is used to produce the highest quality QuickTime animations.

SLAR: Side-looking airborne radar, an imaging technique where radar pulses are sent out from an airplane or spacecraft antenna which illuminate terrain below oriented normal to the vehicle's direction of motion. Two-way travel time of the pulse is used to determine distance to each point, while brightness of the reflected pulse provides information on the composition and surface roughness.

slow-in: Ease-in.

slow-out: Ease-out.

SMPTE: Society of Motion Picture and Television Engineers.

solar wind: A plasma which extends from the outer atmosphere of the Sun throughout the solar system. The solar wind is mostly composed of ionized hydrogen and electrons, at a density of roughly 10 particles per cubic centimeter at a temperature of 1 million degrees Kelvin traveling at an average speed of 400 km/s.

splines: Mathematical descriptions of curves. A variety of control parameters for different types of splines usually permit relatively easy control over specific points along the spline's path, the "tension" of the spline curve along that path, and the various slopes and derivatives along the path.

squash and stretch: An animation technique common to both traditional cel-based animation and computer graphics animation. Simple distortions of the object's height and width can be used to convey a large number of actions, and even imbue animated characters with seeming emotion.

surface-based: Based on objects that are composed of surfaces, usually polygonal, as opposed to volume-based.

surface-modeling: Techniques and tools for building up computer representations of objects by modeling their surfaces, usually as a collection of polygonal facets.

S-VHS: A component-based video standard which uses two components (chrominance and luminance) as its video signal. S-VHS resolution is also higher than ordinary, composite NTSC.

synthetic aperture radar (SAR): Modern terminology for SLAR.

terrain data: A data set in which one has height as a function of horizontal position.

terrain rendering: The process of creating a 3-D looking image of terrain data of an image, generally by texture mapping an image of the region onto the terrain data.

texture map: An image that is mapped onto the surface of a computer graphics object to provide apparent detail without the expense of explicitly modeling that detail. A parametric mapping, specified at the object's vertices, is used to generate the appropriate mapping to the object's surface.

3-D: Three-dimensional.

3-D contours: 3-D isosurfaces. These are the surfaces formed by collections of points at a constant value in a 3-D volume.

tie points: Specially marked points in a sequence of images that are used to force correspondence between features in those images. Used in image interpolation or morphing.

time-code: Standard way of marking each video frame. Usually SMPTE time code is used in broadcast and multimedia applications. SMPTE time code is roughly 30 fps.

tomographic: The noninvasive process of taking volume data of a patient by systematically passing X-rays through the body.

24-bit color: Often called "full-color," 24-bit color simply means that 8 bits of dynamic range are assigned to each of the three colors (R,G,B) in an image or the electron guns in a monitor. The total number of colors available is, therefore, 2^{24} or over 16 million.

2-D: Two-dimensional.

Unix: A common operating system on computers in universities and scientific establishments.

USGS: United States Geological Survey.

UV: Ultraviolet, the portion of the electromagnetic spectrum just above the shortest visible wavelengths (violet).

vector plots: The use of vectors to visualize quantities with a magnitude and a direction.

video: In computer graphics terminology, video refers to the subsystem of the computer responsible for displaying an image on the monitor. More traditionally, video refers to the display of an (NTSC) image on a TV monitor. This ambiguity has often led to confusion among users who thought that their computer could display images on their TV.

video-RAM: Very fast RAM, generally built into the image display system of a computer, which is used exclusively to store image data prior to the data being displayed.

video roll: An effect of "a rolling line" when videoing a screen due to the difference in frame rates between what your screen is displaying and the shutter speed of your camera.

viewing frustum: Viewing pyramid.

viewing pyramid: The pyramidal cone determined by an observer's point of view and field of view.

visible surface determination: The important stage of a computer graphics rendering algorithm that determines which objects are visible from a particular point of view.

visualization: The broad class of computer graphic and imaging techniques used to create visual representations of data.

volume visualization: Refers to computer graphic techniques used to visualize the interior and surfaces of 3-D objects or data structures.

voxel: The 3-D analog of the pixel, the voxel is often treated as the basic graphical unit in volume visualization.

wedging: The practice of recording multiple test versions of a scene to determine optimal (color) parameter settings.

wireframe: A 3-D plot constructed of lines, often used by researchers to represent a function $f(x,y)$. Wireframe views of computer graphic objects are also widely used in the computer animation process. The graphical construct often looks like it is built out of a set of wires.

witness-point tracking: A technique based on monitoring special points in a live-action scene to determine precise positioning of the live-action camera and scene elements, in order to combine the live-action footage with computer-generated imagery.

x-window: A remote windowing standard, based on Unix, developed at MIT in the 1970s.

z-buffer: A memory scheme for rendering a computer graphic image whereby a z-value is stored for each each pixel in the same manner that a color value is stored for each pixel in a frame buffer. As each point on each object is rendered, its color is only retained if it is the frontmost object occupying that pixel.

Barr, A., "Global and Local Deformations of Solid Primitives," *Computer Graphics, ACM SIGGRAPH '84 Proceedings*, 21-30.

Bartels, Richard H., John C. Beatty, and Brian Barsky, "An Introduction to Splines for Use in Computer Graphics and Geometric Modeling," Morgan Kaufmann Publishers, 1987.

Beatty, J.C. and Booth, K.S., eds., *Tutorial: Computer Graphics*, second edition, IEEE Comp. Soc. Press, Silver Spring, MD, 1982.

Blinn, James F., "Models of Light Reflection for Computer Synthesized Pictures," *Computer Graphics, ACM SIGGRAPH '77 Proceedings*, 192-198. Also in Freeman (1980), 316-322.

Blinn, James F., "Simulation of Wrinkled Surfaces," *Computer Graphics, ACM SIGGRAPH '78 Proceedings*, 286-292.

Blinn, James, "Light Reflection Functions for Simulation of Clouds and Dusty Surfaces," *Computer Graphics, ACM SIGGRAPH '82 Proceedings 16(3), 1982.*

Blinn, James F. and Newell, M.E., "Texture and Reflection in Computer Generated Images," *CACM*, 19(10), October 1976, 542-547.

Block, David L. and Richard J. Wainscoat, "Morphological Differences Between Optical and Infrared Images of the Spiral Galaxy NGC309," *Nature*, 353(6339), 1991, 48-50.

Bly, S. A., "Presenting Information in Sound," *Proceedings of the CHI '82 Conference on Human Factors in Computer Systems, pp. 371-375, 1982.*

Breen, D. E., D.H. House and P.H. Getto, "A Physically-Based Particle Model of Woven Cloth," *The Visual Computer*, Vol. 8, No. 5-6 (Springer-Verlag, Heidelberg, June 1992) 264-277.

Bui-Tuong, Phong, "Illumination for Computer Generated Pictures," *CACM*, 18(6), June 1975, 311-317. Also in Beatty and Booth (1982), 449-455.

Buxton, W., "The Use of Non-Speech Audio at the Interface," *Tutorial #10, CHI '89*, pp. 2.1 - 2.15, 1989.

Catmull, Edward A., *Subdivision Algorithm for Computer Display of Curved Surfaces*, Ph.D. Thesis, Report UTEC-CSc-74-133, Computer Science Department, University of Utah, Salt Lake City, December 1974.

Chandrasekhar, S., *Radiative Transfer*, Oxford University Press, 1950.

Clarke, Arthur C. and Hyams, Peter, *The Odyssey File*, Ballantine Books, 1985.

Cline, H.E., Dumoulin, C. L., Hart, H.R., Jr., Lorenson, W. E., and Ludke, S., "3D Reconstruction of the Brain from Magnetic Resonance Images Using a Connectivity Algorithm," *Magnetic Resonance Imaging*, 5, 1987, 245-352.

Cook, R. L. "Shade Trees," *Computer Graphics, ACM SIGGRAPH '84 Proceedings*, 223-231.

Cook, R. L., Porter, T., and Carpenter, L., "Distributed Ray Tracing," *Computer Graphics, ACM SIGGRAPH '84 Proceedings*, 137-145.

Cook, R. and Torrance, K., "A Reflectance Model for Computer Graphics," *ACM TOG*, 1(1), January 1982, 7-24.

Drebin, Robert A., Loren Carpenter, and Pat Hanrahan, "Volume Rendering," *ACM SIGGRAPH '88 Proceedings*, 22(4), 1988, 65-74.

Drewry, D. J., "Antarctica: Glaciological and Geophysical Folio," University of Cambridge, Scott Polar Research Institute, Cambridge, England, 1983.

Dungan, W., Stenger, A., and Sutty, G., "Texture Tile Considerations for Raster Graphics," *SIGGRAPH '78 Proceedings*, 12(3), 1978.

Feibush, E. A., Levoy, M., and Cook, R. L., "Synthetic Textures Using Digital Filters" *Computer Graphics*, 14, 1980.

Fishman, G. and Scheter, B., "Computer Display of Height Fields," *Computers and Graphics*, 5, 1980, 53-60.

Foley, James D., van Dam, Andries, Feiner, Steven K., and Hughes, John F., *Computer Graphics Principles and Practice*, second edition, Addison-Wesley, 1990.

Fournier, A., Fussel, D., and Carpenter, L., "Computer Rendering of Stochastic Models," *Communications of the ACM*, 25, 1982, 371-384.

Freeman, H., ed., *Tutorial and Selected Readings in Interactive Computer Graphics*, IEEE Comp. Soc. Press, Silver Spring, MD, 1980.

Gonzalez, Rafael C. and Richard E. Woods, *Digital Image Processing*, Addison-Wesley, 1992.

Gouraud, H. "Continuous Shading of Curved Surfaces," *IEEE Trans. on Computers*, C-20(6), June 1971, 623-629. Also in Freeman (1980), 302-308.

Grinstein, Georges, Ronald Pickett, and Marian G. Williams, "EXVIS: An Exploratory Visualization Environment," *Graphics Interface '89, London, Ontario*, 1989.

Grinstein, Georges and Stuart Smith, "The Perceptualization of Scientific Data," in *Extracting Meaning from Complex Data: Processing, Display, Interaction*, SPIE - The International Society for Optical Engineering, Bellingham, Washington; 1990, 190-199.

Haber, Robert B., "Visualization in Engineering Mechanics: Techniques, Systems and Issues," in *Visualization Techniques in the Physical Sciences, ACM SIGGRAPH Course Notes (Course 19)*, 1988.

Hanrahan, P., "Volume Rendering," in *Volume Visualization Algorithms and Architectures, ACM SIGGRAPH '90 Course 11 Notes*.

Harris, Lowell D., R. A. Robb, T. S. Yuen, and E. L. Ritman, "Non-invasive Numerical Dissection and Display of Anatomic Structure Using Computerized X-Ray Tomography," *Proceedings SPIE* 152, 1978, 10-18.

Heckbert, Paul, "Filtering by Repeated Integration," *Computer Graphics, ACM SIGGRAPH '86 Proceedings*, 315-321.

Herman, Gabor T. and H. K. Liu, "Three-Dimensional Display of Organs from Computed Tomograms," *Computer Graphics and Image Processing,* 9(1), 1979, 1-21.

Hughes, P. J., *Mars Navigator*, Master's Thesis, University of California Santa Cruz, 1991.

Hussey, K. J., J. R. Hall, and R. A. Mortensen, "Image Processing Methods in Two and Three Dimensions used to Animate Remotely Sensed Data," in *Proceedings of IGARSS Symposium (Zurich, Switzerland, Sept. 8-11, 1986,* ESA Publications, Netherlands, 1987, 771-776.

Jet Propulsion Laboratory, "L. A.: The Movie," *SIGGRAPH '87 Film and Video Show,* 1987.

Jet Propulsion Laboratory, "Mars: The Movie," *SIGGRAPH '89 Computer Graphics Theatre,* 1989.

Kajiya, J. and B. Von Herzen, "Ray Tracing Volume Densities," *Computer Graphics, ACM SIGGRAPH '84 Proceedings* 18(3), 1984.

Kass, Michael and Miller, Gavin, "Rapid, Stable Fluid Dynamics for Computer Graphics," *Computer Graphics, ACM SIGGRAPH '90 Proceedings,* 1990, 49-55.

Kazafumi, K., Kato, F., Nakamae, E., Nishita, T., Tanaka, H., and Noguchi, T., "Three-Dimensional Terrain Modeling and Display for Environmental Assessment," *Computer Graphics,* 23(3) 1989, 207-214.

Kelly, A. D., Malin, M. C., and Nielson, G. M., "Terrain Simulation Using a Model of Stream Erosion," *Computer Graphics,* 22(4), 1988, 263-268.

Knuth, Donald E., *The Art of Computer Programming, Vol. 3: Sorting and Searching*, Addison-Wesley, Reading, MA, 1973.

Laur, D. and P. Hanrahan, "Hierarchical Splatting: A Progressive Refinement Algorithm for Volume Rendering," *Computer Graphics, ACM SIGGRAPH '91 Proceedings* 25(4), 1991.

Levoy, M., "Display of Surfaces from Volume Data", *IEEE Computer Graphics and Applications,* 8(3), 1988.

Levoy, M., "Ray-Tracing of Volume Data," in "Volume Visualization Algorithms and Architectures," *ACM SIGGRAPH '90 Course #11 Notes,* 1990.

Levoy, M., "Efficient Ray-Tracing of Volume Data", *ACM Transactions on Graphics,* 9(3), 1990.

Lewis, J., "Generalized Stochastic Subdivision," *ACM Transactions on Graphics,* 6(2), 1987, 167-190.

Lorenson, William E. and Harvey E. Cline, "Marching Cubes: A High-Resolution 3-D Surface Construction Algorithm," *Computer Graphics (ACM SIGGRAPH '87 Conference Proceedings),* 1987.

Lunney, D. and R. C. Morrison, "High Technology Laboratory Aids for Visually Handicapped Chemistry Students," *Journal of Chemical Education,* 58(3), 1981, 228-231.

Max, N., "Light Diffusion through Clouds and Haze," *Computer Vision, Graphics and Image Processing,* 19, 1986.

Mezrich, J.J., S. Frysinger, and R. Slivjanovski, "Dynamic Representation of Multivariate Time Series Data," *Journal of the American Statistical Association,* 79(385), 1984, 34-40.

Newman, William M. and Sproull, Robert F., *Principles of Interactive Computer Graphics*, second edition, McGraw-Hill, 1979.

Pavlidis, T,. *Algorithms for Image Processing*, Computer Science Press, 1982, 142-163.

Perlin, Ken "An Image Synthesizer," *Computer Graphics, ACM SIGGRAPH '85 Proceedings*, 287-296.

Press, William H., Flannery, Brian P., Teukolsky, Saul A., and Vetterling, William T., *Numerical Recipes: The Art of Scientific Computing*, Cambridge University Press, 1986.

Reeves, W.T., "Particle Systems — A Technique for Modeling a Class of Fuzzy Objects," *Computer Graphics, ACM SIGGRAPH '83 Proceedings*, 359-376.

Reeves, W.T., and Blau, R., "Approximate and Probabilistic Algorithms for Shading and Rendering Particle Systems," *Computer Graphics, ACM SIGGRAPH '85 Proceedings*, 313-322.

Rogers, David F., and J. Alan Adams, *Mathematical Elements for Computer Graphics*, second edition, McGraw-Hill, 1990.

Sabins, Floyd F., *Remote Sensing Principles and Interpretation*, W. H. Freeman, New York, 1978.

Sims, Karl, "Particle Animation and Rendering Using Data Parallel Computation," *Computer Graphics, ACM SIGGRAPH '90 Proceedings*, 405-413.

Smith, Stuart, Georges Grinstein, and Ronald Pickett, "Global Geometric, Sound, and Color Controls for Iconographic Displays of Scientific Data," *Extracting Meaning from Complex Data: Processing, Display, Interaction-Video Supplement, SPIE 1991*.

Snyder, J. and A. Barr, "Ray Tracing Complex Models Containing Surface Tesselations," *Computer Graphics, ACM '87 SIGGRAPH Proceedings*, 21(4), 1987.

Sutherland, I.E., Sproull, R.F., and Schumacker, R.A. "A Characterization of Ten Hidden-Surface Algorithms," *ACM Computing Surveys*, 6(1), March 1974, 1-55. Also in Beatty and Booth (1982), 387-441.

Torrance, I., and Sparrow, E.M. "Theory for Off-Specular Reflection from Roughened Surfaces," *J. Opt. Soc. Am.*, 57(9), September 1967, 1105-1114.

Torrance, K.E., Sparrow, E.M., and Birkebak, R.C., "Polarization, Directional Distribution, and Off-Specular Peak Phenomena in Light Reflected from Roughened Surfaces," *J. Opt. Soc. Am.*, 56(7), July 1966, 916-925.

Tufte, Edward R., *Envisioning Information*, Graphics Press, Cheshire, CT, 1991.

Upson, C. and M. Keeler, "V-Buffer: Visible Volume Rendering," *Computer Graphics, ACM SIGGRAPH '88 Proceedings*, 22(4), 1988.

Wilhelms, J., "Decisions in Volume Rendering," *ACM SIGGRAPH '91, Course Notes, Course 8*, 1991.

Wilhelms, J. and A. Van Gelder, "A Coherent Projection Approach for Direct Volume Rendering," *Computer Graphics, ACM '91 Proceedings*, 1991.

Williams, Lance, "Pyramidal Parametrics," *Computer Graphics, ACM SIGGRAPH '83 Proceedings*, 1-11.

Winkler, D., "Video Technology for Computer Graphics," *ACM SIGGRAPH '90, Course 22 Notes*.

Winkler, D., "Video Technology for Computer Graphics," *ACM SIGGRAPH '92, Course 4 Notes*.

Wolff, Robert S. "The Macintosh Scientific Computing Environment," *Computers in Physics*, 4(4), 1990, 348-361.

Wolfram, Stephen, *Mathematica: A System for Doing Mathematics by Computer*, second edition," Addison-Wesley, 1991.

Yaeger, Larry, Upson, Craig, and Meyers, Robert, "Combining Physical and Visual Simulation—Creation of the Planet Jupiter for the Film *2010*," *Computer Graphics, ACM SIGGRAPH '86 Proceedings*, 85-93.

Yeung, E. S., "Pattern Recognition by Audio Representation of Multivariate Analytical Data," *Analytical Chemistry*, 52(7), 1980, 1120-1123.